CHANGING FORTUNES

CHANGING FORTUNES

Remaking the Industrial Corporation

NITIN NOHRIA
DAVIS DYER
FREDERICK DALZELL

John Wiley & Sons, Inc.

Published by John Wiley & Sons, Inc., New York.
Published simultaneously in Canada.

ISBN 0-471-38481-X

Printed in the United States of America.

10 9 8 7 6 5 4 3 2 1

To Monica, Janice, and Mary-Elise

Contents

Preface

This book develops two major topics: (1) the inexorable drift of the large industrial corporation from the center to the periphery of the modern global economy during the past quarter century, and (2) the implications of that change for the owners, managers, employees, and communities that have depended on the large industrial corporation for rewards and benefits.

During the late 1990s, it seemed to some that a "new economy" of information-intensive companies was eclipsing the "old economy" of traditional industrial corporations. In light of the spectacular tumble of the Nasdaq index during 2000 and 2001 and the failure of many dot-coms, few people now believe that new economy companies will ever dominate the economy as the big industrials once did. The forces that created the new economy, especially the transforming impacts of information technology and social and demographic changes, are still at work, however. These forces continue to drive the shift from an industrial economy based on physical assets and production to a post-industrial economy based on intangible assets and services. The big industrials remain vital economic actors and will in the future, as long as society values tangible goods that are efficiently produced and distributed on a large scale. But they no longer, and never will again, occupy center stage in the economy. They are fading into the background.

The same forces that are driving the big industrials off center stage are also wringing significant changes inside these companies. The principal sources of long-term success—strategies of growth through diversification, hierarchical multidivisional (M-Form) structures, vertical information flows and control systems, the dominance of management in allocating resources and making key decisions, and the unstinting loyalties of owners, employees, and other stakeholders—all came into question. As a result, the big industrial corporation of the early twenty-first century differs markedly from its forebears of decades past. It has a more focused strategy emphasizing core businesses and activities. It features a leaner, flatter organization structure that is more permeable to inside and outside constituencies and pressures. Information and intelligence flows horizontally around business activities and processes, as well as vertically through managerial hierarchies inside the organization. Institutional shareholders, who are demonstrably impatient with what they consider to be poor performance, keep top executives on a tight leash. The impatience of owners illustrates a larger erosion of loyalties among employees, who no longer count on job security and ever-rising real incomes, customers, who no longer blindly trust established brands, and communities, which no longer can expect big companies to generate constantly increasing employment, tax revenues, and charitable giving.

Changing Fortunes portrays the waning of the industrial corporation and its internal transformation in nine chapters, organized topically, each spanning the late industrial and early post-industrial eras. Chapter 1, "The Ordeal of the Industrial Economy," contrasts the stories of Westinghouse Electric and General Electric as emblematic of the forces reshaping the industrial economy since the mid-1970s, as well as the magnitude of changes big companies had to make to survive and prosper. Chapter 2, "Passages and Patterns," discusses the broad economic, technological, and social forces that affected big companies throughout the economy and the particular pattern of responses by the *Fortune* 100 industrials. Chapters 3 through 6—"Strategy: Coping with the End of Growth," "Structure: Crumbling Walls," "Systems: Intelligence Unbound," and "Governance: The Tighter Leash," respectively—thematically break down the changes the big industrials have undergone as they struggled to adapt to the post-industrial economy.

Chapter 7, "Fraying Loyalties," addresses the implications of the receding significance of big industrial corporations for owners and investors, employees, customers, and communities. Chapter 8, "The Churning Mix: The Changing Nature of the Largest American Companies," examines entry and exit from the *Fortune* 100 population and describes and explains changes in the composition of the elite fraternity of the largest American corporations. Finally, Chapter 9, "The Industrial Corporation in a Post-Industrial Age," outlines strategies and actions that seem most likely to ensure the survival of individual industrial companies in an environment of contraction and a future of constrained options. The chapter concludes with observations about society's ongoing search to replace what has been lost.

This book grew out of a research project launched in the mid-1990s by Harvard Business School Professor Nitin Nohria. The project was partly inspired (as many studies of the goals and operations of big companies have been) by Alfred D. Chandler Jr.'s classic work, *Strategy and Structure: Chapters in the History of the American Industrial Enterprise*. Chandler's long, productive explorations into the evolution of big industrial corporations began with a look at trends among the *Fortune* 100 industrials in the late 1950s. In *Strategy and Structure* and subsequent writings, Chandler developed a comprehensive and compelling explanation for the rise and inner workings of the large American industrial corporation during the first half of the twentieth century.[1] His formulation of how these companies successfully grow and change by making fundamental shifts in strategy followed by fundamental shifts in structure (organization) is now almost universally accepted. Although it remains the best explanation of the rise of the big industrial corporation and appears unlikely to be superseded anytime soon, however, Chandler's work deals with the logic of industrial expansion. A question well worth asking by the 1990s was whether the era of industrial expansion had ended. If so, more questions immediately followed: Is there a corresponding logic of industrial decline? If so, what is it? These became the framing questions of Nohria's study.

Nohria began answering the questions by starting where Chandler had, with a statistical profile of the *Fortune* 100, but in this instance focusing on the period between 1978 and 1992. That work, together with a comprehensive literature review, identified many of the major topics and themes explored here, including the most significant changes in corporate strategy, structure, systems, and governance.[2] The study resulted in several articles and working papers, but to extend the research for a book-length study, Nohria sought the perspective of a historian, Davis Dyer, founding director of The Winthrop Group, Inc., and author or co-author of scholarly histories of several big industrial corporations (Hercules Incorporated, TRW, and Corning), as well as other books and essays in business history. Dyer joined the project, which grew in scope to focus on the last quarter of the twentieth century, with some attention to earlier times. At the same time, Nohria and Dyer decided to expand and marry the statistical data with extended case studies of companies included in the *Fortune* 100 in 1974. Frederick Dalzell, another historian, then joined the project, with support from the Harvard Business School and the Winthrop Group. The team quickly meshed in a true, tripartite collaboration, and the authors shared equally in developing the major conclusions of the study and organizing and generating the manuscript.

The major argument of this book is that there is a logic of industrial decline as the large industrial corporation receded from the center of the economy. The logic of industrial growth had been one of opportunity and choice, as the industrial companies faced an environment of abundant opportunities and selected among them, with their choices determining their long-term success. The logic of industrial decline, in contrast, is one of necessity and choice, as the changing business environment demanded that companies make certain changes, with their choices around the particular timing, type, and extent of those changes determining their long-term survival. In general, companies that recognized the necessity to change early *and* made appropriate choices fared much better than the companies that failed to recognize the necessity, or resisted it, or acted too late, or made poor choices in response.

The most successful companies responded swiftly and acted in a tightly sequenced and coordinated manner to alter their goals (from growth to profitability); strategy (from diversification to focus on core businesses, while simultaneously developing or grafting on new capabilities valued in a post-industrial economy); structure (from a stable, multi-layered hierarchy to a leaner, more fluid organization that became more interconnected with suppliers, customers, and partners); internal systems (from vertical information flows supporting hierarchical control functions to horizontal information flows supporting operational activities and processes); and governance (from protecting the autonomy of management to preserving the interests of shareholders). As a shorthand, we describe this pattern as a shift from the multidivisional M-Form organizations (including strategy, structure, systems, and governance) that typified most big industrials in the 1950s and 1960s to a more fluid, networked N-Form of organization in the 1990s and early 2000s.

This book is based on two kinds of information: statistical information about companies in the *Fortune* 100 in 1974, tracked as a panel through time until 1999 and 2000; and a series of historical case studies of individual companies in the panel. The 100 biggest companies comprise a statistically significant sample of large industrial corporations as a group, and we do not expect that our arguments and conclusions would be affected by examining a larger population.

The interior chapters of the book rely on historical case studies of leading competitors in most of the industries represented in the 1974 *Fortune* 100 list as a narrative device to carry the story. In some instances, we follow the stories of two or three companies in an industry; in other instances, just one. This technique is prefigured in Chapter 1, which profiles the contrasting stories of Westinghouse and General Electric—the two leading rivals in the diversified electricals group (five companies) on the 1974 list—between the mid-1970s and the end of the twentieth century, to illustrate the range of changes across the entire population of industrials as a whole. Chapters 3 through 7 use the histories of particular companies to make particular points. To highlight changes in strategy, we follow Dow Chemical, Union Carbide, and Monsanto (three of seven chemical companies on the list), which began the period similar in size and outlook but ended up in very different circumstances. The big three automakers, General Motors, Ford, and Chrysler, are used as vehicles (sorry) to discuss changes in corporate structure. Similarly, the story of Xerox (office equipment) provides an instructive case for discussing changes in systems, USX (néé U.S. Steel, primary metals) for changes in governance, and Eastman Kodak (chemicals and consumer products), for changes in investor, employee, and consumer loyalty, with associated effects on the local community.

Changing Fortunes is a work of synthesis. The story covered here is not so much about individual companies as it is about the large industrial corporation as a type. The historical case studies are based largely on publicly available information and secondary sources, and we rely heavily on academic literature about corporate strategy, organization, systems, and governance. Our professional understanding of how organizations grow and change and our detailed inside knowledge of some companies in the sample also inform our analysis. Even so, the book describes and deals with trends and events that continue to unfold, the outcomes of which may yet surprise us. Still, we believe that it is worthwhile to begin to state some views on the subject. If journalism is the first draft of history, perhaps this book is a second draft.

Finally, a word about the boundaries of our study. We focus on large industrial corporations and present our analysis in the hope that it will be useful to their leaders, who may acquire perspective on the ordeal they are experiencing. At the same time, we recognize that the large industrials are not unique. During the decades covered here, big service companies and smaller industrial corporations confronted the same challenges, although the timing, sequence, scale, and effects of events differed. We hope that the book also interests leaders in service businesses and nascent industries who can expect eventually to encounter the dynamics of decline. For them, the story of how the big industrials coped with a prolonged period of challenge may offer instructive lessons.

CHAPTER 1

THE ORDEAL OF THE INDUSTRIAL ECONOMY

In November 1997, Michael H. Jordan pondered an act that would have been unthinkable for any previous chief executive officer at Westinghouse Electric Corp.: the breakup and sale of the company's core manufacturing operations. George Westinghouse, along with Thomas Edison and Elihu Thomson, had practically invented the modern electrical industry. For more than a century, the Westinghouse name had been synonymous with electrical power and equipment. Yet Jordan, 63, a former McKinsey consultant and senior executive at PepsiCo, now had little choice.

Jordan had come to Westinghouse headquarters in Pittsburgh four years earlier following a boardroom coup that ousted his predecessor, Paul Lego. At first, Jordan had believed that he could transform Westinghouse into "a mobile, aggressive alley fighter," even if it meant selling off some long-standing businesses to pay down the company's crushing debts. To that end, he brought in Fred Reynolds, a former PepsiCo colleague who thrived on making deals, as CFO. Reynolds began immediately to prune Westinghouse's portfolio. Between 1994 and 1996 he raised $5.5 billion by selling an electrical distribution and controls business, a defense electronics business, an office furniture business, and a real estate development subsidiary.[1]

At the same time, Jordan recognized the need to develop or acquire more profitable businesses. The company's biggest earners were its cable-TV unit and radio stations. Looking to expand this base, in August 1995, Jordan announced a blockbuster move: the purchase of CBS Corp., the giant media and entertainment company. The price was $5.4 billion in cash, much of it borrowed. Less than a year later, Jordan followed up with another highly leveraged acquisition, Infinity Broadcasting, for $3.9 billion. The deal brought with it not only the nation's biggest network of radio stations, featuring popular "shock jocks" Howard Stern and Don Imus, but also Mel Karmazin, an ambitious executive and suddenly the biggest individual stockholder in Westinghouse. At the dawn of the Internet age, Karmazin saw innumerable possibilities for CBS and Infinity, and not many for Westinghouse's remaining electrical businesses. He pushed Jordan to get rid of them, a course also favored by stock analysts who hated conglomerates and preferred to track "pure-play" companies.

By the fall of 1996, Jordan was listening attentively to Karmazin and the analysts. Prospects for the media businesses dazzled him, while lingering troubles in the core industrial units weighed heavily on his mind. The problems in the core stretched back for decades, when Westinghouse had diversified aggressively and, in retrospect, foolishly, while chasing faster growth. Management had followed up an acquisition spree in the 1960s with a series of ill-starred and ill-timed moves, selling off properties in down cycles and expanding and venturing into new areas at inopportune moments. The biggest blunder, ultimately Lego's downfall, was the balloonlike expansion of Westinghouse Credit Corp. in the 1980s, based on booming sales of commercial real estate and poor analysis of risk. In the early 1990s, the balloon ruptured with a national recession and the collapse of property values. In the aftermath, Westinghouse absorbed $5 billion in write-offs and restructuring costs, and the board had turned to Jordan for relief.

In November 1996—five months after the Infinity acquisition—Jordan declared his intentions for the company's future. He announced that Westinghouse would be split into two separate companies, one industrial and the other media related, with the former named "Westinghouse Electric Corp." and the latter, the parent company, to take the name and stock symbol "CBS Corp." Westinghouse would remain in Pittsburgh, while CBS would be based in New York City. Jordan initially planned to spin off the industrial company to shareowners, but many observers wondered whether the new company would be viable. By then, not much was left of the historical core: two big power-generation businesses (one conventional, one nuclear), a process control unit, a government contracting operation, and Thermo King, a jewel of a property that manufactured refrigeration equipment for trucks and trains. The total added up to about $5 billion in sales—as contrasted with about $14 billion for the media company.

During the coming months, preparations were made for the spin-off, although the date was postponed several times as pressures mounted on Jordan to pay down acquisition debts. In June 1997, he announced the transfer of Thermo King from Westinghouse Electric back to CBS, a move deemed prefatory to selling the unit separately. Sure enough, a short while later, Ingersoll-Rand agreed to buy Thermo King for $2.6 billion. That left Westinghouse Electric an even less desirable property. In the summer of 1997, the company talked about forming a joint venture in power systems with Siemens, the German industrial giant with a history and product offerings much like Westinghouse's own. The talks broke down, however, when it became clear that Siemens wanted Westinghouse's conventional power generation unit but had no interest in the other divisions.

By November 1997, Jordan believed that he had few options left. Facing deep structural problems in the electric company that would take years to overcome, carrying a big debt burden, acutely aware that his tenure was likely to be short—with Karmazin doing little to disguise his ambitions—Jordan decided to do the unthinkable. He returned to Siemens and arranged to sell the unit Siemens wanted. For all practical purposes, the deal meant the demise of Westinghouse Electric, since it was clear that the remaining properties would be sold in pieces to the highest bidders. The following month, Jordan moved to New York to take up permanent residence with CBS at "Black Rock." He remained there until he retired at the end of 1998, succeeded by Karmazin. And so, an icon of American industry and one of the great business success stories of American history, a 111-year-old company called Westinghouse, vanished into the mists.[2]

A Tale of Two Transformations

In 1973, Westinghouse and its longtime rival, General Electric (GE), ranked among the strongest companies in the American economy, standing as the nineteenth- and eighth-biggest industrials, respectively, in the United States. In 1993, the year Jordan arrived; the company had slumped to number 42 and was slipping fast. Meanwhile, under John F. "Jack" Welch, the charismatic executive who became CEO in 1981, GE had climbed to number 5. Whereas Westinghouse ultimately disappeared in the late 1990s, GE posted revenues of more than $100 billion, and employed nearly 300,000. The company was widely regarded as an exemplar, one of the best managed and most admired corporations in the world—although its portfolio of businesses was far different from what it had been a quarter century before.

It is tempting to dismiss the demise of Westinghouse as a case of mismanagement and an unnecessary corporate tragedy. Some journalists have done just that, focusing on the heavy social costs incurred as a once-mighty employer and contributor to community life in Pittsburgh disappeared.[3] From the shareowner's perspective, however, the picture looks brighter. Jordan's actions pleased holders of Westinghouse stock, who saw it more than double in value between 1993 and 1997, with the surviving company thereafter facing a much more attractive future in the post-industrial economy.[4]

Meanwhile, the GE story demonstrates that there was nothing inevitable about Westinghouse's fate. What was inevitable, both stories reveal, was transformation. In the extreme case at Westinghouse, this transformation was total: an old-line industrial corporation expired, with a new media company rising from the ashes. At GE, the transformation was less dramatic but nonetheless extensive. The healthiest parts of today's company—GE Capital, NBC, plastics, and medical diagnostic equipment—constituted only minor parts of the portfolio in 1973, if they were present at all. The company thrived by grafting elements of the new, post-industrial economy—service and high-tech businesses—to its traditional core operations.

At both companies, the forces propelling transformation were identical. Westinghouse and GE faced common external challenges: energy shocks, recessions, a crisis in American manufacturing competitiveness, shareholder activism, the globalization of competition, the revolution in information technology, and the changing demographics of the U.S. population. All of these contributed to the graying of the industrial economy.

The dimensions of the new, post-industrial economy—and the plight of companies like Westinghouse and GE—are apparent from a glance at Table 1.1, a set of performance indicators that in turn is based on the *Fortune* 100 (F100) list of biggest industrial companies in 1974, a proxy for the larger population of big industrial corporations generally (see Table 1.2). In that year, the F100 industrials accounted for more than a third of the country's economic output; that share tumbled by half by 1998. The proportions and the drop are nearly the same for the population's share of U.S. market capitalization. Where once these industrial corporations employed more than 10 percent of American workers, they came to account for just 4 percent. The same relative decline appears in contributions to total R&D investment, while manufacturing as a whole diminished sharply in importance in U.S. trade. By the late 1990s, clearly, the large industrial companies were no longer centerpieces in the U.S. economy. Rather, they were part of a diverse, information-intensive, and global economy in which services account for more value than goods.

Forced to contend with the necessity of change as the industrial economy underwent its relative decline, both Westinghouse and GE reexamined their strategies, organizations, and ways of operating, and made choices and adjustments. Both undertook steps to de-diversify and refocus on a smaller number of industrial businesses. At the same time, both ventured into new service-oriented businesses that promised greater growth. Both downsized, delayered, and restructured their elaborate multidivisional hierarchies. Both adopted new systems that focused attention on improving quality, productivity, and shareholder returns. Both companies broke long-standing bonds of loyalties with employees, vendors, and customers as they responded to market necessities. In sum, both took gut-wrenching actions to undo a whole system of corporate policies and practices that had been institutionalized over many years of growth and success.

Table 1.1
Waning of the *Fortune* 100, 1955–1998

Category	*1955 (%)*	*1974 (%)*	*1998 (%)*
Share of U.S. GDP	24.4	35.8	17.3
Share of U.S. market capitalization	35.8	32.9	17.1
Share of U.S. employment	9.7	10.7	4.0
Share of U.S. R&D investment	1.40	1.70	0.38
Manufacturing share of U.S. exports	72.4	68.5	50.0

Note: The *Fortune* 100 refers to our study population, the panel of the 100 largest industrial corporations in 1974.

Table 1.2
Composition of the *Fortune* 100 in 1974 by Industrial Grouping

Industrial Grouping	*Companies*
1. Oil and petrochemicals (N = 19)	Exxon, Texaco, Mobil, Standard Oil (Cal.), Gulf Oil, Standard Oil (Ind.), Shell Oil, Conoco, Atlantic Richfield, Occidental Petroleum, Phillips Petroleum, Union Oil, Sun Oil, Amerada Hess, Ashland Oil, Marathon Oil, Cities Service, Getty Oil, Standard Oil (Ohio)
2. Food, beverages, tobacco, and consumer packaged goods (N = 17)	Procter & Gamble, Esmark, Kraft Co., Beatrice Foods, Borden, R.J. Reynolds, Ralston Purina, Philip Morris, General Foods, Colgate-Palmolive, CPC International, Coca-Cola, Consolidated Foods, United Brands, American Brands, PepsiCo, General Mills
3. Metal and glass (N = 11)	U.S. Steel, Bethlehem Steel, Armco Steel, Continental Can, Republic Steel, National Steel, Alcoa, American Can, Inland Steel, Owens-Illinois, Reynolds Metals
4. Chemicals and pharmaceuticals (N = 10)	Du Pont, Union Carbide, Dow Chemical, Eastman Kodak, Monsanto, W.R. Grace, Allied Chemical, FMC, American Home Products, Johnson & Johnson
5. Industrial conglomerates (N = 10)	ITT Industries, Tenneco, LTV, Greyhound, Litton Industries, 3M, TRW, Bendix, Gulf + Western, Textron
6. Automotive and transportation (N = 7)	General Motors, Ford, Chrysler, International Harvester, Caterpillar, Deere, American Motors
7. Aerospace and defense related (N = 7)	Rockwell International, Boeing, United Aircraft, Lockheed Aircraft, McDonnell Douglas, General Dynamics, Raytheon
8. Electrical products (N = 5)	General Electric, Westinghouse Electric, RCA, Western Electric, Honeywell
9. Tires (N = 4)	Goodyear, Firestone, Uniroyal, B.F. Goodrich
10. Paper (N = 4)	International Paper, Champion International, Weyerhauser, Georgia-Pacific
11. Office equipment (N = 4)	IBM, Xerox, Sperry Rand, NCR
12. Other manufacturers (N = 2)	Singer (sewing machines), Burlington Industries (textiles)

Even though both companies eventually undertook similar measures, however, the timing, nature, scope, and extent of these changes proved critical in determining their relative fortunes. GE was more successful than Westinghouse in anticipating the fundamental changes that were necessary. By making difficult decisions quickly and acting aggressively, GE opened up new vistas for growth. In Westinghouse's case, the grudging adoption of difficult decisions only led to a denser thicket of constraints. Ultimately, the only choice that remained was exit and rebirth as a different kind of company. GE traveled a diverging path, one that led to transformation of an altogether different sort.

What Happened to Westinghouse

The unmaking of Westinghouse reached back decades in time, to the late 1960s, when the company had diversified aggressively away from its core business, with few restraints on its growth. When pressures on corporate performance mounted in the early 1970s, culminating in the recession that followed the decade's first energy shock, Westinghouse's leaders proved reluctant to change their ways.

A Grudging Refocus. In 1973, Westinghouse posted nearly $6 billion in sales. The company manufactured and sold more than 300,000 variations of some 8,000 basic products, including nuclear power reactors, steam and gas turbines, radar and other defense electronic systems, industrial motors and other factory equipment, electrical appliances, watches, elevators, air conditioners, and lamps. The company ran 114 subsidiaries and operated 112 manufacturing plants in the United States, as well as 74 other factories in 19 foreign countries. It operated five VHF television stations (the maximum then allowed by the FCC) and seven radio stations. Its diversified units included bottlers of 7-Up, the Longines-Wittenauer Watch Company, Econo-Car International, Host Enterprises, and ventures in land development, education curriculum development, low-cost housing, undersea mining, mass transit, and waste disposal. Westinghouse maintained a network of research laboratories, including a central facility in suburban Pittsburgh, with 1,800 scientists, engineers, and support staff, and satellite labs in Boulder, Colorado, Annapolis, Maryland, and West Lafayette, Indiana, as well as dozens of smaller development labs within the factories themselves. All told, the company employed 184,000 people. Its operations were loosely organized into 135 divisions.[5]

Westinghouse's chaotic sprawl reflected a period of feverish diversification activity that saw sales and profits more than double between 1963 and 1972. Several factors stimulated this activity, including financial analysis that concluded there were limits to growth in "mature" industries like electrical power, antitrust concerns about making acquisitions in core businesses, and high price/earnings multiples that made acquisitions cheap. Meanwhile, there were few checks on Westinghouse's ambitions to grow. Donald Burnham, CEO after 1963, delegated power and responsibility to the division general managers and he eschewed detailed analysis or rigorous long-term planning. At the aptly named Gateway (the company's new headquarters in Pittsburgh's Gateway complex), there was little gatekeeping. When Donald McGannon, head of Westinghouse Broadcasting, decided to go after Longines-Wittenauer (L-W), for example, he made his pitch to Burnham directly; Marshall Evans, who headed the corporate planning staff, was brought in only in the final stages of the deal when he was handed what he later described as a three-page summary consisting of L-W's balance sheet, an earnings statement, and a tally of its product lines. "We had this conviction," senior executive Thomas Murrin later ruefully recalled, "that we could manage anything."[6]

Meanwhile, the company's heady growth masked serious challenges facing many of its businesses, both in core and diversified areas. In power systems, for example, a rash of technical glitches afflicted Westinghouse turbines, and by 1974 nine utilities had filed lawsuits against the company. In appliances, the company's traditionally lackluster marketing performance had become a visible target of analysts, who urged Burnham to sell off the business. In 1968, Westinghouse had begun the process, discontinuing first its TV and then in 1972 its small appliance lines. It stubbornly held on to large appliances—refrigerators, ranges, washers, and dryers—but only by selling at low prices that deeply depressed profit margins. Problems were also beginning to crop up in the Broadcasting, Learning, and Leisure Time division—its very name a sign of its miscellaneous nature. Moreover, some high-profile ventures, including the mail order, car rental, and housing businesses, as well as a French elevator manufacturing subsidiary, posted costly losses.

The energy crisis and deep recession that followed the 1973 Arab-Israeli war hammered Westinghouse and forced Burnham to reexamine how the company operated. By June 1974, the stock was in a free fall from a high of nearly $55 in 1972 to below $20, and the company's price/earnings ratio of nine represented its lowest level in over 10 years. Many analysts called for strong actions and urged the company to divest its appliances line. Rather than concede to this advice, Burnham rejected it out of hand: "This business will definitely not be closed out," he said. Instead, he announced that Westinghouse had earmarked $73 million to modernize production facilities while laying out a new marketing strategy for appliances: The company would stop chasing market share through price cuts and new models, and instead pare its line and simplify remaining models in an effort to streamline production and improve quality. "On Wall Street, the news was greeted with horror," as one analyst put it.[7]

With the company already under intense pressure, it could ill afford more missteps. Unfortunately, another was about to take place. Wall Street got wind of rumors that Westinghouse was facing cash flow problems. Burnham denounced the rumors as "irresponsible and unfounded" but then a few days later, clumsily confirmed them when the company negotiated a bigger line of credit. In the aftermath, a very reluctant Burnham began looking behind the scenes for a buyer for the appliances business. In late December, the company announced a deal with White Consolidated Industries, Inc., selling off five American plants and extensive marketing and service operations.

It was a watershed moment in the history of the company. Westinghouse had sold electrical appliances to consumers since the 1920s. In withdrawing from the field and pulling its trademark "W" out of showrooms, the company was withdrawing in a more basic sense from the consumer market and submerging itself more deeply into the industrial economy below. From 1975 on, with the significant exceptions of lamps (divested in 1983) and broadcasting, Westinghouse's most important customers would be factories, utilities, and governments. At the same time, Burnham and his successors grudgingly accepted the need for further changes in strategy and organization.

A Bad Bet. In 1975, Burnham stepped down as CEO and ushered in his handpicked successor, Robert Kirby, formerly general manager of Westinghouse's Industry and Defense division. Kirby went to work quickly. The company restructured its operations into 37 Strategic Business Units, each responsible for its own marketing, engineering, and manufacturing functions. During the next several years, the company revamped the planning procedures at Gateway, simplifying plan guidelines, extending reporting periods from one to two- and three-year increments, and staggering the timing of submission to headquarters. Kirby and his team also developed a new performance measurement tool called the Value Based Strategic Management system (Vabastram). Intended to regulate future acquisition and resource allocation decisions, Vabastram motivated managers to maximize return on equity: Thus the company sought to shift its priorities from the pursuit of growth to the pursuit of shareholder value.[8]

Kirby also all but admitted that the company's diversification spree in the previous decade had been a mistake. Forecasting robust growth for the company's core energy businesses—he anticipated a major shift from petroleum and natural gas to electricity—he reckoned that the company's best long-term growth prospects lay in nuclear power. He vowed to plow resources back into what was "most vital to [the company's] future and into the technology where it excels—namely, nuclear power." He went on to explain, "That's why I'm trying to get us on an extraordinarily sound financial basis, because, man, we're going to need money. I can't have a whole lot of losing rinky-dink things that I can't get our money out of. Westinghouse and GE are poised on the edge of a whole new surge."[9]

True to his word, Kirby lopped off a number of troubled units on the periphery of the company. Westinghouse discontinued its mail order businesses, divested the troubled European elevator subsidiary, and spun off its car rental business. When Vabastram analysis indicated that Westinghouse's lamp business was slipping, Kirby initiated withdrawal there as well. Over the decade between 1974 and 1983, the company divested units with combined sales of $2.5 billion.[10]

The market applauded Kirby's moves, and during the late 1970s, the company's stock rebounded. Nonetheless, even as Kirby was gathering plaudits, a time bomb was ticking in the nuclear power business. Over the 1960s and into the early 1970s the company had signed long-term contracts with a number of utilities committing Westinghouse to supply uranium at fixed prices averaging $9.50 per pound. The contracts had won business, but at a price that became ruinous after the energy crisis: By 1975, the cost of uranium had climbed to nearly $40 per pound, and the company had not locked up either an inventory or firm supply contracts. Westinghouse tried to pull out of the contracts, and the utilities sued in response. By the time Kirby was preparing his first annual report, the company was facing lawsuits from 27 utilities, and a potential liability worth billions of dollars. The crisis consumed much of Kirby's first four years at the helm of Westinghouse, and the eventual settlements cost the company more than $1 billion.

This was only the beginning. Antinuclear environmental activism was compelling stricter government regulation, which in turn created costs that made nuclear energy uncompetitive with plants fired by fossil fuels. Orders for new nuclear plants in the United States simply dried up. Still worse news followed. An accident at a nuclear power plant in Three Mile Island, near Harrisburg, Pennsylvania, nearly resulted in a meltdown—a scenario eerily foreshadowed in *The China Syndrome,* a popular antinuclear movie that had come out just months before. The accident played into the hands of the antinuclear movement and doomed nuclear power plant construction in the United States. Although some foreign nations continued to embrace the technology, the big bet Kirby had placed on Westinghouse's future had gone terribly bad.

Meanwhile, Westinghouse shifted the focus of its nuclear power business from equipment manufacture, a large, growing, and profitable business, to servicing existing plants, a declining, albeit still profitable business. A similar transformation was underway in the company's conventional power plant business, with servicing contracts growing to some 50 percent of total sales in 1983.

A Deep Disappointment. Outside pressures on Westinghouse continued to mount during the late 1970s and early 1980s with a second energy crisis, an environment of high inflation, and the onset of another recession. The company responded by making more strategic shifts and organizational changes, but it found that it had to go farther still to satisfy its customers and owners.

Westinghouse undertook several productivity initiatives beginning in 1979, when Vice Chairman Douglas Danforth set up a Corporate Productivity Improvement Committee and dispatched teams to study competitors, particularly Japanese companies, and formulate prescriptions for the company. The following year, Westinghouse set up a Productivity Center (eventually the Productivity and

Quality Center), with a staff of 300, to make recommendations to plant and office managers. At the same time, the company established more than 500 "quality circles" on factory floors to identify and solve on-the-job problems.

Meanwhile, the company began to map out new strategic directions for growth, choosing to make several acquisitions. In October 1980, Westinghouse announced the purchase of Teleprompter, a content provider for cable television with properties including Muzak and a share of Showtime, that complemented the company's broadcast properties. Two years later the company moved in a second area, acquiring the robot manufacturer Unimation Inc. for $107 million. Kirby saw the latter move as a first step, part of a larger program to develop factory automation equipment to modernize the company's industrial systems line. "What we envision, in addition to robots," he explained, "is a nucleus of technology-oriented equipment—flexible, computer controlled, sensor-intensive factory machines and peripherals."[11]

In 1983, as the economy and the company began to rebound from the recession, Kirby turned over the helm to Danforth, who came in talking tough and calling for change in the company. The new CEO set ambitious, tangible targets, including yearly sales growth 3 to 4 percentage points above real GNP, operating margins of 8 percent to 9 percent, and record income in 1986, the company's centennial year. He directed a broad restructuring and downsizing that cut the number of Westinghouse's business units from 37 to 26, and extracted layers of corporate staff. Danforth's management team was equally active in the field, overhauling industrial production in the company's power and electrical equipment businesses. Rigorously applying Vabastram analysis, the company consolidated lines, closed plants, upgraded others, and cut out unprofitable products and businesses, selling some and spinning off others as joint ventures. Thus, in its electrical equipment sector, the company merged five SBUs, consolidating both product lines and plants, while it divested a number of unprofitable power equipment lines. "Westinghouse is a changed corporation," Danforth insisted in 1985. ". . . We're convinced that it is possible to manage our businesses to maximize value-creation. . . . We are not wed to any traditional business."[12]

Westinghouse's stock price, however, did not match the chairman's optimism. In the mid-1980s, this was an increasingly dangerous position for the company to find itself in. All around the American economy, large industrial companies, some of them long-standing titans of American business, were losing control of their equity to speculators who bought up large blocks of stock in aggressive raids in order to break up the companies and sell them off piece by piece. At Westinghouse, a takeover became a very real threat. In 1985, Danforth and his financial officers calculated that the company's breakup value (which they estimated at around $9 billion) well exceeded its market value ($7 billion). After consulting with several confidants, Danforth decided to fend off a possible takeover by selling off the company's cable TV content unit (what had been Teleprompter) along with a number of other operations esponsible for total annual sales of $1.2 billion.

These deal enabled the company to purchase 20 percent of its outstanding stock, pay down debt, and cover losses in other businesses.

By these fairly strenuous measures, Danforth was finally able to lift the stock price up to nearly $52 in 1986. Earnings climbed as well, in part because of divestiture-related profit infusions. But the company still faced uneven outlooks in core industries. There seemed to be little likelihood nuclear construction would pick up, power systems was still transforming itself from a construction to a service-oriented unit, and although defense continued to perform robustly, company planners were beginning to cut long-range defense forecasts as the Reagan buildup waned and the end of the cold war loomed.

One trouble spot, Unimation, was especially disheartening. Westinghouse was finding it difficult to regear itself to the pace of business in the rapidly evolving factory automation business. Key managers had left following the buyout. Westinghouse sales teams, more experienced in handling hardware than software, had trouble coordinating effective service and systems integration. Ironically, given Westinghouse's long-standing roots in the electrical industry, Unimation specialized in hydraulic robots while customers were gravitating to electronic robots with electrically driven gears and control systems. The Unimate, Unimation's central product, suffered from a design flaw that caused the robot to vibrate, making its hydraulic components leak. By the mid-1980s, auto manufacturers were switching to other robots that were less expensive to keep running. Westinghouse reacted slowly, taking several years to develop with GM an electric robot, which then proved too small for the market. Even as it was being subsumed into the larger parent company, Unimation's market share in robotics was slipping, from number one (with a 40 percent share) in 1982, when it had been acquired, to number four in 1985. Troubles compounded when the unit's software team quit the company, disenchanted with corporate bureaucracy at Westinghouse.[13]

In 1987, Westinghouse finally admitted failure and divested Unimation in a series of transactions. This outcome represented a portentous retreat for Westinghouse. For nearly a century, the company had been a leading manufacturer of industrial equipment—the machinery and systems that made up the guts of American and international factories—and Westinghouse had acquired Unimation in an effort to stay out on the cutting edge of the business. In hindsight, failure here signaled serious doubts as to the company's industrial future. "It's absolutely sick," Marketing Vice President George Munson would later admit. "It breaks my heart to think of how we lost the industrial robot industry." Thomas Murrin's postmortem, issued from the vantage point of having headed the company's advanced technology group, was sobering: "It was a classic case of trying to merge an entrepreneurial organization into a relatively slow-moving, large American corporation."[14]

A Disastrous Diversification. Everywhere in Westinghouse, pressures built up over the late 1980s. The company's old line businesses were adapting unevenly to changing market conditions, while top management, Vabastram driven, was demanding higher returns on equity. Increasingly, Westinghouse looked to offset troubles in its core manufacturing units by focusing on financial services. At Gateway, strategic thinking inexorably gravitated to Westinghouse Credit Corporation, a subsidiary originally set up to finance consumer lending but in 1986 revamped for higher yield lending in real estate and investment banking. Perhaps services could deliver what manufacturing could not. It would prove a fateful choice.

At first, Westinghouse Credit made good on the bet, generating impressive profits: In 1990 it boasted an asset base of more than $10 billion and earnings of $1.2 billion—each total about double the level in 1986.[15] Expansion proved especially heated between 1988 and 1990, after headquarters engineered a reorganization under which Westinghouse Credit reported directly to the CEO. Even so, the subsidiary operated largely autonomously from what its management referred to as the "Electric Company" eight blocks away in downtown Pittsburgh. John McClester, chairman of Westinghouse Financial Services, caught the tone: "It wasn't their thing," was how he described thinking in the traditional businesses about the new one. "It doesn't hum, doesn't rotate, and you don't plug it in."[16]

By this point, new leadership was in place. In 1987 the company announced Danforth's retirement and replacement by John C. Marous Jr. This turnover, like the ones before it, was tightly controlled, setting up a succession designed to ensure strategic and operational continuity. Marous came from the core of the company, having been president of Westinghouse's Industries and International Group. He and Danforth "agreed on our future strategy," Marous stressed. "It's going to be more of the same." As if to underscore the point, the board of directors went so far as to schedule Marous' retirement for 1990 and designate Paul E. Lego as his replacement. In the interim, Lego was named president and chief operating officer (COO). He too was a career Westinghouse man, having managed the company's lamp and electronic parts divisions.[17]

Marous and Lego had previously collaborated on the overhaul of the Industries and International Group, grindingly driving the company's core manufacturing toward profitability. As CEO and CEO-in-waiting, the pair worked closely together to keep the program on track, touring operations, implementing incremental improvements in quality and productivity that slowly began to show results. The company did manage, for example, to repair relations with nuclear reactor and utility customers, in part by offering service contracts that earned Westinghouse bonuses when plants performed above standards and imposed penalties when they fell short. As quality rose, downtime for plant repairs dropped dramatically. The company also touted its Productivity and Quality Center, calculating that net income per employee had doubled between 1982 and 1987, from $3,100 to $6,600.[18] These hard-won gains permitted the company to make a series of low-profile acquisitions, including several units that specialized in hazardous waste cleanup and toxic waste burning.

As Lego moved into the chairman's office in 1990, however, disquieting signals were emanating from Westinghouse Credit, which was scrambling to cope with a spreading real estate depression. Concerned analysts queried the incoming CEO about the company's exposure. Lego confessed, "It's the area I know the least about."[19] Over the next few months, as Lego took office and the company's stock price started to slide again, he assured worried investors the company was not going to have to absorb any major write-offs. In fact, the credit subsidiary was in serious trouble. During the boom period of the late 1980s, the unit had lent busily and readily. "We were approving loans at 110 percent of value," a former employee admitted. "It was crazy."[20] In February 1991, four months after Lego had reassured investors that Westinghouse had the situation under control, the company was forced to announce a $975 million write-down.

Lego hoped to contain the crisis by selling off some bad debts, restructuring others, and shrinking Westinghouse Credit. But he and his top management team handled the unfamiliar business uncertainly, tentatively. Wary of advice from managers in the unit—"The feeling was that we got them into this mess," one credit executive recalled—Westinghouse executives also declined recommendations from investment bankers at Lazard Frères and Shearson Lehman to spin off the real estate loans in a single transaction. The company invited General Electric's fast-rising Capital unit to make an offer for the unit, but negotiations broke off. Meanwhile, troubles deepened: In November the company was again forced to take a write-off, this one for a shocking $1.7 billion.

"It will take three to five years or longer to dig out of this mess," an executive predicted, but from this point things spiraled downward rapidly.[21] For 1991 the company as a whole posted a loss of $1 billion. As Westinghouse Credit loans continued to sour, corporate executives vacillated over how much of the unit to sell. Citing problems at the credit subsidiary, Standard & Poor lowered the parent company's credit rating. The stock dove further. When efforts to float commercial paper collapsed, the company was forced to draw down its bank credit lines. In October, rumors of liquidity problems and a possible bankruptcy filing flew through Wall Street. By November, with total charges at Credit Corp. reaching $5.2 billion and Westinghouse's bank credit down to $500 million, the company announced that it would accelerate the sale of the unit, withdraw from the business, and put other company units up for sale as well. The news may have relieved investors, but it also substantially reduced the selling value of Westinghouse Credit and other properties. Both Standard & Poor and Moody's responded by lowering the company's credit another notch, down to near junk levels. In December, corporate management again approached GE about buying Westinghouse Credit.

It seemed almost like a replay of the company's troubles two decades before, but this time the story had a very different ending. Between 1974 and 1992, the structure of corporate finance undergirding the company had shifted significantly; Paul

Lego was facing a different group of shareholders than Donald Burnham had confronted. Large blocks of Westinghouse stock now lay in the hands of institutional investors—weighty and increasingly activist powers such as the California Public Employees and State Teachers Retirement Systems (Calpers), along with shareholder groups such as the United Shareholders Association and the Council of Institutional Investors. Westinghouse had raised eyebrows back in February 1991 when it had announced the first Credit Corp. write-off just one month after the board of directors, on the strength of unaudited 1990 earnings, had awarded large bonuses to senior management. As more write-offs emerged, concern spread that Westinghouse management was not grappling realistically with its problems. "This is a company that has been dribbling out the bad news," former SEC commissioner Joseph Grundfest complained in December 1992, "making a practice out of rationalizing reality."[22] Investors began demanding what Daniel DiSenso, Standard & Poor's director of corporate finance, called "radical surgery" in the company.

Lego set up a series of conferences with major shareholder groups, but did not manage in those meetings to lay out a clear strategy for extracting the company from its quagmire. "The board really needs to take hold of this situation," warned Richard Koppes, general counsel of Calpers fund, which held 1 percent of the company's stock. His apprehension only intensified after meeting with Lego: The CEO "seemed to wallow in minutiae," Koppes reported incredulously. "His song is that the company's a mess and it's not his fault. This guy's been there for five years, and now he says it's not his fault."[23]

The company's board of directors could not ignore these very public, increasingly impatient comments indefinitely. In late November 1992, they were prodded to act, though not yet decisively: While leaving Lego in office, the board set up a new president's office to balance the CEO's authority. At the same time, however, the company refused to separate the roles of CEO and board chairman, as many reformers were demanding. Lego, for his part, remained insistently, even defiantly, upbeat: "We're going to be a dynamic, solid operation focused in high-manufacturing-type businesses."[24] But the company posted a loss of $2.5 billion for 1992.

The board was giving him one last chance to sell off Westinghouse Credit. When the second round of negotiations with GE broke off later in December, Lego's fate was sealed. Two outside directors—former U.S. Defense Secretary Frank C. Carlucci and former Amoco chairman Richard M. Morrow—went to work behind the scenes. When the board met on January 27, 1993, Lego was asked to resign, Executive Vice President Gary Clark took over on an interim basis, and the board began to look for a replacement. For the first time in over half a century, it was looking outside of Westinghouse.

The search proved difficult; it took nearly six months before the board finally settled on Michael H. Jordan. It didn't take long after that for Jordan to transform Westinghouse into an altogether different kind of company.

Makeover at General Electric

As Westinghouse foundered and lurched into crises, ultimately undergoing a complete change of character and identity, an entirely different scenario unfolded at GE. GE met and responded to the same challenges threatening to overwhelm its longtime rival, but management recognized the need to change earlier and made better choices across the key dimensions of strategy, structure, and internal systems. GE confronted its necessities and thereby created more opportunities and choices for itself.

Anticipating Change and Refocusing the Portfolio. In 1973, GE seemed on the surface a scaled-up version of Westinghouse. With total sales of $11.6 billion, GE was nearly twice the size, the biggest electrical and electronic equipment manufacturer in the United States. The company held 137 affiliates and operated 210 manufacturing plants in the United States, along with about 80 abroad. These plants produced a vast array of products, including industrial equipment such as turbines, generators, motors, transformers, and switches; a line of household appliances including ranges, refrigerators, dishwashers, televisions, stereo equipment, and lamps; broadcasting stations; aerospace equipment ranging from engines for civilian aircraft to defense weapons systems; x-ray equipment; plastics; process computers; transportation systems; and a swarm of other goods and services. The company also ran more than 100 laboratories and research and development facilities. GE employed 369,000 workers.

The resemblance between GE and Westinghouse, however, was entirely superficial. Where Westinghouse had few controls and would spend much of the 1970s attempting to rein in its decentralized units, GE was more than a step ahead. In 1972, the company was recovering from a decade of problems and losses in three key sectors: nuclear power, commercial jet engines, and computers. In sorting out these problems, the company had drawn on the advice of McKinsey & Co. and had developed organization and management concepts to coordinate all of its businesses. The various operations were sorted into strategic business units (SBUs), each of which constituted a defined business with products that shared the same market, competition, and growth potential. Each SBU formulated annual plans laying out goals for sales and profits, capital investments, market share targets, and new product developments.

By the time Reginald Jones took the helm as CEO in 1972, the new system had been fully implemented and was working its way into managerial habits of thinking throughout company ranks. Jones' ascension to the head of GE, in fact, was closely tied to the company's strategic resolve. A graduate of the University of Pennsylvania's Wharton Business School and a career GE man, Jones had held positions in manufacturing, marketing, administration, and finance, and taken postings in the electrical apparatus, air conditioning, and construction divisions, as well as in distribution and sales. Along the way he had developed a reputation as a financial expert. In 1969, he honed his strategic planning techniques as head of a task force investigating GE's uneven performance in the computer business. After concluding that the company would need a 15 percent market share to compete effectively in the computer market, a target it could not reach without massive changes and investments, Jones' team had decided to pull the company out; GE spun off the business in a deal with Honeywell in 1970. The divestiture, followed shortly by the promotion of the man who had engineered it, sent a strong signal through the company: General Electric was legitimizing exit. "From then on," as one manager later recalled, "it became fashionable to prune businesses."[25]

As he assumed the top post at GE, Jones described "enormous vistas" before the company and announced that "with our new strategic planning process, we are learning how to allocate our resources to the right places, at the right time, for optimum growth and profitability—and at the same time, contain our risks." Possibly he was alluding to Westinghouse when he added, "Many companies claim they do strategic planning, but the process may or may not be anything more than intuitive wheeling-and-dealing by the top man."[26]

Its new systems enabled the company to cope with the energy crisis and ensuing recession with less strain than most American industrials. Earnings dipped by 4 percent in 1975, but the company demonstrated resilience and readiness to adapt: in December, GE announced merger talks with Utah International, a major mining and oil and gas company. Completed the following year, the $2.2 billion merger was the largest in American history to that point. In strategic terms, GE saw the acquisition as a way to expand its global presence, to enter what Jones called "the natural resources industry," and also to hedge the company's overall position against inflation. But GE executives also stressed, and investment analysts at the time agreed, that while the acquisition complemented GE's holdings, Utah International was also a solid company on its own merits, well run, with a firm business base and promising growth prospects.[27]

It did not take long, however, for GE to have second thoughts about the merger. In the late 1970s, many analysts and investors regarded GE as solidly and stolidly planted in the industrial mainstream and so spread out it was unlikely to grow appreciably faster than the U.S. gross national product (GNP) as a whole. Meanwhile, an internal study on technology in 1978 recommended that the company redirect its strategic course away from smokestack industries, including traditional businesses in electrical and industrial equipment, and into electronics and high technology. With hindsight, some executives regretted the decision to pull out of the computer and semiconductor industry. Meanwhile, productivity at GE plastics and jet engines—the company's two highest profile businesses in the global marketplace—trailed that of rising foreign competitors, particularly Japanese companies. Elsewhere in GE, the company's consumer electronics was laboring against stiff competition, power systems growth was off, nuclear construction was dead (the company pulled out in 1980), and Utah International was not generating the kind of growth or earnings the company had expected.

New Leadership and an Urgent Need to Change. GE entered the 1980s with the growing conviction that the company needed to push itself in new directions, to adapt itself to broad changes in the global marketplace. The catalyst for change—the engine of what would become a more-or-less continual campaign of revitalization over the next 20 years—was 45-year-old Jack Welch, who took over as CEO in 1981. An engineer with acute marketing instincts and an aggressive entrepreneurial drive, Welch had come into GE in 1960, through the company's fledgling plastics unit. By 1968, at age 32, he had expanded the operation into a worldwide business selling $40 million, in the process pioneering new industrial and commercial applications. In 1977, with GE's annual plastics sales approaching $500 million, Welch transferred to corporate headquarters, taking with him a boisterous, blunt, often combative style of management. His election as vice chairman two years later, and then CEO two years after that, surprised some observers. This was an appointment from the inside in the sense that he was a career GE man, but Welch was an outsider in the most important respects. He had not worked his way up in the company's traditional core businesses. He was also rougher around the edges and younger than many of his senior colleagues.

Welch came into office convinced the company had grown complacent, and he felt an urgent need to shake things up: "We'll try to adapt GE to a world that we see is on fire," is how he put it a few years later.[28] To begin with, he was convinced that GE had grown top heavy and had to fix more fundamental, internal structural problems. GE employed 25,000 "managers" of one kind or another—500 of them senior managers and 130 vice presidents. Implementing the SBU structure had injected new layers of staff, with another level of management and review—the sector, atop the group and division—added in 1977 to accommodate the company's growing complexity. Nearly 200 senior level planners populated company ranks. Welch recognized that the elaborate planning procedures had helped the company assess performance across a broad range of businesses, but as a bureaucratic apparatus it had grown unwieldy. "We hired a head of planning, and he hired two vice presidents, and then he hired a planner, and then the books got thicker and the printing got more sophisticated and the covers got harder and the drawings got better. The meetings kept getting larger. Nobody can say anything with 16 or 18 people there."[29]

Rising through GE plastics, Welch reached headquarters from out on the periphery of the company portfolio, having built his business without a lot of guidance from the corporate executive office. In the course of this experience, he had developed a few general management principles: "Always meet targets, don't accept mediocrity, embrace change, don't cling to tradition."[30] He was not a man to sit on his convictions. After touring GE operations over his first few months in office, he went to work on the company's structure, cutting out thick slices of middle-level management. In an effort to reconnect line managers to headquarters generally and the CEO's office in particular, Welch extracted the intervening group and sector levels from the organizational hierarchy. Between 1980 and 1984 the company's total workforce shrank from 402,000 to 330,000—with roughly a third of the loss owing to recession cutbacks, and the larger proportion stemming from the company's delayering and downsizing.

The restructuring was deeply painful, earning Welch the sobriquet of "Neutron Jack"— a reference to the bomb that wiped out people while leaving buildings intact. But staff reductions at GE were not driven for the most part by cost cutting. They represented an effort to streamline information flows inside the company. SBU managers now met informally with the CEO and two vice chairman, every 2 to 3 years in the cases of businesses operating in relatively stable markets, more often when businesses confronted rapidly changing conditions. The new process freed line managers from submitting complex, cumbersome annual plans, and put Welch into direct contact with his managers in the field. At headquarters, the planning office reconceptualized itself from being a quasi-supervisory entity to something more akin to an internal consulting firm.

Delayering happened in stages, as the company's top management felt out what would be workable, what could be removed. Before doing away with the sectors, for example, Welch experimented. Initially, to the five existing sectors in 1978 (along with Utah International as a sixth stand-alone unit) he added two more: Technical Systems (including all business units employing microelectronics) and Services and Materials (including the company's fast-growing financial services units). Then in 1984 he cut the number of sectors to four. Finally, in December 1985, the company announced that it was removing the sector level of corporate hierarchy altogether. To review plans and oversee the businesses, the CEO office was enlarged and the Corporate Executive Council (CEC) expanded. Welch described the reorganization as "consistent with our long-stated objective to move to a leaner, flatter, more market-driven structure," better able to compete in "an intensified competitive world, a slower growth world."[31]

A second, central element of Welch's strategic thinking drove the point home: General Electric, top management now decreed, would engage only in businesses in which it held or could obtain a number one or number two share in the market. Uncompromising, upbeat, the dictum struck directly at the suggestion that GE would be content to grow at the rate of the U.S. GNP. Accordingly, between 1981 and 1984, GE began remaking its corporate profile, selling off more than a hundred product lines and businesses—operations worth nearly $7 billion. Among the divestitures was Utah International, the energy and mining unit that had been the centerpiece of Reginald Jones' tenure. There could be no doubt now that Welch was in charge, nor that he had the confidence of the company's board of directors. If the company was going to move aggressively in new target businesses, the new CEO had persuaded top management and directors, it needed a war chest. Welch expected proceeds from the sale of Utah International, as he somewhat blandly stated, to "enable GE to focus these resources on the areas we've identified for future growth."[32]

Rebalancing the Portfolio: Grafting the New onto the Old. Behind the sector clustering and reclustering and the spin offs was an ongoing effort by the company's top management to group GE's diversified businesses around new organizing concepts and, ultimately, a new strategic vision. In 1983, after several years at the helm, Welch drew three overlapping circles—Services, High Technology, and Core—and arranged the company's businesses within and on the margins of the diagram. Core, in his formulation, included lighting, appliances, and turbines, but not large motors, generators, or large transformers, although the company had traditionally manufactured all of these products. If the categories were loose, the signal that went through the company was strong and clear: Welch and his team were winnowing down GE's electrical and industrial sectors, and accelerating development of new ventures in financial services and high technology. As Welch explained, "We have our hands on a simple, understandable strategy for where we are, where we are not, where we can't find a solution, and where we have to disengage."[33]

Welch and his team kept their plans close to their chest initially, examining a host of acquisition possibilities, but the purchases soon came. In 1984, the company picked up Employers Reinsurance Corporation for $1.08 billion from Texaco. On a second front, two years later, the company acquired an 80 percent stake in Kidder, Peabody, and Co., via stock purchase, for about $600 million. (GE acquired the balance in 1990.) The biggest acquisition, however, came in 1986, when GE consummated a merger with RCA for $6.5 billion—the largest non-oil merger to date in American business history.[34] The acquisition represented something like a reunification, since GE had been one of the founding partners of the Radio Corporation of America in 1919 (joining a consortium of companies, including Westinghouse, to develop radio broadcasting technologies and products). RCA circa 1985 shared a number of businesses with GE, including consumer products, electronics, defense, broadcasting, and satellite communications. Still, the merger fundamentally rearranged GE's business profile. At RCA, entertainment generated 30 percent of sales and 40 percent of earnings. RCA's crown jewel and what Welch described as the "key asset" in the deal was NBC, then a popular although not an especially profitable television network. New vistas were opening for the company. "What we bought," Welch crowed, "was prime waterfront property."[35]

The wheeling and dealing continued through the late 1980s. In 1987, GE swapped its consumer electronics unit with Thomson S.A. of France for Thomson's medical equipment business. The French company had put the deal on the table, and Welch had grabbed at it. "We didn't need to go back to headquarters for a strategic analysis and a bunch of reports," he later recalled. "Conceptually, it took us about 30 minutes to decide that the deal made sense."[36] He was delighted to withdraw from an industry roiled by cutthroat competition with Asian companies, even if it meant pulling GE (and RCA) out of an old line business and a manufacturing mainstay.

More moves followed. In 1988, the company acquired Montgomery Ward's credit card operations, paying $1 billion and taking on the operation's $1.8 billion debt. In the same year, GE purchased Boggs-Warner's chemicals businesses. A host of smaller deals gave further definition to the new shape of the company. Welch pointed clearly to the broader, deeper transformation he was overseeing: about half of the company's earnings had come from "core manufacturing" in 1980, the year before he took over. He figured by 1986 the figure had come down to a third.[37] By 1987, the company calculated that nearly 80 percent of its earnings were coming from services and high technology.

From Hardware to Software: An Internal Transformation. In December 1989, Welch pronounced himself satisfied with the remaking of GE's portfolio, stating that the company would slow the pace of acquisitions and concentrate on wringing greater productivity out of existing units. (The company did negotiate a major deal in 1992, selling its aerospace business to Martin Marietta.) GE's industrial core businesses, to be sure, faced tough challenges. Appliances continued to weather fierce competition, power construction was still mired in a soft domestic market, and now aerospace faced sharp U.S. defense cutbacks. But GE had chosen which positions it was going to protect and proved itself capable of restructuring competitiveness into those businesses when they began to lose ground. So, for example, when earnings at appliances slipped under 7 percent in 1993, the company responded swiftly and energetically. Factory workers were taken off assembly lines and reorganized into work teams; the company pumped $140 million into plant overhauls; and engineers and designers retailored products to make them easier and less expensive to produce. The company's line of Maxus washers appearing in 1996 was typical, using 40 percent fewer parts and therefore saving substantial assembly and inventory costs. Essentially similar patterns of responsive restructuring operated in the company's power generation equipment, aircraft engine, and locomotive units.[38]

Meanwhile, the growth businesses the company had cultivated in the 1980s generated new earnings streams. Medical systems, for example, maintained a leading position in imaging technology, and NBC took and held the top network spot through the 1990s. The biggest source of growth, however, came in the company's financial services group, GE Capital. By 1997, revenues at Capital had reached $39.9 billion, making up 44 percent of total corporate sales; the subsidiary's operating profits, at $4.4 billion, accounted for 54 percent of the parent company's earnings.[39] The financial portfolio that generated these impressive results was spread out over a range of services and markets, from credit cards, to equipment leasing, to reinsurance, to computer services. By one analyst's measure, without Capital the parent company would have grown at a fairly pedestrian annual rate of 4 percent between 1991 and 1996, whereas with Capital, GE grew at an annual rate of 9.1 percent.[40]

Like Westinghouse Credit, GE Capital in the 1980s had ventured into the real estate and commercial finance lending markets. Capital, however, had better recognized the risks of overexposure and balanced other more stable financial operations against its high-yield lending. Moreover, Capital had kept a stockpile of reserves—$1.4 billion in 1990—to guard against sudden shocks. Thus GE managed to sidestep the land mines that exploded under Westinghouse in the early 1990s. Capital's diversified portfolio and general stability also enabled GE to absorb sharp losses at Kidder Peabody, an investment banking unit that ultimately was discontinued.

The strength of Capital and other units notwithstanding, in Welch's view the key to GE's success was its intangibles: its managerial ethos and expertise, its relentless drive for productivity and quality—in a word, its people. And it was here that Welch directed his intense energy during the 1990s. In December 1989, the CEO gathered a meeting of 100 top executives to announce that the company's new focus over the coming decade would be on increasing productivity. The first stage of the company's transformation, the "hardware phase," was now largely complete, Welch proclaimed. Now it was time for the "software phase."

It was far from clear at this stage exactly how to proceed. Welch was groping for ways to tap into latent energies within the company, and he was beginning to recognize the need to repair morale in ranks buffeted by restructuring. Brainstorming with close advisors, he concocted a thorough-going internal change initiative called *Work-Out*. The initiative began with a series of gatherings styled like town hall meetings—informal, relatively free-wheeling confrontations between line managers and the clerks, foremen, and floor workers who worked under them. Outside consultants were brought in as facilitators, managers were directed to make brief presentations describing operations as they perceived them, and then employees were invited to put questions, comments, and suggestions to their bosses. The sessions began in March 1989 and carried on unit by unit, office by office, factory by factory, throughout the company. Some workers responded suspiciously, but many more welcomed the opportunity to sound off and ideas poured in. The program worked out some employee frustration, but more importantly it worked innumerable, unnecessary routines out of company bureaucracy. Work-Out quickly became a company tradition and a key mechanism for extending Welch's candid, confrontational style below corporate and middle management ranks, down into the day-by-day, floor-level operations of the company.

For his part, Welch was coming to a grand, overarching articulation of what he saw the company trying to achieve. His vision for GE, he declared in 1990, was that it become a "boundaryless company." The axiom was broad and multivalent.

It described a global company that did business comfortably across national and cultural borders. It described a company that invited both upstream suppliers and downstream customers into collaboration. It described a company readily willing and able to import ideas from the outside. And it described a company in which the membranes of internal organization—hierarchical, horizontal, functional, geographic—became porous, letting ideas and people and initiative flow freely. Most fundamentally, it described the company as an open environment, the antithesis of the slow, stodgy, stiflingly bureaucratic places that critics charged American big businesses were becoming.[41]

Welch demonstrated his openness to outside ideas and his determination to continue pressing for further quality improvements when he launched the company's Six Sigma program in 1995. First conceived at Motorola and then carried over to AlliedSignal, Six Sigma is a statistical measure of quality, although the term also refers to the management philosophy and practices designed to deliver extraordinarily high quality. Six Sigma processes are designed to produce less than 3.4 defects or mistakes per million opportunities. Welch picked up on the idea from Lawrence Bossidy, a former GE vice chairman who had become AlliedSignal's CEO. Somewhat skeptical of quality programs in the past, Welch was nonetheless impressed by Bossidy's enthusiasm, as well as by the breathtaking ambition and stirring simplicity of the Six Sigma goal. Starting with 200 in-company projects in its first year, Six Sigma grew to 3,000 projects in 1996 (delivering $320 million in productivity gains and profits) and 6,000 projects in 1997, making it the largest quality management initiative in corporate America. By this point, the program deployed more than 60,000 part-time "Green Belt" project leaders and nearly 4,000 full-time "Black Belt" and "Master Black Belt" project leaders. More fundamentally, it was etching itself deeply into company identity. Welch embraced the program ardently. "Six Sigma training is quickly becoming part of the genetic code of our future leadership," he proclaimed, speaking glowingly of the rising number of "zealots" the program was creating in company ranks.

He had not invented the concept, but Six Sigma was classic Welch, and it was becoming classic GE. Equal parts bombast and battle hymn, the program was rapidly growing into something like a cult within the company—a proliferation that testified to the company's continuing responsiveness, its enduring ability to mobilize ardent spirit and thunderous energy behind company goals. GE in the late 1990s had grown to be a vast enterprise, but initiatives like Six Sigma suggested it was still strung taut.

A decade earlier, when critics characterized GE's turbulent strategic wheeling and dealing as conglomerate confusion, Welch had protested strongly and tried earnestly to express what he thought held the company together. "A conglomerate is a group of businesses with no central theme. GE has a common set of values," he maintained. "We have [the GE Management Development Institute at] Crotonville, where we teach leadership. We have a research lab that feeds all of our businesses. We have all the resources of a centralized company. Yet we've been able to go in and out of businesses for more than a century and stay ahead of changing times."[42] Later, he added, "GE is greater than the sum of its parts because of the intellectual capacity that is generated in the businesses and the sharing that goes on of that learning and the rapid action on that learning. [The company is] a business laboratory, with ideas everywhere that elevate us to be better than a single-product company could possibly be."[43]

At the dawn of the twenty-first century, the makeover of GE was accelerating. In his final years—he stepped down in 2001—Welch embraced the Internet and e-business with all the fervor characteristic of earlier enthusiasms. "This elixir, this tonic, this e-business" was transforming "the DNA of GE forever," he declared, adding "we are driving the hell out of IT spending. We think it's the lifeblood of the company and that digitization is the most important thing we've undertaken."[44] At the same time, the company was averaging more than a hundred acquisitions per year. Many of these occurred in the service sector, and in 1999, revenues from financial services (51 percent) surpassed those from electrical equipment (43 percent) for the first time, a circumstance that prompted *Fortune*, over Welch's protests, to reclassify GE as a financial services conglomerate.[45]

One of Welch's final acts was an unsuccessful attempt to force another reclassification by announcing plans, late in 2000, to acquire Honeywell, a $25 billion manufacturer of a diverse array of residential, industrial, and defense-related controls, equipment, and systems. Although regulators in Europe rejected the deal on antitrust grounds, GE remained a juggernaut. The company described itself as "a diversified technology, services, and manufacturing company" and posted revenues exceeding $130 billion while employing 313,000 people worldwide.[46] A striking aspect of the company's business portfolio at the dawn of the twenty-first century, given market conditions, was how much of GE's central, historical core survived. The company still manufactured turbines, lamps, and almost everything in between. But the company made, provided, and sold much more: aircraft engines, plastics, broadcasting, a broad array of financial and information services, and industrial and transportation systems.

Less tangibly, GE maintained its role as a leading purveyor of business rhetoric and philosophy. Concepts like Work-Out, the boundaryless organization, best practices, a learning company, Six Sigma, and e-business spread throughout corporate America over the 1990s much as strategic planning had done a generation before. Welch himself became an icon, hailed as one of the greatest corporate leaders of the era. However promotional this stream of press was, it nonetheless highlighted one central fact behind GE's success: this company had managed, unlike many others around it, to survive a sea change in the world around it. Its success required bold reconsideration of a strategy that was working and an organization that was widely admired across industries. It also required a willingness to endure deep pain and a determination to change faster than outside forces dictated.

THE STORY BEHIND THE STORIES

The contrasting stories of Westinghouse and GE exemplify the changing role of the large industrial corporation in the modern American economy, and the resulting dramatic changes in corporate strategy, structure, management systems, and governance. The biggest American industrials faced a stark reality of slow growth in their core businesses, as well as declining significance relative to other sectors of the economy.

In the new environment, giant size and venerable age no longer provided any security, while revolutionary shifts in thinking and acting were required to sustain success. Between 1974 and 2000, almost half of the top 100 industrials disappeared through mergers and acquisitions, bust-ups, and bankruptcies. (See Tables 2.3, 2,4, and 2.5 in Chapter 2 for comparable lists in 1974, 1994, and 2000.) Companies with narrower strategic focus, leaner organizations, and more efficient operations replaced them. Like GE, most of the survivors altered their sales mix to feature higher value-added products and a substantial component of services. Meanwhile, service companies in telecommunications, retailing, financial services, and health care gained new prominence in the economy. In 1995, *Fortune* magazine, which had started compiling its famous list of industrials four decades earlier, took note of the changing revenue streams of traditional industrials and the rise of huge service companies and modified the way it categorized the American economy.[47] Thereafter nearly two-thirds of the new *Fortune* 100 list consisted of service companies like AT&T and SBC Communications, Wal-Mart and Home Depot, Citigroup and Bank of America, and Aetna and Cardinal Health. (See Table 2.6 in Chapter 2 for the list in 2000.) This was but one of many shifts in the symbolic importance of the large industrial corporation: In the 1980s and 1990s, for example, the venerable Dow Jones Industrial Average, one of the most commonly cited indicators of the nation's economic health, leavened its manufacturing-heavy index with service providers in telecommunications, entertainment, retailing, and financial services.[48] (See Table 8.2 in Chapter 8.)

During the past quarter century, decline and change rippled through big industrials, triggering upheaval and pain (see Chapter 2). The biggest problem was finding ways to grow, and survivors in the group fared poorly, producing negligible real revenue growth during the period (see Chapter 3). The pursuit of growth triggered frequent, frantic shifts in strategy and organization, and a few companies, like Westinghouse (Viacom), wholly reinvented themselves. The inability to grow profitably, in turn, triggered massive reorganizations and downsizings and thorough overhauls of internal management systems (see Chapters 4 and 5). Average employment at the largest industrials fell by more than a third (from 100,000 to 65,000), and administrative hierarchies were slashed from an average of ten layers to six. Productivity improvement, total quality management, downsizing, reengineering, enterprise systems, and other corporate change programs and initiatives became a serial way of life. Employees grew anxious about their job security and prospects to earn rising real incomes. By the late 1990s, surveys revealed that 70 percent of employees did not trust their corporate leaders. The *Fortune* 100 no longer automatically attracted the best and brightest graduates into their ranks. Nor were corporate leaders secure in their positions or in the governing arrangements that had long supported them. More than one-fifth of CEOs in the population, like Westinghouse's Paul Lego, were ousted in the 1980s and 1990s, with a much greater likelihood than ever before that their successors, like Lego's, would come from the outside (see Chapters 6 and 7).

The relative decline of industrial companies in the U.S. economy seems likely to continue in the twenty-first century because there is little prospect for a resurgence of growth in aggregate demand for industrial products, especially in the advanced economies. Demand for such products has and will continue to grow faster in emerging and developing economies, but this demand is more likely to be captured by competitors based in late-industrializing countries such as Korea and China or by Western manufacturers willing to make big investments in such countries at the cost of domestic employment and, perhaps, political clout. The institutionalization of production methods and management practices that occurred over time in the advanced industrial countries has made it easier for followers in late-industrializing countries to imitate and absorb these practices.[49] The diffusion of knowledge about how to build, operate, and manage industrial companies has been accelerated by advances in transportation and communication technologies that have made the world, in Marshall McLuhan's famous term, a global village.[50] The spread and internationalization of business schools and management consulting firms further facilitates the transfer and absorption of such knowledge.[51]

New industrial producers can use this readily available knowledge to achieve parity in productivity, while still enjoying a significant labor cost advantage over their older, advanced Western rivals. It is precisely this dynamic that enabled first Japan, then Taiwan and Korea, and eventually China to develop strong industrial companies that first thrived on the growing demand in their own domestic markets and then attacked the advanced industrial markets with inexpensive, reasonable quality exports.[52]

Although the relative contribution of industrial corporations to the American economy began to wane after the mid-1950s, the decline accelerated in the 1970s with the convergence of two adverse trends: soaring energy costs and mounting global competition at home and abroad. On the demand side, the U.S. domestic market stopped growing. On the supply side, the American industrials had to compete against low-cost foreign rivals whose products were steadily, sometimes rapidly, improving in quality. After loudly complaining about the unfair trade practices of foreign competitors, the American industrials slowly began to understand that if they wished to remain competitive they would have to make major gains in productivity and in the quality of their products. The domestic political environment (as we will see in Chapter 2) provided little refuge, generally favoring free market competition over any extended form of protection.

It is often said that necessity is the mother of invention. It certainly appeared to be the case in the U.S. response to global industrial competition. New information technologies (such as computer-controlled machines and equipment) enhanced labor productivity through automation. Other forms of information technology improved managerial productivity by enabling the reengineering of business processes to reduce the need for the information transfer and coordination tasks that managers traditionally had performed. Once the productivity frontier began moving outward, it continued to do so with newer applications of information technologies and continuing process improvements.

Unfortunately, although they realized these productivity gains, the big industrials were unable to capture the value they created.[53] Rather, this benefit was split between consumers, who got ever better products at lower prices, and by investors, who took their returns and transferred them to companies in higher-growth sectors. For example, the price of a mid-sized car barely kept pace with inflation after the mid-1970s. At the same time, quality (as measured by defects) and durability (as measured by the length of standard warranties) more than doubled in the same period.

Even though they eventually recovered some of the ground lost to their foreign rivals,[54] the big industrial-companies confronted a new necessity—they had to come to terms with the dynamics of decline, of shrinking in the face of rapid productivity gains that outstripped anemic demand growth. Unfortunately for the managers of these companies, the dynamics of decline turned out to be quite different from their historical experience of the dynamics of growth. Those that understood the necessities of decline, like GE, were able to respond in ways that enabled them to prosper again. Those that resisted this dynamic, like Westinghouse, became casualties of this era of changing fortunes.

FROM GROWTH TO DECLINE: FROM THE M-FORM TO THE N-FORM

During the first half of the twentieth century, as the historian Alfred D. Chandler Jr. has vividly documented, U.S. industrial companies enjoyed a period of extraordinary growth.[55] The United States is a large country endowed with rich natural resources and a growing population well linked and supported by transportation and telecommunication networks. This created a large and steadily increasing demand for all types of industrial products, which in turn fueled the growth of those companies that could reliably and consistently produce and distribute such products. It was only toward the end of the 1960s that the demand for industrial goods began to taper off. By then, most American households had at least one car and television, a rich variety of household appliances, and a kitchen stocked with goods packaged in paper, plastic, metal, or glass containers—the result of a long wave of industrial expansion.

Before the market matured, matching the burgeoning demand for industrial goods with stable supply required careful coordination of a large number of interdependent investment intensive decisions. A series of coordinated investment decisions was necessary to ensure the reliable supply of relevant inputs; to transform these inputs cost-effectively (exploiting economies of scale) into outputs; and to market and distribute these outputs to customers. Chandler's central proposition is that, in the face of the uncertainty prevailing in these growing markets, the visible hand of managers who internalized these coordination problems within the boundaries of the corporation best accomplished the coordination of these interdependent investment decisions. [56]

Accordingly, the first type of industrial corporation to emerge at the turn of the century was the unitary or U-Form organization. Its strategy was to exploit economies of scale in the production of a single or narrow line of products. The corporation was organized functionally, with each function coordinating one important activity (e.g., purchasing, manufacturing, sales and marketing, finance). The functions all reported to a president or CEO, who assumed responsibility for coordinating among them using budgets and other vertical control systems. In many of these early industrial companies, the CEO was the founder and primary owner rather than a professional manager. Principal-agent problems, which arise with the separation of ownership and control, were not very significant. Hence, the contemporary conceptualization of corporate governance problems as a misalignment between shareholders' and managers' interests was not a significant concern.[57] Andrew Carnegie's Carnegie Steel (forerunner of U.S. Steel) and Henry Ford's Ford Motor Company were prototypical examples of the U-Form industrial corporation.

As large industrial companies developed a broader range of products and expanded into multiple market segments, they discovered that the U-Form organization was not suited to this increasing complexity. To better exploit these emerging economies of scope (across multiple businesses or markets) in addition to earlier economies of scale, some industrial companies, such as Du Pont and General Motors, starting in the 1920s, pioneered a new form of organization, which has been labeled the M (multidivisional)-Form. The main features of the M-Form include:

1. A *strategy* of growth based on exploiting economics of scale and scope. The large industrial company thus became increasingly diversified, both vertically and horizontally.

2. A *structure* designed to support this strategy and the increasing complexity of the corporation's activities. It involved the creation of semiautonomous operating divisions organized along product, brand, or geographic lines, each responsible for managing operating affairs. Overseeing these operating divisions was a corporate headquarters consisting of a number of powerful general executives and large advisory and financial staffs whose role was to monitor divisional performance, allocate resources among divisions, and engage in strategic planning.[58]
3. A *system* of budgeting, resource allocation, and performance evaluation that served to coordinate the corporation's various activities. Divisional or operating managers generated requests for resources in consultation with planning and financial staff at the headquarters. Senior executives at the corporate headquarters reviewed these competing requests and allocated resources according to their strategic merits, holding divisions accountable for producing results commensurate with the resources allocated to them. The primary information flows were vertical between division managers and top corporate executives, with the corporate staff playing a mediating role.[59]
4. *Governance* shifted to the hands of professional managers. Gradually, there was a virtually complete separation of ownership and control in large industrial corporations.[60] Even though the board of directors remained nominally responsible for overseeing the actions of managers and serving the interests of shareholders, the corporation's management typically appointed board members. Even outsiders on the board were usually part of the inner circle of senior corporate executives.[61] Thus the direction of the corporation was exercised not by the owners of capital, but by the managers who ran it. Indeed, the widespread diffusion of the M-Form went hand-in-hand with the rise of managerial capitalism.[62]

By the end of the 1960s, virtually every large industrial corporation, including GE and Westinghouse, had adopted these features of the M-Form, albeit with minor variations on each dimension.[63] The ubiquitous adoption of the M-Form provides powerful support for Chandler's hypothesis that economies of scale and scope can be best realized if industrial activity is coordinated by the visible hand of managers within the boundaries of the M-Form corporation.

Our analysis of the historical evolution of the large industrial corporation during the last quarter of the twentieth century suggests that Chandler's proposition hinges on a key contingency that has not been explicitly recognized. The hypothesis is valid only under conditions of growth. It does not hold under conditions of decline. In fact, based on our analysis, we hypothesize that the marginal value of managerial coordination is contingent upon growth. Managerial coordination has increasing returns when markets are expanding and companies are growing, but diminishing returns once markets mature and start contracting.

When demand stops growing, several things occur that invalidate Chandler's hypothesis. First, the growth of the corporation can no longer be met by related diversification that offers additional economies of scope. The stream of innovative new products emanating from any particular technological trajectory (for example, exploiting advances in polymer chemistry to create a series of important new plastics) slows down. While there is always room for minor product enhancements, the prospect of major product breakthroughs diminishes. Few industrial companies in our 1974 panel of *Fortune* 100 industrials successfully introduced blockbuster new products during the period of our study. New geographic markets or untapped customer segments also become more difficult to find and more fiercely contested when available.

The only option big industrials had to sustain growth was to venture into businesses that were unrelated to their core operations. Having lived through an age in which growth was their only experience and one of their main business imperatives, managers of industrial companies sought growth wherever it was available. During the late 1960s and early 1970s, companies like GE and Westinghouse vastly altered the scope of their businesses, entering many in which they had no particular experience or expertise (GE proved shrewder than Westinghouse choosing which service businesses to enter, as well as more adept in learning how to manage them.) At the same time, highly diverse, conglomerate corporations like ITT and Teledyne appeared. Under the direction of CEO Harold Geneen, ITT entered into over 50 unrelated business segments. The conglomerate represented the distorted apogee of Chandler's proposition—that industrial activity of any nature was best carried out through managerial coordination within the boundaries of an M-Form corporation.[64]

In a world in which capital and labor markets were becoming increasingly deregulated and more efficient, it was hard for conglomerate managers to claim credibly that they were better at managing activities far afield from their core competence than other managers who focused their energies solely on managing a particular business segment. The ease with which investors could diversify risk through investment portfolios (spurred by the rise of mutual funds in this period), made the risk management argument for conglomerates untenable.[65] It was little surprise that conglomerates enjoyed a short heyday and began to be dismantled during the 1970s.

By this time the management practices required to coordinate the activities of a large industrial organization had become widely known and highly institutionalized.[66] The uncertainty of making large interdependent investments that reliably matched demand and supply, which was quite acute in a rapidly growing market, diminished substantially as markets matured and stabilized. There were simply fewer such investment decisions to be made. The key decisions were no longer which new product to introduce, or which plant or distribution facility to invest in, but which existing operations to shut down. The major decisions did not have to deal with the uncertainties of seizing opportunities in a growing market but rather with confronting the painful certainty of shrinking to serve a declining market. Under conditions of decline, markets rather than managers gained the upper hand. By understanding and accepting the power of financial markets, Jack Welch was able to maintain control over GE's destiny. By resisting that power (among other mistakes), the leaders of Westinghouse doomed their company.

It became easier to coordinate activities through arm's-length or market contracts late in the twentieth century because the coordination issues were by then well known. The increasing viability of market contracting in relation to managerial coordination triggered the horizontal and vertical de-integration of the complex M-Form enterprise. [67] In the arena of strategic management, this trend was framed as refocusing the corporation on its core competencies.[68]

The institutionalization of industrial production and managerial practices also enabled increasing productivity. When practices and processes become relatively well defined, they also become more susceptible to automation. New information technologies that emerged in the 1970s and proliferated rapidly—especially decentralized computing power—facilitated such automation. As a result, both blue- and white-collar employment could be reduced.[69] The new ability to perform both production and managerial tasks more efficiently created a growing surplus of both workers and managers.

When demand is not growing fast enough to accommodate this labor surplus, productivity gains are first realized by downsizing and business process reengineering within a single company. The sooner these gains are recognized, as GE did well before Westinghouse, the more time the company buys to turn around its fading fortunes. But once these opportunities have been recognized and the ways to realize them have been learned, the obvious next opportunity to achieve productivity gains involves the merger of two entities, which affords further opportunities to reduce overhead and consolidate operations. Indeed, a careful analysis of mega-mergers reveals that the major benefit is neither new revenue streams (although this is often touted) nor higher prices through increased market power (although this is often presumed). The principal benefits of mergers are the cost-savings and productivity gains that result from eliminating redundant production or distribution capacity and laying off not only front-line workers but also substantial numbers of middle managers and senior executives. As a rough rule of thumb, when two companies of approximately equal size (in terms of revenues and employment) merge, after three years, the company will have revenues equal to the sum of its two constituent entities, but only one-and-a-half times the number of employees that either entity had before the merger.

Once consolidation begins in an industry, there is a natural tendency for other competitors to follow suit. In industry after industry, a merger between two major rivals inevitably triggers other competitors to follow suit. By insisting that every company in GE's portfolio be first or second in its industry, Welch ensured that these units would always remain ahead in this race toward consolidation. One rationale can be found in Harrison White's conception of markets as role structures in which producers orient themselves toward each other and toward customers by arranging themselves on a size spectrum.[70] A substantial change in the relative size of any major competitor created by an event such as a big merger disturbs this role equilibrium. Matching an initial merger between rivals enables other rivals to remain competitive and restore the earlier relative-size equilibrium and ordering in the market.[71]

Other factors may also contribute to this bandwagon effect. One is that companies compete intensely to attract and retain the attention of important stakeholders, such as investors, customers, and employees. A company that finds itself suddenly much smaller than a previously comparable competitor may fear (sometimes understandably, sometimes irrationally) that it could lose status in the eyes of its major stakeholders.[72] For example, following a merger, investment bankers may spend more time calling on the now much larger competitor, neglecting smaller rivals in the process. Customers may be attracted to the presumed stability of the larger company. Employees may wish for the security of working for the acquiring party in a merger, because post-merger layoffs inevitably are greater in the entity that is viewed as having been acquired (even in a deal that is framed as a merger of equals).

Another explanation for the bandwagon effect in mergers is that the CEOs of large companies have large egos and are highly motivated to restore parity among their peers if it appears that they have fallen behind. They may be especially motivated to maintain relative size, because historically CEO pay has been tightly linked to company size.[73] In this view, mergers that result in consolidation may simply reflect the hubris of CEOs and have little economic merit.

We believe all these explanations of industry consolidations are at least partly valid. But the underlying driver of the strategic refocusing and consolidation of large industrial companies is the diminishing returns to managerial coordination when markets stop growing and begin to decline. Not only do these diminishing returns to managerial coordination change the strategic trajectory of the M-Form industrial corporation, but they also change its structural characteristics. Important structural consequences include the downsizing and delayering of elaborate M-Form hierarchies. Such moves are particularly devastating to middle managers and headquarters staff, whose coordinating roles have been greatly reduced. As companies strategically refocus and consolidate, the need for corporate strategists who helped manage and monitor resource allocation decisions across a diverse portfolio of businesses simply disappears.

The renewed emphasis on productivity and profitability also means that strategy shifts to identifying ways to optimize operating efficiencies from ways to optimize resource allocation across a portfolio of businesses. Power flows back from the corporate headquarters to the operating units.[74] At GE, Welch spotted this trend early and quickly dismantled the company's elaborate corporate hierarchy. At

Westinghouse, the powerful corporate headquarters bureaucracy remained intact much longer.

With the coordination of activities no longer the responsibility of a heavily staffed corporate headquarters or a steep, vertical managerial hierarchy, teams now carry out this work. These may include self-managing production teams or executive teams that bring together managers from different parts of the business to coordinate interdependencies and share best practices to increase productivity. Horizontal and informal relationships rather than vertical and formal relationships increasingly define the official structure of the organization. The resulting structure thus resembles more a network (N-Form) as opposed to the hierarchical M-Form, even though the skeleton of the M-Form remains.

Management systems and processes are also reconfigured. Systems and processes that managed the flow of information up and down the organization to help coordinate activities across a hierarchy of managers are no longer useful because of the reduced marginal value of such coordination. These centralized systems are supplanted by more decentralized information systems that enable operating workers and managers to be better informed and act more autonomously. Information systems also become network-like to reflect and support changes in the strategy and structure of the organization.

When demand for industrial goods was growing in the United States, Chandler's managers were rightfully the dominant actors on the economic stage. By coordinating large-scale enterprises that exploited economies of scale and scope to produce a reliable and expanding supply of goods, managers as agents created great value that benefited all major stakeholders. Because the challenges of coordinating such enterprises were novel and as yet unclear, agents who possessed the skills to manage such complex enterprises had great value to principals who recognized the investment opportunity but did not themselves possess the requisite management skills. Competent professional managers became valuable economic agents. Thanks to their skills, consumers could buy goods that enhanced the quality of their lives, investors saw a growing return on their investment, and employees got rising real wages, job security, and good prospects for upward mobility in a growing organization.

In a growing market, opportunities to create value abounded, and managers were granted considerable autonomy to pursue them. As long as managers maintained respectable track records of capturing these opportunities, they continued to enjoy this autonomy. In a positive-sum game, it is easier to keep everyone happy and stakeholders tend to be more forgiving of occasional lapses. In these circumstances, it is not surprising that we witnessed the separation of ownership and control. Nor is it surprising that managers became a powerful elite, who acted in ways to consolidate and preserve their power.

Managerial capitalism becomes more problematic when growth stops. Now the problems rather than the virtues of agency become more salient, as managers may pursue strategic choices that are at odds with what shareholders believe is necessary. During decline, the task for corporate managers is more obvious but less palatable. It is to oversee cost cutting and continuous gains in productivity. There is less room for strategic choice and the value of the visible hand diminishes. Society prefers that its resources, which include capital, labor, and managerial talent, be reallocated to emerging growth sectors, where their marginal value is much greater. The autonomy that managers previously enjoyed now needs to be curtailed.

Few people willingly give up their autonomy and power, and managers are no exception. Moreover, it is far more exciting to oversee growth than to oversee decline. The latter takes a greater emotional toll because it inevitably involves breaking commitments or resetting expectations formed during periods of growth.

As we saw at Westinghouse, the senior managers who rose to power during a period of growth, found it difficult to come to terms with the necessities of decline. They continued to pursue growth wherever they thought they could find it. Skilled at managing industrial growth, they did not really know how to manage industrial decline nor how to identify, enter, and manage businesses in emerging growth sectors. GE under Welch provided a sharp contrast. Ultimately, forceful external intervention was required to reduce managerial autonomy and refocus management priorities in most big industrials. This was precisely the role first played by takeover artists, then large institutional investors, and finally independent boards of directors. They had no choice but to replace management if it was unwilling to adapt to the necessity of managing decline. Often outsiders, like Michael Jordan at Westinghouse, could take a more objective look at the emerging reality, untainted by the prior history of growth, and proved better suited to the new task at hand. The balance of power thus slowly but surely shifted back from agents to principals, from managers to investors.

In sum, the M-Form was the product of an era of growth. As growth diminished, the advantages of the M-Form were lost. In its place, a new form—the N-Form industrial corporation—emerged (see Table 1.3).

The remainder of this book describes the historic transformation of the large industrial corporation in greater detail. We start by discussing the various forces that combined to trigger the fading fortunes of large industrial companies in the United States (see Chapter 2).

The new strategies (Chapter 3), structures (Chapter 4), systems (Chapter 5), and governance arrangements (Chapter 6) that emerged from this period of turmoil combined to define a big industrial corporation that was qualitatively different from its forebears: leaner, faster, more interconnected and interdependent with other institutions and more responsive to market forces.

Meanwhile, as the industrial corporation receded from the center of the economy, all the constituencies that had prospered under its sway—owners, managers,

Table 1.3
From the M-Form to the N-Form

	M-Form Corporation	*N-Form Corporation*	*Adaptive Actions*
Strategy	Growth through economies of scale and scope; vertical and horizontal diversification	Emphasis on profits and productivity; focusing on core businesses and activities	Divestitures and mergers leading to consolidation, alliances, and outsourcing
Structure	Hierarchical, multidivisional structures; large corporate headquarters	Flatter, network like structures; lean corporate headquarters	Downsizing, delayering, reduction of white-collar employees
Systems	Vertical systems designed to optimize strategic resource allocation decisions	Horizontal and networked systems designed to optimize operating business processes	TQM systems, reengineering, decentralized information technologies
Governance	Managerial capitalism; managers enjoy considerable autonomy	Investor capitalism; managers on a tight leash	Concentration of capital in the hands of institutional investors; tight corporate governance
Loyalties	All stakeholders benefit; reciprocal bonds between companies, employees, consumers, and investors.	Zero-sum game; arm's-length contracts between companies, employees, consumers, and investors.	Market forces prevail over long-term commitments

employees, customers, and communities—were forced to look elsewhere to obtain the benefits and assurances now lost (Chapter 7). A new set of companies and industries captured the imagination of customers, employees, and investors, and occupied center stage in place of the large industrials (Chapter 8). That development, in turn, carried enormous implications for the large industrials, as well as for the non-industrial institutions now expected to fill their historic role (Chapter 9).

CHAPTER 2

Passages and Patterns

Fred Crawford, the legendary leader of Thompson Products before it merged with Ramo-Wooldridge in 1958 to become TRW, the automotive supply and aerospace powerhouse, once compared leading a business to riding a bicycle: keep moving or you fall down. The observation remains as true at the dawn of the twenty-first century as it did decades ago. The most constant consideration for any business organization is dealing with change: new people, products, markets, customers, competitors, industries, public policies, technologies, techniques, ideas, and mistakes jostle with the old in a continuous churn. The saga of GE and Westinghouse in Chapter 1 is a case in point. Although the story focuses on the period beginning in the mid-1970s and carries it forward to the present, we do not wish to imply that these companies—or any other company in the *Fortune* 100, or any business organization at all, for that matter—ever enjoyed a time to relax and coast. There is no such thing as stasis in business. But there are stretches of greater and lesser turbulence. And for the large American industrial corporation, the period since the mid-1970s has been emphatically a time of great turbulence.

Some forces that gathered and merged to create the storm naturally have deeper roots than others. In addition to the everyday drivers of change just mentioned, several long-term trends converged to alter the business environment. To begin with, the structure of the entire economy has been shifting inexorably over time. Between about 1880 and about 1920, the United States moved from a nation whose wealth depended on agriculture to one reliant on manufacturing.[1]

The primacy of manufacturing proved short lived, however. By 1955, the year after *Fortune* began tracking the largest industrials (meaning companies engaged primarily in manufacturing, mining, and construction), this sector of the economy accounted for 45 percent of total economic activity in the United States. (See Figure 2.1.) By 1974, the percentage slipped to 36 percent, and by 1998, to 24 percent. These data prompt several observations.

First, the rate of relative decline in the industrials proved roughly constant over the entire period between 1955 and 1998. The industrials lost 25 percent of their share in the 19 years between 1955 and 1974 and another 33 percent in the 24 years between 1974 and 1998. No matter what these companies tried—and they tried many different things—they proved powerless to reverse their relative decline.

Figure 2.1
U.S. Economy by Sector

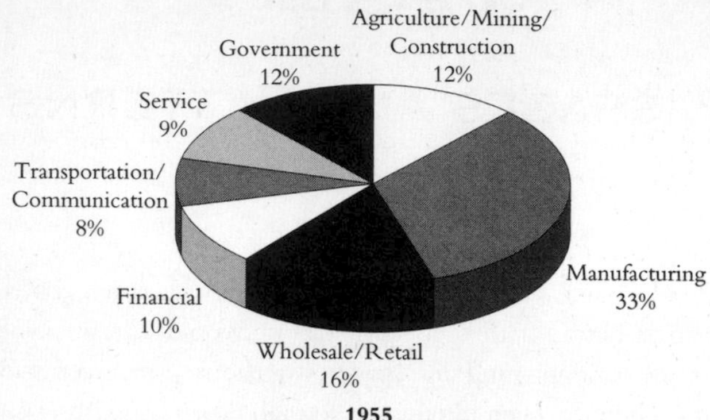

1955

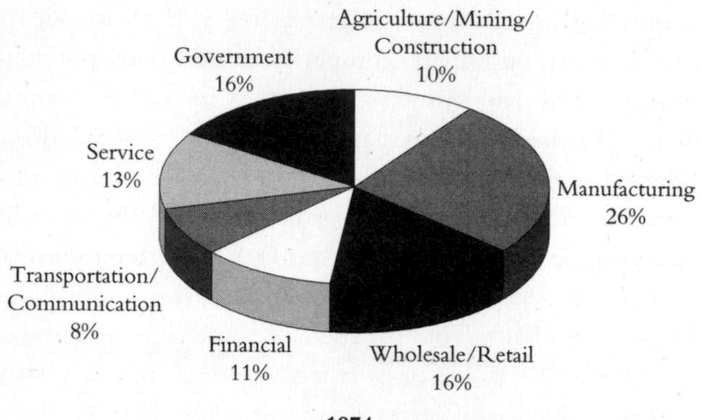

1974

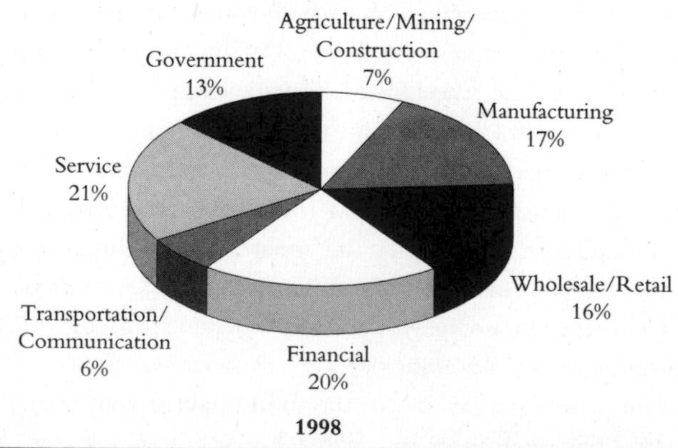

1998

The agricultural component of the "Agriculture/Mining/Construction" category amounted to only 5 percent in 1955 and has continued to drift slowly down since then. These graphs are based on information available in U.S. Bureau of the Census, *Historical Statistics of the United States* and *Statistical Abstract of the United States 2000* (Washington, DC, 2000).

Second, significantly, the relative contributions of government, the transportation and communications sector, and the wholesale/retail trade sector remained more or less steady during the period. In the case of the government, the constancy indicated by the endpoints of the data masks a period of expansion in the 1960s and one of retrenchment in the 1980s. In the transportation/communications and the wholesale/retail trade sectors, the constancy is surprising, especially given technological change, competitive dynamics, and other upheavals of the era.

Third, the service industries have been the big gainer in the economy, with traditional services (professional, real estate, shipping, etc.) growing steadily and financial, health care, and media and information technology services surging dramatically in the 1980s and 1990s.

Finally, and most fundamentally, these trends illustrate a secular change in the basis of economic activity as the U.S. economy continues to migrate from a foundation in manufacturing to a dependence on services.[2] In 1998, government and services accounted for more than three-fourths of the U.S. GDP. Whatever is going on here is working against the fortunes of the industrials and benefiting other actors in the economy.

That the makeover of the economy is proceeding at a constant pace is not to say, however, that the period since the mid-1970s has been a mere continuation of what went before. Quite the contrary: The voyage remains under way at constant speed but the passage has become much more perilous. That is the result of other long-term factors at work.

THE GATHERING STORM

Economists and historians frequently divide the period since World War II into two halves: a stretch of robust economic growth between the late 1940s and the mid-1970s, and a more troubled time since the mid-1970s.[3] The energy crisis in 1973 and 1974 is often pinpointed as a watershed moment because it triggered an unusually long and deep recession and because it was followed by many years of upheaval in the industrial sector of the economy. Moreover, the oil crisis coincided roughly with other significant events that seemed to cap the postwar era, especially the Watergate scandal, which toppled the presidency of Richard Nixon and called into question leadership in all kinds of institutions, and the winding down of the Vietnam War, which emphasized the limits of American power and influence abroad. The mid-1970s thus hastened to a premature end "the American century" (a phrase coined by *Time* magazine's Henry Luce in the 1940s) of unparalleled prosperity and geopolitical dominance.

Like most generalizations, this one exaggerates. The economy before 1973 was hardly static or wholly benign, and since then it has featured many trends beneficial to big companies. Before 1973, as noted previously, the basis of the U.S. economy was already shifting away from manufacturing toward services. At the same time, the composition of the industrial economy was changing, as evidenced by Tables 2.1 and 2.2, which list the 100 biggest industrial companies in 1917 and 1955.[4] In the earlier year, the industrial economy was heavily dependent on a few salient industries: the extractive industries (including energy and mining), primary manufacturing (metals, rubber, chemicals), production of heavy machinery and equipment (e.g., transportation equipment, electrical equipment), and food, tobacco, and clothing. By 1955, the mix had shifted somewhat, with many of the same industries still well represented but with several newcomers—especially aircraft equipment, defense contracting, and electronic equipment—now figuring substantially. The arrivals owed much of their fortune to the rise of the U.S. government, especially the Department of Defense, as a major customer. Most of the companies that disappeared from the list by 1955 came from the extractive and primary manufacturing industries, indicating the industrial sector's migration toward provision of higher value-added goods and services. Although no one at the time used the term, the industrial base was shifting from capital-intensive production to science-based and knowledge-intensive work.[5]

This pattern was not yet evident in the early post-World War II years, which are often considered a "golden era" in American industrial history. The contribution of manufacturing to gross domestic product peaked between 1953 and 1957.[6] U.S. manufacturers had emerged from the war as the world's biggest and most powerful, and they possessed many compelling advantages. They were flush with cash and carried little debt on their balance sheets. They had learned to manage rapid growth, organize and train large numbers of employees, and plan for the future. They operated large, modern facilities bristling with the latest, most advanced machinery and equipment. They parlayed numerous wartime inventions and innovations into new or greatly expanded industries in electronics, aircraft, defense, pharmaceuticals, and synthetic materials.[7] At home, they sold into the world's biggest, most affluent, and most homogeneous market. And abroad, in an effort to promote democratic capitalism and check the rising influence of communist nations, they shared products, technology, and management techniques with war-ravaged nations in Europe and Asia, as well as with developing nations around the world. All this combined to generate a period of unparalleled profitable growth for big industrial corporations.

Meanwhile, high growth rates and low rates of inflation and unemployment created a benign macroeconomic environment. Although several recessions punctuated the 1950s and 1960s, these were mere hiccups: none lasted as long as a year before giving way to a return of vigorous prosperity. Between 1948 and 1973, the U.S. economy boomed at an average annual rate of 3.7 percent per year, with big industrial corporations clearly accounting for much of it.[8] The growth rate in aggregate sales among the *Fortune* 500 after 1954 consistently outpaced growth of the U.S. economy as a whole.[9] Over the same 25-year period, total factor productivity climbed at an annual rate of 2.5 percent per year, helping weekly take-home wages

Table 2.1
The 100 Largest Industrial Corporations in 1917

1. U.S. Steel
2. Standard Oil (New Jersey)
3. Bethlehem Steel
4. Armour & Company
5. Swift & Company
6. Midvale Steel & Ordnance
7. International Harvester
8. Du Pont
9. U.S. Rubber
10. Phelps Dodge Corporation
11. General Electric Company
12. Anaconda Copper Corporation
13. American Smelting & Refining
14. Standard Oil (NY)
15. Singer Manufacturing Company
16. Ford Motor Company
17. Westinghouse Electric & Manufacturing
18. American Tobacco Company
19. Jones & Laughlin Steel Company
20. Union Carbide and Carbon
21. Weyerhaeuser Timber Company
22. B.F. Goodrich Company
23. Central Leather Company
24. Texas Company
25. Pullman Company
26. Gulf Oil Company
27. Kennecott Copper Corporation
28. American Sugar Refining
29. Chile Copper Company
30. General Motors Corporation
31. American Can Company
32. Consolidation Coal Company
33. American Car & Foundry
34. Standard Oil (Indiana)
35. Standard Oil (California)
36. American Woolen Company
37. Magnolia Oil
38. Western Electric Company
39. Republic Iron & Steel
40. Lackawanna Steel Company
41. Willys-Overland Company
42. Pittsburgh Coal
43. Corn Products Refining
44. Liggett & Meyers Tobacco
45. Ohio Cities Gas Company
46. United Fruit Company
47. Aluminum Company of America
48. Prairie Oil & Gas
49. Wilson & Company
50. Philadelphia & Reading Coal & Iron
51. Chevrolet Motor Company
52. W.R. Grace
53. Youngstown Sheet & Tube
54. Colorado Fuel & Iron Company
55. Virginia-Carolina Chemical Company
56. Sinclair Oil & Refining
57. Morris & Company
58. Crucible Steel of America
59. U.S. Smelting, Refing, & Mining
60. Calumet & Hecla Mining
61. Ohio Oil Company
62. American Locomotive Works
63. Cuba Cane & Sugar
64. Pan American Petroleum
65. Goodyear Tire & Rubber
66. American Agriculture Chemical Company
67. Lehigh Coal & Navigation
68. Utah Copper Company
69. Associated Oil
70. International Paper
71. Union Oil Company of California
72. Vacuum Oil Company
73. New Jersey Zinc
74. United Shoe Machinery
75. Baldwin Locomotive Works
76. National Biscuit Company
77. Deere & Company
78. Studebaker Corporation
79. Cudahy Packing Company
80. Eastman Kodak
81. P. Lorillard Company
82. International Nickel Company
83. Procter & Gamble
84. Atlantic Refining Company
85. Greene Cananea Copper Company
86. National Lead
87. Inland Steel Company
88. General Chemical Company
89. United Motors Corporation
90. Distillers Securities Corporation
91. United Verde Ext. Mining Company
92. Allis-Chalmers Manufacturing Company
93. Great Western Sugar Company
94. Crane Company
95. Midwest Refining Company
96. Firestone Tire & Rubber
97. Cuban-American Sugar Company
98. Maxwell Motor Company
99. Dodge Brothers
100. United Verde Copper

Note: Companies are ranked by total assets.
Source: Alfred D. Chandler Jr., *The Visible Hand: The Managerial Revolution in American Business* (Cambridge, MA: Harvard University Press, 1977), pp. 503–512.

Table 2.2
The 100 Largest Industrial Corporations in 1954

1. General Motors
2. Standard Oil (New Jersey)
3. U.S. Steel
4. General Electric
5. Swift
6. Chrysler
7. Armour
8. Gulf Oil
9. Socony-Vacuum Oil
10. Du Pont
11. Bethlehem Steel
12. Standard Oil (Ind.)
13. Westinghouse Electric
14. Texas Company
15. Western Electric
16. Shell Oil
17. National Dairy Products
18. Standard Oil (California)
19. Goodyear Tire & Rubber
20. Boeing Airplane
21. Sinclair Oil
22. International Harvester
23. RCA
24. Union Carbide
25. Firestone Tire & Rubber
26. Douglas Aircraft
27. Procter & Gamble
28. Republic Steel
29. Cities Service
30. Phillips Petroleum
31. General Foods
32. U.S. Rubber
33. Borden
34. Lockheed Aircraft
35. Alcoa
36. International Paper
37. Wilson & Company
38. Sun Oil
39. United Aircraft
40. American Can
41. General Dynamics
42. North American Aviation
43. Eastman Kodak
44. B.F. Goodrich
45. Continental Can
46. Bendix Aviation
47. Atlantic Refining
48. Inland Steel
49. Armco Steel
50. Allied Chemical
51. American Metal Products
52. American Tobacco
53. Continental Oil
54. Allis-Chalmers
55. Jones & Laughlin Steel
56. General Mills
57. National Steel
58. Curtiss-Wright
59. Olin-Mathieson Chemical
60. American Smelting & Refining
61. IBM
62. Anaconda Copper
63. Tide Water Associated Oil
64. Cudahy Packing
65. Briggs Manufacturing
66. Sperry
67. R.J. Reynolds Tobacco
68. Pittsburgh Plate Glass
69. Dow Chemical
70. Youngstown Sheet & Tube
71. Kennecott Copper
72. National Lead
73. Standard Brands
74. W.R. Grace
75. Caterpillar Tractor
76. American Motors
77. Ralston Purina
78. American Cyanamid
79. Pullman
80. Pure Oil
81. Borg-Warner
82. Nabisco
83. Avco Manufacturing
84. Union Oil
85. Philco
86. Burlington Mills
87. Monsanto Chemical
88. Campbell Soup
89. Owens-Illinois Glass
90. Pillsbury Mills
91. Singer Manufacturing
92. Hormel
93. Hygrade Food Products
94. Republic Aviation
95. Carnation
96. American Sugar Refining
97. Reynolds Metals
98. John Morrell
99. Standard Oil (Ohio)
100. American Radiator & Standard Sanitary

Source: Fortune, July 1955, Supplement, "The Fortune Directory," and pp. 96–97.

Note: Several large companies, most notably Ford Motor, were not included in the original list of the top 500 because they did not publish sales figures. For purposes of subsequent analysis in this book, Ford is considered part of the sample for this year and American Radiator & Standard Sanitary is not.

Holdovers since 1917: (48) U.S. Steel, Standard Oil (NJ), Bethlehem Steel, Armour, Swift, International Harvester, Du Pont, U.S. Rubber, General Electric, Anaconda Copper, Am. Smelting & Refining, Standard Oil (NY) [Socony-Vacuum Oil], Singer, Ford, Westinghouse, American Tobacco, Jones & Laughlin, Union Carbide, B.F. Goodrich, Texas Co., Pullman, Gulf Oil, Kennecott Copper, American Sugar Refining, General Motors, American Can, Standard Oil (Ind.), Standard Oil (Cal.), Western Electric, Republic Iron & Steel, Willys-Overland [American Motors], Alcoa, Wilson, W.R. Grace, Youngstown Sheet & Tube, Sinclair Oil, Goodyear Tire, International Paper, Union Oil, National Biscuit, Cuddahy Packing, Eastman Kodak, Procter & Gamble, Atlantic Refining, National Lead, Inland Steel, Allis-Chalmers, Firestone Tire, Maxwell Motors [Chrysler].

Arrivals since 1917: (52) Chrysler, Shell, National Dairy, Boeing, RCA, Douglas Aircraft, Cities Service, Phillips Petroleum, General Foods, Borden, Lockheed Aircraft, Sun Oil, United Aircraft, General Dynamics, North American Aviation, Continental Can, Bendix Aviation, Armco, Allied Chemical, American Metal Products, Continental Oil, General Mills, National Steel, Curtiss-Wright, Olin-Mathiesen Chemical, IBM, Tide Water Associated Oil, Briggs Manufacturing, Sperry, R.J. Reynolds Tobacco, PPG, Dow Chemical, Standard Brands, Caterpillar, Ralston Purina, American Cyanamid, Pure Oil, Borg-Warner, Avco Manufacturing, Philco, Burlington Mills, Monsanto, Campbell Soup, Owens-Illinois Glass, Pillsbury, Hormel, Hygrade Food Products, Republic Aviation, Carnation, Reynolds Metals, John Morrell, Standard Oil (Ohio).

Departures since 1917: (52) Midvale Steel, Phelps Dodge, Weyerhaeuser, Central Leather, Chile Copper, Consolidation Coal, American Car & Foundry, American Woolen, Magnolia Oil, Lackawanna Steel, Pittsburgh Coal, Corn Pdts. Refining, Liggett & Meyers Tobacco, Ohio Cities Gas, United Fruit, Prairie Oil & Gas, Phil. & Reading Coal, Chevrolet, Colorado Fuel & Iron, Va.-Carolina Chemical, Morris & Co., Crucible Steel, U.S. Smelting & Refining, Calumet & Hecla Mining, Ohio Oil, Am. Locomotive, Cuba Cane & Sugar, Pan Am. Petroleum, Am. Ag. Chem., Lehigh Coal, Utah Copper, Associated Oil, Vacuum Oil, New Jersey Zinc, United Shoe Machinery, Baldwin Locomotive, Deere & Co., Studebaker, P. Lorillard, International Nickel, Greene Cananea Copper, General Chemical, United Motors, Distillers Securities, United Verde Ext. Mining, Great Western Sugar, Crane, Midwest Refining, Cuban-American Sugar, Maxwell Motor, Dodge Bros., United Verde Copper.

climb an average of 2.9 percent per year—higher sustained rates than any seen since the beginnings of industrialization.[10]

In qualitative terms, the famous admission of "Engine" Charlie Wilson (to distinguish him from his contemporary "Electric" Charlie Wilson, head of GE), the president of General Motors, well expressed the primacy of the big industrial corporation. Testifying before the U.S. Senate in 1952, when President Eisenhower had nominated him to become Secretary of Defense, Wilson denied any potential conflict of interest, acknowledging that "for years I thought that what was good for the country was good for General Motors, and vice versa. The difference did not exist. Our company is too big. It goes with the welfare of the country."[11] This was no mere boast: the economy whirled around an industrial axis stretching from Pittsburgh to Detroit, and Big Steel and Big Autos served as financial bellweathers. (The Dow Jones Industrial Average, the most frequently cited index of the nation's economic health, was composed heavily of manufacturing companies until the 1980s, when financial services companies like American Express and Citigroup were added.[12])

The big industrials dominated public awareness of business and economic activity—hence *Fortune* magazine's decision in 1954 to begin tracking them as a group. The motives and inner workings of these giants became fodder for popular authors (Ayn Rand), stage (*Death of a Salesman, How to Succeed in Business Without Really Trying*), and screen (*The Man in the Gray Flannel Suit*), as well as for astute social commentators like C. Wright Mills, William H. Whyte, and Peter Drucker. Several influential books portrayed the big industrials as nearly invincible actors. In 1959, Harvard economist Edward S. Mason, an expert on monopolies, edited a collection called *The Corporation in Modern Society* that became a staple on college and business school reading lists. Contributors to the book accepted as given that the business (industrial) corporation had swelled into a mighty and largely uninhibited force capable of dictating terms to owners, employees, and unions, while paying little heed to the government.[13] A few years later, Mason's colleague, the liberal economist John Kenneth Galbraith, published *The New Industrial State,* a treatise warning against the unchecked economic and political clout of the industrial giants. Simultaneously, the French political journalist Jean Jacques Servan-Schreiber issued *Le defi americain* (*The American Challenge*), a widely circulated work that alerted French and European readers to the might of American industrial management and predicted that world markets and foreign cultures would soon be overwhelmed.[14]

Yet even as the triumph of the big corporation was being written, countervailing currents were eroding its foundations. The portrayal of big companies in alarmist terms reflected an enduring strain in American culture, especially suspicion of concentrated wealth and power. And in the late 1950s and early 1960s, government policies began to tilt against the big corporations, with major antitrust settlements against AT&T and IBM and an embarrassing price-fixing scandal involving GE and Westinghouse. The Celler-Kefauver Act (1950) prohibited any merger that reduced or "substantially lessened" competition "in any line of commerce." An important test of the statute came in the 1962 U.S. Supreme Court decision *Brown v. Kinney Shoe,* which outlawed a proposed combination between a leading shoe manufacturer and a leading shoe retailer.[15] The effect on big companies was pronounced: As growth rates tapered off in the mid- and late-1960s amid concerns that core technologies were maturing, a wave of mergers unfurled. But companies avoided making deals within their core industries—a course that might have produced renewed gains in efficiency and productivity—instead using them to diversify into new and unrelated areas. Between 1949 and 1969, the number of *Fortune* 500 companies that derived the majority of their revenues from a single or dominant business dropped by half (from about 70 percent to about 36 percent), whereas the number that gleaned revenues from activities unrelated to their original core business more than doubled (from about 30 percent to about 64 percent). When the strategy was carried to its extreme, it resulted in conglomerates like Textron, ITT, Gulf + Western, Teledyne, and LTV. (Between 1965 and 1969, Teledyne alone completed 125 acquisitions, the vast majority of which were unrelated to the company's original business.)[16]

In the meantime, the political and economic environment was turning more hostile. Starting in the mid-1960s, the federal government spawned a host of administrative agencies designed to regulate corporations, including the Occupational Health and Safety Administration (OSHA), the National Transportation Safety Board (NTSB), the Consumer Product Safety Commission (CPSC), and the Environmental Protection Agency (EPA).[17] In each instance, agencies formed in response to specific problems and abuses, but they held broad mandates to regulate business corporations. Critics of big business typically led and staffed the agencies, a factor that tinged proceedings and hearings with adversarial hues. Collectively, the agencies triggered a sharp rise in corporate operating costs. In response, many large companies opened "public affairs" offices in Washington, DC, and contributed to the swelling budgets of industry associations and other lobbying groups formed to combat and ease the pressure.

In the late 1960s and early 1970s, other factors combined to dampen the fortunes of the big industrials. President Johnson's decision to prosecute the Vietnam War while also funding the expanded domestic programs of the Great Society, all without raising taxes, caused ballooning deficits and unleashed inflationary pressures. The consumer price index more than quadrupled between 1964 and 1970 (from 2.9 percent to 5.7 percent). President Nixon attempted to reign in the economy through strong measures. His New Economic Policy attacked inflation through a complex system of wage and price controls (1971 and 1974) that tended to constrain strategic options, raise corporate operating costs (among other ways by compliance with new and sometimes cumbersome bureaucratic requirements), and depress earnings. The growing strength of the major European and Asian economies, now fully recovered from the devastations of World War II, prompted Nixon in

August 1971 to end the convertibility of the dollar into gold and terminate international financial agreements that for a quarter century had governed trade in the noncommunist world. The short-term result was a significant devaluation of the dollar against the German mark and Japanese yen and a temporary surge in U.S. exports. The long-term effect was to introduce new uncertainties into U.S. trade and financial policy and prompt American companies to accelerate overseas investments as a means of hedging against fluctuating exchange rates.[18]

Congress, for its part, helped keep big companies on the defensive. The Foreign Corrupt Practices Act (1972), for example, outlawed abuses, created new compliance costs, and helped reinforce a growing public perception of big companies as fundamentally untrustworthy. The Watergate scandal, which culminated in Nixon's resignation, also triggered fresh congressional scrutiny into corporate political activities and donations and resulted in new legislation governing these matters. Meanwhile, the U.S. Federal Trade Commission (FTC) enacted new accounting rules for disclosure in acquisitions valued above $10 million. The rules tended to discourage large deals such as those that had flourished in the late 1960s.

The final insult was the sudden rise in energy costs resulting from the 1973 Arab-Israeli War and the transformation of the Organization of Petroleum Exporting Countries (OPEC) from a weak information-sharing body into a militant cartel. During 1973 and 1974, OPEC hiked oil prices nearly fourfold, with devastating effects on the U.S. economy and consumer confidence. The economy tumbled into recession for 16 months—the longest stretch of hard times since the Great Depression—and consumers suddenly became aware of U.S. vulnerability to foreign energy sources and to the impact of energy costs on the costs of living and conducting business.

TIMES OF TURMOIL: THE PERIOD AFTER 1974 CONSIDERED AS A WHOLE

In retrospect, it seems clear that the energy crisis of 1973 and 1974 accentuated trends adversely affecting the big industrials. But it also ushered in an era that the industrials perceived and experienced as new, qualitatively different, and mostly hostile. U.S. economic growth stagnated for a decade, and when it resumed, prosperity did not come from the traditional drivers, the big industrials, but rather from recent entrants in high technology, as well as the service sector. The big industrials continued their drift from the center toward the periphery of the economy. The direction and pace of change became painfully evident to owners, managers, employees, and other stakeholders.

The changing circumstances and fading fortunes of the *Fortune* 100 are apparent in the official lists and rankings of the era. (See Tables 2.3 through 2.6.) Comparing the 1954 list (Table 2.2) and its counterpart in 1974 (Table 2.3) uncovers several patterns. The trend toward higher value-added manufacturing remained evident,

Table 2.3
The *Fortune* 100 in 1974

1. Exxon
2. General Motors
3. Ford Motor
4. Texaco
5. Mobil
6. Standard Oil (California)
7. Gulf Oil
8. General Electric
9. IBM
10. ITT Industries
11. Chrysler
12. U.S. Steel
13. Standard Oil (Indiana)
14. Shell Oil
15. Western Electric
16. Conoco
17. Du Pont
18. Atlantic Richfield
19. Westinghouse Electric
20. Occidental Petroleum
21. Bethlehem Steel
22. Union Carbide
23. Goodyear
24. Tenneco
25. Phillips Petroleum
26. International Harvester
27. Dow Chemical
28. Procter & Gamble
29. LTV
30. Esmark
31. RCA
32. Eastman Kodak
33. Kraft Co.
34. Union Oil
35. Rockwell International
36. Caterpillar
37. Sun Oil
38. Amerada Hess
39. Boeing
40. Firestone
41. Xerox
42. Beatrice Foods
43. Monsanto
44. W.R. Grace
45. Greyhound
46. United Aircraft
47. Borden
48. R.J. Reynolds
49. Lockheed Aircraft
50. Ashland Oil
51. Armco Steel
52. Continental Can
53. Litton Industries
54. McDonnell Douglas
55. Ralston Purina
56. International Paper
57. Philip Morris
58. General Foods
59. 3M
60. Marathon Oil
61. Cities Service
62. Getty Oil
63. Republic Steel
64. National Steel
65. Alcoa
66. Singer
67. American Can
68. Honeywell
69. Colgate-Palmolive
70. Sperry Rand
71. CPC International
72. Champion International
73. Weyerhauser
74. Coca-Cola
75. Deere
76. TRW
77. Bendix
78. Inland Steel
79. Georgia Pacific
80. Consolidated Foods
81. Burlington Industries
82. Uniroyal
83. Gulf + Western
84. United Brands
85. Allied Chemical
86. American Brands
87. Standard Oil (Ohio)
88. Owens-Illinois
89. Textron
90. PepsiCo
91. FMC
92. American Home Products
93. American Motors
94. General Mills
95. Reynolds Metals
96. B.F. Goodrich
97. NCR
98. General Dynamics
99. Johnson & Johnson
100. Raytheon

Source: Fortune, May 1974.

Holdovers since 1954: (62) General Motors, Exxon [Standard Oil (NJ)], Ford, U.S. Steel, General Electric, Chrysler, Gulf Oil, Mobil [Socony-Vacuum Oil], Du Pont, Bethlehem Steel, Standard Oil (Ind.), Westinghouse Electric, Texaco [Texas Co.], Western Electric, Shell Oil, Standard Oil (Cal.), Goodyear Tire, Boeing, International Harvester, RCA, Union Carbide, Firestone Tire, Procter & Gamble, Republic Steel, Cities Service, Phillips Petroleum, General Foods, U.S. Rubber, Borden, Lockheed, Alcoa, International Paper, Sun Oil, United Aircraft, American Can, General Dynamics, Eastman Kodak, B.F. Goodrich, Continental Can, Bendix, Atlantic Refining, Inland Steel, Armco Steel, Allied Chemical, Conoco [Continental Oil], General Mills, National Steel, IBM, Sperry, R.J. Reynolds, Dow Chemical, W.R. Grace, Caterpillar, American Motors, Ralston Purina, Union Oil, Burlington Industries, Monsanto, Owens-Illinois Glass, Singer, Reynolds Metals, Standard Oil (Ohio).

Arrivals since 1954: (38) ITT Industries, Occidental Petroleum, Tenneco, LTV, Esmark, Kraft Co., Rockwell International, Amerada Hess, Xerox, Beatrice Foods, Greyhound, Ashland Oil, Litton Industries, McDonnell Douglas, Philip Morris, 3M, Marathon Oil, Getty Oil, Honeywell, Colgate-Palmolive, CPC International, Champion International, Weyerhaueser, Coca-Cola, Deere, TRW, Georgia Pacific, Consolidated Foods, Gulf + Western, United Brands, American Brands, Textron, PepsiCo, FMC, American Home Products, NCR, Johnson & Johnson, Raytheon.

Departures since 1954: (38) Swift, Armour, National Dairy Products, Sinclair Oil, Douglas Aircraft, Wilson, North American Aviation, American Metal Products, American Tobacco, Allis-Chalmers, Jones & Laughlin Steel, Curtiss-Wright, Olin Mathiesen, American Smelting & Refining, Anaconda Copper, Tide Water Associated Oil, Cudahy Packing, Briggs Manufacturing, Pittsburgh Plate Glass, Youngstown Sheet & Tube, Kennecott Copper, National Lead, Standard Brands, American Cyanamid, Pullman, Pure Oil, Borg-Warner, National Biscuit, Avco Manufacturing, Philco, Campbell Soup, Pillsbury Mills, Hormel, Hygrade Food Products, Republic Aviation, Carnation, American Sugar Refining, John Morrell.

Table 2.4
The *Fortune* 100 in 1994

1. General Motors	35. Lockheed	69. Ralston Purina
2. Ford Motor	36. Georgia-Pacific	70. Monsanto
3. Exxon	37. Phillips Petroleum	71. Unisys
4. IBM	38. Allied Signal	72. Deere
5. General Electric	39. IBP	73. Whirlpool
6. Mobil	40. Goodyear Tire	74. Pfizer
7. Philip Morris	41. Caterpillar	75. Sun Oil
8. Chrysler	42. Westinghouse	76. Compaq Computer
9. Texaco	43. Anheuser-Busch	77. Colgate-Palmolive
10. Du Pont	44. Bristol-Myers Squibb	78. H.J. Heinz
11. Chevron	45. Rockwell International	79. Kimberly-Clark
12. Procter & Gamble	46. Merck	80. Hoechst Celanese
13. Amoco	47. Coastal	81. CPC International
14. Boeing	48. Archer Daniels Midland	82. Borden
15. PepsiCo	49. Ashland Oil	83. Campbell Soup
16. ConAgra	50. Weyerhauser	84. Miles
17. Shell Oil	51. Martin Marietta	85. Eli Lilly
18. United Technologies	52. Raytheon	86. Kellogg
19. Hewlett-Packard	53. Citgo Petroleum	87. Cooper Industries
20. Eastman Kodak	54. Alcoa	88. Johnson Controls
21. Dow Chemical	55. Baxter International	89. Honeywell
22. Atlantic Richfield	56. Intel	90. Levi Strauss
23. Motorola	57. Textron	91. Amerada Hess
24. USX	58. Texas Instruments	92. Warner-Lambert
25. RJR Nabisco	59. Abbott Laboratories	93. PPG Industries
26. Xerox	60. American Home Products	94. W.R. Grace
27. Sara Lee	61. American Brands	95. Quaker Oats
28. McDonnell-Douglas	62. Emerson Electric	96. Litton Industries
29. Digital Equipment	63. General Mills	97. Coca-Cola Enterprises
30. Johnson & Johnson	64. Occidental Petroleum	98. Dana
31. 3M	65. Hanson Industries	99. Gillette
32. Coca-Cola	66. Unocal	100. American Cyanamid
33. International Paper	67. Apple Computer	100. Raytheon
34. Tenneco	68. TRW	

Source: Fortune, April 18, 1994.

Holdovers since 1974: (63) Exxon, General Motors, Ford, Texaco, Mobil, Chevron [Std. Oil (Cal.)], General Electric, IBM, Chrysler, USX [U.S. Steel], Amoco [Std. Oil (Ind.)], Shell, Du Pont, Atlantic Richfield, Westinghouse, Goodyear, Phillips Petroleum, Dow Chemical, Procter & Gamble, Eastman Kodak, Unocal [Union Oil], Caterpillar, Sun Oil, Boeing, Monsanto, W.R. Grace, United Technologies [United Aircraft], Borden, RJR Nabisco [R.J. Reynolds], Lockheed, Ashland Oil, McDonnell-Douglas, Ralston Purina, Int'l Paper, Philip Morris, 3M, Citgo Petroleum [Cities Service], Alcoa, Honeywell, Colgate-Palmolive, Unisys [Sperry Rand], CPC International, Weyerhaueser, Coca-Cola, Deere, TRW, Georgia-Pacific, Allied-Signal [Allied Chemical], Sara Lee [Consolidated Foods], American Brands, Textron, PepsiCo, Am. Home Pdts., General Mills, Johnson & Johnson, Raytheon.

Arrivals since 1955: (37) ConAgra, Hewlett-Packard, Motorola, Digital Equipment, IBP, Anheuser-Busch, Bristol-Myers Squibb, Merck, Coastal, Archer Daniels Midland, Martin Marietta, Baxter International, Intel, Texas Instruments, Abbott Laboratories, Emerson Electric, Hanson Industries, Apple Computer, Whirlpool, Pfizer, Compaq Computer, H.J. Heinz, Kimberly-Clark, Hoechst Celanese, Campbell Soup, Miles, Eli Lilly, Kellogg, Cooper Industries, Johnson Controls, Levi Strauss, Warner-Lambert, PPG, Quaker Oats, Coca-Cola Enterprises, Dana, Gillette, American Cyanamid.

Departures since 1955: (37) Gulf Oil, ITT, Western Electric, Conoco, Bethlehem Steel, Union Carbide, Navistar [International Harvester], LTV, Esmark, RCA, Kraft Foods, Firestone, Beatrice Foods, Greyhound, Armco, Continental Can, General Foods, Marathon Oil, Getty Oil, Republic Steel, National Steel, Singer, American Can, Champion International, Bendix, Inland Steel, Burlington Industries, Uniroyal, Gulf + Western, United Brands, Std. Oil (Ohio), Owens-Illinois, FMC, American Motors, Reynolds Metals, B.F. Goodrich, NCR, General Dynamics.

Table 2.5

The 100 Largest Industrial Corporations in 2000

1. General Motors
2. Exxon Mobil
3. Ford Motor
4. General Electric
5. IBM
6. Philip Morris
7. Boeing
8. Hewlett-Packard
9. Compaq Computer
10. Lucent Technologies
11. Procter & Gamble
12. Texaco
13. Merck
14. Chevron
15. Motorola
16. Intel
17. Du Pont
18. Johnson & Johnson
19. USX
20. Lockheed Martin
21. Dell Computer
22. United Technologies
23. ConAgra
24. International Paper
25. Honeywell International
26. Conoco
27. PepsiCo
28. Bristol-Myers Squibb
29. Sara Lee
30. Raytheon
31. Coca-Cola
32. Microsoft
33. Caterpillar
34. Xerox
35. Dow Chemical
36. Georgia Pacific
37. TRW
38. Alcoa
39. Pfizer
40. Johnson Controls
41. 3M
42. Coca-Cola Enterprises
43. Archer Daniels Midland
44. Emerson Electric
45. Eastman Kodak
46. IBP
47. Phillips Petroleum
48. American Home Products
49. Dana
50. Abbott Laboratories
51. Atlantic Richfield
52. Kimberly-Clark
53. Warner Lambert
54. Goodyear Tire & Rubber
55. Lear
56. Weyerhauser
57. Cisco Systems
58. Deere
59. Sun Microsystems
60. Anheuser-Busch
61. Textron
62. R.J. Reynolds
63. Whirlpool
64. Monsanto
65. Eli Lilly
66. Gillette
67. Texas Instruments
68. Illinois Tool Works
69. H.J. Heinz
70. Schering-Plough
71. Colgate-Palmolive
72. Paccar
73. Northrop Grumman
74. General Dynamics
75. Oracle
76. Nike
77. Navistar
78. Gateway
79. Bestfoods
80. Ingersoll-Rand
81. Sunoco
82. Eaton
83. Solectron
84. Nabisco
85. Coastal
86. PPG Industries
87. Crown Cork & Seal
88. Occidental Petroleum
89. Unisys
90. Smurfit-Stone Container
91. Tyson Foods
92. American Standard
93. Baxter International
94. Pharmacia
95. Ashland
96. Fort James
97. Rockwell International
98. Amerada Hess
99. Kellogg
100. Boise Cascade

Ranked by revenues; adapted from *Fortune* 500 list, April 17, 2000.

Holdovers since 1994: (72) General Motors, Exxon Mobil, Ford, General Electric, IBM, Philip Morris, Boeing, Hewlett-Packard, Compaq Computer, Procter & Gamble, Texaco, Chevron, Motorola, Intel, Du Pont, Johnson & Johnson, USX, Lockheed Martin, United Technologies, ConAgra, International Paper, Conoco, PepsiCo, Bristol-Myers Squibb, Sara Lee, Raytheon, Coca-Cola, Caterpillar, Xerox, Dow Chemical, Georgia Pacific, TRW, Alcoa, Pfizer, Johnson Controls, 3M, Coca-Cola Enterprises, Archer Daniels Midland, Emerson Electric, Eastman Kodak, IBP, Phillips Petroleum, American Home Products, Dana, Abbott Laboratories, Atlantic Richfield, Goodyear, Weyerhaeuser, Deere, Anheuser-Busch, Textron, R.J. Reynolds, Whirlpool, Monsanto, Eli Lilly, Gillette, Texas Instruments, H.J. Heinz, Colgate-Palmolive, General Dynamics, Sunoco, Coastal, PPG Industries, Occidental Petroleum, Unisys, Baxter International, Ashland, Rockwell International, Amerada Hess, Kellogg.

Arrivals since 1994: (28) Lucent Technologies, Dell Computer, Conoco, Microsoft, Lear, Cisco Systems, Sun Microsystems, Illinois Tool Works, Schering-Plough, Paccar, Northrop Grumman, Oracle, Nike, Navistar [International Harvester], Gateway, Bestfoods, Ingersoll-Rand, Eaton, Solectron, Nabisco, Crown Cork & Seal, Smurfit-Stone Container, Tyson Foods, American Standard, Pharmacia, Fort James, Boise Cascade.

Departures since 1994: (28) Mobil, Chrysler, Amoco, McDonnell Douglas, Digital Equipment, Tenneco, Westinghouse, Martin Marietta, Citgo Petroleum, American Brands, General Mills, Hanson Industries, Unocal, Apple Computer, Ralston Purina, Deere, Hoeschst Celanese, CPC International, Borden, Campbell Soup, Miles, Cooper Industries, Levi Strauss, Warner Lambert, W.R. Grace, Quaker Oats, Litton Industries, American Cyanamid.

Table 2.6
The *Fortune* 100 in 2000

1. General Motors
2. Wal-Mart
3. Exxon Mobil
4. Ford Motor
5. General Electric
6. IBM
7. Citigroup
8. AT&T
9. Philip Morris
10. Boeing
11. Bank of America
12. SBC Communications
13. Hewlett-Packard
14. Kroger
15. State Farm Insurance
16. Sears Roebuck
17. American Intl. Grp.
18. Enron
19. TIAA-CREF
20. Compaq Computer
21. Home Depot
22. Lucent Technologies
23. Procter & Gamble
24. Albertson's
25. MCI WorldCom
26. Fannie Mae
27. Kmart
28. Texaco
29. Merrill Lynch
30. Morgan Stanley DW
31. Chase Manhattan
32. Target
33. Bell Atlantic
34. Merck
35. Chevron
36. J.C. Penney
37. Motorola
38. McKesson HBOC
39. Intel
40. Safeway
41. Ingram Micro
42. Du Pont
43. Johnson & Johnson
44. Costco Wholesale
45. Time Warner
46. United Parcel Service
47. Allstate
48. Prudential Insurance
49. Aetna
50. Bank One
51. USX
52. Lockheed Martin
53. Metropolitan Life Ins.
54. Goldman Sachs Group
55. GTE
56. Dell Computer
57. United Technologies
58. Bell South
59. Cardinal Health
60. ConAgra
61. International Paper
62. Freddie Mac
63. AutoNation
64. Berkshire Hathaway
65. Honeywell International
66. Walt Disney
67. First Union
68. Wells Fargo
69. Duke Energy
70. New York Life Insurance
71. American Express
72. Loews
73. PG&E
74. Conoco
75. Cigna
76. PepsiCo
77. AMR
78. Bristol-Myers Squibb
79. Sara Lee
80. FleetBoston
81. Sprint
82. Raytheon
83. Coca-Cola
84. Microsoft
85. Caterpillar
86. UnitedHealth Group
87. Xerox
88. Lehman Bros. Holdings
89. Dow Chemical
90. UtiliCorp United
91. Electronic Data Systems
92. J.P. Morgan
93. CVS
94. UAL
95. Walgreen
96. Georgia-Pacific
97. Federated Department Stores
98. Sysco
99. Supervalu
100. Bergen Brunswig

Source: Fortune, April 17, 2000.

Holdovers from 1994 list: (33) General Motors, Exxon Mobil, Ford, General Electric, IBM, Philip Morris, Boeing, Hewlett-Packard, Compaq Computer, Procter & Gamble, Texaco, Merck, Chevron, Motorola, Intel, Du Pont, Johnson & Johnson, USX, Lockheed Martin, United Technologies, ConAgra, International Paper, Honeywell, Conoco, PepsiCo, Bristol-Myers Squibb, Sara Lee, Raytheon, Coca-Cola, Caterpillar, Xerox, Dow Chemical, Georgia-Pacific.

with producers of computers, electronic equipment, specialty chemicals, and materials, and defense contractors recording continuing gains. Notable arrivals by 1974 included Xerox, Honeywell, TRW, and Raytheon, while computers, electronics, and software now propelled the businesses of IBM, Sperry Rand, and Singer. At the same time, a dozen conglomerates made the list, many of them at the expense of producers in industries that consolidated, such as primary metals, aerospace, and food products. By 1994—the last year in which *Fortune* compiled its traditional list of industrials (Table 2.4)—most of the conglomerates had long since disappeared, while arrivals included Hewlett-Packard, Motorola, Digital Equipment, Intel, Texas

Instruments, Apple Computer, and Compaq. Another set of companies arrived from pharmaceuticals (Merck, Bristol-Myers Squibb, Pfizer, Eli Lilly, Warner-Lambert) and health care (Abbott Laboratories, Baxter International). As before, the new entrants illustrated the burgeoning trend toward high-tech manufacturing and knowledge-based industries. And the trend apparently continues. Although *Fortune* changed its specifications for the list in 1994, a fabricated top 100 industrials list based on the list published in 2000, Table 2.5, reveals another strong showing for high-tech companies, including new arrivals Dell, Microsoft, Cisco Systems, Sun Microsystems, Oracle, and Solectron in computers and software, and with many departures due to industry consolidation in foods, energy, and chemicals. Foreign acquirers accounted for some prominent disappearances (Chrysler, Amoco).

The trend not captured in Tables 2.1 through 2.5—the shift of the economy as a whole away from manufacturing to services—is evident in Table 2.6, the actual *Fortune* 100 list for 2000. About two-thirds of the companies now officially listed, including many competitors in financial services, telecommunications, retailing, entertainment, health care, and energy distribution, are service companies. The traditional manufacturers still in the mix recall familiar, enduring categories in transportation equipment, energy, electrical equipment, chemicals, food and tobacco, and paper—although many of these companies also have substantial units and operations devoted to services. The primary metals industry, which once dominated the list, was down to a single representative (USX), and the rubber industry, which had three competitors well placed as recently as 1974, had none.

The explanation for these changes and movements is necessarily involved and particular to individual companies and industries. But the changes and movements also have roots in the business environment after 1974, which, although it affected all companies and industries, rewarded some and penalized others differentially.

To begin with, macroeconomic conditions, which had become a concern in the late 1960s, worsened and remained worrisome. After growing at a compound annual growth rate of 3.96 percent between 1948 and 1973, gross domestic product (GDP) slowed markedly, dipping to just 3.14 percent between 1974 and 1999. At the same time, after 1973 the percentage of GDP accounted for by manufacturing dropped from 23.7 percent to 17.1 percent.[19] Meanwhile, overall productivity of the U.S. economy slowed to an average of 1.4 percent per year between the mid-1970s and the mid-1990s—less than half of its rate during the postwar golden years. Put another way, the standard of living in the United States doubled between 1948 and 1973, a single generation, while at the post-1973 rate, it would not double again until the 2020s, or after two generations.[20] The relative decline in standard of living became apparent almost immediately. After climbing steadily since the late 1940s, real weekly wages began a slow and sustained fall that lasted for more than 20 years.[21]

Looked at more closely, the years since 1974 fall into two parts: a time of unusual difficulty between 1974 and the mid-1980s, and a somewhat gentler period thereafter, notwithstanding a sharp recession in 1990 and 1991. During the first period, unusually high energy prices, inflation, interest rates, and unemployment levels prevailed. In the aftermath of the 1973 and 1974 oil shock, the price of a barrel of crude oil tripled. Following the 1979 Iranian revolution and a second oil crisis, the price reached a level 10 times higher than in 1973. Higher energy prices translated into rampant inflation (by U.S. standards): Growth in the consumer price index climbed into double digits, peaking at 13.5 percent in 1980. During the 1950s and 1960s, the federal funds interest rate charged by the Federal Reserve Bank averaged between 3 and 4 percent, although an upward trend was noticeable. After the energy shocks, interest rates also hit double digits, peaking above 19 percent in the summer of 1981. Finally, the unemployment rate, which had averaged well below 5 percent during the 1950s and 1960s, surged above 8 percent in 1975 and climbed to a peak of 9.7 percentin 1982.[22] The Dow Jones Industrial Average, which first broke the 1000 barrier in 1972, did not reach that level again on a sustained basis until 10 years later.[23]

Squeezed between rising costs of inputs, on the one hand, and increasingly price-sensitive customers on the other, the big industrials had limited room to maneuver. Meanwhile, investment capital became unusually expensive and hard to come by and employees pushed hard for pay and benefits to keep pace with inflation. These were painful years that a double-dip recession in 1980 and 1981 and 1982 only worsened. Big employers like International Harvester, Bethlehem Steel, and Chrysler avoided bankruptcy through last-minute interventions such as federal loan guarantees. The once-mighty economic axis stretching from Detroit to Pittsburgh took on a new appellation: "the Rust Belt."

Harsh economic conditions finally began to lift in the mid-1980s. A combination of conservation measures and more fuel-efficient usage broke the OPEC cartel and oil prices tumbled to tolerable levels. The U.S. Federal Reserve Board's aggressive monetary policy (high interest rates) managed to wring inflation out of the economy. By the late 1980s, the economic signs returned to normal, with strong growth rates, low inflation, low interest rates, tolerable levels of unemployment, and a stock market once again on a sustained rise, subject to occasional sharp checks, as in October 1987.[24]

Meanwhile, the administrations of the period were strongly pro-business, regardless of the president's political roots. Presidents Carter and Reagan launched campaigns to deregulate industry. The Reagan administration all but ceased policing business and relaxed enforcement of the antitrust laws. Thereafter, mergers and acquisitions, sometimes hostile, within industries resumed and spread rapidly. Reagan and his successors generally adopted policies supportive of trade and investment. The government encouraged *maquiladora* assembly plants situated in low-wage areas just across the Mexican border, with goods shipped into the United States without tariffs. The *maquiladora* program had originated in the 1960s to aid economic development in Mexico; in the 1980s, it became a vehicle of economic assistance for ailing U.S. manufacturers. The next step was the North American Free Trade Agreement (NAFTA) initiated under President Reagan and implemented under President Clinton. In 1993, President Clinton and Congress agreed on a budget package, a combination of spending cuts and tax increases, which proved effective in reducing the federal deficit. In 1998, the government reported its first surplus in more than three decades.

These improvements dovetailed with a slowdown in Asia, where a revalued yen, real estate crises, and other factors helped slow the Japanese competitive onslaught. By the late 1980s, and certainly after the 1990 and 1991 recession, life for most American companies became much easier. In the 1990s, GDP grew at nearly 4 percent per year, a level comparable to the "golden" years of the post-World War II era. Productivity rates also returned to high levels characteristic of the 1950s and 1960s. Inflation and unemployment rates remained low.[25]

In such circumstances, the population of the *Fortune* 100 showed marked improvement, especially on the bottom line, where more than a decade of productivity, total quality, and reengineering initiatives wrought significant savings. But the better conditions of the late 1980s and 1990s did not bring with them renewed growth, optimism, or a reversal of the relative decline of the industrial sector.

Roots of Relative Decline

Business leaders in the *Fortune* 100 were well aware of fundamental shifts in the world around them. In countless speeches and communications with employees, shareholders, and the public, chief executives focused on the "unprecedented" challenges facing them: increasingly fierce, increasingly global competitive rivalry, a shift in the balance of power from sellers to buyers, an accelerating pace of change. Many of these claims were overstated and rhetorical, designed to energize employees and prod the internal pace of adaptation to catch up with the external rate of change.[26] But these executives were also right in sensing that some factors at work in the business environment were qualitatively different from those characteristic of earlier eras, and that the big industrials would never regain the dominant position in the economy they had enjoyed in the post-World War II era.

Six factors gathered and merged in ways to threaten the large industrial corporation. These factors include:

1. Information technology and digital convergence, which blurred the traditional boundaries between industries, companies, suppliers, customers, and competitors and transformed the internal systems and processes of organizations;
2. The relative decline of transportation and shipping costs, which lowered barriers to regional and international expansion;

3. The resulting globalization of trade and competition, which, initially, particularly affected industrial companies adversely;
4. The changing composition and expectations of the workforce, which industrial companies proved ill-suited to address;
5. The explosive growth of business information, which industrial companies were ill-equipped to manage; and
6. The rising concentration and mobility of capital, which posed grave threats to the independent leadership of industrial companies.

This list is not surprising. It is hardly news, for example, to take note of the impact of information technology on companies, or of the globalization of trade and competition, or of the rise of institutional investors. However, these phenomena emerged, accumulated, and interacted at particular times and in particular ways to pose particularly tough challenges to big industrial corporations. This process unfolded in a manner that affected all companies but seemed to have hit the big industrials especially hard. Large service companies, apparently, were not hurt as badly.

The point becomes clearer upon consideration of each of the factors in turn.

New Information Technology and Digital Convergence

The thoroughgoing, transformative impact of information technology on companies is readily apparent from a simple comparison between the uses of computers in the early 1970s and the late 1990s. Before the first energy crisis, big companies maintained large, central computer installations that were used to process large amounts of data, typically automating routine, paper-based processes such as payroll and accounting. R&D organizations also employed computers for scientific research and complex calculations. Then, in rapid sequence, came a series of revolutions: minicomputers, which provided real-time control of industrial processes; personal computers, which decentralized information and computing power and at least partly automated office work; small-scale networks, which linked companies with suppliers, partners, and customers; and large-scale networks, including the Internet, which opened information pipelines between anyone, anywhere, at any time, on virtually any subject.[27] As a result, no function, process, or activity inside a company remains untouched by information technology. The conduct of work, if not its object, has been, and is being, unalterably changed.[28]

The past quarter century has witnessed a steady stream of fundamental information technology breakthroughs: the improbable, open-ended continuation of Moore's Law (named for Intel cofounder Gordon Moore, who posited in 1965 that, for the same cost, the computing power of microprocessors would double every 12 months for the next 10 years); a host of ancillary electronic devices such as memory chips, signal converters, and network devices; increasingly powerful and flexible software;

communications satellites and microwave transmitters and antennas; fiber optics, semiconducting lasers, and photonic devices; digital wireless communications. The gathering, transporting, storing and accessing, processing and analyzing, and displaying of information have become fully digitized.

As noted in Tables 2.2, 2.3, and 2.4, the information technology industry has been the major beneficiary of change in the *Fortune* 100 population since the mid-1950s. Between 1973 and 1998 total IT industry revenues skyrocketed from $99.2 billion to $920.1 billion (est.)—a 25-year compounded annual growth rate (CAGR) of 9.3 percent that outpaced the growth of the economy as a whole by a factor of three. At the same time, the industry has been a major driver of change in the economy as a whole. Over the same period, total U.S. investment in computer, business, and telecommunications producers' equipment soared from $104.3 billion to $781 billion—a CAGR of 8.4 percent.[29]

The full impact of this huge investment is hard to measure—although there is no shortage of claims. A consultant waggishly pointed out that the value of new technology becomes manifest in organizations at about half the speed of the technology's development—"Demi Moore's Law."[30] Nonetheless, according to a recent estimate, shrewd use of information technology by leading companies in the 1980s and 1990s repeatedly halved the cost of production, doubled the quality of products and services, and permitted the development and bundling of many new, attractive, and profitable features with products and services. At the same time, sales per employee (SPE) grew by factors between 1.5 and 30 in the 1980s and 1990s, a circumstance largely attributable to information technology (IT).[31]

Although the big industrials clearly benefited from their IT spending, evidence suggests that other types of businesses may have benefited more. The major savings in manufacturing companies occurred in process control and in more efficient management of the supply chain. The leverage IT created in savings and capabilities among some service companies was notably bigger. Between 1978 and 1997, the SPEs of General Electric and Pfizer grew by multiples between four and six; the SPE of American International Group, an insurance and financial services giant, in contrast grew by a factor of 70.[32]

Declining Relative Costs of Transportation and Shipping

The late twentieth century also witnessed another, less obvious, revolution in the infrastructure of the economy in transportation and shipping. In the 1950s and 1960s, the revolution began in mundane areas such as highway programs and containerized shipping, which substantially reduced the relative costs of domestic shipping—a trend interrupted by the energy crisis but then resumed through more fuel-efficient internal combustion and diesel engines. The revolution expanded to ocean transport. The development of more, bigger, and more efficient tankers and container ships

Table 2.7
Indices of Trade and Shipping

	1955	*1974*	*1998*
Merchant vessels in service worldwide (number and capacity in gross tonnage [000 lbs.])	29,967 [100,069]	52,444 [227,490]	84,264 [507,873]
Waterborne cargo tonnage (thousand short tons)	1,016	1,731	2,339
Ton miles flown (thousands)	0.2	2.4	20.0

Source: U.S. Bureau of the Census; Air Transport Association, Annual Report 1999; U.S. Army Corps of Engineers, Waterborne Commerce of the United States.

dramatically lowered costs and raised the volume of international trade. (See Table 2.7.) These innovations, in turn, helped hasten the demise of American industrial companies engaged in mining and primary manufacture of commodity materials.

In the late 1960s and early 1970s, a new generation of powerful turbojet engines enabled aircraft manufacturers to introduce much bigger and faster aircraft for carrying people and freight over long distances. A short span of years saw the premieres of four new "wide body" aircraft: the Boeing 747, DC-10, and L1011 Tristar in the United States and the A-300 in Europe. These aircraft more than doubled the lifting power and range of previous long-range aircraft and helped to usher in a new era of international commerce.[33] In the 1980s and 1990s new aircraft from Boeing (757, 767, and 777) and Airbus (A-330 series) extended the revolution with yet more powerful and fuel-efficient engines.

The spread of containerized shipping, the advent of larger, more efficient merchant vessels and large jet aircraft provided a powerful stimulus to foreign trade. So did the emergence of air freight companies such as Federal Express, Airborne Express, and DHL, as well as augmented air services from United Parcel Service (UPS) and the U.S. Postal Service.

The Globalization of Trade and Competition

Cheaper, more powerful information technology and declining relative costs of transportation helped to replicate on a bigger scale the phenomenon that had occurred on a regional and national scale a century earlier: the linking of once distinct, market "islands" into a single, huge market. In the nineteenth century, the arrival of the telegraph and railroad had created the infrastructure for a national market in the United States.[34] The integration of a national market laid the groundwork for national competitors operating with scale and scope advantages and the passing of local and regional manufacturers. (See Table 2.8.)

In the last third of the twentieth century, new information technology and jet aircraft produced a similar effect on a supranational and global scale. For the big

Table 2.8
Indices of Globalization

	1955	*1974*	*1998*
International travelers in the U.S. (millions)	0.7	4.2	46.4
U.S. travelers abroad (millions)	1.1	12.4	56.3
U.S. direct investment abroad (billions)	NA	$110.1	$2,140.5
Foreign direct investment in the United States (billions)	$5.1	$25.1	$2,194.1

Source: U.S. Bureau of the Census, 447, 829–830; 1085.

American industrial corporations, this was both good news and bad: good, in the sense that it increased the accessibility of foreign markets (including, eventually, former communist countries in central and eastern Europe and Asia, as well as formerly protectionist countries like India); bad, in the sense that foreign competitors found it easier to reach customers in the United States. Although global competition also roiled service companies—witness the troubles of American banks abroad—it hit first and hardest in manufacturing, where some foreign producers enjoyed significant cost advantages over American industrials. As had occurred among local and regional manufacturers a century before, weak competitors fell by the wayside. (See Table 2.9.)

The bad news, naturally, received greater publicity. The combination of high energy and labor costs—as well as, in retrospect, dubious or unmade investments—all but wiped out American producers in industries such as consumer electronics, machine tools, and rubber, while causing serious crises in the auto and steel industries. The competition from Europe and Asia (and especially Japan), pushed many U.S. manufacturers, including perennial top 25 industrials International Harvester, Bethlehem

Table 2.9
Competitive Decline of U.S. Industries, 1960–1990 (in Percent)

*Industry/World Market Share**	*1960*	*1970*	*1980*	*1990*	*2000*
Automobiles	83	66	42	38	34
Chemicals	68	40	31	23	21
Computers	95	90	86	70	42
Electricals	71	59	44	11	21
Iron and steel	74	31	26	12	9
Textiles	58	44	41	21	18

*World Market Share is an estimate based on a proxy: percentages refer to the U.S. share of output of the top 12 producers worldwide.
Source: Lawrence G. Franko, "Global Corporate Competition: Is the Large American Firm an Endangered Species?" *Business Horizons* (November–December 1991), as quoted in Nitin Nohria and James D. Berkley, "Whatever Happened to the Take-Charge Manager?" *Harvard Business Review* (January–February 1994), p. 131; various sources for 2000.

Steel, and Chrysler, to the brink. The American companies first blamed outside forces—foreign subsidies and trade policies, a strong dollar, and myopic U.S. government policies—for their troubles. As the crisis deepened, however, it became obvious that these companies were fundamentally uncompetitive and that their industries were consolidating on a global scale.

The Changing Composition and Expectations of the Workforce

During the last quarter of the twentieth century, significant changes in the U.S. labor market continuously challenged traditional ways of organizing and managing in big companies. The arrival of the baby boom—the 76 million Americans born between 1946 and 1964—into the workforce constituted the first challenge. This generation of young people was better educated than any in history and somewhat more skeptical of received wisdom as a result. They were also less inclined than their parents to seek careers in factories or big companies.[35] But when they did enter the workforce, starting in the mid-1960s, the boomers swelled management ranks and strained pyramidal, hierarchical structures. Big companies adapted to demographic pressure by decentralizing organization structures and promoting "quality of work-life" initiatives, teamwork, and other collaborative ways of working.

As the boomers aged—with the average age of the workforce approaching 40 in the early 2000s—they presented employers with a different set of problems: demands for greater services and benefits. Labor costs in the United States remained among the highest in the world, a circumstance that launched employers on an anxious, ongoing search for labor-saving techniques and methods and hastened the development of knowledge-intensive industries.[36]

Meanwhile, the demographic profile of the workforce changed dramatically. Although white males remained the biggest single group in and entering the labor market, their relative lead over other groups declined steadily during the second half of the twentieth century. Between 1950 and the late 1990s, the proportion of adult women in the workforce doubled (from about 32 percent to more than 60 percent), with enormous implications for work and family life. The ethnic and racial composition of the workforce also changed in important ways, with increasing numbers of people of color and people speaking native languages other than English competing for jobs and advancement.

Big industrial corporations, like all employers, adapted to these changes by making costly adjustments in hiring, training, development, and compensation and benefits policies, especially in areas such as day care and family leave. But the industrials did not accommodate change easily. In part, their difficulty reflected entrenched assumptions and practices. These institutions, after all, were long-time bastions of white male culture. Top executives generally embraced diversity in the workforce, but the process of opening up and moving beyond minimum compliance with laws and regulations proved slow and uneven. It took many years to shatter "glass ceilings" and remove barriers to advancement, and few impartial observers would even now, several decades after enactment of the equal opportunity statutes, acknowledge that the process is complete. In the meantime, the high visibility of the big industrials made them prominent targets of lawsuits, often resulting in costly legal settlements.[37]

The Explosion in Business Information

If a manager from a 1950s-era *Fortune* 100 company were, like Rip van Winkle, to awake from a decades-long nap in the early 2000s, he would surely recognize the timeless issues and challenges of management: to achieve results, to beat the competition, to motivate employees. But differences from his own time, especially the overwhelming volume of business information to be sifted, sorted, and acted upon, would also surely bewilder him. The bottomless resources of the Internet, to mix metaphors, constitute the tip of the iceberg. Public agencies, think tanks, industry associations, consulting firms, and academic institutions published and maintained extensive data sets. The explosive growth of business education (much of it based on case studies) and the business press, the meteoric rise of the consulting industry, the proliferation of headhunters and job-hopping, and the routine nature of mergers, acquisitions, joint ventures, and alliances, meant that not only information but knowledge and expertise became widely available, often at little or no cost. (See Tables 2.10 and 2.11.) In the 1950s, most executives made their careers with a single employer, working their way up from entry level.[38] By the late twentieth century, the number of companies that continued to promote exclusively from within had dwindled to a tiny number. Senior executives typically had backgrounds that featured stints with multiple employers, including consulting and other professional service firms. They brought with them experiences and relationships that extended their employers' networks and facilitated freer and faster flow of information.

Table 2.10
Degrees Conferred, 1955–1998

	1955	*1974*	*1998*
B.A. or equivalent	285,841	945,776	1,184,406
MBA	3,500 (est.)	32,820	102,171
Masters in engineering	4,483	15,385	25,936
Masters in computer science	NA	2,299	11,246

Source: Digest of Education Statistics (2000), Table 255.

Table 2.11
The Explosion in Business Information, 1982–1992

	1982	*1992*
Consulting industry		
Number of consultants	30,000	81,000
Total consulting revenues	$3.5 billion	$15.2 billion
Corporate training		
Number of people trained	33.5 million	40.9 million
Total training hours	1.1 billion	1.3 billion
Total corporate expenditures	$10 billion	$45 billion
Business media		
Number of business stories	125,000	680,000
Number of new business books	1,327	1,831
Sales of business books	$225 million	$490 million

Source: Nitin Nohria and James D. Berkley, "Whatever Happened to the Take-Charge Manager?" *Harvard Business Review* (January–February 1994), p. 130.

In a world awash in business information, with multiple, handy techniques and mechanisms to transfer it across industry and corporate boundaries, it became increasingly difficult for companies to preserve differentiated strategies and protect distinctive advantages, even trade secrets.

The Rising Concentration and Mobility of Capital

The most important trends in corporate finance during the second half of the twentieth century were the concentration of financial capital among institutional investors and the willingness of those investors to trade frequently in large blocks.[39] In 1950, institutional investors—banks, insurance companies, mutual funds, and pension funds—held less than 10 percent of publicly listed securities. By the early 1990s, mutual funds and pension funds together held more than 60 percent. With growing concentration of ownership came bigger and more frequent trades. Block trading—trading in large lots—a phenomenon virtually unknown before the late 1970s, became a frequent daily occurrence. In the 1950s, a typical day on the New York Stock Exchange witnessed about 2 million shares traded; by the mid-1980s, the number skyrocketed to more than a billion shares per day, mostly in blocks.[40]

The new owners were notoriously impatient for results. Portfolio managers were evaluated and compensated according to formulas based heavily on the financial returns they generated quarterly and annually. This time horizon created a dynamic tension between owner-representatives and managers. The problem was especially acute in industrial companies, where capital investments and R&D expenditures typically paid off years down the road. It is no coincidence that industry and corporate restructuring began in the industrial sector of the economy in the 1980s. Nor is it a coincidence that boards of directors were much more likely to dismiss the CEO of a big industrial company than the head of a service company or nonprofit organization.

In summary, each of the six factors driving change in the *Fortune* 100 demanded companies to make creative responses. In combination, they built up and reinforced each other to pose momentous challenges to business corporations. The globalization of trade, for example, depended on advances in information technology and transportation; the advances in IT were a necessary precondition for the explosion of business information (as were the professional aspirations of baby boomers) and the concentration and mobility of capital. In sum, the six factors combined and interacted in ways that challenged all business organizations, but especially the big industrials.

In the late 1960s and early 1970s, however, the nature and extent of their coming ordeal was hardly apparent to the population of the *Fortune* 100 as they attempted to deal with what they perceived as the onset of a cyclical downturn, to be met with cost cutting and productivity initiatives.

STAGES OF TURMOIL: THE PERIOD AFTER 1974 EXPERIENCED IN PARTS

The big industrial corporations did not experience the period after 1974 as an integrated whole. Although the companies felt continuously under pressure and sought continuously to find better ways to operate, the nature of the pressure altered over time, as did the nature of their response. The changes undertaken by the *Fortune* 100 were eventually and cumulatively dramatic, but they unfolded episodically and in piecemeal fashion. This pattern of evolution is captured in a chronological sequence of four stages.

In the first stage, from the early 1970s to about 1980, companies slowly recognized the end of the prosperity and stability of the post-World War II period and a transition into a new era. In an environment of higher costs (especially energy) and high inflation, these companies tried various strategies to regain equilibrium: They adopted formal strategic planning systems, cut costs, launched productivity improvement initiatives, diversified farther afield, and then curtailed diversification as nothing seemed to work. At the end of this stage, American industrials were in retreat and disarray as foreign (especially Asian) competitors gained market share in industry after industry.

In the second stage, from about 1980 to about 1990, the big industrials launched the painful and protracted process of restructuring. Intensifying global rivalry was part of the problem. In addition, the regulatory reforms of the Carter and Reagan administrations facilitated the emergence of corporate raiders who stood ready to acquire and disassemble underperforming conglomerates. Once-great companies such as Chrysler and Bethlehem Steel teetered on the brink of bankruptcy. Other once-mighty industrials—Gulf Oil, Bendix, and RCA, among them—fell prey to takeovers. The survivors responded in various ways. Some, in industries such as steel and transportation, sought drastic reductions in their costs. They shut down plants and laid off workers in unprecedented numbers, with serious social dislocations in cities like Pittsburgh, Pennsylvania, and Flint, Michigan. In other industries such as chemicals, there was a renewed emphasis on diversification to escape commodity markets and enter into higher margin specialty products. In yet others, such as oil, the fear of raiders led to divestitures of previously prized acquisitions.

At the same time as they responded to market forces (each in different ways), the *Fortune* 100 companies also mounted a counterattack. They lobbied to protest dumping by foreign competitors and pursued other trade remedies such as voluntary restraint and orderly marketing agreements. They sought to turn back raiders through the adoption of poison pills and other antitakeover defenses. Finally, all of the *Fortune* 100 industrials began making significant internal changes in organizational structure and management systems, with the total quality movement the rubric for many of these. By the late 1980s, the industrials were flatter, leaner, more productive, and more competitive.

The third stage of response opened in the early 1990s, when the *Fortune* 100 companies finally and fully recognized the magnitude of their ordeal. The cause of a deep recession in the early 1990s originated in good news: the end of the Cold War. However, an expected peace dividend did not materialize. Instead, the shrinkage of the defense industry dragged down other industrial sectors. As they groped for ways to offset decline, leaders of the big industrial companies began to understand that their problems were caused not by government policies, foreign competition, or shareholder activists, but rather by all of these together and something more: a shift into a fundamentally different sort of economy in which knowledge and human resources represented the only sources of sustainable advantage. In the 1990s, the big industrial corporations came to terms with the global economy and investor capitalism by making sweeping changes in operations. This became an era of refocusing, downsizing, delayering, reengineering, and boundaryless organization, with new information technologies playing prominent roles in each development. In marked contrast to earlier periods of retrenchment, the management reforms of the 1990s exacted a heavy toll not only on blue-collar employees but also on their white-collar counterparts. The reforms resulted in significant gains in productivity and efficiency, but they produced negligible real growth.

The fourth stage in the evolution of the *Fortune* 100 is unfolding now, as the big industrial company is coming to terms with a new economy founded on speed, flexibility, rapid response, knowledge assets, and superior service. The very nature of the *Fortune* 100 has been fundamentally altered, with the group now including financial service companies, health care providers, retailers, media conglomerates, and software and Internet giants, as well as traditional manufacturers. The choices that these companies make in strategy, structure, and systems, and the views of investors, employees, and public policy makers toward these, carry profound implications for the future evolution of the economy and American society.

CHAPTER 3

STRATEGY: COPING WITH THE END OF GROWTH

The final years of the twentieth century witnessed breathtaking changes in the U.S. chemical industry. In 1997, Lyondell Petrochemical Company, which had come into existence a dozen years earlier as a petrochemical subsidiary of ARCO, formed a joint venture with Millennium Chemicals (a spin-off of loosely related properties once part of the conglomerate Hanson Plc) to pool their commodity chemicals operations. The following year, the new venture, called Equistar Chemicals, added a third partner when Occidental Petroleum contributed its petrochemical business to the mix.[1] The formation of Equistar, with $7 billion in assets and $6 billion in sales, sent shockwaves through the chemical industry. The new company immediately became a strong competitor to Dow Chemical and Union Carbide, with comparable advantages of scale and superior access to petroleum-based feedstocks. Nearly concurrent announcements of huge mergers by a number of the world's biggest oil companies—BP, Amoco, and ARCO; Chevron and Texaco; and the granddaddy of them all, Exxon and Mobil—caused still more tremors among chemical producers.[2]

These deals and the pressures behind them constituted not so much a wave as a tsunami of change that completely transformed the structure and competitive dynamics of the chemical industry in the United States. In August 1999, Dow and Union Carbide, respectively the second and third largest American producers, announced plans to merge, while many smaller rivals were gobbled up or put themselves on the block. A few competitors had anticipated the tsunami and had sought to escape its impact by reinventing themselves as producers of pharmaceuticals, biotechnology, or something else vaguely described as "science-based." When asked for comment on the announcement of the Dow-Union Carbide merger, for example, a spokesperson at Du Pont, long the nation's biggest chemical company (potentially number two in chemicals after the merger), sniffed that "The term 'chemical company' doesn't accurately reflect the Du Pont of today. Du Pont is a science company with a highly diversified portfolio, and there are few areas where we compete with either Dow or Union Carbide."[3]

Another erstwhile chemical giant—Monsanto, which had been the fourth-biggest competitor in the industry during most of the second half of the twentieth century—had also endeavored diligently to make itself over into a different sort of enterprise, a "life-sciences" company. During the 1980s and 1990s, Monsanto shed most of its traditional chemical businesses while developing, through a combination of acquisitions and accelerated research, major positions in agricultural biotechnology, pharmaceuticals, and food products. It was a bold, ambitious strategy, much admired in the business press, and it worked—to a point. In December 1999, Monsanto announced that it, too, would merge. Its new partner and, it turned out, temporary owner, was Pharmacia & Upjohn, itself the product of a four-year-old merger of Swedish and American pharmaceutical companies. Pharmacia Corporation, as it soon rechristened itself, remixed Monsanto's portfolio, combining the pharmaceutical operations with its own and disposing of other businesses. Late in 2001, Pharmacia announced plans to divest Monsanto, which would resume its independent life in 2002 as a pure-play agricultural bioengineering company.[4]

Although the upheavals and transformations in the chemical industry were unusually dramatic, they exemplified the fading fortunes and strategic struggles of big American industrial corporations in the late twentieth century. Corporate leaders could hardly have realized the problem a quarter century ago—and perhaps would have doubted their sanity if they had—but they were facing a stark reality: the end of growth. In the aggregate, annual revenues of the companies listed as members of the *Fortune* 100 in 1974 grew at an anemic rate of 1.6 percent through 1999. And net income grew only slightly more rapidly, at 2.4 percent. Meanwhile, other sectors of the economy, especially financial and health care services, expanded at much faster rates.

These circumstances sorely tested and eventually invalidated assumptions that the big industrials had long taken for granted. The end of growth meant the end of easy opportunity and the onset of a new necessity to adapt to a vastly altered world. Although growth rates for most industrials began to slacken in the 1960s, the growth challenge proved particularly difficult in the chemical industry. All of the major competitors relied heavily on petroleum feedstocks, and the first energy crisis in 1974 proved devastating. Suddenly inputs that had accounted for 30 percent of manufacturing costs now accounted for 70 percent. The second energy crisis that followed the Iranian Revolution in 1979 made matters much worse. By 1980, the cost of fuel and feedstocks had surged 585 percent above its level a decade earlier.[5]

As demand for chemical (especially petrochemical) products slowed with soaring prices, the chemical companies confronted an immediate and indefinite future of restricted growth. They responded first by attempting to diversify, the strategy pioneered and long-since proven in the industry. As they discovered limited room to grow in other markets and sectors, however, the chemical companies retreated and refocused on core operations, slashing costs, exploring downstream, value-added applications of their products, and searching for more profitable niches. Some, like Du Pont and Monsanto, sought to reinvent themselves based on new technologies in the life sciences. Most of the chemical companies formed strategic alliances with erstwhile competitors, pursuing N-Form strategies. Sometimes, like Dow and Union Carbide, they merged in hopes that bigger would be better. This pattern of diversification, then retreat and refocusing, restructuring, and networking proved especially vivid in the chemical industry, but most big companies across the industrial landscape eventually followed suit.

THE LOGIC OF DIVERSIFICATION

The big industrials initially responded to the end of growth by continuing to pursue strategies of diversification: If the core business was no longer generating significant growth opportunities, then why not look elsewhere? This line of thinking had originated a half century before at Du Pont. Between 1908 and 1920, Du Pont had executed a series of mergers, acquisitions, and capital allocations that redefined both the company and the possibilities of corporate strategy in fundamental and far-reaching ways. For more than a century after its founding in 1802, the company had been almost exclusively a maker of explosives. The onset of World War I, however, brought dramatic changes to Du Pont. Business boomed and the company expanded capacity exponentially to supply the Allies, but in doing so it created the prospect of a sharp postwar contraction. In a preemptive response, executives rapidly assembled plans to preserve the sudden gains by preparing the company to enter new markets as the war ended. By the time peace arrived, Du Pont was acquiring and developing a series of operations making products that employed the nitrocellulose derivatives of its explosives manufacturing processes, including businesses in artificial leather, pyroxylin (Celluloid), varnishes, paints, and dyestuffs. Farther afield, the company also bought a major stake in General Motors, then consolidating its position as the nation's largest automobile manufacturer and hence a leading customer for Du Pont's protective coatings. In effect, Du Pont was executing a deft lateral shift, transforming its sharp increase in scale into a sudden expansion of scope.[6]

The strategy worked, and it validated a new approach to business planning and organization. In the aftermath of World War I, Du Pont managed to establish itself in a ring of adjacent chemical markets. And as it did so, it demonstrated that powerful new possibilities of strategic maneuver were opening to big business as the American industrial economy matured. Du Pont established a multidivisional (M-Form) structure with autonomous divisions responsible for managing distinct businesses, while executives and staff at the corporate headquarters formulated strategy and allocated resources to support the corporation as a whole. Although the full implications of the strategic and structural changes at Du Pont would not become evident for decades, they enabled an entirely new way of thinking about and organizing the corporation. The M-Form structure liberated top management from the concerns of individual business units. Corporate leaders became free to develop and acquire new businesses that could be managed as new units in an expanding portfolio of divisions. Cash flow from high-performing units could be used to fund growth in new areas. Lower-performing divisions could be sold or spun off, with the proceeds reapplied in the continuing quest for growth. Senior executives became responsible for optimizing the mix of businesses to ensure sufficient returns to investors in the short term while simultaneously positioning the company to remain prosperous in the long term.

The Du Pont model of strategy and structure proved powerfully appealing in the chemical industry as well as among industrial corporations generally. As Alfred D. Chandler Jr. has so richly documented, nearly all large American industrial corporations adopted diversification strategies and M-Form structures during the middle decades of the twentieth century. Particularly after World War II, which conferred new technological and managerial capabilities on many firms, the strategy of growth through diversification gathered momentum.[7] Powerful economies of scale drove the trend. Added impetus came as a rationale, a compelling sense of corporate logic, formed around the concept of the diversified corporation. Strategists began to think in terms of companies' intangible assets—their technologies, brand identities, managerial capabilities, and administrative infrastructures—and became concerned with exploiting those assets, with leveraging them, and with protecting them from the vicissitudes of fluctuations in particular markets.[8] Diversification promised to reinforce companies' market power by enabling them to cross-subsidize businesses, bring predatory pricing powers to bear on their competitors, and enforce mutual forbearance in the context of multipoint competition.[9] Economies of scope, both real and conjectural, thus began to work in concert with economies of scale.

Initially, corporate diversification took place within bounded industry contexts. Over the middle decades of the twentieth century, for example, chemical companies like Du Pont, Dow, Union Carbide, and Monsanto all developed or bought their way into a range of chemical businesses such as plastics, polymers, and artificial fibers that were related through common feedstocks or process technologies although their customers and end uses were often vastly different. Some venturesome producers also took steps toward vertical integration; Union Carbide prospected upstream and staked out raw material and mineral supplies, even a hydroelectric plant. By and large, however, the chemical companies tended to stay within relatively clear industry boundaries through the 1950s.

During the 1960s, the scope of activity broadened dramatically as corporations began to expand into unrelated industries, principally by means of acquisition. As we saw in Chapter 2, enforcement of the Celler-Kefauver Act of 1950 discouraged horizontally and vertically related acquisitions (buying competitors, buyers, or suppliers). Companies seeking growth were thus obliged to diversify into other industries, fueling waves of mergers.[10] The M-Form structure easily accommodated unrelated diversification because newly acquired businesses could be tacked on as new divisions in the corporate structure. By the late 1960s, conglomerates—umbrella corporations, encompassing numerous businesses widely dispersed across industrial sectors—were proliferating and other large industrial companies in general were expanding their scopes of operation. As we saw in Chapter 1, Westinghouse had taken on hotels, car rentals, and mail-order record clubs. Exxon, the energy titan, entered office equipment markets, pitting Vydec word processors, Qyx typewriters, and Quip fax machines against the likes of IBM, Xerox, and Wang. By 1980, less than a quarter of the *Fortune* 500 confined their business exclusively to a single two-digit Standard Industrial Classification (SIC) industry, and more than half operated in three or more.[11]

The economic merits of unrelated diversification and the conglomerates it spawned were hotly debated from the start. Financial economists argued that the diversification of risks was best left to investors to accomplish through financial markets rather than through conglomerate corporations. They contended that unrelated diversification simply reflected the self-interest of managers who benefited from such strategies because their compensation and prestige were often tied to company size and because diversification reduced their employment risk.[12]

Others took a more favorable view. Citing limitations of the external capital markets such as underinvestment in growth businesses, incomplete information, and insufficient monitoring incentives, they argued that the internal capital market created by the diversified companies offered better access to high quality information and resulted in better resource allocation choices.[13] In addition, it was argued, highly diversified companies benefited shareholders by pooling earnings streams across different businesses, thereby making them more predictable and reliable. This reduced volatility in earnings, it was believed, would lower the cost of raising capital as well as reduce the amount of taxes paid.

The management consulting industry further helped promote the idea of the corporation as a portfolio of businesses with different financial profiles. Firms such as the Boston Consulting Group and McKinsey & Co. created a host of compelling portfolio-planning tools and methodologies that the biggest diversified companies quickly embraced. Most of these tools categorized business units according to structural characteristics of the markets they served, including attractiveness (growth, margins) and competition. Such analysis generated a steady stream of numbers that combined with other financial metrics to allow executives to track performance and balance their portfolios. By the end of the 1970s, portfolio planning had become the dominant strategic tool in most *Fortune* 500 corporations.[14]

The typical industrial corporation became a diverse entity consisting of scattered businesses, many of them recently acquired and still unfamiliar. It was planning intently, by the numbers, its executive attention fixed on financial targets. It was broadly confident in its strategic powers and, as global competition intensified, as the energy crisis hit, and as business conditions that had supported decades of growth began to deteriorate, its first reaction, more often than not, was to apply the strategies it already knew. Du Pont, for example, pursued diversification with mounting intensity. During the 1970s and early 1980s, the company made a series of strategic moves nearly as dramatic as those it had taken during World War I. It acquired Remington Arms, New England Nuclear Corporation (which manufactured radioactive chemicals for medical systems), Solid State Dielectrics, Elit Circuits, Inc., and the agrichemicals divisions of SEPIC. In 1981, Du Pont stunned followers of the chemical industry by acquiring the energy giant Conoco for the unheard-of price of $7.8 billion. At the time, the deal represented the biggest transaction in American business history, and it secured for Du Pont a reliable source of feedstocks. By the mid-1980s, the company was running 90 major businesses, and annual reports were regularly updating investors on the financial prospects of the company's portfolio.[15]

With vast resources at its disposal, Du Pont could take advantage of opportunities like the Conoco deal relatively easily, without unduly disrupting either its core operations or other diversification ventures. But Du Pont's competitors in the chemical industry—companies like Dow, Union Carbide, and Monsanto—struggled and searched for opportunities more urgently as the energy crisis hit and the end of growth became manifest. These companies occupied roughly similar positions in the mid-1970s, each harboring major businesses in commodity chemical lines, each casting about for ways to generate growth in newer lines of business. Dow and Union Carbide followed a path typical of most big industrial companies, which sought to revive growth by intensifying diversification, only to encounter more trouble and eventually face the necessity to refocus on their traditional core businesses. The story of Monsanto told later in this chapter illustrates a different path, as the company strived to reinvent itself through internal development and a few carefully placed bets on acquisitions.

DIVERSIFICATION AND REFOCUSING AT DOW AND UNION CARBIDE

In the quarter century after the first oil shock of the 1970s, Dow and Union Carbide slowly faced up to the challenges posed by the end of growth. At both companies, responding to the challenges eventually entailed wholesale rejection of the strategies that had undergirded their growth in the post-World War II era. Confronting the necessity to change, both would abandon efforts to diversify and choose to refocus on the chemical businesses they knew best. The starting points, motivation, timing, and extent of these changes differed in the two long-time rivals, but the outcome proved the same—just as it did for most of their peers among the *Fortune* 100 industrials.

The Logic of Diversification at Dow

Dow Chemical, Du Pont's most aggressive domestic rival through the 1970s, presented a very different kind of company, in temperament as well as strategic circumstance. Dow was three-quarters of a century old in 1973, but it still did business more like a hungry upstart than a venerable giant. An episode from the company's earliest years of growth set the tone of business for decades to come: in the early twentieth century, when Herbert Dow first tried to wedge his way into European bromide markets, the powerful Deutsche Bromkonvention retaliated by slashing their prices in the United States to levels far below production costs. Dow fought back, going deep into debt to match the dumping prices. And Dow struck offensively as well, buying up the bromide his German and British competitors were dumping in the United States and shipping it back to Europe to resell there at prices that substantially undercut those of local producers.[16]

That kind of tactical savvy and single-minded, hard-nosed competitive drive was still very much in evidence at Dow in the 1960s and early 1970s, a period of heady expansion. The company borrowed freely, laid out heavy capital expenditures, pushed continually into new international markets. By 1973, the company had been betting more-or-less continuously on market growth, and meanwhile managing to offset rising costs (in labor, raw materials, and construction) with technological gains.[17] "Dow gambled the company on debt, did well, and got its deserved success," Du Pont chairman Irving Shapiro conceded, somewhat backhandedly, in 1977. "He's right," former Dow chairman Carl Gerstacker responded. "But Du Pont did not have to take such risks. They were rich and Dow was the poor boy."[18] By the time the two men were trading these barbs, Dow had surged past Du Pont in profitability and seemed well poised to consolidate and exploit its years of growth.

That growth had been fairly focused, however. Strategically speaking, Dow still occupied a distinct segment of the industry. Historically known as "the chemical company's chemical company," Dow had staked itself in commodity chemical lines—that is, in the bulk manufacture of basic chemicals (such as ethylene) from which other chemicals were crafted. Chemicals and metals accounted for nearly half of the company's sales in 1973, and plastics and packaging for another third. Dow did little business in the retail marketplace; its principal customers were industrial, many of them other chemical companies, including Du Pont. The company's most significant consumer product, Saran Wrap®, had emerged almost in spite of corporate strategists: Dow originally developed the product for the Navy, to wrap arms and equipment being transported from ship to shore, and declined to market it commercially. Only after two Dow chemists, acting on their own initiative, found a ready market for household-sized rolls of "Clingwrap" among housewives in Midland did the company commit to commercial distribution. All told, consumer products and bioproducts (including pharmaceuticals and some agricultural chemicals) made up just under 18 percent of Dow's earnings in 1973.[19]

The energy crisis demonstrated how vulnerable this strategic ground was becoming. The first oil shock increased Dow's production costs substantially, though the full impact was not apparent for a few years. Through the mid-1970s, high levels of demand enabled the company to pass higher costs along to its customers; Dow increased prices in 1974 and again in 1975, though sales were beginning to slip by then. The company tried a third round of price hikes in 1976, but failed to keep pace with still-rising hydrocarbon costs, and earnings began to fall. Wall Street grew concerned and Dow's share price began to drop, from a 1976 high of 57 to around 37 by early 1977.[20]

By the late 1970s, the commodity chemical market was saturated and Dow was struggling to cope not only with industry overcapacity, but also repeated OPEC price increases and lingering U.S. stagflation. As a low-cost producer and price leader, Dow initially fared better than many of its competitors. The company's geographic spread also helped to buffer the impact; strong operations in Latin America and the Pacific generated much-needed earnings through the mid-1970s. But the company's long-term (and long-held) strategic ground seemed increasingly shaky. And it was getting crowded, too. Petroleum companies, which enjoyed ready access to feedstock supplies, were establishing petrochemical capacities of their own. Windfall energy crisis profits gave these competitors formidable resources, as well as powerful incentives to hedge themselves against the cyclicality of oil prices.[21] Moreover, national companies were by now forming in various OPEC nations. For a cluster of energy crisis-related reasons, then, Dow's historic strategy was growing more expensive and its options more constrained. The mainstay of its business, commodity chemicals, had always been a cyclical market, but as both the company's scale and the intensity of its competition grew, the cycles were becoming more violent, harder to manage strategically.

In May 1978, Paul Oreffice took over as Dow's president and CEO, and he perceived the necessity to change. Oreffice was a chemist, like virtually all of Dow's top management, but he had made his reputation within the company for his financial acuity. As financial vice president between 1970 and 1975 he had steered the company through the first phase of the energy crisis with a steely nerve, steadily hiking Dow's prices as material costs increased. Still, he knew the numbers too well to imagine that those kinds of tactics were going to work indefinitely.

Within months of assuming office, Oreffice braked petrochemical construction and convened a summit of Dow's top 30 executives in Shanty Creek, Michigan. "What does Dow have to do to be a great company in the year 2000?" the new CEO asked the gathering. By his later account, what "came out as the absolute essential" was diversification. Executives resolved to reduce Dow's dependence on commodity chemicals and take the company into specialty chemicals, setting a realignment target of 50 percent for specialty chemicals earnings by the mid-1980s. Oreffice himself strongly backed the new strategic direction. "I felt it was absolutely important for Dow to get away from being strictly a basic chemical and plastic company, that we needed to go downstream," he later recalled. "Where was the big action, the big opportunity? We had a base for pharmaceuticals—it was too small, too miserly—but that was the place we ought to go. So I thought we ought to expand downstream in pharmaceuticals, number one; that was my first priority. And let's put more resources into consumer products and ag chemicals, and into specialty chemicals."[22]

In November 1980, Dow cut the first in a series of major deals in specialty chemicals when it acquired Richardson-Merrell's pharmaceutical business. At $260 million, the purchase price amounted to more than twice the unit's asset value, but Dow saw great possibilities in Merrell's research portfolio. Dow's Human Health Group, reformulated as Merrell-Dow Pharmaceuticals, Inc., now possessed "a sufficient sales base to support the volume of research needed to compete in today's drug industry," Dow's 1981 Annual Report claimed, adding that Merrell's salesforce, product line, and geographic mix dovetailed nicely with Dow's.

The next several years, at least, seemed to vindicate the diversification strategy. Dow's commodity chemicals and plastics business languished, and declines in real energy prices weighed down the company's oil and gas ventures, but strong earnings in drugs, pesticides, and consumer goods helped buoy Dow's overall financial performance. In 1982, Oreffice pushed the company further downstream when he cut off several major commodity chemicals ventures. Dow sold off its oil and gas reserves and its interests in several foreign national petrochemical joint ventures. This last step sent a particularly strong signal through the ranks of the company. "There was a faction, a strong faction on the board and in the company," Oreffice would admit, looking back, "that felt that that's where Dow's future was. They felt that Du Pont had done the right thing by buying Conoco, and that we were going wrong by going downstream—we should be backward-integrating. I wanted to avoid that route."[23]

Oreffice was not yet done. "Dow has established several diversification teams and acquisition committees to identify and evaluate business opportunities," the company reported to its shareholders in 1983. "We haven't been involved in many acquisitions in the past, but we will be much more aggressive in the specialties area."[24] True to its word, Dow announced late the following year it was acquiring Texize, a specialty chemicals unit, from Thiokol, including that unit's Fantastik® and Spray 'n Wash® lines. The move doubled the size of Dow's consumer products business, to nearly $600 million in sales.[25] Oreffice's retirement and replacement by Frank Popoff in 1987 did nothing to slow the trend. That year the company reconstituted its consumer products units as DowBrands.

Dow also pressed into agricultural chemicals during this period, another line of business that seemed to hold high, noncyclical growth possibilities. Headquarters pumped substantial R&D allocations into various pesticide and herbicide projects through the 1980s. The sector attained a new place within the company, though, in 1989, when Dow joined forces with Eli Lilly in a combination that effectively doubled the size of its agricultural chemicals operations. With first year sales of $1.5 billion, DowElanco vaulted into place as the sixth-largest producer in the field globally.

Dow's pharmaceutical line also strengthened by way of acquisition in 1989, incorporating a 39 percent stake in Marion Labs. At $2.2 billion, the acquisition was Dow's largest to date, and once again it paid top dollar. Analysts questioned the move, noting that several of Marion's key patents were scheduled to expire shortly and that it had nothing of note in the pipeline.[26] But for their part Dow's corporate strategists expressed eminent satisfaction with the progress of their diversification program. Record sales ($17.6 billion) and net income ($2.49 billion) in 1989, the company reported to its shareholders in 1989, signified strong growth. And even more important from a strategic standpoint, half of those earnings were now coming from consumer products: pharmaceuticals, and specialty chemicals. "Dow," the report concluded, "has diversified globally, emphasizing value-added products resistant to economic cycles and markets to provide growth in the 1990s."

By the end of the 1980s, Dow had put itself on a new strategic footing. Through a decade of energetic dealing it had built up a diversified portfolio of specialty chemical businesses to augment its commodity chemical operations. As "the chemical companies' chemical company" it had been securely lodged well upstream, but powerful currents were eating away at that ground and driving the company downstream, into new markets. It was a signal transformation. For decades through the mid-1970s, Dow had mastered business at the industrial heart of the chemical sector. By manufacturing bulk chemicals and selling them to other chemical companies and industrial clients, and particularly by doing so more skillfully and more efficiently than its competitors, Dow had built itself up into a major corporate power. Over the late-1970s, however, its leaders perceived the necessity to change, concluding that business would not sustain the same kind of growth in the future. They saw the end of growth coming and took anxious steps to thwart it.

Rethinking the Portfolio at Union Carbide

During the 1970s and 1980s, Dow sought to counteract disturbing trends in its core business by diversifying away from it. At the same time, Dow's long-time rival, Union Carbide, was already diversified when the energy crisis hit and caused a slowdown. As a result, Union Carbide confronted necessity and made a different choice. It sought to rethink the strategy of diversification and reexamine possibilities in its traditional operations. In so doing, Union Carbide started down a path that many other big industrial companies, including Dow, would later follow. A tragic accident in Bhopal, India, in 1984 increased the urgency of Union Carbide's efforts to change but also constrained its strategic options.

In 1973, strong commodity chemical operations anchored Union Carbide, but it also managed a range of specialty chemical lines and several well-developed consumer businesses. Union Carbide had formed in 1917 through a merger of four companies, each operating in distinct market segments. From its earliest years, the company's business had been closely tied to the steel industry: One of the founding four companies, Union Carbide, made calcium carbide (used to manufacture metal alloys), and customers in the primary metals industry still accounted for a fifth of corporate revenues in 1973. From its earliest years, the company had also produced acetylene, oxygen, and other gases and chemicals for industrial uses. But its portfolio also included the National Carbon Company, which in the late nineteenth century had manufactured and marketed the first commercial dry cell battery, and Prestone Antifreeze®, a popular additive to automotive cooling systems developed in the 1920s.

Spread from its earliest years along a range of businesses, Union Carbide approached the last quarter of the twentieth century by way of distinct strategic patterns of operation. From its very inception, it had expanded aggressively, and somewhat haphazardly, in both scale and scope. Internal development had created products such as vinyl and phenolic plastic, while acquisitions had carried Union Carbide into a series of new chemicals markets and upstream as well: In the middle decades of the twentieth century, the company bought up mineral operations, raw material deposits, and even hydroelectric plants. By the late 1960s, the company had evolved into a full-blown conglomerate, with businesses in petroleum, pharmaceuticals, semiconductors, mattresses, and undersea equipment, along with its core operations in chemicals, plastics, gases, and batteries.

Strategic coordination of this assemblage of markets and businesses had traditionally been loose. Operated for decades as a holding company, Union Carbide restructured in 1949, consolidating its subsidiaries into an operating company, though individual business units continued to function with a good deal of autonomy. Poor decision making at the corporate level had cost Union Carbide leading market shares in a series of product lines, which it had originally dominated, including vinyl, phenolic plastic, ethylene, polyvinyl chloride (PVC), and polystyrene.[27] Headquarters had tried repeatedly to impose some degree of central control over the company's various processes of resource allocation, but business planning remained highly decentralized until the late 1960s, when headquarters began applying more formal mechanisms of strategy making to company operations. In 1970, the company established a new business development department to oversee nonchemicals and nonplastics businesses, and two years later it established a central management committee to oversee all the businesses. The structural move fortified the company's commitment to defend its market share in polyethylene and ethylene oxide, but at a heavy price: Profits in those core businesses deteriorated badly.

In the mid-1970s, CFO F. Perry Wilson sought vigorously to shift the company's strategic focus from market share to profitability and to break the company's various businesses into strategic planning units (SPUs). General Electric (GE), of course, had popularized formulation along similar lines, and at Union Carbide as at GE (along with a host of other diversified companies during this period), the restructuring was designed to plant new strategic discipline into business operations throughout the company. Like most other industrial corporations that embraced strategic and portfolio planning during the 1970s, Union Carbide came to view its operations as a business portfolio, trying to develop its "stars," milk its "cash cows," and terminate its "dogs." In Union Carbide's terms: "We have sorted out our businesses according to criteria such as profitability and growth potential," the annual report for 1974 assured shareholders. "We have proceeded to categorize these businesses on a scale of relative attractiveness, ranging from those that are superior and merit full support to those that are weak, or declining, and call for consideration of withdrawal. With this done, we have allocated our resources—particularly construction capital and research and development effort—preferentially to the more promising businesses."[28]

Over the next few years, corporate headquarters proceeded to execute this strategic realignment, albeit somewhat ambiguously at first. The company targeted medical systems and electronic materials and components as two markets with high growth potential, for example, and began to channel development funds in those directions. In 1975, the company pointed out that 60 percent of its sales originated in growth category businesses, and that those businesses would get the lion's share—80 percent—of "forecasted construction expenditure." In a similar vein, though somewhat less ambitiously, Union Carbide announced the following year that it was directing one-third of its R&D spending toward "new business opportunities," including such diverse projects as municipal waste systems, chemical production from coal and synthesis gas, medical diagnostics systems, pesticides, and specialty chemicals for increasing oil well outputs. At the same time, the company reconstituted its agricultural chemicals operations as a dedicated Agricultural Products Division, buttressed by the acquisition of Rorer Amchem's Amchem Products subsidiary.

The ascension of William Sneath as CEO in 1977 intensified the campaign to reposition the company's business portfolio. During the late 1970s, Sneath engineered exits from several dozen businesses, pulling Union Carbide out of aluminum automobile radiators, brain scanners, and shrimp fishing. "We are in too many things," Sneath explained, "most of them growing very rapidly and demanding a lot of cash, and therefore you begin to limit each business."[29] Some divestitures shed peripheral ventures. Salmon farming, for example, clearly had taken the company into unfamiliar waters. "That type of thing we've stopped," Sneath announced. "In the long run we would be in a narrow sector of the frozen food business and who would our competitors be?" Experienced big food companies, Union Carbide's strategists were coming to realize, who would hold clear competitive advantages in the form of well-developed marketing and distribution infrastructures.[30] Other strategic withdrawals, though, took the company out of businesses it had been mining for decades. In 1978, for example, the company pulled out of polyvinyl chloride, a polymer Union Carbide had practically invented, though one that had become a fiercely competitive and barely profitable business. Even more strikingly, two years later, amid a flurry of divestitures, Union Carbide sold off its calcium carbide operations—the business that had formed the basis of the original parent company—to fund its investment program.

By this point, Union Carbide had been pared down to a handful of core businesses—"a trimmer and better-balanced company," it declared—grouped around graphite electrodes, batteries, agricultural chemicals, polyethylene, and industrial gases. Corporate planners remained committed to diversification, but within bounds. They relied heavily on state-of-the-art strategic planning disciplines to project market growth business by business and position the company to "Go where the action is," in the words of the annual report for 1982. "That may be toward an industry with good growth potential, or toward a niche or industry segment that is growing faster than the market as a whole."[31]

In the chemical industry, as far as Union Carbide (along with Dow, Allied, Hercules, Eastman, Hunt, Morton Thiokol, and other companies) could see, moving "where the action is" meant shifting out of petrochemicals and into specialty chemicals, and thereby shifting the company out of price-based competition, into service- and knowledge-based competition.[32] Wilson put high stock in Union Carbide's consumer products, with evident satisfaction proclaiming, "The supermarket has become a very important outlet for Union Carbide Products." Other "entrepreneurial segments" of the portfolio included such specialty projects as polycrystalline silicon (a chemical used in semiconductor production) and oilfield service chemicals. Thus, even as it was shedding underperforming and peripheral businesses, and meanwhile maintaining its longstanding operations in commodity chemicals, plastics, and industrial gases, Union Carbide was trying to shift the center of the company downstream, where specialty markets seemed richer and less crowded.

Union Carbide's efforts to remake its portfolio accelerated dramatically and involuntarily following a tragic accident in December 1984 at a plant owned by a subsidiary in Bhopal, India. Poisonous gas leaking from the plant killed several thousand people in nearby neighborhoods. In the aftermath of this tragedy, Union Carbide itself faced terrible consequences. Within days the company's stock plunged from $49 to $35 a share, and the *Wall Street Journal* speculated that litigation would force Union Carbide to declare bankruptcy.[33] Inevitably, predators began circling the wounded prey. The attack began eight months later, when GAF CEO Sam Heyman revealed he was acquiring piles of Union Carbide stock. Should he gain control, Heyman announced, he would sell off large chunks of the company, including its metal and carbon, technical service and specialty products units, (which Union Carbide itself was now planning to sell), as well as its consumer products division (which Union Carbide hoped to retain).

Union Carbide eventually defeated Heyman's bid but paid a heavy price for its victory. To survive, the company was forced to abandon the strategy it had spent the past 10 years developing. Union Carbide took on extraordinary levels of debt and committed to sell businesses that only a few years before had seemed its most promising. During 1986, Union Carbide spun off the battery division, the home and automotive lines, a 50 percent stake in the electrical carbon business, and its worldwide agricultural chemicals unit.

Just one ray of light brightened the company's bleak prospects, but it may well have been a critical one: By 1986, commodity chemicals and plastics markets were reviving due to falling energy prices. The revenue stream was welcome, indeed urgently needed. But the sense of hope, the renewed perception of opportunity, might have been even more important at this point. At the very least, the earnings purchased some modest degree of strategic flexibility. The company hazarded a small acquisition in 1987, picking up a hydroxyethylcellulose business. Soon afterward it began exploring joint venture possibilities in some business lines. Earnings remained strong. By 1988, Union Carbide had compiled $1 billion in cash and a new strategy was beginning to take shape.

The company was still in hock. At $3.2 billion, its debt amounted to 64 percent of total capital, and many investors expected that the new profits would be applied to reducing that debt. Nevertheless, in April 1988, Union Carbide announced fairly ambitious plans for capital expenditures. Company analysis had determined that the upswing in the commodity market stemmed from "fundamental supply and demand," declared CEO Robert Kennedy (who had taken over in early 1986, following the takeover battle), and Union Carbide was moving to take advantage. The company would double capital spending in chemicals and plastics to $400 million for 1988, while holding carbon-products spending level and taking industrial gas spending down slightly. Union Carbide had become a "significantly simpler organization . . . with few delusions about itself," Kennedy added. "We've been to the brink, and when you've been to the brink, it changes your attitude."[34]

Indeed, Union Carbide was now crafting a very different strategic sense of itself and its opportunities. When asked in 1988 where the company's greatest growth markets lay, Kennedy promptly responded: "In chemicals and plastics, there is just no end to the invention of new molecules and new processes in response to market needs and the search for lower manufacturing costs." In other words, Union Carbide was rededicating itself to a longstanding area of expertise.

Kennedy knew he was working within a narrow time frame. Union Carbide, it seemed, was chaining itself to the inevitable down-cycle in commodity chemicals. As if on cue, demand stagnated in 1989 and earnings began to fall. There was little choice but to ride things out, by applying superior technology and doing whatever else it took to be the low-cost producer. So Union Carbide centralized inventory management, cut inventory and shipping costs by tightening distribution, overhauled plant maintenance procedures, pared executive perks, and ruthlessly reengineered operations. Critically, the company's Unipol processing technology, which permitted chemical reactions at lower pressure and so was much more energy efficient, enabled deep additional cuts in plant operation costs. "We've proven this business can be at the top of the industry in the good years," Kennedy declared resolutely to shareholders in 1990; "It is our intent to prove that we can achieve strong relative performance in a downturn, ranking us among the leaders over the full business cycle."[35]

A final round of divestitures and refocusing accompanied the commitment to chemicals and plastics. Just before the downturn, Union Carbide had restructured itself as a holding company comprising three independently operating subsidiaries—Union Carbide Chemicals and Plastics, Union Carbide Industrial Gases, and UCAR Carbon Co. (which manufactured graphite electrodes)—the company promptly began preparing the nonchemicals units for divestiture. "You guys are worth more than what we're getting credit for," Robert Krauss, chief executive of UCAR Carbon, later remembered Kennedy telling him. "Go away. Go find your own worth." Krauss moved decisively. First he brought in Mitsubishi as a partner, negotiating an agreement under which the Japanese firm purchased a 50 percent stake in the subsidiary, now a joint venture. Then he began streamlining and reengineering operations. ("Let's pretend we're a raider," the CEO told his staff as they rolled up their sleeves and set to work.) Within several years, operations had grown more efficient, more profitable, and eminently more salable. In 1993, Blackstone Group purchased a 75 percent share in the business (half of Union Carbide's stake and all of Mitsubishi's, which sold for a healthy profit), and the following year it brought UCAR public.[36] Meanwhile, Union Carbide also spun off its industrial gases subsidiary to shareholders in 1991.

In sum, Union Carbide took on a "new identity. . . . No longer the large conglomerate of past years, we've become a tightly focused basic chemical company." It still had a handful of "noncyclical" chemicals businesses, including wire and cable insulation, solvents and coatings, technology licensing deals, and several specialty chemicals. But its sales were heavily weighted, and the company's strategic focus was distinctly committed, to commodity chemicals. "We are planting our flag in basic chemicals, the very segment of the petrochemical industry that a number of other companies are abandoning," the company declared, "because it's the segment in which Union Carbide can, by any measure, be the best in the business."[37]

So, in a process that was perhaps as much alchemy as it was chemistry, Union Carbide made choice out of necessity, and profits out of commodity chemicals. By

1993, having shed all of its nonchemicals businesses and ruthlessly reengineered what remained, Union Carbide had made itself a substantially smaller, leaner company. Revenues had shrunk by half, and its workforce by 90 percent, from mid-1980s levels. Fifty percent of the company's earnings now stemmed from polyethylene and ethyl glycol, and despite the down cycle, Union Carbide was still able to report profits, largely due to cost cutting: Over the early 1990s, the company squeezed $575 million worth of overhead out of its operating budget. With an upswing in core markets in 1994, profits rose dramatically, though executives resolutely maintained, even intensified, the cost-cutting campaign. By 1997, the company had raised its cost reduction target (based on 1993 cost structures) to $1.1 billion by the year 2000, and was already more than three-quarters of the way there.[38]

Reckoning and Refocusing at Dow

Even as extrinsic necessities were driving Union Carbide from the specialty chemicals field and forcing the company to refocus on its commodity chemical core, Dow was also discovering the limits of diversification and the desirability of retreat to the traditional chemical businesses. Recognition of the necessity to refocus occurred somewhat later than at Union Carbide, however.

Through the late-1980s, as demand for commodity chemicals surged, Dow continued to feed and expand its pharmaceutical, agricultural, and consumer products lines, busily preparing for the next down cycle. By 1990, Dow had indeed managed to insulate itself fairly well from the downturn, earning $1.4 billion, 45 percent lower than the previous year's net income but better than most chemical companies. The company settled in, tended its specialty chemicals businesses, and waited for commodity chemicals markets to improve. While Union Carbide was streamlining operations and overhauling cost structures, Dow was focusing on moves like expanding its DowBrands line, putting new skin lotions, shampoos, and premium-grade tomatoes on supermarket shelves.

The strategy did bring new pressures, however. Dow's forays into the supermarkets, for example, put it in a league with consumer-savvy companies like Procter & Gamble and Unilever, which were highly skilled at promoting and managing brands. In order to keep pace, Dow had to make substantial new research and advertising expenditures.

Consolidating the company's pharmaceutical expansion also demanded a growing commitment of strategic resources. Through the 1980s, Merrell-Dow performed strongly, sales reaching $1.3 billion by the end of the decade, surpassing $2 billion with the addition of Marion Laboratories in 1989, and climbing to $3.3 billion by 1993.[39] Marion Merrell Dow (MMD) "made a bundle of money for us when we needed it the most, in 1991, 1992, and 1993," Frank Popoff affirmed, adding that

Dow as a whole was "really less vulnerable to the business cycle than we were in the early 1980s."[40]

Stability at Dow proved short lived, however. The pharmaceutical industry, it appeared, was prone to its own cycles, and Dow was hitting a downswing just as the structure of the industry was undergoing dramatic change. When Glaxo Group Ltd, a British firm, bought Wellcome & Company in 1995 for $15 billion it became the largest pharmaceutical firm in the world. "The definition of 'big' changed," Popoff ruefully reported. "The definition of big was a $5 billion company not so long ago. The definition of big now is $10 or $12 billion."[41] Companies on the scale of Glaxo Wellcome were large enough to "rationalize, and spread your research costs across a whole lot more sales," Temple added. "You had to be big . . . or you were going to be eaten alive by these companies that were going through the mega-mergers."[42]

Dow, it seemed, faced a choice: either take the next step and make another substantial pharmaceuticals acquisition, or sell off MMD. Corporate strategists explored their options, identifying Hoechst as a candidate for "possible strategic alliance" and approaching people there about a deal. "Dow was looking at an $11 to $14 billion acquisition," Temple reported[43]—in other words, a strategic move on a scale, as Popoff realized, that "would have turned Dow toward pharmaceuticals to such a degree that it would have overshadowed everything else in the company."[44] In any event, Hoechst was not interested in being acquired; in fact, MMD had turned up on Hoechst's list. Negotiations opened, but now Dow found itself playing the role of seller, not buyer. The company eventually sold off MMD for $5.2 billion. "I'm ambivalent about Dow getting out of the pharmaceutical business after we put so much talent and time into building it up," Popoff admitted. "As we went along in that business every hurdle we came to was higher."[45]

Strategic ambivalence eventually betrayed itself in DowBrands as well. Through the mid-1990s the unit weathered fierce competition in retail markets like skin care and household products. Eventually corporate strategists decided it was time to pull out. In 1996, the company sold off its personal care line, disposing of all consumer products save those which the company had been initially marketing: food protection and specialty cleaning chemicals. It had been a "good business," CEO William Stavropoulos reported to shareholders in 1997, but Dow lacked "the critical mass to achieve world leadership."[46]

Dow did remain committed to its agricultural chemicals business, however. Even as it completed the sale of its personal care and household consumer products, the company bought out Eli Lilly's 40 percent stake in DowElanco, renaming it Agro-Sciences LLC, and meanwhile increased its share of Mycogen, a biotechnology firm, to 63 percent. All in all, the annual report for 1997 (Dow's centennial year) claimed, the company was generating about half of its sales in "our targeted group of performance businesses (those that produce more stable earnings)."

Dow entered its second century of business searching for new strategic bearings. The company had plunged into a series of specialty markets, most of which had grown too expensive or demanding to sustain. Diversification may well have distracted corporate executives; it certainly delayed restructuring of the company's commodity chemicals businesses. Dow was notably late in applying the kinds of cost cutting and reengineering that revitalized Union Carbide. Belatedly, though, the company did begin to formulate a new, refocused strategy for fortifying its operations in commodity chemicals. By 1999, the company was implementing what it termed "bottom-of-the-cycle planning," meaning planning for profitability through the trough of the next down cycle. Dow was no longer strategizing to escape the next downturn—was no longer trying to dodge necessity. Instead it was preparing itself to do business within the boundaries of necessity, reducing costs, cutting (or preparing for rapid cuts in) capacity, carving out layers of management, and so on. And in an effort to discourage short-sighted up-cycle capital investment, Dow was now figuring profitability in terms of economic profit, that is, factoring in cost of capital, and setting returns-on-assets targets for the next downturn.[47] Dow, too, eventually bowed before the forces that had overtaken Union Carbide a decade before and began to refocus its strategic energies on its chemical operations.

REFOCUSING THE INDUSTRIAL CORPORATION

Strategic thinking at Dow, Union Carbide, and other industrial companies evolved in response to specific industry and company circumstances. In the cases of both Dow and Union Carbide, the particular challenges of managing commodity chemicals businesses created a distinct sequence and timing to diversification and eventual refocusing. An industrial accident forced Union Carbide to face choices that Dow kept at bay for another decade but was finally unable to avoid, choices even mighty Du Pont could not forestall indefinitely. Whatever the specifics, whatever the timing, the biggest industrial companies were facing up to a difficult challenge: the decline of real growth in a more competitive, maturing global economy.

The path that Dow and Union Carbide trod in these circumstances proved well worn among big industrial companies generally, as they finally began to confront the necessity of managing in an environment of limited growth and declining future prospects. The result was a reexamination of the role of strategic planning, the gradual divestiture of unrelated businesses, and a heightened focus on the company's core businesses and competencies. Many industrials that had set up large strategic planning departments in the 1970s scaled them back dramatically in the 1980s. GE, the pioneer in establishing such departments, became the pioneer in disassembling them. The planning function itself, which had usually been lodged in central staffs, was dispersed to operating units and made a responsibility of senior line managers who best understood their businesses. A small number of executives at headquarters—sometimes only an individual—pulled together divisional plans and added a corporate perspective.

At the same time, the big industrials threw off the acquisitions an earlier generation of corporate planners had negotiated. According to one calculation, as many as three-quarters of unrelated acquisitions in the industrial economy were divested by 1987. Other measures reinforced the trend of reversal and retrenchment. In 1980, more than three quarters of the *Fortune* 100 had deployed themselves in multiple two-digit SIC codes; by the mid-1990s, over two-thirds had withdrawn to strongholds within single designations.[48] The median overall level of diversification among the *Fortune* 100 firms, moreover, declined by about 30 percent during the 1980s and 1990s.

Refocusing did not mean an end to mergers and acquisitions. Indeed, a rush of activity accompanied the shift in strategy, as companies bought, sold, spun off, and swapped operating units in order to bring themselves into new alignment. Between 1978 and 1996 the average *Fortune* 100 firm engaged in 24 acquisitions, costing some $412 million each (on average). Unlike the deals of the 1960s, however, as many as half of which were unrelated, the acquisitions of the 1980s and 1990s tended (65 percent) to occur in related businesses—meaning they fell within the primary four-digit SIC code in which the acquiring firm operated.[49] (Figures for 1978 through 1992 indicate even stronger refocusing tendencies: 81 percent of these acquisitions occurred in related businesses.) Rather than marking a company's entry into new markets, acquisition now served to shore up defensive positions in existing markets, often by consolidating competing businesses. (See Table 3.1 and Figure 3.1.) These related deals became possible during an era of relaxed antitrust enforcement.

The pattern of divestitures was equally dramatic, particularly over the late-1980s. The average *Fortune* 100 firm made 33 divestitures, meaning in sum that it made more exits than entrances. (The mean divestiture value, moreover, was larger than the mean acquisition value.) A little more than half of the divestitures (56 percent) cast off business falling outside of parent companies' primary operating SIC categories—another indicator of refocusing, but a somewhat diffuse one; the fact that almost half of the divestitures were related might suggest that companies were making particularly close, careful assessments of their core competencies.

Several forces and factors accounted for these trends. To begin with, companies with strategies, structures, and operations premised on growth proved surprisingly vulnerable to attack when growth slowed down. Starting in the late 1970s, what became known as "bust-up takeovers"—in which raiders used highly leveraged debt to acquire control over undervalued companies in order to split them up into parts and sell them off individually at a significant profit—began to proliferate (more about this in Chapter 6). The laissez-faire regulatory reforms of the Reagan administration in

Table 3.1
Acquisitions, Divestitures, Joint Ventures among *Fortune* 100 Companies, 1974–1996

	Mean Number per Firm	*Mean Dollar Value*	*Percentage Related*
Acquisitions	24	$412MM	65
Divestitures	33	450MM	44
Joint ventures	34	270MM	50

Note: These data are available for only a subset of the full sample. They are based on 687 acquisitions, 707 divestitures, and 243 joint ventures.

the early 1980s facilitated the trend. Antitrust enforcers no longer prevented horizontal mergers merely because they would increase industry concentration. Several landmark court decisions, including the 1982 *Edgar vs. MITE* decision, which limited the ability of state governments to protect local companies from out-of-state raiders, helped to smooth the way for hostile takeovers. Meanwhile, a large increase in the high-yield debt market enabled raiders to raise large sums of capital with relative ease, further boosting their activity.

Many raiders employed analytical techniques such as the "chop-shop" model of corporate valuation to determine how much a diversified company could be worth, should it be broken up and the parts sold off.[50] Much as the portfolio-planning

Figure 3.1
Acquisitions, Divestitures, and Joint Ventures by the *Fortune* 100 Firms, 1978–1996

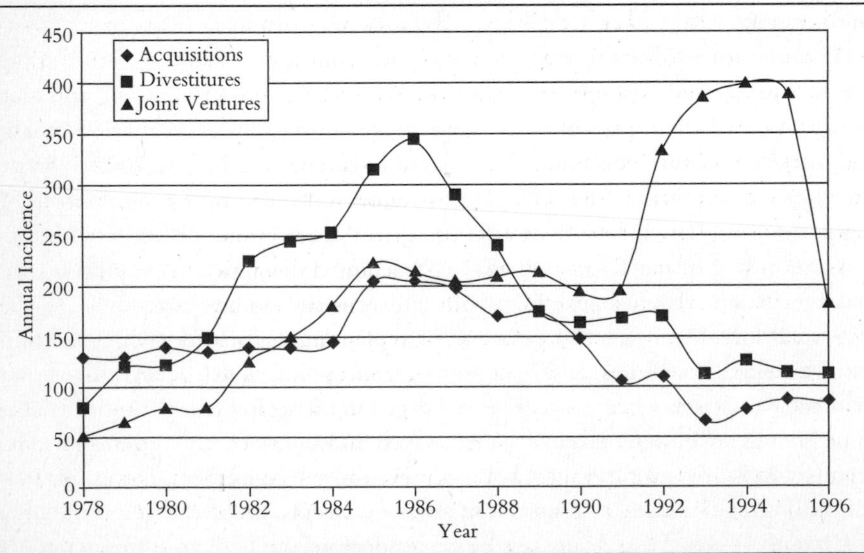

models that strategic management consultants earlier advanced had promoted diversification strategies, the spread of chop-shop types of valuation models spurred the takeover movement and corporate refocusing. Armed with such models, raiders were able to identify undervalued companies with readily separable parts, find buyers for the parts in advance of the takeover attempt, secure short-term debt financing to complete the takeover, and then quickly retire some or all of the debt with the proceeds of the bust up. This strategy enabled even small companies or groups of individual investors to make very large acquisitions. And the threat of takeover prompted voluntary refocusing at many companies, which applied the valuation models to themselves.

As events at both Union Carbide and Dow suggested, broader changes in the operating environment made the imperative harder and harder to resist in any event.[51] Mounting competition in core product markets forced corporate leaders to pay more detailed attention to their business operations. The pressures of the era demanded no less. Senior executives could not afford to occupy themselves exclusively with long-term planning and making resource allocation decisions. They had to focus their attention on increasingly urgent competitive issues such as improving their cost positions and increasing operating efficiencies. Meanwhile, any informational advantage that leaders of diversified corporations once enjoyed over external markets in allocating business resources declined as capital markets became more efficient and reporting requirements for publicly held companies grew more stringent.[52]

The stock markets, for their part, supported and encouraged the refocusing of the *Fortune* 100 companies. Given the threat of takeovers, corporate executives grew increasingly concerned about how the markets reacted to their strategic moves. What they found was that markets clearly favored transactions that increased corporate focus. Although markets tended to react negatively to acquisitions, for example (see Table 3.2), they greeted news of related acquisitions with relative equanimity, and responded harshly to unrelated acquisitions. Conversely, announcements of divestitures usually won market approval. Indeed, markets reacted essentially similarly to news of related and unrelated divestitures, suggesting that investors welcomed any form of refocusing, even if it meant exiting from operations in a firm's core business.

As refocusing gathered force, moreover, it acquired theoretical underpinnings that in turn made it yet more compelling, both to executives and investors. Over the late-1980s and early-1990s, strategic and portfolio planning became suspect, diversification fell into disfavor, and as these strategic concepts declined in relevance a new resource-based view of the corporation emerged in the strategy literature.[53] Michael Porter's work on competitive advantage played an important early role, and something like a theoretical culmination was achieved in the concept of "core competencies" by 1990.[54] Working in combination, these concepts directed strategic attention away from a company's position in various product markets. To be successful, a new

Table 3.2
Two-Week Cumulative Excess Returns for Different Transactions

	Total	*Unrelated Transactions*	*Related Transactions*
Acquisitions	−0.15%	−0.50%	+0.01%
	(n = 1788)	(n = 535)	(n = 1253)
Divestitures	+0.23%	+0.08%	+0.40%
	(n = 2292)	(n = 1208)	(n = 1084)
Joint ventures	−0.08%	−0.24%	+0.03%
	(n = 1985)	(n = 829)	(n = 1156)
Joint ventures	(n = 2292)	*Transactions*	*Transactions*
	(n = 2292)	(n = 1208)	(n = 1253)
	−0.08%	−0.08%	+0.40%

Note: A transaction is related if it occurs in a 4-digit SIC code segment in which the company has at least 20 percent of its assets.

generation of strategic thinkers maintained, companies needed to be more introspective, needed to assess and exploit their distinctive skills and assets. Inasmuch as it strained credulity to claim that a company might simultaneously enjoy distinctive competencies in a number of unrelated businesses, the resource-based view presented a strong case for a return to specialization.

N-Form Strategy: Alliances and Joint Ventures

A host of forces—financial market pressures, operational demands, and a new cluster of strategic theories—pulled corporations out of noncore businesses and away from the expansive ambitions of an earlier business era. It was a hard strategic reckoning, for it demanded that companies not only take apart what they had built, but also figure out how to rebuild. For if business exigencies increasingly restricted traditional strategies and tactics, business opportunities continued to appear—indeed they surfaced and sank more rapidly and more fluidly than ever before. Businesses that failed to recognize and adapt to necessity failed to survive, but businesses that merely bowed to necessity, that did only what they had to do in order to stay in business, only postponed the reckoning. The times called on the corporation not only to adapt to strategic necessity, but also to continue to find and make appropriate strategic choices and institutional responses, including the revival of a venerable mechanism, the joint venture, as a means to pool scarce resources and enhance market presence.

These were the dynamics working on chemical companies, for example, as they struggled in the trough of the down cycle between 1990 and 1994. Harder pressed, by fiercer competition, more expensive development costs, and a longer wait for recovery, they were forced to devise creative, flexible strategies, both to sustain presence in a range of markets and to develop new growth opportunities. Acquisitions had become more and more expensive, and the costs, moreover, were reverberating: disenchanted with the pursuit of "synergy," investors were responding increasingly negatively to acquisition announcements. Still, shifting market conditions continued to open tantalizing possibilities for growth. New market and industry convergences seemed to be forming, in biotechnology, for example. Unable, in many cases, to shoulder the weight of acquisitions, companies turned to building networks through alliances and joint ventures.

The turn, in this case, was actually a *re*turn. Joint ventures had long played a major role in the chemical industry. Companies like Dow entered the 1970s engaged in some joint ventures that were already decades old. And the energy crisis had extended the strategic trend, encouraging new, often highly articulated alliances between chemical companies trying to shore up supplies of hydrocarbon feedstocks and oil companies developing petrochemical capacities of their own. Dow, for example, undertook elaborate negotiations in the 1970s with both Saudi Arabia's Sabic and Iran's National Petrochemical Company to build major petrochemical complexes in those nations. But through the mid-1980s, companies preferred, when possible, to assume direct control over those businesses they targeted as strategic priorities, either by developing necessary technologies and production and marketing resources in-house, or by acquiring existing businesses, or by some combination of the two. The expansion into specialty chemicals of the 1980s thus took the familiar form, for the most part, of build or buy.

The industry depression of the early 1990s, however, demonstrated both the risks and the limits of acquisition as a primary growth mechanism. This time the down cycle was sharper, more prolonged, more widespread among global markets. Intense foreign competition, not just globally but in domestic markets, had bid up the costs of both development and acquisition. And this time the costs of exit seemed high, too. "What can be done with a major business that is underperforming or growing slowly?" the industry's most prominent trade journal, *Chemical Week,* asked its strategists. "Sell it? That is not always a sensible option, particularly during a downturn, and it may result in giving up significant technology position. Can a company make an acquisition to gain critical mass? If the sector is underperforming, it will probably only increase exposure."[55]

Chemical companies responded by forging a new round of joint ventures, these ones subtly but qualitatively different than earlier alliances. Union Carbide played an important early role. Its strategic options severely constricted in the wake of Heyman's raid, the company was forced to improvise, to find new ways to protect its stake in its core industries without expending substantial new resources. In 1988, Vice Chairman Clayton Stephenson discounted the possibility Union Carbide would undertake any "megabuck acquisitions" in the near future, then added the company was looking at "joint undertakings" as a more realistic tactic.

Sure enough, Union Carbide energetically explored the possibilities of joint venturing over the coming years. By 1993, with the industry deeply mired in stagnant, saturated demand, and the company meanwhile preparing to embark on what CEO Kennedy was calling "the growth phase of our strategy,"[56] Union Carbide was developing joint ventures with a range of international partners. The company was working with Asian partners to build a glycol unit in Alberta, Canada; was negotiating to build "a world-scale petrochemical complex" with Petrochemicals Industries Company of Kuwait; and was laying plans to reenter the European market the following year via "Aspen Polymeres," a 50–50 polyethylene joint venture with Elf Atochem, and Polimeri Europa, a joint venture with EniChem. Union Carbide was looking, the company declared, "not simply to get bigger, but to boost productivity, spread technological costs over a larger sales base and add value increasing our stake in profitable markets." And it was proceeding chiefly by way of "joint ventures in which our superior technology would represent a large share of our equity contribution."[57]

In sum, Union Carbide was leveraging its technology, its expertise, and building network relationships to reenter global markets. What it brought to the table was highly advanced, low cost manufacturing technologies, most notably its proprietary process for manufacturing polyethylene efficiently and cheaply. In one sense the strategy was a natural extension of Union Carbide's willingness a decade before to license proprietary process technologies to its competitors (a tactic rivals such as Dow had resisted). And to some extent it also reflected the company's reduced circumstances—really Union Carbide was unable to develop or acquire substantial new businesses on its own. But the strategy was also in synch with trends that were transforming the entire industry. By 1995, joint ventures had become "state of the art industry thinking," proclaimed *Chemical Week* in a cover story.[58] Conferring partners with the benefits of combined strategic resources—market presence and infrastructure, technology, geographic position, manufacturing capacity, and experience—the alliances (in the best cases) enabled companies to draw on each other's strengths and overcome strategic weaknesses. Even more critically, given current conditions, joint ventures spread out the costs of development, which had been growing progressively heavier.

Dow, for its part, had tended to guard its proprietary technologies more closely than Union Carbide, in part simply because for a time it could afford to do so. But gradually it became clear to executives that the company could no longer shoulder growth all by itself, and Dow too undertook several substantial joint ventures. DowElanco, for example, the company's efforts to expand its agricultural chemicals line in 1989, initially took the form of a 60–40 joint venture with Eli Lilly. Especially striking, though, was the company's announcement in February 1995 that it was combining its elastomers operations (manufacturing synthetic rubbers) with those of rival Du Pont. Engage, as the venture was eventually called, pooled Du Pont's facilities (that company supplied most of the venture's fixed assets and 80 percent of its workforce) with Dow's new Insite process technology. From Dow's point of view the venture represented an opportunity to jump-start its business, which it had spent the past year or so building after devising the underlying technology. From Du Pont's perspective, the alliance offered a way to inject a growth technology into a business in which it had developed a substantial stake, but one that needed revitalization.[59]

Already well accustomed to growth through alliance, the chemical industry took naturally to joint ventures in the early 1990s. But now they were joined by numerous other companies, in a string of other industries. By one calculation, more strategic alliances formed during the 1980s than in the entire prior history of the industrial enterprise.[60] Among the *Fortune* 100, the average company entered 34 joint ventures between 1978 and 1997—meaning that it struck alliances significantly more often than it made acquisitions (24), though the average investment in these joint ventures ($270 million) was substantially smaller than the sums companies typically invested in acquisitions. (See Table 3.1.)

Alliances and networks offered the prospect, at least, of broad benefits. They opened access to complementary assets in other companies and enabled partners to share risks, mitigate competitive uncertainties, generate real options for entry into new markets and technologies, and learn partnering skills. The strategy also became a transitional device for resolving information asymmetries inherent in acquisitions and divestitures.[61] Some critics described joint ventures as little better than substitutes for unrelated acquisitions, pursued by self-interested managers interested in growth for its own sake rather than for the value it created.[62] Still, the networking strategy grew increasingly popular. In a wary financial market, in an era of strategic retrenchment, in a business environment that was constantly growing faster-paced, more competitive, more punishing, alliances created ways of hedging choices.

The twin emphasis of focusing on core competencies and forming alliances as necessary suggests that the strategy of the modern industrial corporation after about 1990 can be conceived in network terms. The competitive landscape no longer resembled what it looked like in the 1970s, when large diversified companies competed with each other to capture expanding markets and growth opportunities. Instead, the structure of industries became defined in terms of competition and cooperation among focused companies linked to each other through a web of alliances.

THE BID FOR REINVENTION AT MONSANTO

By the mid-1990s, most of the *Fortune* 100 was in strategic retreat, dismantling diversification campaigns and pulling back from forays up- and downstream. "Core competence," and "stick to the knitting," the watchwords of a new era, warned against corporate hubris and discouraged strategic moves that tried to vault companies into entirely new businesses. But was refocusing and the formation of new alliances the only solution to the end of growth? The story of Monsanto, a company similar in 1973 to Dow and Union Carbide, illustrates an alternative strategic option, although not, ultimately, a safe harbor.

Entrenched in 1973 in high volume, low margin commodity chemicals businesses, Monsanto made a sustained effort over nearly 20 years to reinvent itself into a "life sciences company" in high growth pharmaceutical and biotechnology markets. The technology underlying this transformation was the revolutionary advance in genetics, and the strategy exploiting the technology entailed the genetic recoding of Monsanto itself.

As of 1973, at least, Monsanto seemed like an unlikely candidate for dramatic strategic reinvention. Established in 1901 to manufacture saccharin, the company expanded within a few years to the production of caffeine, vanillin, and eventually acetylsalicyclic acid (aspirin), then gradually integrated backward into raw materials production. By the 1950s it had evolved into a multinational integrated chemical company. Still, the Monsanto that approached the last quarter of the twentieth century was a fairly stolid commodity chemical company, producing little in the way of proprietary products or technology. Of total sales in 1973, two-thirds came from low-end bulk commodities including fibers, industrial chemicals, and polymers.

Monsanto was not entirely mired, however, in commodity chemicals. Agricultural chemicals generated 14 percent of total sales in 1973. Monsanto had established its Agricultural Division in 1960, and then spent a decade nurturing it before seeing profits in 1969 with the commercial release of the herbicide Lasso®. Perhaps that experience, that long initial period of gestation and cultivation, helped prepare the company's strategists for what was to come. In any event, it had cleared new strategic ground—outlying fields in which Monsanto would eventually plant some of its most exotic seeds.

Recognizing and developing growth potential in agricultural chemicals would become a driving force for reinvention at Monsanto. A second impetus came with leadership change. In 1972 the company brought in a new CEO, John Hanley. Coming from Procter & Gamble, Hanley was the first outsider to head Monsanto. Over the 1970s, while trying to maintain the company's traditional commodity and plastics lines, Hanley husbanded substantial expansion of the Agricultural Products Division as that business moved in new high-tech directions. Through a venture capital unit called Innoven (set up in 1972 with St. Louis neighbor Emerson Electric Co.), Monsanto developed ties to a series of small new companies undertaking genetic reengineering research—Genentech, for example, founded in 1976.[63]

Hanley was thinking less in terms of reinvention than of diversification, at this point, and exploring other specialty chemicals prospects as well. Innoven also channeled funds to other high-tech firms, and Monsanto began building up its silicon capacity over the same period, anticipating major growth in electronic chemicals. But Hanley did move methodically, framing strategic transformation as a thoroughgoing process that would have to work internally on the company. Monsanto, in other words, was not going to try to simply acquire its way into new businesses. Fatefully, Hanley committed the company to developing a substantial in-house molecular biology research effort, in 1979 bringing in Howard Schneiderman, the dean of the School of Biological Sciences at the University of California at Irvine, to run R&D.

Schneiderman brought high-profile scientific credibility to Monsanto's push into molecular biology, and Hanley saw to it he received strong funding support as well. The company built a major new research lab in St. Louis to house the program. Schneiderman began recruiting hundreds of scientists from leading universities, and Monsanto set up an alliance with the Washington University Medical School, funding its efforts to study and isolate proteins and peptides regulating cellular functions.[64] By the early 1980s, Monsanto was repatterning its strategic allocations, reducing capital spending on plant construction, and steadily increasing R&D outlays.[65]

Schneiderman, for his part, was spending his money widely, drawing in a series of research partners, such as the Washington University Medical School. Monsanto also drew on its partnerships with companies like Genentech during this period, providing funding in exchange for development and licensing rights (under royalty structures) for resulting commercial products. "We decided we would get technology and products from wherever we could," Schneiderman related. "There was no problem of NIH (not-invented-here)."[66] In 1982 Genentech successfully isolated bovine somatropin (BST), a protein that increased dairy cows' milk production. Monsanto promptly exercised its option and began commercial development.

But if he was open to outside research, Schneiderman, like Hanley, remained committed to developing a strong R&D capacity within Monsanto. In part, the conviction stemmed from tactical caution. "Unless you build internal capabilities," Schneiderman recognized, "you don't know the right price for technology you acquire from the outside. You don't know whether a discovery is significant and durable or whether it is ephemeral. You don't know what the best procedure is, where the bottlenecks are." But in a deeper sense, Schneiderman was thinking not so much of how best to handle a string of potential acquisitions, as how to work more fundamental and lasting transformation on the company as a whole. As far as Schneiderman was concerned, grafting biotechnology onto Monsanto was going to mean more than merely adding a new set of star businesses to the company portfolio. The company was going to have to acquire new instincts, new outlooks, not only in the labs, but in its executive suites and its boardroom. "Some companies have bought other companies and have essentially tried to assimilate them—with varied degrees of success," Schneiderman was aware. "We are building our technology internally, and I think that way is working for us. The research is part of the company—not separate. There is no 'we' versus 'they.' Everything is 'we.' "[67]

By 1983, when Hanley retired and Richard Mahoney stepped up as CEO, a decade of grinding competition in Monsanto's commodities businesses and steady building in its specialty and nonchemical lines had shifted the company's strategic center of gravity by several degrees. Its fibers businesses had been losing money consistently for nearly a decade and plastics were barely profitable; in both lines, despite substantial outlays Monsanto was struggling to sustain what had become marginal market positions. The Agricultural Products Division, meanwhile, had become the largest selling unit (21 percent of total company sales) and by far the most important source of earnings (90 percent). Recognizing the shift, anxious to set up what he called "a menu of opportunities," Mahoney restructured operations and promised to continue pursuing diversification. "By the early 1990s," the new CEO proclaimed, "we project that we'll be one-third in chemicals, one-third in the biological sciences, and one-third in mechanical goods."[68]

The middle leg of that triad, "biological sciences," obviously referred to Monsanto's agricultural chemicals businesses, as well as whatever the company's more exotic ventures in genetic engineering might generate. Mahoney's phrasing was studied, for company strategists by this point were thinking (just as Dow's planners were, at the time) along pharmaceutical lines. Indeed, Mahoney was already scouting around for acquisition possibilities, with the goal of building a $2 billion drug business over the next decade. When G.D. Searle, an ethical drug company, went into play in 1984, Monsanto quickly opened negotiations, hesitated when Searle's executives insisted that any deal include its NutraSweet operation (which was profitable but scheduled to lose patent protection soon), and eventually, in 1985, decided to plunge. At $2.75 billion (19 times earnings, and 5.5 times Searle's book value), the acquisition was expensive, particularly for a company whose product line, analysts noted, consisted largely of off-patent drugs losing market share to generic competitors. But Monsanto was going to need a distribution network to market some of the biotechnology it was nurturing. Moreover, the company needed a new revenue stream. Petrochemical earnings had dwindled, and markets for the company's leading agricultural products—the herbicides Roundup and Lasso—were maturing. Monsanto's biotechnology ventures needed more time to bear fruit. Company planners had expected that its factory automation business (a unit centered on Fisher Controls) would help tide revenues over until biotech began to pay off, but Fisher was not generating hoped-for earnings. "We're in a situation where no one is making money," admitted Nicholas Reding, head of agricultural chemicals.[69] Now, it seemed, Searle's NutraSweet revenue stream might sustain what was becoming an increasingly demanding strategic focus on biotech. "We're going to run the NutraSweet business," Mahoney announced as his staff worked out the details closing the Searle acquisition. "It's one of the fastest growing products around and it's very profitable." They had at least seven years to work with, under that strategy: NutraSweet's patent ran out in 1992.[70]

A series of sell-offs followed the Searle acquisition, as Monsanto continued to intensify its commitment to biotechnology by methodically shedding businesses. Between 1985 and 1995, Monsanto divested, in sequence, its oil and gas properties (1985), its polyethylene bottle business, its electronics materials operations in the United States, Japan, Malaysia and the United Kingdom (1988), Fisher Controls (1992), and its plastics business (1995). Meanwhile, the company again escalated research funding levels substantially. Investment analysts following Monsanto were by turns intrigued, impressed, and anxious. "Monsanto's spending so much and counting so heavily on research for their future," Anantha Raman observed in 1986, when R&D expenditures had climbed to $520 million (of which 57 percent was earmarked for life sciences, $100 million specifically for biotechnology). "And that's a double or nothing kind of bet."[71] By 1990, the company had spent nearly $1 billion on biotechnology, with nothing yet to show for it. Efforts to obtain regulatory approval for the commercial release of its first genetically engineered product, BST, had stalled, and signs of resistance were appearing among dairy farmers and consumers. Two years later, on schedule, the NutraSweet patent expired.

There was nowhere to go but forward, really. What had started as one part of a multifaceted diversification program had become a tightly focused strategic drive to transform Monsanto via biotechnology. Perhaps the most important force sustaining the drive, at this point, was what corporate executives knew was not only in the lab, but by now in the pipeline and slowly approaching commercial readiness. In 1994, Monsanto at last cleared the final regulatory hurdles and launched BST commercially, marketing the product as Posilac. Dairy farmers were still wary, and some retailers, too, but Monsanto, at least, was finally in the business of selling genetically engineered products.

Soon after BST went into commercial release, Mahoney announced his resignation. As if it were taking a collective breath, Monsanto prepared for the final stage in its reinvention. Robert Shapiro, Mahoney's replacement, was a company insider but not a chemical engineer, coming in by way of Searle, where he had been vice president and corporate counsel when that company had been acquired by Monsanto. His business acumen, however, had since proven itself when Shapiro headed the NutraSweet business, where he had prepared the product for commercialization, and Monsanto's agricultural chemicals unit. Since 1993 he had been serving as president and Mahoney's heir apparent and was fully committed to the company's strategic program. "I think we're on a good course, it's showing itself in our results, and we're going to go on," he declared as he prepared to take over executive leadership.[72] Observers on Wall Street applauded, in part because many expected that Shapiro would sell off Searle, where performance seemed lackluster. But buyers willing to pay what Shapiro considered fair value did not step forward, and the new CEO refused to sell the unit at fire sale prices.[73]

Events now began to pick up momentum. Two years after Shapiro's ascension, in 1996, Monsanto rolled out genetically engineered tomatoes, potatoes, and cotton. In a particularly deft stratagem, the company was now able to market "Roundup Ready" seeds—meaning seeds for crops that had been genetically treated to resist Monsanto's leading herbicide. Once marketed for conservation tillage, Roundup received new life as a "row-crop" herbicide. And Monsanto bloomed in the American business imagination. Stock prices shot up by 74 percent in 1995, then 71 percent in 1996, lifting Monsanto past Dow in market value. "Five years ago," Shapiro marveled, "we were a Roundup company that was spending a lot of money on biotechnology stuff that was never going to happen, a cyclical-chemical company and the world's only money-losing pharmaceutical company." No longer. Searle was posting profits; NutraSweet was holding market share, though earning less; even BST seemed to have turned the corner, registering its first profits. Above all, the agricultural products group, and especially Roundup, were thriving—generating almost half of the company's operating income off of only a quarter of total sales in 1995.[74]

In September 1997, Shapiro completed the company's strategic transformation, spinning off its old-line chemical businesses as Solutia Inc. In the process, Monsanto shed a chrysalis of $3 billion in commodity chemicals operations and emerged as a $7 billion company comprising agricultural products (generating about half of 1997 sales, with Roundup accounting for 40 percent of total earnings), pharmaceuticals (roughly a third of sales), and food products (less than 20 percent of sales, with NutraSweet as the leading product).[75] The company's annual report that year proclaimed "A New Era of Value Creation" and characterized Monsanto as a "life sciences company"—a label that conspicuously avoided the term "chemical." Indeed, Monsanto now occupied (and had played no small part in forming) fertile strategic ground at the nexus of a new market convergence, situated somewhere between chemical, pharmaceutical, and food industry boundaries.

Shapiro clearly relished the ensuing rush of attention from the popular business press and certainly exploited it to promote Monsanto's financial prospects, but he could not afford to rest on the company's accomplishments. Indeed, if anything, the pace of strategic action accelerated dramatically, as Monsanto rushed to consolidate its new position. Competitors and would-be competitors were already encroaching on the new ground the company had carved out for itself, including much larger rivals. Assessing the situation, Shapiro determined that Monsanto needed to integrate backward and acquire major seed companies, both to more tightly knit together the production of seeds and their bioengineering, and to acquire ready-made global marketing networks. "The next big increment in value," he announced in March

1997, as he intensified his wheeling and dealing, "is in trying to manage as a coherent system the entire process, from seed to crops to food to health and wellness."[76] In 1996, the company acquired Asgrow (the number two producer of soybean seeds), a 40 percent stake in DeKalb Genetics (number two in corn seed), a controlling interest in Calgene (another agricultural biotech company), and Holden Foundation Seeds. The following year Monsanto added cottonseed giant Delta & Pine Land, the remaining 60 percent stake in DeKalb, and a controlling interest in the Brazilian seed company Sementes Agroceres S.A. Shapiro was also striking alliances, both within and beyond industry boundaries. Monsanto was working with IBM, for example, to "apply advanced information technologies to genomics research on plant groups and human diseases," and with companies like Frito-Lay, where a product development venture "aimed at improving the quality of potato varieties grown for snack foods."[77]

Monsanto's campaign of strategic reinvention was decades, not years, in the making. Company executives put events in motion as early as 1960, when they formed an agricultural chemicals division, though the "strategy" only gradually, incrementally took form as anything like a vision of remaking Monsanto into a "life sciences company." Indeed, through the 1980s, it would have been hard to distinguish strategies at Monsanto from those at Dow or Union Carbide. The three companies were roughly equal in size and started in essentially similar strategic positions in 1973. All three pursued diversified ventures in an effort to lessen dependence on cyclical commodity chemicals earnings. To all outward appearances, they were on the same strategic trajectory. Then Bhopal and the GAF raid forced Union Carbide off that trajectory; Dow raced on, for a time, before starting to fear that it was being carried off course and loosening itself from a series of diversification projects; while Monsanto decided ultimately to abandon not diversification, but the core businesses from which it had launched diversification.

Why did these trajectories diverge? When, and how, did Monsanto's strategy of diversification becoming a strategy of reinvention?

In part the answers lie in the nature of the company's commitment to its strategic choice. Somewhere along the line Monsanto decided—and decided not just by executive fiat, but collectively—that its prospects and indeed its only hope for a future lay in biotechnology. At that point, diversification became something more than a means of balancing the company portfolio and evening out revenue streams: it became a platform, a middle stage, a way to prepare the company for another, more radical strategic transformation.

Robert Shapiro emerged as something of a business hero between 1996 and 1998, as the company's biotech products began to roll out and the company's stock shot up. But the heart of this story took place over the late-1980s and early-1990s, before Shapiro took over, when no one was paying much attention to Monsanto apart from skeptical analysts and impatient investors, when the company's exotic ventures in biotechnology were making no money, when they were in fact sucking up increasingly large amounts of corporate resources. It was the company's resolution through this dark period, its sense of itself and its faith in what it was growing, that sustained the strategy. As expenses mounted, the company's other diversification ventures had to be sold off to support it. Eventually, Monsanto faced the choice of either abandoning or totally committing itself to what it was doing. Monsanto stayed the course because its scientists, engineers, managers, and executives all believed in each other. And by implication, it was the efforts of people like Howard Schneiderman to plant an ethos and instinct for research throughout the ranks of the company, to weave high technology into its corporate DNA, that transformed the strategy from one of diversification to one of reinvention.

CONSOLIDATIONS AND CONCLUSIONS

By early 1998, the strategic cost of reinvention at Monsanto had reached $6.7 billion and analysts were questioning whether or not the company would be able to survive independently.[78] Other companies—chemical giants—were also acquiring biotech firms and looking to develop transgenic agricultural chemical lines of their own. Whether Monsanto would be able to assemble enough critical mass to fortify itself against the onrushing competition remained unclear. In June 1998, the company agreed in principle to merge with American Home Products. The move would have substantially expanded the company's financial resources (AHP was nearly twice Monsanto's size) and at a stroke extended its markets globally, putting the new life sciences businesses in the hands of an experienced marketer with a proven record in the sale of over-the-counter and prescription drugs. But the deal fell apart, and Shapiro resumed his own acquisitions and divestitures.[79] "We certainly have the wherewithal to be independent, if that's the best thing for our shareholders," maintained CFO Gary Crittenden in early 1999. "But if the right opportunity came along, we would be crazy not to consider it."[80]

That strategic uncertainty continued to hover over Monsanto, despite the company's dazzling and diligent transformation, demonstrates how completely the business world around it had changed over the previous quarter century. The company had found a way to reinvent itself, had taken hold of what had seemed like strategic necessity and reformulated it as strategic choice. In other contexts, at other points in the history of the industrial corporation, it would have been a relatively straightforward matter to consolidate the new businesses as a platform, the foundation for a new period of growth and industry leadership. In the strategic context of the late twentieth century, in the twilight of the industrial era, however, all Monsanto had accomplished was to position itself within a new sector of the economy that had better growth prospects but that was already becoming as fiercely competitive as the commodity chemicals sector the company was leaving behind. Monsanto had jumped out to early leads both technologically and in terms of market share, but it needed to fight fiercely to preserve those leads. The vision of Howard Schneiderman, the foresight of John Hanley, the skillful stewardship of Richard Mahoney, the charismatic promotion of Robert Shapiro, the adroit strategic decision making of 20 years, had secured for Monsanto only a narrow window of opportunity, only the chance to keep trying.

Monsanto did not quite manage to pull it off. By December 1999 shareholders were stepping up pressure to break up Monsanto's agricultural and pharmaceutical businesses. Building out distribution for the agricultural products was getting prohibitively expensive, and meanwhile popular wariness about genetically engineered foods was creating growing market problems, especially in Europe. On the pharmaceutical side of the business, moreover, senior executives were becoming concerned Monsanto lacked the marketing and distribution infrastructure it would need to capitalize on the drugs it was preparing to bring to market. After exploring merger possibilities with Novartis AG, a large Swiss drug firm, Shapiro approached Pharmacia & Upjohn Inc., itself recently formed in the 1995 union of Swedish and American drug companies. Thus Monsanto was finally engulfed by the necessity of consolidation. Although the company would survive in name, when Pharmacia announced plans late in 2001 to divest it, the new Monsanto would emerge shorn of its pharmaceutical businesses, which remained part of its erstwhile parent, and some other businesses that Pharmacia sold off. The new, smaller Monsanto would compete as an agricultural biotechnology company, a far cry from its roots in industrial chemicals and its mid-twentieth century success in petrochemicals.

Meanwhile, the formation of Equistar and the tsunami of mergers in the chemical industry noted at the beginning of this chapter occurred at a particularly bad time for Union Carbide. The company had been earning healthy profits through the mid-1990s on the peak of the commodity chemicals cycle. But higher prices had encouraged another boom in capacity construction, at Union Carbide and other companies. By the late 1990s a new series of larger, more efficient petrochemical plants was coming on line, just as commodity prices began to decline. A severe economic crisis in Asia exacerbated conditions. And at Union Carbide the strategic crisis was compounded by an outbreak of local operational setbacks at several of the company's plants overseas. For all of its earnest efforts at rededication to its core business, the company continued to struggle. Much as with Monsanto, Union Carbide was a victim of timing as much as anything else. At an earlier point, under different conditions, a tightly run middle-tier commodity chemical company might well have been able to keep things going through a few setbacks. Not in the late 1990s, though, with the tsunami washing over the chemical industry. William Joyce, the company's CEO and chairman, took stock of the situation and contacted William Stavropolous, a close friend and, not incidentally, CEO of Dow. Would Dow be interested in discussing a merger?

Joyce's overture came at an interesting point for Dow. Stavropolous had overseen a fairly rigorous round of restructuring in which the company had pulled out of pharmaceuticals and consumer goods, and overhauled its commodity chemicals units. Strategic recommitment to the core had tightened up Dow's operations, making the company one of the industry's most efficient producers. At the same time, Dow had not given up on diversification altogether. It continued to nurture an agricultural chemical line with promising possibilities, though its investments in biotech had not matched the multibillion dollar acquisitions ventured by both Monsanto and Du Pont. Dow had not assembled anything like critical mass, in other words, and if it wanted to stay in the new field, it was going to have to do it working from a solid base in commodity chemicals. From that point of view, the pressure from Equistar, ExxonMobil, and others threatened Dow just as strongly as it did Union Carbide.

So Union Carbide and Dow, after a century of independent operation, and after decades of increasingly urgent strategic formulation and reformulation, found each other matched in an almost fated union. As the industry's leading trade journal observed, "Once Equistar was in place, a union of the two remaining big U.S.-based petrochemical players that were not parts of an oil company seems to have been predestined."[81] In August 1999, Dow and Union Carbide announced the two companies would merge under Dow's umbrella. The deal, which cost Dow $11.6 billion (structured as a stock swap), along with $2.3 billion in acquired debt, created a commodity chemical giant with combined revenues of just over $24 billion.[82]

From headquarters at both companies, the rhetoric was upbeat. The deal's principal participants could not afford to sound anything other than optimistic, under the circumstances. Both Joyce ("Union Carbide's shareholders have really received a fine package here: near-term gains and a fine future") and Stavropolous ("This merger jump-starts the growth phase of our strategy") sounded all the right notes.[83] Analysts, meanwhile, approved the deal, too. Observed one: "The complementary nature of many of the businesses should enable Dow Chemical to attain meaningful cost reductions and operational synergies, increasing the prospects for sustaining above-average profitability in an increasingly competitive global chemical industry."[84]

The Dow-Union Carbide merger culminated a tumultuous period in the American chemical industry. It also signaled the distance two of the major competitors had traveled since the energy crisis in 1974 forced them to reevaluate their strategies and eventually to confront the end of growth. Diversification failed to protect Dow and Union Carbide. Rather, they and most of their competitors were obliged to restructure their portfolios, reengineer their operations, and pursue new opportunities in related technologies and downstream product applications, sometimes via joint ventures and network relationships. None of the chemical companies succeeded in pharmaceuticals and none experienced more than modest or fleeting success in their diversified activities. At the dawn of the twenty-first century, their future—like that of other big industrials—appeared to lie in technologies and markets closely related to their traditional expertise.

The experience of the leading American chemical producers during the last quarter of the twentieth century proved typical of the largest industrial companies generally. The purpose and practice of corporate strategy changed profoundly as these companies encountered limits to growth and the M-Form corporation mutated into the N-Form. Industrial leaders discovered slowly and painfully that traditional thinking about how and where to grow, and about how to plan, organize, and manage, was ineffectual and obsolete. That thinking had been based on the logic of growth, of chasing abundant opportunities, and choosing among them. But these leaders now dealt with a different dynamic: the logic of industrial decline. To remain profitable in an era of diminishing prospects, they had to grapple with hard necessities, and they had fewer, more difficult choices. Opportunities proved scarce. Diversification was rarely as successful as it was at GE; complete metamorphosis, as at Westinghouse and Monsanto, was fraught with risks. The best hope lay in refocusing and restructuring, a path that entailed relentless cost reduction and productivity improvement, bundling services with products, and acquisitions and alliances to defend old businesses and develop new and related ones. How fast and how well the big industrials negotiated this path determined their success or failure.

CHAPTER 4

STRUCTURE: CRUMBLING WALLS

The onset of post-industrialization forced deep changes in the way large industrial corporations structured their business. Companies took themselves apart and put themselves back together more-or-less continuously over the final decades of the twentieth century, sometimes in bursts of spirited experimentation, often in atmospheres of crisis as growth declined, competition sharpened, and shareholder pressure mounted. Under intense structural stress, what had once been organizing principles, literally and figuratively, were excavated, examined, tested, and refashioned if not discarded altogether. Needing to make themselves faster and more efficient, companies overhauled their internal organizations. Needing to make themselves more mobile and strategically maneuverable, they reconfigured their external boundaries. Integral attributes of the classic M-Form structure gave way as companies *downsized, delayered,* and bridged functional silos with *cross-functional teams.* External and extra-structural elements of traditional corporate organization also crumbled as companies *dismantled vertically integrated* formations, *outsourced* once-centralized functions and capacities, opened processes in new *extended enterprise* configurations, and *globalized* operations.

It was a violently wrenching process. Mighty and monumental structures were giving way from within, swaying dangerously, even threatening to topple under their own weight. By the end of the century, though, as the large industrials found their bearings in the emerging post-industrial economy, a new structural framework of corporate organization was taking form. Multidivisional M-Forms were painfully but inexorably transforming themselves into networked constructions—N-Forms—bound together in more fluid patterns and flexible architectures.

The chapter that follows tracks this process, using Chrysler, Ford, and General Motors as vehicles for telling the story. In the mid-1970s, as Detroit's "Big Three" wheeled around to meet an energetic challenge from oncoming foreign competitors such as Toyota, Nissan, and Honda, they found themselves so heavily encumbered, organizationally speaking, that they were starting to stagger under their own massive weight. What they were facing, it became clear, was not just a mortal competitive threat, but a profound structural crisis as well—a crucible in which they would have to reforge themselves, foundation and frame.

In response, each of the Big Three undertook drastic restructuring measures. Ford, facing the very real prospect of utter collapse in the early 1980s, tore down its functional silos and rebuilt its processes from the ground up. Chrysler skirted bankruptcy, barely escaped, overhauled its supplier relations and internal workings, and ultimately accepted absorption in a new global mega-structure, DaimlerChrysler. Even the largest and seemingly the most solid of the three, GM, undertook a series of jarring reorganizations, blew up the car divisions that had formed its central structural pillars, and by the end of the 1990s was in the process of stripping out Delphi, its automotive parts unit. Foundational elements were rattling, if not quite falling to pieces—in Detroit and Dearborn and indeed across the industrial landscape.

It was, especially in the case of GM, a distinctly resonant turn of events because GM had been one of the original and most influential architects of the M-Form, more than half a century before.

THE M-FORM TAKES FORM

The classic outlines of the American corporation coalesced in the early decades of the twentieth century, as companies like Ford and General Motors assembled businesses of massive new size and complexity and learned how to run them steadily, rationally, and profitably. Operations like Ford's River Rouge plant and assemblages like GM's interlocking array of car companies and parts makers were capable of mass production and mass distribution on a vast scale and scope. But making them work smoothly posed daunting structural challenges. Gradually and somewhat messily, solutions emerged.

That story has been told before,[1] but its highlights are worth reviewing briefly, for the original construction of the corporation shaped efforts to find new solutions to new structural challenges in the twilight of the industrial age, some three-quarters of a century later.

Billy Durant assembled the basic components of what would become General Motors piecemeal, in several headlong expansion drives in 1908 to 1910 and (after Durant lost and then regained control over the company) 1915 to 1920. He was a salesman and an entrepreneur, though, not an engineer, and Durant only loosely bolted his acquisitions together. Even after 1917, when he changed GM from a holding to an operating company, it remained an atomized, uncoordinated cluster of essentially autonomous minicompanies.

The need for some mechanism of corporate coordination became inescapably apparent when a recession struck in 1920, the auto market contracted sharply, and GM suddenly found itself it the midst of a crisis. As inventory piled up in immense lots of unsaleable automobiles the company was forced to shut down its plants, freezing cash flow even as financial obligations pressed in. Finances and operations lay in chaos; no one had reliable accounting data; no one could even calculate information as basic as how many cars the company was making or holding. "In short," recalled Alfred Sloan, the man who was tapped to sort out the mess, "there was just about as much crisis, inside and outside, as you could wish for if you liked that sort of thing."[2]

To meet the crisis General Motors reorganized its operations, welding together in the process one of the prototypical M-Form organizations. Unlike Durant, Sloan was methodical and precise, an engineer by training, process-oriented by instinct. By the mid-1920s, after several years of experimentation and refinement, he and his executive team had worked out the basic outlines of an effective structure. GM's various operating units (essentially, the individual automobile and automotive components companies Durant had bought up) were reconstituted as autonomous divisions, each staffed with individual support functions (sales, purchasing, and so on), each headed by a general manager responsible for administering divisional operations and accountable for profits or losses in the unit. At the same time, above the divisions, Sloan overlaid a headquarters apparatus, equipped with staff specialists, patched in to uniform statistical and accounting reporting from the field, to strategically coordinate and set direction for the company as a whole. (See Figure 4.1.)

The M-Form Multiplies and Mutates

For GM, the M-Form proved an ideal strategic as well as structural fit. Over the early-1920s, under Sloan's leadership, the company remodeled its car divisions, tailoring them to specific segments of the American auto market. This enabled GM to stake out a comprehensive market presence, from the low end (Chrysler) to the high end (Cadillac).[3]

But the M-Form proved highly adaptable to any number of corporate strategies. Whereas nineteenth century industrial companies had structured themselves as unitary U-Forms organized along functional lines (e.g., purchasing, manufacturing, sales), the generation of new, more complicated enterprises that emerged in the early twentieth century found it necessary to spin out parallel line operations—divisions—equipped with independent functional capabilities. Divisions might be built around product lines, as at GM, or contoured to geographic territories (as happened, for example, when Sears reorganized its operations over the 1920s).[4] Various companies worked out initial formulations in the 1920s, including DuPont and Standard Oil (New Jersey) along with General Motors and Sears. Permutations varied, but in each case, the M-Form separated headquarters from divisions, vesting control over strategic direction in the former and responsibility for day-to-day operations in the latter.

This divisionally-decentralized, centrally-coordinated structure became the dominant model of industrial organization after World War II. General Electric,

Figure 4.1
General Motors Organization Chart, 1925

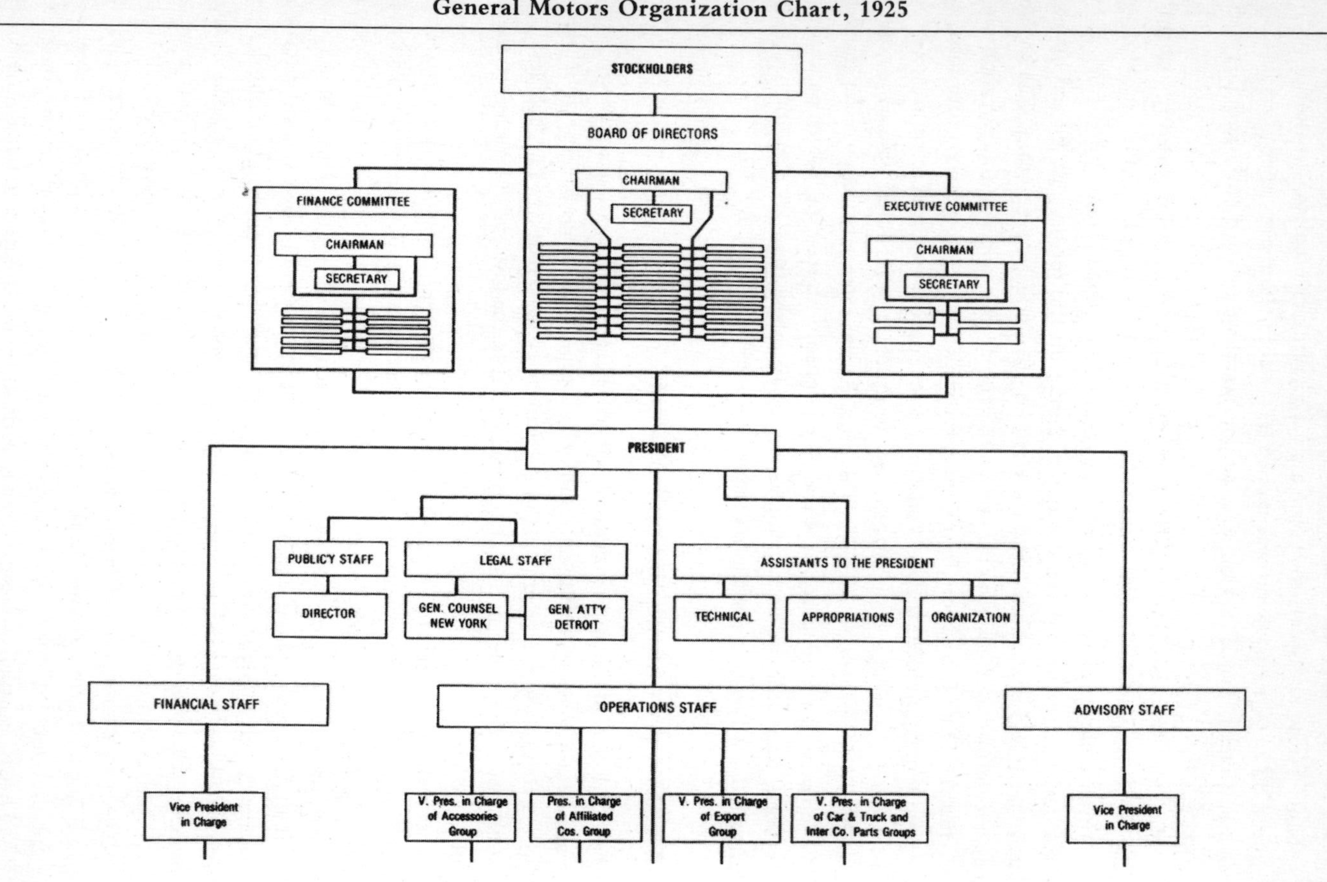

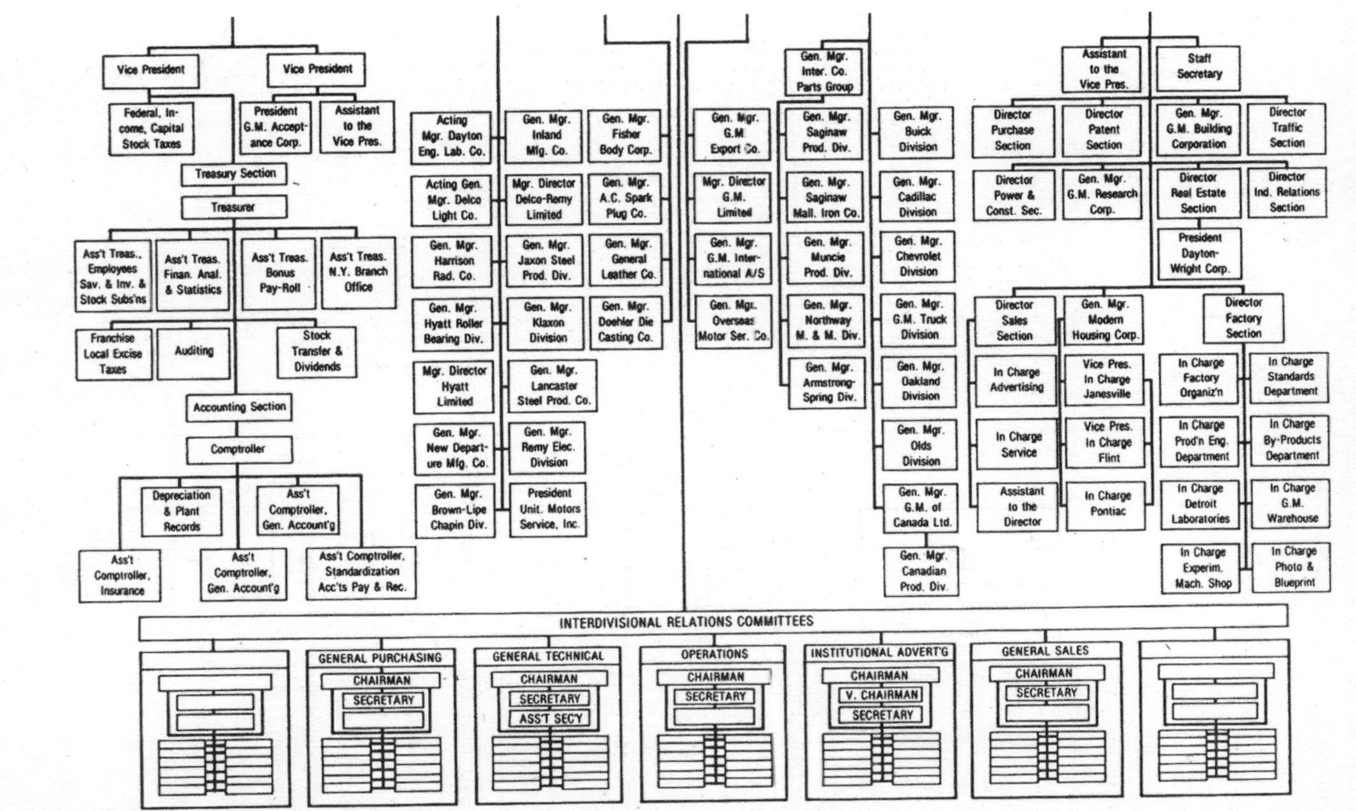

Source: C. S. Mott, "Organizing a Great Industrial," *Management and Administration,* May 1924.

for example, set up similar channels and chains of command in the mid-1900s. Many other large companies, both American and foreign, followed suit. By 1972, as Peter Drucker reported, it was "the rare business that has not been made over in the image of GM.[5]

The M-Form multiplied rapidly and widely in the postwar environment because it proved ideally suited to the strategy of diversification. During the 1950s and 1960s, as the large industrial corporation developed and acquired more and more independent businesses (see Chapter 3), it grew increasingly complex to operate. Senior managers found themselves unable to keep up with the burdens of administration on the one hand and the new, demanding challenges of strategically managing the firm's "portfolio" on the other. They turned to the multidivisional structure, and turned their companies into M-Forms, as a way of alleviating the strain and formalizing the new assignment of responsibilities.

Company by company the M-Form proliferated, and *within* companies it multiplied, too. Corporate management grew considerably more complex, information processing needs burgeoned, and, in the course of diversification, coordination between the divisions and the central corporate office demanded increasingly large and sophisticated information bureaucracies. As M-Form companies grew, they acquired larger corporate staffs and more layers of middle management. The structure grew more differentiated, both vertically and horizontally. By the late 1960s, the largest industrial corporations had evolved into nested multidivisional hierarchies. What had been divisions had split into multiple divisions, organized into Groups; then Groups clustered in Sectors. By the time the industrial corporation lumbered into the 1970s, a series of intermediate layers separated the operating divisions from corporate headquarters.[6]

Delineating Exterior and Super-Structural Dimensions

As the M-Form took shape internally, other structural attributes of corporate organization coalesced at its margins. At more or less the same time as companies like GM assembled headquarters and divisional structures, they were extending outward and backward, encompassing widening scopes of operation. This delineation of corporate boundaries had important structural implications. Indeed, it became itself a key structural dimension of the industrial corporation. The most successful and powerful of the industrials tended to engross as much of a given value chain as they could to regulate inflows of supplies and outflows of product.

So, for example, while Durant focused initially on acquiring competing automakers (Olds Motor Works, Cadillac, and Oakland [Pontiac], in the first round of acquisition), he then turned upstream, directing his second round of expansion at absorbing—literally incorporating—companies that manufactured automobile components, including Hyatt Roller Bearing (which was how Sloan came into GM),

Fisher Body, and Delco. By the end of the 1930s, GM was manufacturing more than 50 percent of the materials and components that went into its cars. Ford depended more heavily on outside suppliers of parts and components. GM's rival did, however, manufacture the bulk of the steel, glass, and lumber that went into its cars, and seriously contemplated internalizing rubber manufacturing as well. Indeed, Ford's most monumental industrial edifice, the vast, sprawling River Rouge plant, was celebrated as a monument to vertical integration, from the steel mill at one end to the cars that rolled out the other.[7]

Not all industrials accomplished such complete integration. Indeed, few managed to vertically integrate as fully as GM or Ford. The automakers' example was typical, though, in its assumptions about how a corporation defined and held its ground within the larger economic landscape. Specifically, the industrial statesmen of the early twentieth century accepted as implicit the principle that their businesses needed to achieve as much control and as much autonomy as they could lay claim to. They operated, in other words, on the assumption that their corporations were essentially closed structures. The common view of industrial companies took them to be black boxes: Raw materials went in, finished products came out, everything in between was kept tightly contained. Thus corporations commonly designated interactions with outside companies as transactions rather than shared processes. In obtaining components from suppliers, for example, the automakers typically worked up detailed sets of specifications internally, then put them out to bid, often multisourcing and tending to favor short term contracts so as to avoid becoming captive buyers. This was a strategic decision, of course, but one with important structural implications. GM, Ford, and other industrial corporations constructed fairly stout, clearly drawn outer walls—invisible aspects on the edges of organization charts that nevertheless figured powerfully in shaping corporate processes and flows.

Another structural element not depicted on organization charts like GM's was the company's blue collar workforce. The scheme took labor for granted, in a sense, as being plugged in at the bottom of the chart, and distinctly not an element that impinged on the sphere of "management." Again, this dimension of corporate structure was invisible but formative. As the auto industry geared itself for mass production on assembly lines over the 1910s, companies like Ford systematically de-skilled the work of manufacturing itself and methodically shifted control of production processes from workers to foremen and department managers. Workers, for their part, eventually turned to unions as countervailing mechanisms for protecting their interests. This extra-structural arrangement solidified in the auto industry over the 1930s and 1940s, as the United Auto Workers (UAW) established itself as the collective bargainer for Detroit's autoworkers. The UAW thus became a kind of shadow structure hovering in the background of organizations like GM and Ford. And within the companies themselves, meanwhile, the distinction between "workers" and "management" hardened into one of the most durable and impervious elements of corporate organization.[8]

Finally, given the events that followed, it bears adding that although all three American automakers had established international operations by the end of the 1920s, they did not structure their operations along global lines. Through the mid twentieth century Detroit executives remained preoccupied with the American market (which was enormous, after all). In any event, stiffening protectionism over the late 1920s and 1930s, as the world depression battered local economies, made any sustained effort to integrate operations across national borders unfeasible. Through mid-century the international automobile market remained divided in discrete nationally-defined zones, and automakers organized their operations accordingly, setting up foreign ventures as autonomous subsidiaries, disconnected from other divisions.

Breaking Down the Elements of Structural Change

In these basic characteristics, the structures adopted by GM, Ford, and Chrysler were prototypical. By roughly mid-century, the classic outlines of the American M-Form had solidified and spread throughout American industry. At its core, commonly, the industrial corporation organized its businesses in a multidivisional structure defined by a highly elaborated grid of horizontal (functional and divisional) and vertical (hierarchical) boundary lines. It was vertically integrated to a relatively high degree—at least insofar as circumstances permitted. Along its external boundaries it was surrounded by a clearly defined and generally impermeable shell. Internally, it maintained equally rigid barriers between labor and management. And it arrayed its international operations in segregated units.

Such were the structural parameters by which corporations organized their business as the industrial economy matured. Even as it was fully assembled, however, it was all about to come apart. During the last quarter of the twentieth century, in the face of unprecedented foreign competition and increasingly unstable market conditions as the economy shifted from an industrial to a post-industrial footing, American industrials disassembled key structural underpinnings of the M-Form and reassembled them in new, networked configurations:

1. They *downsized* substantially and repeatedly through these years—a process that typically started in blue-collar ranks, but soon penetrated middle management enclaves and eventually engulfed headquarters themselves.
2. They implemented a series of "quality of work life" and related *employee involvement* initiatives, trying to break down distinctions between "workers" and management.
3. They undertook strenuous efforts to *delayer,* to streamline corporate bureaucracies, in order to make themselves faster, more efficient, and more responsive.

4. They broke apart functional structures based on specialties such as marketing, R&D and manufacturing, reassigning employees in *cross-functional teams* organized around specific projects, products, or customers.
5. They *reconfigured main perimeters,* opening systems and processes to outside partners in order to tighten coordination with suppliers, distributors, and the like.
6. They *outsourced* functional aspects like IT, human resources, and a host of other "auxiliary" capacities, shedding what had once been considered integral components of corporate management.
7. They took substantial steps toward *vertical de-integration,* dismantling the up- and downstream assemblages by which they had regulated mass production and distribution.
8. They *globalized,* or started to, drawing once disparate international operations into tighter, more coordinated alignment.

In sum, industrial corporations recast themselves as N-Form organizations—organic structures that resembled networks more than hierarchies.

Breaking out the various elements of this transformation in list form suggests, perhaps, that it unfolded evenly and rationally, according to plan. It did not. It was a lurching passage. Inside these companies people were scrambling, reeling, drawing up schemes, throwing together makeshift solutions, and just plain scurrying for cover as corporations groped for organizational answers.

Such was the case, certainly, with Chrysler, Ford, and GM. Like most other big industrials, they responded unevenly and in some confusion, slow at first to accept just how dysfunctional their organizations had grown over years of complacent, oligopolistic competition.

CRISIS AND CONTAINMENT IN THE AUTO INDUSTRY

In the case of the automakers, M-Form structures began to shake loose in the 1970s, as successive energy price shocks triggered a series of jarring shifts in the American auto market. The OPEC embargo in 1973 sent oil prices sharply upwards, catching GM, Ford, and Chrysler with product lines bloated with mid- and full-sized cars. GM, as the largest producer, was particularly badly positioned, with cars that ranked last in average fuel economy at 12.2 miles per gallon, versus 14 miles per gallon for the domestic industry as a whole. As rapidly as it could the company responded, downshifting, cutting production, laying off factory workers, and simultaneously accelerating production of smaller car models, which were selling more quickly than they could be made.[9] First two, then three, then four assembly plants converted from large and intermediate to compact car production. Slowly and painfully the company lumbered through the turn, converting assembly plants, retooling factories within its assembly division and among its components divisions. "The average car contains about 15,000 parts," GM reminded shareholders in its 1973 Annual Report.[10] Then, almost as abruptly, the market shifted again: oil prices receded and Americans flocked back to what Detroit executives called "full-sized" cars. Indeed, through an Indian summer from 1975 to 1978, the American appetite for larger, better-appointed automobiles seemed stronger than ever. Then the second oil shock hit, much harder. Gasoline prices doubled; long lines sprouted at gas stations; the federal government set up a stand-by oil rationing program; and customers retreated to smaller, more fuel-efficient cars. Again GM found itself laboring to adjust, caught in the early stages of a downsizing program that was reducing the size of its cars but not yet positioning the company to take advantage of the new demand. Events were outpacing the company's ability to adapt. GM, it was becoming inescapably clear, was no longer able to maneuver responsively in the marketplace.

How had GM grown so slow and sluggish? Theoretically the company's decentralized, multidivisional structure should have equipped it to work close to the ground, respond flexibly to market shifts, despite is bulk and sprawl. Sloan's once supple structure had ossified over the years, however, particularly in areas like product development. By 1973, GM's car and truck divisions (Chevrolet, Pontiac, etc.) submitted vehicle designs to a separate division, Fisher Body, where they were engineered and passed along, in turn, to a third division, General Motors Assembly Division (GMAD), for actual assembly. Fisher had acquired broad, pan-company engineering responsibility shortly after being acquired by GM in 1926, an arrangement that in theory helped standardize components across GM's seven car divisions. The company had set up GMAD in 1965, over the objections of the car division heads, to rationalize manufacturing and, in part, to make antitrust dismantling by the federal government more difficult.

Whatever the benefits of rationalization, going through Fisher and GMAD made vehicle development an extended, complicated, often contentious process. Designs now had to climb not one but three lines of command; in structural terms, design, engineering and manufacturing functions became insulated from each other, encased within separate structural strongholds. Development frequently degenerated into turf battles. "Guys in Fisher Body would draw up a body and send the blueprint over and tell the guy, 'Okay, you build it if you can, you SOB,' " recalled GM CEO Roger Smith, with evident exasperation. "And the guy at GMAD would say, 'Well, Jesus, there's no damn way you can stamp metal like that and there's no way we can weld this stuff together.' "[11]

Even within the divisions, territorial mentality ruled. Fisher Body in particular was honeycombed with structural vestiges of the formerly independent companies it had acquired. For years after Fisher acquired Ternstedt (a trim maker), for example, the unit resisted full incorporation. "Those Ternstedt guys were alive and well within Fisher Body," GM executive John Debbink reported. "It was natural, because they were responsible for a specific part of the body of the car, and they had a pride in their organization. When they were absorbed by Fisher, they simply circled their wagons and did their own thing. The Ternstedt people were still *Ternstedt people,* even though they were being paid by Fisher Body."[12]

GM, in short, was channeling product development awkwardly and inefficiently through functional silos it had meshed into its multidivisional grid. The growing influence of the company's finance staff over the 1950s and 1960s exacerbated the bureaucratic bloat. "Unless you're working on the Fourteenth Floor [where senior executives presided]," one plant manager complained, "you have about a zillion bosses. Every small thing requires approval up the line. They have thirteen thousand checkers in this company to make sure things are done right. Hell, they have checkers to check the checkers."[13] The most damning insider's account of GM management at the top level came from John DeLorean, a "car guy" (a transmission engineer, fittingly) who rose through the Chevrolet division to become group vice president for North American operations before resigning to set up, infamously, his own car company. DeLorean described GM's Fourteenth Floor as a muted, muffled place, filled with droning committee meetings in which the company's highest executives deliberated endlessly over administrative minutia. A short-sighted financial mentality dominated planning and management, DeLorean complained, insulating headquarters from the marketplace and bogging down car and truck development. Urgent product development decisions had to be cycled through a laborious, time-consuming series of committee meetings on the fourteenth floor, while engineers and plant managers in the field waited helplessly, then scrambled to get back on schedule when a decision finally came down from the executive heights.[14]

In an earlier, more comfortable era, such ponderousness would not necessarily have cost GM all that much. But by the late 1970s American automakers were losing the luxury of adapting at their accustomed, plodding pace. They had much sharper competition to deal with. Japanese imports, once considered cheap, were establishing themselves in the American market as reliable and high quality alternatives to American cars, which year after year it seemed had to be sent back to the manufacturer for expensive and disillusioning recalls. In 1976 Japanese auto imports surged from under 700,000 units to 1.7 million; by 1980 they exceeded 2.5 million. That year marked a turning point globally, in fact. Total Japanese motor vehicle production in 1980, at 7 million, brushed just under total U.S. production of 7.2 million, while both Toyota and Nissan jumped past Ford to become number two and three, respectively, in world vehicle manufacturing. This was suddenly serious encroachment. Awakened to the growing precariousness of their position, all three of the American automakers began mapping out responses that fairly quickly assumed structural dimensions.

GM: Structural Adaptation as Choice

GM posted a $763 million loss in 1980—the first calendar year loss GM had incurred in sixty years, the first in fact since the crisis in the early 1920s that had precipitated Sloan's original reorganization. Unlike Ford and Chrysler, though, GM was still holding onto its market share (46 percent of U.S. sales in 1980), and had the financial wherewithal to absorb the loss. The company was shaken; people within the company recognized they needed to redesign their cars and factories. Only slowly and unevenly, though, did they come to grips with the need to remake GM itself.

The company's first impulse was instinctive. As it had before when confronting downturns, the company downsized its capacity, idling plants, reducing shifts, laying off factory workers, and working up plans to shutter some of its older, less efficient factories. GM slashed its U.S. hourly employment by 20 percent in 1980. On the white-collar side, the company contented itself with suspending merit increases for salaried employees and bonuses for management. The thrust and the instinct of the initial response was crisis containment by cost reduction: much as GM was "downsizing" its cars by simply making them shorter and lighter, without necessarily redesigning them from the wheels up, the company was downsizing itself, without restructuring its undergirding organizational architecture.[15]

So, for example, people within the company increasingly recognized that structurally walling its workers off from its managers was cutting off a vital resource for improving efficiency and quality. GM's factories were notoriously inefficient, littered with inventory and scrap, rife with quality breakdowns, and deeply alienating places in which to work. In the 1970s, Quality of Work Life (QWL) initiatives had begun breaking through the barriers, inviting workers to give input on how production processes might be improved and tentatively giving them modest measures of control over production itself. The onslaught of Japanese competition, which pitted cars of much higher quality (statistically speaking) against GM's, lent QWL initiatives some urgency. Ultimately, however, the momentum behind the idea flagged. Commitment remained sporadic, taking root where particular plant managers actively supported programs, but elsewhere lapsing. Lacking sustained impetus from senior management and a collective sense of urgency, GM did not manage to transform its labor relations in any meaningful, structural sense.

Instead, impetus for restructuring GM's factories gathered behind an alternative approach: automation. In 1980, Roger Smith assumed executive leadership of GM and promptly began laying out major investments to modernize the company's production lines with state of the art robots and computer control systems. Automation of GM's factories, Smith predicted, would reduce the company's high labor costs and restore its competitiveness. "Technological leadership is what will keep us ahead in world competition," he maintained, "and it's one of the things that is going to make the difference between high and low profit margins."[16] By late 1981, GM had already stationed some 1,200 robots on its shop floors and was busily installing more.[17] In 1983, GM accelerated the program when it entered a 50–50 joint venture with Fujitsu Fanuc to develop a new generation of industrial robots and pilot them in GM's plants. GM's investments in automation yielded mixed results in terms of productivity, though, as bugs crashed systems and workers and plant managers struggled to adapt to the new technology. Meanwhile, the automation drive further alienated GM's blue collar workforce, undercut QWL progress, and betrayed the company's continuing preoccupation with controlling production rather than integrating its workers more evenly in collaborative drives for quality or efficiency. In structural terms, the effort to automate its factories reinforced the barriers separating GM's workers and managers.[18]

A similar ambivalence about undertaking drastic structural reform betrayed itself in GM's approach to dealing with the Japanese. By 1980, it was becoming clear that companies like Toyota were somehow making cars better and more efficiently than GM. Significantly, though, GM perceived the problem in fairly limited terms: as needing to relearn how to make *compact* and *subcompact* cars. Soon after taking office Smith shut down the company's "S-car" program, which had been developing a new compact car for launch in 1985, and began exploring joint ventures with various Japanese companies. GM crafted a venture with Suzuki to market Suzuki-made, Chevrolet-marketed "Sprints," and with Isuzu to design and produce another subcompact line, the "Spectrum."

Smith undertook his most ambitious venture along these lines in partnership with Toyota. In March 1983 the two companies announced the formation of New United Motor Manufacturing, Inc. (NUMMI). Under the agreement, GM and Toyota reopened a plant GM had shuttered in Fremont, California, tooling it to stamp and assemble Toyota-designed "Novas" that incorporated a substantial proportion of Japanese-manufactured components (including such high value-added parts as engines and transaxles).

Attempting to placate American critics accusing GM of surrendering the field to the Japanese (and profiting on the surrender in the bargain), Smith underplayed the significance of the venture. NUMMI was "a short-term thing for us," he stressed. "It's a one-shot deal. . . . We had an empty plant and they had an empty car, you might say, and we put the two together." Actually, Smith hoped for much more from GM's $100 million investment. He wanted a chance to observe Japanese cost structures and plant operations at close hand. He wanted to get an inside view not only of how competitors like Toyota operated, but also whether their methods could be transplanted to the United States. Once the Nova plant was running, GM dispatched company managers to Fremont in batches to tour the Nova plant.[19]

Launching Saturn

Experiences like NUMMI demonstrated strikingly different kinds of structures in action. Japanese industrial companies tended to mix up functional specialists, creating small teams that worked in collaboration on specific projects and processes. Workers sat at the same tables as managers; engineers worked alongside designers; few horizontal or hierarchical impediments separated people within the company from one another.

Meanwhile, elsewhere within GM, a direct assault on the company's layered and walled structures was forming. In May 1982, looking for new ways to develop a compact car internally, Smith plucked out a skunk works project led by Alex Mair. The project initially went under the nondescript label "Advance Product Manufacturing and Engineering Staff," but team leaders, taking as their inspiration the NASA program that propelled the United States past the Soviets to reclaim the lead in the space race, adopted a new name: Saturn.

Saturn began as a small 16-person research team and a structural anomaly, set apart from the company's existing staffs and divisions. That organizational context, or lack thereof, quickly became a defining aspect as Saturn broadened both in membership and the scope of its mission. "We looked at all the disciplines to find out what we needed to do differently to become competitive," team member Neil De Koker recalled, "and the bottom line was that it wasn't just design, engineering, and manufacturing that needed to change, but *the entire business of running the business*."[20] Management invited union representatives, and then shop managers and factory workers into what became the "Group of 99." At the end of 1984, seeking to protect their autonomy, the team recommended that they be formally broken off from the rest of the company. In 1985, GM's senior management endorsed the move, creating GM's first new car division since the acquisition of Chevrolet in 1918.

Gathering planners, designers, engineers, plant supervisors, and a sizable number of UAW representatives and plant workers, Saturn represented an assemblage dramatically different from anything GM had constructed before. Within their bubble, working in a fluid, boundaryless ambience, the team formed plans, sketched out designs, began welding body panels onto prototypes—not just of their car, but of the M-Form itself. Distinctive patterns of management and teamwork took shape within Saturn. Resolved to improve quality, to incorporate worker involvement, and to cut as much bureaucracy out of its processes as possible, the program broke participants down into self-directed work units of 6 to 15 people. Each of these small teams was led by a charter team member (CTM), and each operated under the principle of consensus, meaning that 70 percent of a team had to approve a decision before it could be implemented. The CTMs represented their teams in larger "decision circles" that organized around the basic building blocks of production: the cooling system, paint processes, and so on. And the decision circles in turn fed into one of three overarching "business unit committees": the Manufacturing Action Council (overseeing production), the Technical Development Action Council (steering engineering and design) and the Customer Action Council (handling marketing, sales and service functions). The top management team at the center of these three inner circles, the Strategic Action Council (SAC), gathered Saturn's president, the local UAW president, and representatives of the business unit committees.[21] (See Figure 4.2.)

The resulting picture represented a new structural paradigm: when Saturn drew itself it depicted overlapping circles, not hierarchical trees. True to its promise,

Figure 4.2
Saturn Corporation Organization Chart

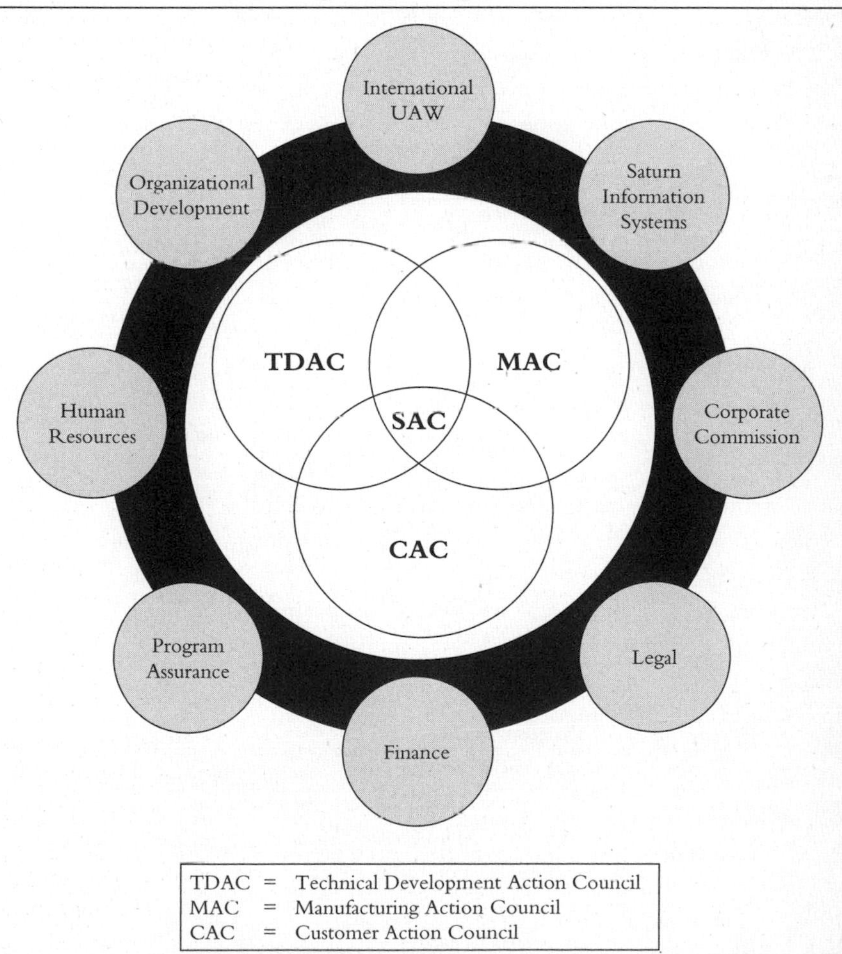

TDAC	=	Technical Development Action Council
MAC	=	Manufacturing Action Council
CAC	=	Customer Action Council

Source: Anita McGahan and Greg Keller, "Saturn: A Different Kind of Car Company," Harvard Business School case study, 1994.

Saturn did indeed create a space in which GM's management and workforce could align itself in new, collaborative structural arrangements. "Every Saturn employee is going to be a decision maker," program executive Guy Briggs declared. "Every manager. Every machine operator. Every skilled tradesperson. Every secretary and maintenance person."[22]

Reorganization on a Comprehensive Scale

Saturn put truly revolutionary structures into operation—albeit, in a small, isolated pocket of the company. GM as a whole grappled more ambivalently with the idea of comprehensive and thoroughgoing restructuring. At the executive level, the conviction slowly took hold over the early 1980s that the company did need to shake itself up. The result was GM's most substantial reorganization since the initial construction of the M-Form. In 1984, after several years of quiet planning, the company announced it was reorganizing its operations in a new structure clustering the company's various car divisions within two super-groups, a Buick-Oldsmobile-Cadillac group (BOC) designing and making larger, high-end cars, and a Chevrolet-Pontiac-GM of Canada group (CPC) specializing in low-end small cars. Each of the super-groups would assume responsibility for overseeing development of its own vehicles, including body and assembly engineering; the plan subsumed both Fisher Body and GMAD within the two super-groups. More generally, the plan called for a renewed dedication to the company's historically decentralized patterns of operation. The new organization deployed engineers and managers in product development teams (PDTs) that collected design and manufacturing engineers, purchasing agents and suppliers. "There will be a big change in our systems, a big change in our management philosophy," Roger Smith promised. The reorganization was going to transfer "decisions down to the guy who is closest to the marketplace . . . Too many decisions have been coming up too high in the organization."[23]

Breaking down Fisher Body and GMAD in particular promised to make GM's development procedures leaner, flatter, and more responsive to the marketplace. Tellingly, though, the company declined to set a timetable for the transformation, and indulged in some temporizing on the ultimate fate of Fisher Body. GM president Jim McDonald affirmed that the head of Body and Assembly Group "has to work himself out of a job," but also predicted "the name Fisher Body will always have an identity in General Motors. How we preserve it, we still have to determine."[24] In a similar vein, Roger Smith speculated that twin Fisher Bodies would somehow survive in each of the super-groups: "They will each have a Fisher department, but I don't know if they'll call it that." The Fisher name, Smith added, was a valuable asset that GM would certainly not abandon.[25]

GM was also vague on how long it would take to implement the reorganization. Perhaps three to five years, company executives predicted, it was hard to know.

"This is a big undertaking," one official pointed out. "It's going to take a lot of care and thought to get us from where we are today to where we want to be eventually. We might make some false starts. It's not going to be easy with a company this big."[26] From the margins of the company, GM dealer William L. Crawford Jr., of Champion Chevrolet in Manhattan Beach, California, concurred. "The corporation moves in such a ponderous fashion it could be three or four years before we see any change," he predicted. "It's kind of like turning a supertanker around."[27]

REVOLUTION FROM WITHIN: FORD, 1980–1984

GM approached restructuring, through the mid-1980s at least, somewhat tentatively, as a matter of importance but not exactly urgency. What still seemed like choices at GM, though, had already become driving necessities at Ford. Between 1980 and 1982 Ford posted losses totaling $3.3 billion, a figure that represented 43 percent of the company's net worth; shareholder equity melted from $10.6 billion to $6 billion; the company's debt-to-equity ratio climbed from 19 percent to 79 percent; and its credit rating skidded from AAA to BBB. GM had troubles, serious ones, but few people within that company doubted that things would eventually turn around. Ford was fighting for its life. "Talking was going on everywhere," Don Petersen would later recall of those dark days. "The discussions ranged widely, but what the conversations kept coming to was 'Why are we doing so badly? Why are our results so poor? What's wrong with us?' "[28]

In search of answers, Ford sent teams to Japan to investigate operations at Mazda (in which Ford held a minority stake), Toyota, Nissan, and other companies, trying to figure out how their competitors were doing so successfully what Ford no longer seemed able to manage. Some 10 percent of Ford's top managers participated in the Japan tours, along with hundreds of other employees and hourly workers. They had company: General Motors and Chrysler also dispatched reconnaissance missions to Japan in the early 1980s. But Ford's emissaries saw different things, took different lessons from their visits. They came away impressed above all by Japanese management methods and working dynamics, particularly the relationships their competitors fostered between middle managers, floor supervisors, and workers. In Petersen's words, "the real secret was how the people worked together—how the Japanese companies organized their people into teams, trained their workers with the skills they needed, and gave them the power to do their jobs properly. Somehow or other, they had managed to hold on to a fundamental simplicity of human enterprise, while we built layers of bureaucracy."[29] In short, Ford's Japanese visits focused thinking on the company's structure and what kind of process it shaped.

Like GM's, Ford's structure was highly articulated, both vertically and horizontally. Thus, while Ford had no institutional equivalent of Fisher Body, it nonetheless wrestled through "near legendary . . . disputes between Design and Car Body Engineering," recalled Jim Manoogian, the company's director of quality assurance. "Though their buildings were adjacent on the Ford 'campus,' officials of the two departments communicated by memo, refusing to meet face to face."[30] Similarly, although Ford had not broken off production into a divisional equivalent of General Motors' GMAD, its manufacturing engineers and factory managers were nevertheless deeply divided from other staff. "If a guy in engine development came up with a way to make a lighter engine, or one that was more fuel efficient, there was little incentive to consult with manufacturing so they could prepare themselves for different assembly parameters," a company executive explained. "So the car would come together and the pieces wouldn't fit."[31] A plant manager agreed; "The games we played were amazing. We'd sabotage the other's projects. We'd freeze the other side out of discussions, swear, blow up, ignore people, or simply not show up at meetings."[32]

Within Ford, the functional partitions were called "chimneys," and by 1980 they had embedded themselves deeply in the company, running through middle management and reaching all the way up into headquarters. "An entire layer of people at the chimney tops—the equivalent of the divisional presidents—had come up through their respective chimneys and had enormous loyalty to their former colleagues," one executive related. "It was civil war at the top."[33]

The crisis atmosphere that enveloped the company in the early 1980s, however, rapidly broke down the chimneys, at all levels of the company. In 1980 a new executive leadership took over, headed by a triumvirate of Philip Caldwell as CEO, Don Petersen as president, and Red Poling as executive vice president of North American Automotive Operations, all of whom recognized the need for reorganization. As a starting point, Caldwell and Petersen appointed a Blue Ribbon Committee in 1980, initially to study ways to streamline the company's engineering staff as a cost-cutting measure, eventually to design a delayered and downsized managerial organization for the company as a whole.

Meanwhile, on the shop floor, Ford's factories restructured labor relations and began to reengineer production in a burst of grassroots Employee Involvement (EI) initiatives. The movement started in the company's Transmission and Chassis Division, under local labor relations manager Stan Sturma, who began convening hourly meetings in which groups of workers offered supervisors and plant managers suggestions about how their work areas and routines could be made more efficient. Sturma modeled the sessions on a Quality of Work Life program over at GM. At Ford, however, EI was to take much deeper root, and to work a much deeper and more lasting transformation. By 1981, with the active endorsement of both Ford management and the UAW, a thousand EI problem-solving groups in 68 Ford plants were tapping the input of more than 10,000 employees. It was an astonishing level of participation, particularly in an atmosphere of sharp contraction and steep layoffs. It was borne of desperation, a series of frantic local efforts to boost quality in order to stave off shutdown. And as management came to appreciate, it came from below. Plant by plant, accordingly, Ford executives opened company books to union representatives, set up steering committees peopled by equal numbers of managers and employees, drew in outside consultants to facilitate, and began regrouping people in clusters of teams.

"You can never underestimate how scared we were," one Ford executive remembered of the early 1980s. "We *really* believed Ford could die. From top executives through middle management and down to the hourly employees, a lot of people got religion. It enabled us to deal with the turf, the egos, and the 'not invented here' attitudes that were killing us."[34] Initiatives like EI, in other words, took hold as quickly and widely as they did because they represented lifelines.

For the same reason, the impulse spilled over the company's factory floors and spread through the ranks of middle management. When EI reached Ford's Diversified Products Operations (DPO) in 1979, the company was warning the unit's managers that they would be closed down if they could not bring their quality levels up to competitive standards. The executive vice president of DPO—a man named Tom Page ("Gentle Tom," Petersen called him)[35]—seized EI, or at least in its underlying principles, as a way to nurture a new operating dynamic in his managerial ranks. Working closely with Nancy Badore, a DPO manager with a doctorate in industrial psychology, Page began sponsoring a round of free-wheeling executive workshops within the subsidiary's business units. Ideas poured in. As momentum built up behind DPO, Page and Badore, with Petersen's authorization, set up a Change Task Force to export the program throughout Ford. By 1983, the task force was making its presentation in top management circles, trying as one member put it "to get people thinking about Ford" by creating "a systematic picture of successful organizations. We didn't say anything bad about Ford but left it to the listeners to draw their own conclusions."[36] From there the project, dubbed "Participative Management," spread broadly across the organization, working its way through middle management unit by unit, section by section. Seminars created cross-functional forums, common meeting ground above the landscape of chimneys. Marketing managers put questions to engineers, and engineers to marketers; designers tapped into the experience and the frustrations of production specialists, and vice versa. Ford's vast and varied field of middle management began to think in team terms.

Taurus and Teamwork

"Working at Ford in the early 1980s was like participating in a social revolution," one comrade reminisced. "There was a tremendous upwelling of initiative from the ranks. Somehow we channeled it constructively."[37] The company was fighting for its life, plant by plant, dealership by dealership, office by office. Employee Involvement and Participative Management were in the air, beginning to articulate new organizational principles predicated on cross-functional cooperation and delayered decision making. In this atmosphere of stark crisis and structural ferment, Ford launched its most ambitious and costly car development program ever. Initially code named Monica, then Sigma, the car ultimately adopted the name Taurus. "We didn't really set out to use these new approaches for the development of this particular car," Petersen stated in retrospect, "but that's pretty much what happened."[38]

The goal was to develop a new ("clean sheet") $15,000 sedan, marketed to young and middle-aged car buyers. Ford budgeted $3.25 billion for the project, more than three times as much as it had ever before spent on a new car program. It was a substantial stake for any auto company in any market; for Ford in the early 1980s, losing billions of dollars, it amounted to betting the company. And the symbolic stakes may have been even higher. The mid-sized sedan lay at the heart of the auto market, as far as the Big Three were concerned. What Taurus represented was nothing less than Ford's effort to recapture the automotive American imagination.

From the first, this car took form differently. Don Petersen encouraged designer Jack Telnack to venture daring, aerodynamic stylings, and Philip Caldwell put Lew Veraldi in charge of the team carrying the project through development. Veraldi had developed a reputation within the company as an individual who could work across the chimneys, with both production managers and design engineers. In assembling the Taurus team and defining its development process, Veraldi built on his experience in Ford of Europe, where programs like the Fiesta had enlisted salespeople, production specialists, and other representatives from across the company to work closely with planners, designers, and engineers. Veraldi's initial team of 25 enlisted not only planners, designers, and product engineers, but manufacturing engineers, marketing experts, service managers, and repair personnel. Marketers worked with planners to tailor the car more closely to customer wants and needs; factory specialists worked with component and body engineers to model a car that would be more easily and reliably manufactured.[39]

Members of Team Taurus reported to a Car Program Management Group headed by Veraldi. But Ford's corporate management was careful not to insulate the project from the rest of the company. Taurus was structured to draw in "people who were in the mainstream of the company . . . but not remove them from their regular work," according to John Risk, the team's car development planning director.[40] In other words, Team Taurus formed what Veraldi described as "a kind of *ad hoc* group with program managers who functioned as team leaders in their respective areas but, rather than working separately, they worked together within the entire process."[41] At the very top, Caldwell and Petersen gave Veraldi broad latitude to handle what Petersen called "all the day-to-day decisions," and took pains to preserve continuity on the team.[42]

Taurus broke open all kinds of structures within the company. Ford had its various divisions compete to make the car's major components, often pitting them against outside companies. All suppliers were brought into the process early in development in a series of meetings—MSBs (Must See Befores)—to review prototypes and go over how the pieces were going to fit into the vehicle. And well before production began, the Taurus team sent managers and engineers to the primary assembly plants in Chicago and Atlanta to get input from hourly workers, sending along plastic see-through prototypes to show workers how the pieces fit together as a whole. In the spirit of employee involvement, the company solicited ideas for making the car easier to build, and fielded 1,401 suggestions. Each one was carefully reviewed, and over 700 were eventually adopted. For example, following worker suggestions, the team reduced the number of body side panels and enlarged interior plastic trim pieces to make them easier to install.[43] The efforts to reduce manufacturing glitches and problems paid off: Only 1 percent of Tauruses coming out of the assembly plants needed rework, as compared to a 10 percent norm.[44]

Taurus was launched December 26, 1985. The program came in below budget ($3 billion spent vs. $3.25 billion budgeted). Far more importantly, it produced a superior car. Taurus won the 1986 Motor Trend Car of the Year and, the following year, became the best-selling car in the United States. Ford had forecast an 8.5 percent return on investment for the project; Taurus returned 11 percent.

The less tangible returns were no less important. Taurus had become a central drama within Ford, an effort at restructuring and renewal that people throughout the company—workers, managers, and executives—were watching closely. The car's triumph vindicated not only the company's automotive expertise, but also the new organizational structure that had shaped Team Taurus.

EXTERNAL DELINEATIONS: THE CASE OF CHRYSLER

Necessity was forcefully remaking Ford's internal structures. Dire exigencies were forcing even more radical measures at Chrysler, the smallest and most vulnerable of the Big Three. The same crisis that rattled GM and shook Ford rocked Chrysler to its foundations. The company skirted bankruptcy and forestalled utter collapse only with the assistance of timely financial intervention by the federal government. Chrysler, like Ford, overhauled organizationally, creating lean, cross-functional, platform-centered teams to design and develop its cars. But it could not afford to stop there. Chrysler depended on outside suppliers to provide significantly higher proportions of the vehicles it manufactured than either Ford or GM: Detroit's smallest automaker in fact "made" only 30 percent of its cars. By necessity, then, the impetus for overhaul reached beyond the formal boundaries enclosing Chrysler proper. The company had to draw its suppliers into the project of restructuring, and in the bargain redesign its outer structural shell in fundamental and (literally) far-reaching ways.

Like other Detroit automakers, Chrysler had studied Japanese competitors in the early-1980s. In Chrysler's case, it was Honda that provided important lessons, particularly in how it handled suppliers. Like other Japanese firms, Honda worked closely with what was, by Detroit standards, a small number of suppliers. The firms providing Honda's systems and components set up their manufacturing plants alongside Honda's plants, planning and tooling on the security of long contract cycles. Honda held substantial investment stakes in its largest suppliers. The Japanese automaker made it a habit to invite engineers from its suppliers' ranks onto Honda's product development teams. The two sides coordinated their operations, in sum, in a close, collaborative, organic relationship—a network—that the Japanese called a *keiretsu*.[45]

Chrysler's senior management doubted, initially, that a networked supplier structure could be made to function in an American setting. American automakers typically designed components and systems in-house, drawing up detailed specifications and then putting them out to bid. Whereas Honda selected suppliers on the basis of previous quality and reliability track records, Chrysler, like Ford and GM, typically went with low bidders. This system made the relationships between American automakers and their suppliers inherently competitive, antagonistic, predicated on mutual suspicion. Each side fought to dig as much profit out of the contract as it could. Each side blamed the other when cars broke down.

But Chrysler had to figure out how to make cars that did not break down. And events over the late 1980s suggested that Japanese methods might in fact survive transplanting to an American context. In 1987, Chrysler acquired AMC, an even smaller automaker that had fostered relatively close, even Japanese-like supplier relationships. Engineers and manufacturing specialists from both AMC and its suppliers had been working for several years on integrated teams developing the Cherokee, Premier, and Comanche—working, indeed, far more productively than Chrysler's own development teams over the same period. Progress on Chrysler's LH program to develop midsize car models to compete with the Ford Taurus team (around the company "LH" was coming to stand for "last hope") was then stalled, $1 billion over budget. Under the circumstances, the AMC experience was intriguing.

In any event, the company had to take drastic measures of some kind, particularly as Chrysler veered back into financial crisis in the late 1980s. Robert Lutz, who had taken control of the company as president of operations in 1988 (coming over from Ford, like a lot of new Chrysler managers), overhauled the LH team and decided to use the project as an experiment in recrafting Chrysler's supplier relationships along AMC lines. Relocated out of Highland Park and stocked with design, engineering, manufacturing, procurement, marketing and finance staff, including representatives from major suppliers, the LH team made impressive, rapid progress, coming in below budget in the bargain.

Once the concept had proven its feasibility, the key for Chrysler became institutionalizing the dynamics that had made the Jeep and LH projects so successful. In a word, the challenge became structural: the company needed to devise infrastructure to support the new relationships that Chrysler executives now sensed were becoming workable, indeed, indispensable. Teams had to be not just cross-functional, but cross-company, in order to generate close and sustainable collaboration. Gradually, painstakingly, Chrysler coaxed wary suppliers into partnership. As the program matured over the 1990s and relations with specific suppliers deepened, Chrysler began inviting proven partners to design components and craft prototypes, promising to confer contracts extending over the life of a particular car model as incentives. And by the mid-1990s it was looking to suppliers not just for savings or quality improvements, but also for input on reducing vehicle weight and complexity.

The result was not so much a Japanese keiretsu as an American hybrid. Chrysler still dealt with more suppliers than Toyota or Nissan, and unlike the Japanese automakers it did not formally invest in its major suppliers. Still, Detroit's smallest automaker was restructuring itself on several dimensions. What had been a closed unit was becoming an "extended enterprise" interlaced within a broader network of companies. What had been an exoskeletal shell was becoming a permeable membrane.

GM VERSUS FORD: CHOICE AND NECESSITY

Structural responses at Ford and Chrysler were both creative and committed—in large part because these companies were fighting for survival. GM, meanwhile, found its initial efforts at restructuring bogged down fairly quickly. While Ford buzzed with concepts like EI and Participative Management, GM's middle management struggled with the dislocation of reorganization. "It's coming slow," Roger Smith conceded in April 1985, over a year after the reorganization had been launched. "The easy thing is moving the boxes around on an organization chart. The hard part is changing the system."[46] For the first six months of 1984, implementation team meetings consumed much of everyone's time. And confusion and disarray prevailed well into 1985, with many managers still working out of their briefcases, sitting at bare tables with telephones.

Then, even as the dust settled, the automotive economy revived and enthusiasm for reform evaporated. Actually, if anything GM's structure grew more bureaucratically constricted in the wake of the 1984 reorganization. Marketing and engineering functions, for example, were now staffed at corporate, group, and division levels; by injecting a new "group" layer and a new executive group vice president office into the organization chart, the 1984 reorganization had actually thickened the hierarchy.[47] Operational decisions still labored up a long, winding ladder of administrative command, manager by manager, meeting by meeting. If a designer wanted to make even a minor change, say, a modest headlight redesign, the proposal had to make its way from design through engineering, then through marketing. Then it went to the car division level (say, Chevrolet), then on to a pre-work group meeting, then to a work group meeting. Those that survived passed on to a plan review, followed by a business review (where finance first weighed in). Then, finally, the proposal reached the corporate level—where it wound its way first through the corporate marketing staff, then through a preproduct program review, then a program review, then through pre-executive staff, then past the executive committee, and finally to the management committee, where the final authority rested. It took fifteen meetings, in other words, to approve a designer's suggestion tinkering with the look of a car's headlight. Fifteen meetings, and the ultimate arbiter, GM's president, sat in on the last five.[48] "GMers look at the way they do business as a sacred cow and don't realize that they aren't functioning internally," complained one outside management consultant after working with the company. "More time is spent on meetings than any place I've ever seen, but less is accomplished."[49]

Saturn, meanwhile remained an island of innovation, enchanted, but cut off from the mainland. The project's structural lessons in particular did not seem to penetrate the parent company. Or rather, GM ultimately looked to the Saturn experience for different kinds of lessons. Judging by GM's corporate gloss on the project, as well as subsequent press coverage, what seemed instructive about Saturn were its (equally innovative, to be sure) efforts to establish new industrial relations with organized labor and to overhaul production methods. GM executives, Saturn spokespeople, and business reporters waxed far more eloquently about Saturn's modular assembly methods, about the harmony the project was engendering between local UAW leaders and GM managers, about robots and computers, about one-price, hassle-free car dealerships, than they did about the project's distinctive organization.[50]

A comparison between GM's Saturn project and Ford's Taurus project is instructive. Both programs developed over roughly the same period, in response to the same industry crisis. Both represented pilot car programs, in the sense that they were set up not only to make new cars, but more fundamentally to restructure the underlying process of making cars. Both were located off of their parent companies' existing organizational grids. And both arrived at much the same internal structure. Small, cross-functional, product-centered teams formed the heart of both programs; both Saturn and Taurus managed to set up spaces in which designers, engineers, factory workers, and a host of other participants worked side by side on projects.

Important differences, however, separated Saturn and Taurus. For its pilot project Ford had chosen a mid-sized family sedan, staking its "clean-sheet" program on a bid to reclaim the heart of the automotive market. With Saturn, on the other hand, GM looked toward the low end of the market, the compact car segment, where profits were traditionally lean and cars utilitarian. GM was aiming more directly at its Japanese competition (as it was arrayed in the mid-1980s, at least). But it was also consigning its pilot effort to what American automakers still considered to be the periphery of the market. And in a parallel sense, Saturn came to occupy a distinctly peripheral place within GM, compared to Taurus's place within Ford. Taurus' success vindicated and accelerated the spread of initiatives that were working broadly throughout Ford—employee initiative, participative management, and the like. As a company drama, Taurus took stage at the center of Ford and instructed the entire company. Saturn, by contrast, remained a relatively isolated experiment, albeit a successful one. Both Saturn and GM executives seemed more concerned to protect the subsidiary from the parent company's bad habits than they were to disseminate the project's innovations beyond Saturn's boundaries into the vast reaches of General Motors. Moreover, as Saturn drew near to actual production in the late 1980s, GM's corporate executives grew nervous about saturation in the compact car market, and about Saturn's production cost projections. In what must have been a strong signal to the rest of the company, GM cut its capital investment in Saturn in half and scaled back from two to one assembly lines.[51]

GENERALIZING FROM GENERAL MOTORS

GM may have still been balking at the prospect of organizational overhaul as the 1980s wound down, but by that point the necessity was beginning to overtake large industrial corporations everywhere. Most were coping with severe pressures of their own, and setting up experiments and expedients quite similar to those underway inside Chrysler, Ford, and Saturn if not GM generally. Cross-functional team structures, often growing up outside of existing channels, as "swat teams," "skunk works," and the like, were becoming basic building blocks for new organizational models. Corporate staffs were shrinking in size. One survey of companies headquartered in New York, for example, found that the typical company had reduced headquarters staff from more than 500 in 1980 to a median size of 90 in 1989.[52] More fundamentally, corporate managements were trying to delayer, to shorten chains of command and control, to push authority and initiative down into their field operations. Key underpinnings of M-Form organization, including horizontal specialization and vertical, multilayered hierarchical supervision, were bending here, compressing there. (See Figure 4.3.)

Restructuring initiatives were protean, evolving industry by industry, company by company, management team by management team. And they were often painful, confused, well intentioned but uneven experiences. Consider the organizational evolution of AlliedSignal, a conglomerate of widely diversified businesses ranging from aerospace to automotive components to engineered materials. In 1991 the company came under the aggressive, hard-driving control of Lawrence Bossidy, who was brought in from GE to boost the company's performance. Determined to get Allied's business units performing as individual profit centers and market leaders, Bossidy ratified a reorganization that sharply reduced the number of divisions and cut several

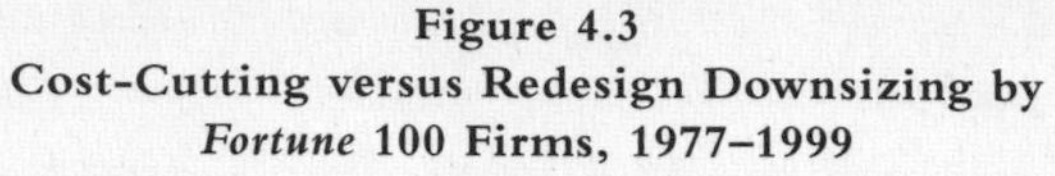

Figure 4.3
Cost-Cutting versus Redesign Downsizing by *Fortune* 100 Firms, 1977–1999

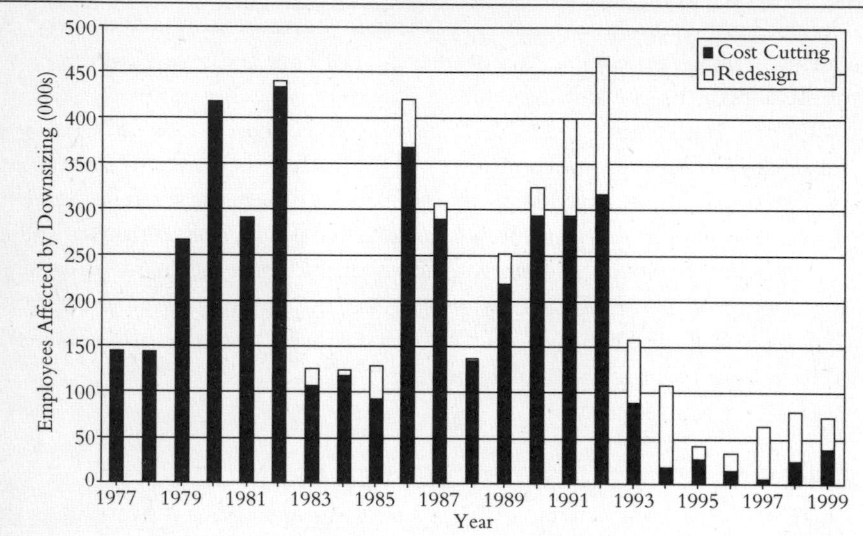

layers of management out of the company's hierarchy. At the same time, he devised new horizontal channels that cut through the company's divisional structures, including intercompany, transdivisional "trade shows" in which group officials showcased technologies that might have cross applications. "We have programs set up to break down the barriers—to break down the silos," Senior Vice President Ernest Linneman affirmed, "so we can truly become one company and take advantage of the fact that we do have a diversified corporation that serves multiple markets."[53] AlliedSignal also found distinct applications for the team concept, forming cross-functional teams not only in product development, but also in purchasing, in the form of "commodity teams" that mobilized the collective input of manufacturing engineers, designers, and purchasing and financing experts. Clustering around such broad categories as castings, electronic gear, machine parts and raw materials, the commodity teams picked and then oversaw relations with AlliedSignal's suppliers.[54]

At Procter & Gamble (P&G), dedicated, cross-functional teams deployed *down*-stream, affixing themselves to the company's largest customers (Wal-Mart and Kmart, for example) in collaborative efforts to streamline the supply chain. The device was one of number of structural innovations implemented under CEO John Smale in the late 1980s as P&G overhauled its marketing, sales, manufacturing and distribution structures. Its national sales force, for example, had been arranged along

11 product lines, meaning retailers had to contend with 11 different P&G sales reps and a clamoring confusion of uncoordinated promotions. A 1987 reorganization switched "from a product to a customer approach," as sales executive Mike Milligan put it, setting up teams of personnel from finance, distribution, manufacturing and other functions to handle transactions with given customers in "the trade." The company also streamlined brand management by creating "category managers" with spending power and executive authority to respond below the corporate level to fast-changing market conditions. And P&G set up product supply managers, who also received authority to make on-the-spot decisions as they coordinated manufacturing, engineering, distribution, and purchasing staff in product development.[55]

Something clearly *was* happening to the M-Form. It was adapting, it was resisting; everywhere it was coming under stress and in a few companies it seemed to be coming apart altogether. Sweeping rhetoric and suspiciously vague buzzwords surfaced. Jack Welch's clarion call for GE to make itself a "boundaryless company" in 1990 for example,[56] represented something more like a vision, an ideal, than a model of reorganization. Certainly GE continued to operate along chains of command, through tightly focused business units, in 1990 and to this day. But the urgency with which the idea spread, through GE and beyond, the breadth of its appeal, the intensity of the competitive business atmosphere that formed its context, no company could afford to dispute by the time Welch sounded the call.

DISINTEGRATION: GM, THE CAR DIVISIONS, AND DELPHI

GM may have looked for a time as though it might somehow avoid drastic restructuring measures, then, but time was running out. The company lurched and rattled its way into another industry downturn in the early 1990s, this one steeper and more dangerous than in the previous decade, since by this point GM was beginning to lose market share as well as sales. As a corporate engine, General Motors was straining harder and harder, yet generating less and less drive. The pieces no longer seemed to mesh smoothly together, and GM's top managers, it became increasingly clear, did not know how to reassemble them in a way that would. Word surfaced that GM was preparing another round of reorganization dismantling the super-groups—the CPC and the BOC—it had erected less than a decade before, in an effort to de-layer its bureaucracy. Few within senior management seemed to relish the prospect of more structural turmoil, but events were slipping out of their hands. In April 1992, the directors forced out President Lloyd Reuss, putting CEO Robert Stempel on sharp notice that they wanted action. Even as Jack Smith replaced Reuss and the company floated $2.9 billion in common stock on the financial market, the company announced that it would rip out the super-group level, set Cadillac off as a separate division, keep Saturn independent, and consolidate all of the other domestic car groups within a new structural unit, North American Operations (NAO). More details emerged a few months later, shortly after the board intervened again to depose Stempel and install Jack Smith as CEO. Three automotive units would form inside NAO, company spokespeople reported, each around a distinct set of platform specifications. Within these units, cross-functional "platform teams" would merge engineering, manufacturing, and styling functions on a platform-by-platform basis.[57]

Yet more radical structural moves lay ahead. In 1998, as its share of the U.S. market slid dangerously close to 30 percent and second place status, GM announced another round of reorganization, this one consolidating the company's five marketing divisions and thus dismantling the last remnants of the old car divisions. At the same time, the company revealed plans to spin off Delphi Automotive Systems, an auto components unit that was doing $31.4 billion in business annually and employing roughly 200,000 workers—nearly one-third of GM's total workforce.[58]

Clearing out the remains of the car divisions represented a fairly minor move, by 1998, but the decision to spin off Delphi was historic. Delphi represented a substantial and once vital dimension of General Motors, both strategically and structurally. In effect, incorporating Delphi within GM had signaled the vitality of the M-Form, testifying to headquarters' ability to orchestrate the corporate whole. By the reverse token, the decision to spin it off signaled just how dysfunctional GM's M-Form management had grown in the years since. In the context of post-industrialization, it was too heavy a load to carry, too broad a scope of industry to operate competitively and profitably. According to veiled accounts in the business press, the main trick had been reconciling organized labor to the idea. Once that point had been finessed, GM had gratefully relinquished the responsibility. "We are going to be a much faster company," vowed Jack Smith, "focused on our core business of building cars and trucks." It may have made good bottom-line sense, but the sentiment revealed just how radically GM's conception of its "core business" had shrunk. The decision to spin off Delphi "represent[ed] nothing less," Smith conceded, "than a fundamental shift away from vertical integration."[59]

Extending the Enterprise

Vertical De-Integration implied not just a narrowed sense of the corporation's scope and structural parameters, but an awakening awareness to the possibilities of functioning as an extended enterprise. Chrysler had backed into the idea over the 1980s. Now GM was implicitly committing itself to the concept. Signifying the interlacing of interfirm relationships along supply chains (between autoparts manufacturers and automakers, for example), the notion of extended enterprises subtly but definitively reshaped the boundaries delineating the industrial corporation over the 1990s. Ford, for example, began purchasing entire door assemblies from suppliers, delivered ready to be bolted onto frames and painted. The doors were opening on Ford's cars, and into Ford's processes. The emergence of powerful and pliant new information system technologies (see Chapter 5) enabled the trend, hard-wiring firms together in ways that allowed them to interact more effectively. (In cases like Chrysler's and Ford's, for instance, joint engineering with suppliers would probably have been impractical without access to digital networks and CAD systems.) As firms experimented, honed techniques, created and celebrated "best practice" cases, the concept gained credence and spread widely through American industry.

It was a powerful organizing idea, with broad structural ramifications. It opened, for example, the possibility of outsourcing a whole host of functions that corporations had once maintained internally. When the M-Form had held sway, in the heyday of the corporate headquarters, staffs had swelled with functional specialists. The role of headquarters, after all, was to apply functional expertise and state of the art management techniques to the divisions below. As new areas of expertise emerged, accordingly, corporations folded new specialists in—strategic corporate planners, for example, in the 1950s and 1960s; IT officers in the 1970s and 1980s. When Roger Smith determined that computer expertise was becoming a critical competitive edge in the 1980s, he promptly acquired Ross Perot's EDS and folded it into GM. Within a handful of years, however, the company's strategic choices grew starker and its headquarters began inexorably to shrink. Like other large industrials GM was straining by the 1990s to focus its energies as tightly on its core as possible—in GM's case, on the business of making cars. Bowing to the new structural logic, GM spun off EDS. IT remained a vital component of GM's business, to be sure, but evidently not one the company felt compelled to maintain in-house. It no longer made sense, after awhile, to carry a unit like EDS. GM was not in a position to make itself a world-class IT company. It needed world-class IT, however, and the best way to get it was by dealing with equally focused, independent world-class providers, not blinkered and beleaguered corporate staff.

A series of other companies made essentially the same decision, outsourcing functions such as strategic planning, IT, human resources, marketing, logistics, R&D, product design, and production engineering to consulting firms and other specialized providers. In extreme cases, even manufacturing itself migrated out of some firms—in the electronics industry, for example, where specialized providers such as Flextronics began running factories for corporate customers. Metaphorically speaking, it was as if little pieces of the M-Form were breaking off, clustering together in specialty clumps, and orbiting like satellites around the old-line industrials. Corporations no longer ran business in-house; they choreographed it, configuring intricate meshes of internal and external activity, and aligning themselves as they did so in fluid, highly-integrated networks of shared processes.

TOWARD GLOBAL STRUCTURES

The process of structural transformation radiated concentrically outward. First corporations overhauled their internal management structures. Then they reconfigured their external relations with suppliers and customers. By the early 1990s, the process was extending yet farther, across oceans, as corporations began to align their dispersed international operations in tighter, more integrated patterns. In a word, industrial corporations went global.

Each of the Big Three adapted differently to this new wave of structural transformation. They had all, as noted earlier, long done business internationally. But through the 1980s, they structured their foreign operations as distinct, parallel structures. Ford, for example, developed, manufactured, and marketed a separate line of cars in Europe, maintaining parallel structures overseas to handle that aspect of the business. Which made, of course, for considerable overhead and not a little duplication. Yet if, say, Toyota managed to make and sell essentially the same car around the world —the Camry, for example—couldn't Ford? It was a tantalizing question, and it was Ford, in fact, that took up the challenge most aggressively.

Ford's first attempt to make a "world car," the Escort of the early 1980s, was not a success. The company fielded parallel development teams in Europe and the United States and, predictably, ended up with two different cars made from two different sets of parts. (Two's were wild, it seemed; the two different Escorts ended up sharing a grand total of two parts.) The company tried again a few years later in what was known internally as the CDW27 program, which became the Mondeo in Europe and the Contour and Mystique in the United States. The program was messy, expensive, and slow in producing a car. But it taught the company important lessons and prepared managers for more comprehensive structural reform.[60]

In 1994, Ford took the next step, announcing "Ford 2000," a program to globalize product development. Specifically, the company stated it would establish five Vehicle Centers (VCs), each responsible for development of world cars based on designated platforms. The VC for developing small front-wheel drive cars would be located in Europe; the others in Dearborn, Michigan. It was a radical and ambitious undertaking, and one that faced a rocky implementation. But Ford's senior management, at least, and in particular its hard-driving CEO, Jacques Nasser, were convinced it was going to have to happen, sooner or later.

Certainly for Chrysler the prediction was on the mark. In the mid-1990s, following a harrowing corporate raid from Kirk Kerkorian (which the company did manage to fend off), Chrysler's management concluded that its international operations were too small to achieve critical mass, and that without a capacity for global growth it would not be able to survive. Thus in what was perhaps the most dramatic structural development of the decade, Chrysler agreed in 1998 to merge with German automotive giant Daimler-Benz, creating DaimlerChrysler. The Americans insisted as they did so that they were effecting a marriage of equals; the Germans nevertheless went on to consolidate managerial control by 2000. Whoever won or lost was less important, though, than the broader structural implication: Chrysler had joined something bigger than an American or a German entity. It had become part of a global mega-structure.[61]

CONCLUSION: DRAWING THE NEW STRUCTURE

By 2000, the world around industrial corporations had changed forever, and so too had the world within them. They were unlimbering and unlumbering themselves. The 1980s and 1990s was a period of fertile and frantic structural experimentation as companies tried with mounting urgency to make themselves leaner, flatter, faster, more efficient, and more maneuverable. These imperatives compelled corporations to reconceptualize the forces and relationships that held them together.

The master image of the traditional M-Form corporation was the organization chart, vertically oriented, stacking boxes on top of each other and connecting them, from the single box on the top to those arrayed in neat rows and multiplying columns below, all the way down to the bottom. The picture was designed to depict complex allocations of authority, across broad scopes of action, up and down multi-tiered hierarchies of command and control. For command and control lay at the heart of the classic corporate organization, structurally speaking.

The onset of post-industrialization forced deep changes in this view of the corporation, however. In structural terms, the most important relationships within the corporation became not the formal, vertical relationships but the horizontal and informal ones. The defining unit became the team, cross-functional, working close to the ground, equipped and authorized to make rapid decisions. Command and control did not wither away altogether. It did, however, become significantly less central to the effective operation of the corporation. Whether by necessity or by choice, companies drastically downsized their headquarters and corporate staffs over the last quarter of the twentieth century, significantly de-layered their vertical structures, and systematically dismantled their horizontal ones. Cumulatively, these changes unmade and remade corporate organization itself. M-Form components buckled and bent, while N-Form structures proliferated in the opening interstices. If the central metaphor describing traditional corporate structures was the organization chart, the metaphor for the structures that grew among, across, and through them during the 1980s and 1990s was the network, binding relationships together in more lateral, more fluid, more organic patterns.

The process of N-Formation, moreover, rearranged business not just within corporations, but along their edges and out past their borders. As extended enterprises spread through the post-industrial landscape, processes and pieces of business de-clustered from corporate constructions and reclustered in networked patterns. Over time, the transformation redelineated the very ground corporations occupied. It became harder to distinguish interior and exterior aspects—and less important, too. Structure became infrastructure. What had been a forest of free-standing organizational chart "trees" became a dense jungle, woven together by innumerable vines.

CHAPTER 5

SYSTEMS: INTELLIGENCE UNBOUND

The fast-paced, relentless, on-the-fly renovation of the large industrial corporation during the last quarter of the twentieth century extended well beyond strategies that refocused on core businesses and structures that became smaller, flatter, and more permeable. The internal systems of these behemoths also underwent a massive overhaul. To borrow a metaphor from residential construction, while the structural changes demolished walls and ceilings and opened doors and windows, the wiring and plumbing were also constantly upgraded and occasionally ripped out and replaced. What companies measured, how they measured it, and how and to whom they reported this information were critical management issues as the big industrials adapted to inexorable pressures in the world around them.

The ongoing revolution in information technology, which moved out of the backroom and centralized data processing centers into factories and onto desktops produced the most obvious changes in internal management systems. By the 1990s, vital business information was being generated at critical points of production and sale and fed back in real time to decision makers at multiple levels and locations inside companies. The advent of the personal computer and local area networks, as well as large-scale private and public networks, enabled information to flow instantaneously to decision makers anywhere, anytime, and enabled fundamental changes in the ways companies managed their operations, activities, and businesses.

But these were hardly the only changes to management systems. Total quality management (TQM) called for tighter horizontal coordination across functions and locations and connected companies in new ways with their suppliers and customers. Activity-based cost accounting and business process reengineering established new units of analysis inside organizations and new metrics. The imperatives to learn faster and better ("the learning organization") and capitalize on proprietary knowledge ("knowledge management") stimulated new "information architectures" and more new metrics for tracking the use and value of intangible assets. These new metrics combined with financial measures such as Economic Value Added, and human resource and customer satisfaction metrics in "balanced scorecards" that signified new ways of managing in many companies. Finally, the advent of collaborative software and object-oriented databases spawned a host of new tools and measurements for managing the flow of information, goods, and services throughout the supply chain, as well as the flow of proprietary information inside companies. Enterprise Resource Planning (ERP) systems and their close relatives, Enterprise Information Systems (EIS), Customer Relationship Management (CRM) systems, and other similar packages and systems wrought continuing, extensive changes in the way companies organized and conducted their business.

To borrow another image, the classic U-Form and M-Form organizations of the mid-twentieth century operated like an advanced, if familiar, organism. The headquarters organization constituted the brain into which most significant information—usually financial data—flowed for processing and was then sent back in the form of orders to various parts of the body for action. The traditional vertical information systems supporting the traditional structure served as the central nervous system. In contrast, the network or N-Form organization of the late 1990s was more akin to some kind of alien organism with multiple brains, including one at the center and perhaps many others elsewhere in the body, and they tracked a variety of financial and nonfinancial measures. Any of these multiple brains could stimulate orders for action, and they were linked to each other through a variety of horizontal and vertical systems in a complex distributed nervous system.

As this biological analogy suggests, the transformation of the U-Form and M-Form into the N-Form was hardly a simple matter. It did not follow a straightforward evolutionary path. And the necessity for the organism to remain alert and focused while undergoing major surgery on the brain and nervous system made the path more complicated still.

The first stirrings of change in corporate management systems began in the late 1950s and early 1960s, when two F100 companies, one in its infancy, announced the introduction of startling new products. Little did the leaders of Xerox and IBM imagine the transforming impact on their customers and themselves of the forces they were about to unleash.

SOME PRODUCT ANNOUNCEMENTS

In early autumn 1959, with fairly modest fanfare, an obscure company named Haloid unveiled a new document copier for office use, the Haloid 914. It was the size of a desk, an intricate piece of machinery, cumbersome to maintain. It was easy to use, though, and unlike other products on the market, it rendered sharp, clear copies on plain paper, using an arcane technology Haloid called "xerography."

The impact registered quickly. The copier market was crowded, different technologies were jostling with each other, Haloid was coming in as a tiny, unknown player, pitting itself against the likes of 3M and Kodak. Still, editors at *Business Week* decided that the appearance of a machine that made plain paper copies simply and affordably was big news, and they devoted a cover story to the Haloid 914. "Every year, businessmen drown in a deeper sea of paper," the story opened. "There was a time when the American businessman needed little more in the way of records than a ledger and a balance sheet. Today he needs paper by the truckload—information on prices, sales, markets, production, inventory, transportation."[1] Indeed, corporate information systems were burgeoning and clogging, and office managers already urgently needed what xerography offered. Haloid's sales, $33 million in 1959, climbed to $100 million by 1963 and reached the half billion mark three years later. "My first day as a salesman back in the 1960s," one company executive would later recall of that heady early growth, "I walked out of the office and looked up at all the buildings around me and thought, 'Every one of those offices wants what I have to sell.'" Within only a handful of years, Haloid became Xerox, Xerox became one of the largest industrial corporations in the world, and the Xerox copier became a mainstay of the corporate office.[2]

File that for later.

At about the same time as the plain paper copier spread through the offices of the industrial corporation, another information technology was also making its way into the business mainstream. In 1961, two years after the Haloid 914 hit the market, IBM's top management began planning to launch an ambitious new line of computers. Up into the early-1960s, the typical computer took up most of a room, required painstaking reprogramming to switch functions or even formulas, and could share neither peripheral gear, software, nor data with other kinds of computers. A few large, information-intensive companies tended these behemoths—insurance companies, for example. IBM foresaw much broader market possibilities and committed itself to developing a new line of next generation computers.

It was a high stakes play, a gambit that would either position IBM to dominate a huge new market or ruin the firm, possibly beyond repair. The project consumed massive resources in development costs—$5 billion within a few years. Meanwhile, competitors were pressing uncomfortably close, announcing new, versatile computer products of their own. By early 1964, IBM executives decided they had to strike preemptively. In April, while company engineers hurried to finish the machines and code the software, IBM dramatically (and with far more fanfare than Haloid had been able to muster back in 1959) unveiled the System/360 line of mainframe computers.[3]

The System/360 line employed (hybrid-)integrated circuits (as opposed to transistor chips), equipping its computers to handle more complicated, more powerful, and more flexible programming. Moreover, these computers were designed to be compatible up and down the line: data, software, and peripherals (disk drives, storage devices, printers and so on), could be transferred from one System/360 computer to another. The new computers were expensive, but at lease rates they were priced to fit corporate budgets, and business customers deluged IBM with orders. Within two years the company had shipped 4,000 and was working on a 20,000 backlog. It was a business triumph, making millions and ultimately billions for IBM. It was also a watershed event in the history of business systems. With its flexible programming and system compatibility, System/360 transformed the computer from an exotic, rarified technology into standard business equipment. By 1966, *Fortune* magazine was proclaiming that "The computer is recognized as the most vital tool of management introduced in this generation."[4]

So two new technologies, the copier and the mainframe computer, infiltrated corporate systems in the early-1960s. Taken together, they marked both the culmination of one era of corporate information, and the beginning of the onset of a new one. The "Xerox machine" became a fixture of the corporate office, equipping companies to generate paper far more quickly in much bigger batches, and thus reinforcing the architecture of information that companies were busily extending to support multidivisional coordination across a widening scope of diversification. The *Fortune* 100 company rested on informational foundations that were made of paper, and the Xerox machine buttressed that foundation. As did the IBM System/360, for while the mainframe computer converted data to electronic forms, it still kept information within tightly controlled, hierarchically-oriented channels. This equipment was designed, or at any rate applied, principally to strengthen and further centralize the resource allocation process that had emerged, by the 1960s, as the central function of corporate management.

But the strategic and structural underpinnings that had shaped corporate information systems were about to start breaking down. As companies refocused on core operations, and as they started to restructure, to delayer, to break down functional barriers, the information architectures that they had built to support resource allocation within a multidivisional corporate framework began to show signs of serious stress. If the arrival of the Xerox machine marked the apex of traditional systems, the emergence of corporate computing signaled the beginning of a protracted, painful, ultimately systemic transformation in the way information moved through corporations. Particularly as pressing new information needs emerged over the 1980s, companies tried with mounting urgency to rewire their systems. At the same time, powerful new technologies emerged, creating tantalizing visions of radically altered information dynamics. As things turned out, both Xerox and IBM would play pivotal roles in the proliferating market for these new technologies. Xerox, in particular, would struggle to adapt—both externally, to digitize its product lines, and internally, to wire in a new information architecture that would equip the company to do business in an increasingly competitive and turbulent marketplace. The company's story thus becomes a double-sided parable of the industrial firm as it tried to take apart and reassemble its systems, tried to capitalize on IT opportunities, tried to unbind its intelligence.

THE ORIGINS AND EVOLUTION OF INDUSTRIAL CORPORATE INFORMATION SYSTEMS

For all of their innovative technological sophistication, the Xerox machine and mainframe computer were profoundly traditional tools, at least as corporations first applied them. As such they were extending what was, by 1959, nearly a century of evolution in office systems. We tend to think of "systems" as signifying computers, but in fact, the concept needs to be tracked further back, to the late-nineteenth century, when an earlier generation of information technologies first equipped the large industrial firm to do large industrial business. The original information technologies of the industrial age may not seem as glamorous or high-tech as the computer or copier, but they had played a vital role in the growth and expansion of the corporation. They were the typewriters, filing cabinets, tabulating machines, adding machines, and telephones, that around the turn of the century went under the collective term of "office appliances."

The typewriter, for example, which speeded up and systematized both writing and reading, quickly became a central mechanism of big business. Entrepreneur-inventors first developed typewriters that could be mass-produced during the late-1860s and early-1870s; by the mid-1870s, Remington Rand was establishing itself as the leading producer. Sales were slow for a decade or so. Then they took off, and seemingly overnight the new machines became office fixtures—a development that seemed as portentous in the late-nineteenth century as the spread of computers would one hundred years later. Remarked one observer in 1887, "Five years ago the type writer was simply a mechanical curiosity. Today, its monstrous click can be heard in almost every well regulated business establishment in the country. A great revolution is taking place, and the type writer is at the bottom of it."[5]

Actually, the typewriter was working in tandem with a convergence of larger economic forces. It was no coincidence that the new machine entered industry in substantial numbers around 1880, for it was just at that point that the scale and pace of business began to escalate dramatically, approaching modern industrial proportions. If Remington Rand found customers in substantial numbers beginning in the mid-1870s, it was because new kinds of businesses were rapidly developing new kinds of systems needs. In the 1870s, both the McCormick Harvesting Machinery Company and the Singer Manufacturing Company began building national branch offices networks. In 1881, Swift & Company began putting together a national distribution web for its meat packing business; almost immediately Armour & Company went to work on a parallel structure of its own. In 1885, James Buchanan Duke began making cigarettes using new continuous process machinery, honing the mass production and distribution techniques he would expand five years later through the American Tobacco Company. In these and dozens, then hundreds of other businesses, operations mushroomed and multiplied. Running companies like McCormick or Singer required intricate coordination of supply, production, traffic, and distribution.

Economies of scale became decisive, never-slackening throughput became imperative, and in the process, conducting business became a series of highly complex logistical challenges. Pen and paper, ledger books, and clerks were soon overwhelmed. The new enterprises created and confronted what one historian has called a "crisis of control," and adopted a powerful new series of information technologies to cope with that crisis.[6]

IBM, for example, learned the lesson late, in the mid-1960s, as it geared up to full production of the System/360 computers. Before the 360, the company had assembled its computers from components produced by suppliers; IBM was not so much a manufacturer, originally, as it was a design, assembly, and business services firm. With the shift to the 360, IBM integrated backwards, building up substantial in-house manufacturing operations to make internal components for its computers. The company hired 50,000 new employees and built six major new plants, including facilities to manufacture the intricate integrated circuitry on which the 360 ran. In a sense, this marked IBM's real initiation into the ranks of the large industrials.

It was a fundamental transformation, and it created chaos within the company. Building and running the integrated circuits plants in particular proved much more difficult than IBM planners had allowed for. Unanticipated glitches repeatedly interrupted production, even as demand for the new computers outstripped the company's manufacturing capacity. By 1965, IBM's factories were going all out, field technicians were scrambling to install machines, and the project's software engineers were falling way behind schedule. Shipments slipped weeks, then months. In the headlong rush to assemble and ship machines, financial controls fell apart almost completely; when executives tried to close the company books for 1965, large sums remained unaccounted for. "What we didn't realize," CEO Thomas Watson Jr., later admitted, "was that our accounting system was an anachronism, left over from the days when IBM had just a few plants and each was responsible for its own set of products. With the 360 the plants had become interdependent—about two thirds of all our factory shipments were unfinished goods that went on to other factories for more work. We had no system for keeping tabs on this inventory moving around the company. [IBM president] Al [Williams] guessed that the amount in question might be $150 million—but the data he was getting were so vague as to be useless." Efforts to clamp down, to do something as basic as calculate inventory levels, taxed and vexed the company's financial analysts; even after polling all of the company's plants, Watson recalled, executives "couldn't get the numbers to add up." Finally upper management "insisted that each factory manager take a physical inventory—which means clerks with clipboards walking through the factories counting things. We'd never done that before. But that was how [we] finally discovered that the accounting system had gone completely out of whack. We had almost *six hundred million dollars* of work-in-progress inventory, and none of the factory managers wanted to claim it."[7]

These sorts of problems were new to IBM in 1965, but they were not new to American industry. Companies like Du Pont and General Motors had been working through them for decades, and had evolved elaborate information systems for managing them. They had learned to use typewriters, memos, reports, routing slips, and committee meetings, building an infrastructure of information that grew highly articulated and rigidly routinized. As would prove equally true in the computer age, the "software" proved just as important to master as the "hardware." Consider, for example, the impact made in 1893 at the Chicago World's Fair by the introduction of the vertical filing system, an innovation that garnered wide approbation and a gold medal.[8] It was a prosaic "technology," to be sure, but the file cabinet would arguably prove as powerful and transformative as the dynamo that so famously transfixed Henry Adams during his visit to the same fair.[9] For file cabinets, in combination with typewriters, gave corporate managers the tools they needed to create and store files—the basic building blocks of business bureaucracy. As the industrial firm grew larger in size, wider in scope, more complicated structurally, more sophisticated in functional specialization, professional managers had to figure out how to distribute massive amounts of complex information efficiently and reliably through the organization. In short order the new "office appliances" affixed themselves to and extended new patterns of communication: report gathering, statistical and financial analysis, committee meetings, circular letters, memoranda, and the like. Business bureaucracies themselves became elaborate forms of information-processing technology—became, in other words, knowledge systems, designed to generate, channel, and evaluate information efficiently and accurately.

More specifically, corporate bureaucracies and the machines that powered them were designed to inform executive management. Variations evolved, firm by firm, but in their broad outlines the systems adopted by the multidivisional industrial corporation followed a basic pattern. By mid-century the dominant information channels within the corporation were the resource allocation systems that supported corporate planning, budgeting, and performance measurement processes. These systems were designed to draw data—sales, share data, costs, projections, budget figures, and so on—from field units through the operating divisions up the corporate hierarchy to senior management for evaluation, analysis, and executive decision. The central documents circulating within these systems were divisional and departmental plans and budgets, making their way upward toward headquarters, passing through successive stations on the chain of command, continuously reprocessed along the way, with additional filtration by corporate staff specialists. By the time they reached senior management they had been highly refined, usually prepared to fit a standard corporate format, often integrated with other plans or budgets. Then, following executive review and decree at headquarters, a parallel set of systems carried executive decisions in the reverse direction, back down into the divisions and through the lower reaches of the divisional chains of command. The system as a whole was circulatory, drawing information into, and then carrying out from, corporate headquarters at its heart.[10]

Among the various data streams in circulation, the most important were the flows of financial information. By the 1960s, when the copier and computer began to make their way into these systems, the typical large industrial firm was running its business on the basis of highly complex, growth-oriented financial metrics. Headquarters controlled resources, and what weighed most heavily at headquarters were numbers such as return on investment and discounted cash flow within each of the various business units below. Companies like General Electric were making "strategic business planning" an intricate and influential science. Companies like Dow and Union Carbide were squinting at their "business portfolios." Companies like Ford and General Motors had come under the decisive sway of the "Finance Guys."

Built principally to sustain the resource allocation process, the systems of the industrial corporation took on certain defining characteristics. They tended to be vertically-oriented, laid out along corporate chains of command. They also tended to be functionally-compartmentalized, containing data within specific silos or staff channels such as finance, production, or personnel. Vertical orientation and functional compartmentalization implied that systems were fragmented, dispersed through the firm. Overlaying and reinforcing the structural lineaments of the firm, corporate systems formed, in essence, maps of authority: They marked off decision rights within functional jurisdictions and aligned corporate processes along hierarchical chains of command and control. And they ran under the tight control of information resource managers, typically titled EDP (electronic data processing) or DP managers.[11]

In theory, laying out systems along these lines made optimal use of the operational or "specific knowledge" possessed by managers running a firm's businesses, while freeing up senior managers, with their presumed strategic or "general knowledge," to focus on making the trade-offs that maximized value.[12] Over time, however, these systems had the effect of fragmenting information across the various levels of the organization. Each higher level was progressively removed from the detailed information and assumptions that supported the plans or budgets proposed by department and division managers. And each lower level was progressively removed from the strategic thinking and process by which choices were made.

Inevitably, too, organizing information flows along these lines tended to foster interdivisional rivalry as various units competed for approval of resources outlined in their plans and budgets from a limited corporate pool. The tight link between the planning and budgeting systems and the performance appraisal and rewards systems tended to intensify this rivalry.

Another latent problem was the bias inherent in the financial orientation of these systems, which used targets and measures based on discounted cash-flow (DCF) methodology. By 1978, 87 percent of large U.S. corporations reportedly used DCF methods to evaluate capital projects.[13] These techniques were well suited for making choices among competing projects that were independent of each other, a condition that was largely satisfied in companies that were diversified in unrelated businesses. But these methods were ill suited for making investments in organization-wide capabilities necessary to achieve superior performance in terms of quality, speed, flexibility, and innovation. And, as famously argued by Robert H. Hayes and William J. Abernathy, DCF and other forms of controls based on calculations of financial return tend to bias decision makers against investments with distant pay-offs—the very types of investments manufacturing companies must make to ensure their long-term competitiveness and survival.[14]

Still, for all of their limitations, the resource allocations systems in fact served the strategic goals of the industrial corporation quite nicely—at least, in the context of growth and unrelated diversification. In their heyday, industrial corporations commanded broad confidence. They and by implications the systems that sustained them seemed to be highly effective instruments for making capital decisions—more effective, it was thought, than financial markets in generating the information necessary to make short-term, fine-grained choices among competitive projects.[15]

Take Xerox, for example. The copier company in effect signaled its arrival, its maturing as an industrial corporation, when it brought over Archie McCardell, one of the "Whiz Kids" who had overhauled Ford following the Second World War, and installed him in 1966 as group vice president of finance and control. With McCardell came Melvin Howard, who assumed the post of chief financial officer, and Gary Bennett and Jim O'Neill, who took up high stations in the company's finance and sales units. Xerox managers called them "the Ford Men," and they quickly made their stamp on the company. McCardell and his lieutenants installed rigid new financial controls, along with state-of-the-art new financial systems to operate, monitor, and fine-tune those controls. The balance of power within Xerox shifted decisively from the company's engineers and marketers to its financial analysts. David Kearns, entering the company's executive circle from IBM in 1971, shortly after McCardell assumed the president's office, arrived just as the Ford Men were consolidating their grip. "Trend analysis and financial controls," he would later recount, became "the most important tools in guiding decisions" at Xerox. As far as McCardell was concerned "numbers shone a spotlight into the belly of the corporation and revealed everything."[16]

ADDING COMPUTERS, ADAPTING CORPORATIONS

Their fierce conviction in executive management on the basis of financial measures made McCardell and Xerox's other "Ford Men" enthusiastic computer users. They seized on the newer, more powerful computing possibilities offered by mainframes such as IBM's System/360, tinkered a bit, and made them integral parts of their planning regime. An elaborate computer model called "Shazam" ran the numbers at Xerox headquarters, calculating and comparing projected impacts of various product and pricing alternatives. Among the company's old guard, Shazam became infamous, demanding, devouring hundreds, thousands of facts and assumptions in making its forecasts. Any marketer or project engineer wanting to take on finance at Xerox had better come armed with piles of computer printout, though if finance remained skeptical it was likely to run the numbers again, using its own set of data points.[17]

IBM, meanwhile, was modifying its computers and software to handle just this kind of application. "Use a Computer to Improve your Decision Making," one IBM programmer suggested in a promotional article in 1973. "Where are we in terms of resources, output, and return on the investment in resources?" Julio Bucatinsky had his hypothetical manager asking. To assist in formulating a "planning matrix" IBM had designed "packaged planning systems" to run on corporate mainframes, Bucatinsky reported, allowing corporate managers to "significantly speed up both the model-building function and the repeated iterations or runs that make the 'what if' game useful and valuable." So, for example: "One firm with a number of operating units is developing five-year plans for each division and subsidiary and is consolidating the individual plans into a corporate five-year operating strategy. When management is in a planning session, new views can be produced within half an hour, permitting the 'what if' game to go on at length until management is satisfied with the objectives it has defined and with the strategies adopted to achieve them."[18]

It was a scenario of scenario-making perfectly suited to the corporate thinking of the era: the mainframe computer was configured to crunch the numbers for corporations running business by the numbers. Drowning in "seas of paper" as they assumed increasingly broad resource allocation responsibilities and applied increasingly sophisticated metrics, senior managers readily latched on to the new equipment. Indeed, insofar as these technologies lightened the burden of managing corporate resource allocation, Xerox machines and mainframe computers encouraged further extension and articulation of vertical control systems. So, for example, moving accounting functions from general ledgers onto mainframes enabled companies to drive complex accounting calculations down to the divisional level. Decentralized profit-and-loss accountability, and sophisticated return on investment (ROI) measurements, became possible on a running business-by-business basis. Companies were now able to deepen their data collection, creating much more sophisticated capital budgeting capabilities. Corporate strategists readily took the opportunity to expand their planning regimens.[19]

But if the computer was initially adapted to existing infrastructures and information flows, it was ultimately destined to play a more fluid and far more transformational role in rerouting corporate information systems. The concept of what a "computer" was just beginning a period of rapid and revolutionary transformation as System/360 ramped up.

It would have taken a truly gifted prophet to see it all coming from, say, the executive heights of senior Xerox management in 1976, as the company ceremonially marked the processing of the last U.S. order for the 914. Fundamental changes were certainly in store, executives realized. They were exhorting each other to prepare Xerox to equip a paperless office of the future, they were trying to move the company into computer technologies, they were convening events like 1977's grand "Xerox World Conference" to explore the impact new information technologies might have on corporate systems. They had also set up a major research laboratory in Palo Alto—Xerox PARC—to incubate futuristic office technologies.[20]

Meanwhile, the company was continuing to make and sell paper copiers. But that core business was growing uncomfortably competitive, by the late-1970s. In fact, the company was sliding into a serious crisis, even as it probed into new technologies. By the time it phased out the blockbuster product that had propelled it into the business mainstream, Xerox was in a race for its very life. At first the race seemed to be one of high strategy and high technology. Gradually it dawned on the company it was facing a more basic crisis, more internally rooted, more deeply systemic.

COMPETITION AND QUALITY: XEROX, 1972–1988

While its senior managers were using the mainframe computer to reinforce vertical control systems at Xerox, a new competitive reality was dawning, and it would pressure the company to develop a vastly improved level of horizontal coordination among scientists, engineers, manufacturing managers, and marketing personnel.

The first signs of crisis at Xerox emerged at just about the same time as corporate America's wider industrial reckoning began to set in. In December 1972, the FTC filed a complaint accusing Xerox of restraining trade and illegally monopolizing the market for plain paper copiers. A negotiated settlement in 1975 forced the company to license copier patents to its competitors and to offer customers the option of buying, rather than just leasing, their machines. In any event, even as the FTC suit was getting underway, Canon introduced a liquid toner copier and promptly began licensing the technology to other companies. IBM had entered the copier market in 1970; in 1975, Xerox's Rochester neighbor, Kodak, came in as well, joining some 20 companies now in the fray. Suddenly, within the space of half a dozen years, Xerox found itself doing business in a sharply competitive marketplace.[21]

Company strategists marked the change, of course, but they paid more attention initially to Kodak and IBM, underestimated the Japanese threat, and most critically, misgauged the nature of the challenge and what it would require of Xerox. The company had anticipated the entry of American rivals; it was already girding itself for battle with Big Blue and the Yellow Giant. The full implications of the Japanese competition, however, only gradually dawned.[22] "Within the span of a few years," Kearns recalled, a memory of bewilderment still coloring his tone years later, "something like ten Japanese companies were suddenly active in the copier business, all armed with similar strategies of under-pricing us. We tended to refer to them collectively as Japan Inc."[23] As they did in other industries, the Japanese entered the copier market at the low end, taking advantage of Xerox's disinterest in producing stripped-down machines, not to mention the superior cost-effectiveness of Japanese production methods. In 1975, Savin unveiled its 750—"a real dazzler," Kearns would admit in retrospect, a small Japanese-made liquid toner copier that worked slowly but very reliably. Savin marketed the machine for sales, rather than leasing; it cost two and a half times less than comparable Xerox products.[24] A ripple of uneasiness went through Xerox's upper ranks. Still, the company remained fairly complacent, even as its market position began to slip. In 1981 Canon introduced a line of middle-volume copiers. The Japanese were beginning to move up the market spectrum. By this point, Xerox's market share had shrunk to less than 50 percent.[25]

"What no one at Xerox seemed to have any good grasp of," Kearns would later realize, "was the level of quality and the low cost of manufacturing that the Japanese were destined to achieve."[26] In other words, the crisis at hand was a trial of process, of system—a crisis that caught Xerox unprepared and ill equipped. Over its formative years of booming growth, the company had paid little attention to product quality. Its copiers frequently broke down, but with its proprietary control over key technologies and its captive customer base (nearly all of Xerox's customers leased, rather than bought, their copiers), the company felt no real pressure to improve quality. Xerox made profits servicing breakdowns; in fact, often customers felt compelled to lease extra machines as backups, yielding even more revenue.

In any event, Xerox had no systems in place for comprehensively measuring or controlling quality. Xerox's senior managers were studying instrument panels that prominently displayed data on sales and sales growth, but no readings for field failure rates or customer satisfaction. As a result, uneven quality patterns had worked their way deeply into the organization. Joseph Juran, a consultant who had helped design Japanese systems and industrial processes, conducted a battery of tests on Xerox copiers in the early 1980s and found that they tended to break down for the same reasons, regardless of the model. In other words, the company was xerographically reproducing its problems, product by product. Many of these were bugs design engineers might have corrected fairly easily. But design engineering came under the organizational jurisdiction of product managers, whose overriding goal was to sell copiers with more features, not copiers that held up. "From the very beginning," Kearns eventually conceded, "Xerox had built an organization that wasn't centered on quality and reliability of the product. The early emphasis was on ease of use, because other duplicating equipment was anything but easy to use."[27]

The Japanese Revelation

Xerox faced a drastic situation, but it still held powerful assets. The one that may have been most important at this critical juncture, though few senior managers fully appreciated it yet, was Fuji Xerox. Xerox had set up its Japanese subsidiary in 1962, originally as a joint venture to penetrate Japanese and East Asian markets. Fuji Xerox operated more-or-less autonomously from its American parent, adapting products and manufacturing methods to Japanese patterns. "In its first ten years," as Kearns put it, "Fuji Xerox took what Xerox and Rank Xerox [a British subsidiary] had to offer, reengineered it and manufactured it for the Japanese market."[28] Which meant that Fuji Xerox was well positioned to provide its American parent with crucial perspective on its capable new competitors. Itself hard-pressed by competition, the subsidiary in 1976 had launched what it called the "New Xerox Movement," which targeted ambitious quality goals and 50 percent reductions in development cycles and manufacturing costs.[29] The results were impressive. And they began to draw attention from the United States as a sense of crisis took hold within the parent company's corporate ranks.

The shock that shook Xerox out of complacency was the arrival in U.S. markets of mid-sized Japanese copiers for less than $10,000. At first Xerox executives were convinced their competitors were dumping. But Xerox's new manufacturing chief, Frank Pipp, who had been a Ford manufacturing manager and who was just coming into headquarters from a Europe posting, believed there was more to the story and decided to take a team across the Pacific to investigate. Significantly, Pipp enlisted a broad cross-section of Xerox's senior line and staff management for the trip, including plant managers, financial analysts, engineers and manufacturing specialists. Pipp was determined to make an impression where it would count, and to document it with the full force of Xerox's expertise. The revelations were sobering. Surveying operations at other companies and digesting information from Fuji Xerox, the team discovered that their Japanese counterparts had far outpaced them in both quality and efficiency. "We can't be that bad," Chairman Peter McColough protested. "We are," Pipp replied. Xerox's Japanese competitors carried between six and eight times less inventory. The quality of the parts they purchased from suppliers averaged over 99 percent, as compared to 95 percent at Xerox. Their overhead was half what Xerox's was. They made, assembled, packed, and shipped product with much leaner managerial staffs. "In category after category," Kearns exclaimed, "the difference wasn't 50 percent better or anything like that; it was almost always over 100 percent!" In sum, it cost the Japanese manufacturers about two-thirds of what it cost Xerox to produce a copier "That statistic was absolutely astonishing," Kearns admitted. "When we understood that, we were terrified. We had no idea they were making machines that much cheaper. That was no gap. That was a chasm."[30]

What Xerox's American managers found when they toured Japanese factories was a radically different set of production processes and systems. They found no quality inspectors, nor the various troubleshooters, the replacement workers, inventory runners, machinery and tool repair personnel, that tended to hover over American assembly lines. Nor did they find the extensive rework areas, the piles of scrap waiting to be discarded, the large lots of inventory waiting to be used, that cluttered the shopfloors of Xerox plants. And yet they found humming enterprises, turning out top quality products.

They found, in sum, factories that had been built around what Japanese companies called Statistical Process Control (SPC), a bundle of principles that in the United States would assume the label Total Quality Management (TQM). SPC techniques had spread through Japan in the rebuilding years after World War II, under the assiduous sponsorship of the Japanese Union of Scientists and Engineers and the widely influential tutelage of U.S. consultants like W. Edwards Deming and Joseph Juran. Initially, Japanese companies had gone after quality problems by building up elaborate inspection systems. But they soon shifted their attention from reactive detection to proactive prevention: With ardent commitment and resourceful creativity, Japanese companies taught themselves to root out and rip out quality breakdowns at their sources, and to anticipate future potential quality problems.[31]

The policies and systems the Japanese followed to manage quality contrasted sharply with the top-down, hierarchical information and control systems embedded in most U.S. manufacturers. The Japanese defined quality in terms of what customers, internal and external to the organization, wanted, as opposed to what engineers and manufacturing managers might have considered adequate. The Japanese then managed this different (and usually more exacting) standard of quality through policies and systems that decentralized decision-making and fostered horizontal coordination across the entire supply chain. For example, Japanese R&D personnel worked across functional boundaries with manufacturing engineers and production workers to design products to facilitate defect-free manufacturing. On the assembly lines, Japanese production workers tracked data about parts and assemblies that enabled them to catch problems at an early stage and take quick, informed actions to fix them. Groups of workers and first-level supervisors met frequently in quality circles to review performance and suggest improvements. Just-in-time (JIT) inventory management required manufacturers and suppliers to maintain tight communication links and synchronize their actions.

As a result of these and other policies and systems, Japanese manufacturers could assemble products much faster, with many fewer defects, and at much lower cost than their American rivals. They could also develop new products, and significant improvements much faster. The quest for better quality, in other words, delivered a multitude of powerful economic benefits and advantages.

Leadership Shakeup

The Japan expeditions encouraged change. Further impetus came with turnover in Xerox's senior management. Around 1980 a cadre of executives returned to Stamford from postings at Rank Xerox in Europe, where the battle with Japanese competitors had been raging especially fiercely. Bill Glavin, Dwight Ryan, and Wayland Hicks reentered headquarters troubled and restless. They became important members of a new executive team solidifying around David Kearns, who took over as CEO in 1982. The new chief was deeply impressed with the need to shake up Xerox. Indeed, he feared for the very survival of the company. "The institution was more than threatened; it was terminally ill," Kearns later remembered feeling during those dark days. "We were drifting into highly dangerous waters, and it became evident that only drastic measures would work."[32] Casting about for answers, Kearns traveled to Japan himself in 1982 to preside over the twentieth anniversary of Fuji Xerox and take in the results of the New Xerox Movement. Perhaps something like that was what the company needed. With some trepidation, the new CEO decided to commit Xerox as a whole in the same direction, launching what the company called its Leadership Through Quality (LTQ) program.

To an extent that is difficult to appreciate in retrospect, LTQ represented a real risk on Kearns's part. "Quality" suggested luxury, yet Xerox was in the midst of a desperate crisis, slashing costs, laying off thousands of workers, fighting for survival. Under the circumstances, many within the company's executive ranks felt that focusing on quality would be extravagant, if not a waste of time. In the abstract it sounded laudable, but actually committing major resources, making it a strategic priority—could Xerox really afford to mount a sustained quality drive?

Kearns decided Xerox could not afford not to. He unveiled the program at an annual conference of Xerox executives in Leesburg, Virginia in February 1983. He met considerable skepticism, yet launched an intensive multistaged training program designed to reach throughout the massive organization, from top to bottom. Senior managers first took the training as students, in a session that lasted a week, then turned around and taught the program to middle managers. The process cascaded from top management down through the ranks, steadily gathering force over 1984 and into 1985.[33]

Quality training called on Xerox's executives, managers, supervisors, office- and factory-workers to reconceptualize their roles in terms of customers—whether external (purchasers of Xerox products) or internal (the shipping units that received products from a manufacturing unit, for example). It set up rigorous new techniques for identifying and tracing defects, glitches, and breakdowns back to their source, as soon as they appeared, if not before they even happened. In place of broad, unquantified commitments to the name of quality, it demanded that the company formulate and closely monitor new statistical controls.

From a systems point of view, the shift to a quality regimen required a radical reorientation of information. LTQ put new kinds of questions to Xerox. Some were obvious: How often did the company's machines break down, and for what reasons? Others were less obvious, growing out of the company's glimpses into highly honed Japanese operations. How much, for example, was Xerox's rework and scrap costing the firm? How much work-in-progress inventory were plants carrying, and how much did that cost? How about inspection and warranty work, or customer and vendor complaint resolution? What kind of elapsed production times were plants posting? How did work processes map out, on factory floors in offices? How much distance did products travel as they were assembled?

Those kinds of questions gnawed at Xerox's managers as the scope of the challenge before them grew clear. Awakened to their company's deeply ingrained habits of operational underperformance, they—like many of their peers in corporate America—were straining by the early-1980s to peer down into the guts of their factories, warehouses, shipping routes, sales offices, and service centers. Kearns could no longer afford to wait for filtered information to make its tortured way to him via the traditional chain of command. He needed access to continuous data—he and, as he quickly learned, thousands of other people within the company.

QUALITY SYSTEMS TAKE ROOT WITHIN THE F100

One after another over the 1980s and into the 1990s, the industrials joined the quality movement. Xerox was one of the first; other early corporate converts included Motorola and Hewlett-Packard. Initially a bold choice, TQM rapidly became a competitive necessity as more and more companies recognized—or could not afford to ignore—the compelling economic logic. During the 1980s, TQM swept through nearly all of the F100 industrials. (See Figure 5.1.) Although their commitment to TQM varied, as did the effectiveness of their initiatives, all of them faced the challenge to develop new systems to support the decentralized decision-making and coordinated action involved. This constituted a dramatic change in thinking about management systems generally.

Whereas traditional planning and budget systems emphasized financial measures, quality systems emphasized customer satisfaction and resource productivity measures. Rather than focusing on the financial hurdles imposed by the internal resource allocation process, the new systems focused on performance hurdles set by customers in product markets. They also emphasized paying attention to total

Figure 5.1
Adoption of TQM Systems by the *Fortune* 100 Companies

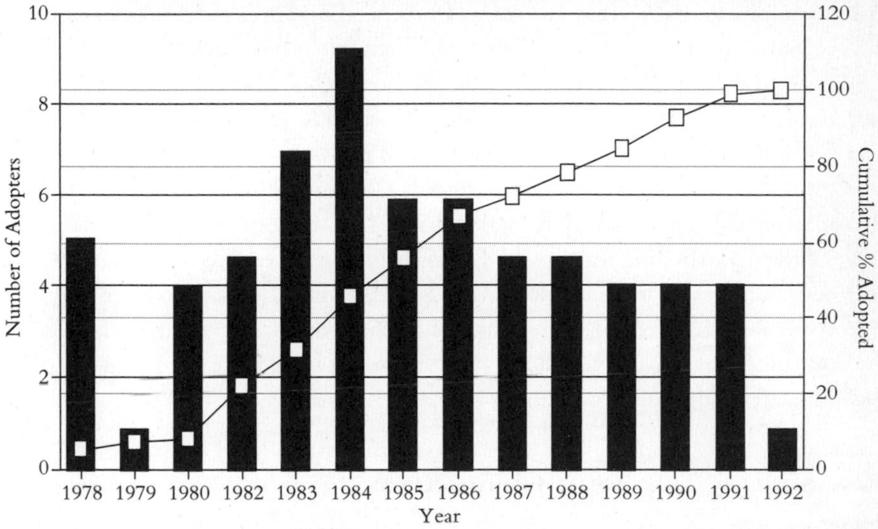

Number of Adopters
Cumulative % Adopted
1978 1979 1980 1982 1983 1984 1985 1986 1987 1988 1989 1990 1991 1992
Year

Note: This graph is based on telephone interviews with senior executives in each company.

factor productivity, as companies drove themselves to locate and minimize inefficiencies in the use of capital, labor, materials, and time.

They reflected new points of emphasis, and routed information along fundamentally new directions. Traditional resource allocation systems had followed vertical lines within the organization, affixing themselves to chains of command and lines of reporting. Quality systems reoriented axes of information horizontally as the new "customer" mentality, and in particular the notion of internal customers within the firm, opened new information channels. All kinds of people had to learn to share information: factory workers and service personnel, engineers and sales reps, "customers" across the firm. The push to increase total productivity broke down functional categories, forcing attention onto horizontal processes such as production, product-development, order-fulfillment, and other supporting business processes. As they dug into their processes companies learned that inefficiencies typically arose out of costly transfers between the various parts of these horizontal processes. Eliminating those inefficiencies required better coordination among everyone involved in the overall execution of a process—and that, inevitably, meant sharing information more broadly and more fluidly, across the firm.

The emergence of cross-functional teams represented the structural manifestation of this insight. (See Chapter 4.) On a systems level, the teams that took root in firm after firm over the 1980s represented efforts to collect and pool information that the company's traditional planning and budgeting systems had fragmented and dispersed. The pooling of information, in turn revealed all kinds of latent opportunities for performance improvements that cut across traditional organizational boundaries.

Another consequence of the quality movement, the restructuring in teams, and the new systems they spawned, was to push decision rights down the organization. Senior managers—at least, those that "got it"—quickly learned that the key to improving quality was digging into the flawed process-points that created quality problems, and that meant equipping people as close to the source as possible with the information and the authority to make changes on the spot. It meant enabling factory workers on the line to stop the line as breakdowns erupted, for example. And on a structural level, it meant delegating broad decision powers to team members, who were almost always far better positioned than top management to anticipate or root out problems. The new systems thus wrested control from managers in finance and other staff functions, restoring it to operating managers.[34]

New Systems Take Root within Xerox

As these new imperatives made themselves felt within Xerox, the company found itself busily installing new systems initiatives and experiments. Indeed, even as Leadership Through Quality was still taking form as a company mission, Xerox plant managers were wiring in new, more automated material management systems. In retooling Building 200 in its Webster manufacturing complex, for example, to produce the 10 Series copiers (a sophisticated new line of copiers run by embedded microcircuitry), the company substantially overhauled and updated the plant. "The notion," explained one production engineer, "is that to build a 10 Series of copiers you also need a 10 Series line of factories. The latest in technology." Indeed, the new plant "circuitry" in Building 200 was as intricately networked as the microcircuitry housed within the copiers it was building. Engineers installed a state-of-the-art materials handling system, for example, that streamlined Xerox's assembly lines and whittled down work-in-progress inventory. "I hate to say it," admitted Bob Sternberg, the plant's supervisor, "but in the old days we used to receive a part in Webster, handle it, pay for the storage, bring it back in, handle it again, store it, bring it to the line, and put it in the machine."[35] Those were exactly the kinds of transfer-points where inventory clutter, inefficiency and quality breakdowns bred. To streamline the process, Xerox began bar-coding parts packages for the 10 Series and scanning them into a computer system as they came into Building 200, to determine where they were headed and when they would be needed. Thus incoming parts could automatically be either relayed directly to assembly lines or sent to a new on-site warehouse designed for rapid and automatic delivery by overhead shuttle cars, conveyors, and wire-guided vehicles. It was a high-tech version of what the Japanese (who were not yet using the high technology) called *kanban*. As part of the system, Xerox began dispatching trucks on daily rounds to those vendors situated within 40 miles of the plant, picking up parts needed for the next day.[36]

Automated material management at Webster did not initially go under the name of quality, but it clearly bore the imprint of the Japanese benchmarking expeditions. The system was designed to pare out production clutter, streamline inventory, and tighten links with suppliers. It folded neatly into LTQ as that program took shape, and continued to evolve over the 1980s. By 1989, plant managers at Webster were drawing workers into problem-solving teams, posting daily reports detailing the previous day's defects, and bringing the number of defective parts caught on the line down from 10,000 per million down to 360. In the meantime, supervisors had shifted their focus. "Just in time is probably our No. 1 strategy right now," reported Jim Horn, vice president of manufacturing at the plant, in 1990. The company was using pull systems and smaller lot sizes to dramatically reduce work-in-progress, making mistakes much less costly. Thus, for example, plant operators had cut the number of units between the machining and welding stations from 300 sets to 10; "now if there's a problem," one engineer stated, "we don't have to rework 80 or 100 frames."[37]

Meanwhile, far above the company's factories, Xerox's senior managers were coming to grips with the stranglehold their traditional systems had put on information and decision-making authority. In the early 1980s, in Kearns' first years as CEO, he and other Xerox executives resolved to take turns manning the customer complaint lines at headquarters. Each of the company's top two dozen corporate officers had to spend "a day in the tank," dealing directly with customers. No call could be transferred; the individual had to stay in the tank and try to work through the problem. It was a revelatory experience. "Fairly quickly," Kearns reported, "the program had the effect of raising the sensitivity level among management to our inability to satisfy our customers. We . . . came to realize how little freedom we gave our own employees in the branches to fix problems, even when the solutions were patently obvious."[38]

Time "in the tank," the incremental improvements that grew out of quality drives, the cross-functional sharing of information as teams gathered, gradually it all started to add up to a larger phenomenon. The company, collectively, discovered how much information it had locked up within its various constituent parts, how tightly its existing systems had been throttling its people and its information. Coming to grips with that realization, and working out more flexible systems, was a protracted and often disruptive process.

LTQ nonetheless delivered tangible results at Xerox, helping to reverse its competitive decline. Aided by a revaluation of the yen, which raised the price of Japanese exports, LTQ enabled Xerox to become the first major U.S. manufacturer to reclaim market share lost to the Japanese. In 1989, Xerox's Business Products &

Systems unit won a Malcolm Baldrige National Quality Award. The citation noted that Xerox had regained the global lead in copy-machine quality.[39]

FROM VERTICAL CONTROL TO NETWORKING

The decentralized, horizontally-linked management processes and systems of TQM developed simultaneously and symbiotically with new information systems architectures. During the 1980s, the personal computer revolution took hold, placing PCs and workstations on most desktops in offices and scattering them throughout warehouses and factories. Decentralized computing power supported decentralized decision-making. A revolution in computer networking followed hard on the revolution in personal computing, with Xerox reprising its role as a driving force.

In 1973, a team of researchers led by Robert Metcalfe at Xerox PARC began hooking computers together on lines of cheap coaxial cable, enabling them to send and receive radio signals. This was "a prototype information system involving linked, interactive machines." Subsequent work at PARC, at other computer companies, and in government laboratories extended the development of local area networks (LANs) that enabled computers to communicate and share information. By the mid-1980s, several competing standards for the technical interfaces and information protocols had emerged, with the most promising one defined by Xerox and its partner, Digital Equipment Corporation. The Xerox-DEC "Ethernet" eventually won out as the standard governing LANs. Meanwhile, the continuing advance of data processing—ever more computing power in ever more compact packages—merged with LANs to establish a new "client-server" information architecture in companies. Central servers maintained software packages and databases accessible to client PCs throughout the network.[40]

The net effect was to unseat corporate EDP managers, rupture vertical control systems, and redistribute information in much more plastic configurations. In some confusion, but under virtually irresistible pressures, the American industrial corporation unbound its information—released it from file cabinets and insulated data processing centers, as corporate managers came to realize that managing information was no longer a question of lodging it in the "proper" place, so much as making it available wherever and whenever it might enable coordination and exchange within and across the boundaries of the firm.

This kind of thinking was very much in evidence at Xerox by the late-1980s. When IT executive Paul Strassman had lobbied for budget allocations in the 1970s, the executive committee had grumbled about how expensive the computer department was growing. Initiatives like LTQ, however, coupled with the dawning awareness of what ethernet could do for internal communication, completely recast Xerox's sense of its "computer department." By the late-1980s, on the other side of Xerox's crisis of competitiveness, information had grown into something more central, more basic than a support function. It had come to seem instead like a vital aspect of business—and, for Xerox, an incalculable opportunity, too. "IS was once an independent slice of overhead, seemingly out of control, growing at 40 percent per year while the rest of the company grew at 20 percent," Kearns confirmed. "Today it is an integral part of Xerox's corporate strategy."[41] Vice Chairman Bill Glavin echoed the sentiment, identifying information technology as "a critical resource that can help us simplify our business processes and further streamline our organization."[42]

THE REENGINEERING RESPONSE

So new systems proliferated throughout Xerox over the 1980s, taking root locally, incrementally, not as part of any single grand plan or architecture at first, but as experiments and applications to solve discrete problems, achieve concrete results. The company was struggling to meet competition, adapting imported operating techniques, and tinkering at the same time with devices its own lab had been devising. It was starting to collect new kinds of data and trying to figure out how to apply that data. And meanwhile, exotic new technologies were expanding the ways in which data could be channeled and manipulated. By 1990 the company was systematically and systemically dismantling itself, taking itself apart process by process, system by system, and trying to see how the pieces could be put together so that they worked more cleanly and efficiently. As were many other large American industrials.

By the late 1980s, TQM and decentralized information systems together were wreaking a radical transformation in the ways big companies managed themselves. This process accelerated following a sharp recession in the United States in 1990 and 1991. Although TQM programs had made internal operations more efficient and helped to streamline entire supply chains, the recession exposed continuing cost problems. Companies responded with a massive wave of restructuring, downsizing, and plant closings, and, for the first time in generations, shed thousands of white-collar employees. (See Chapters 4 and 7.)

The scale of the downsizing was as significant as its manner. Companies confronted the necessity to shrink and get leaner by embracing a new management technique called "business process reengineering," or, simply, "reengineering."[43] As the label implied, reengineering involved breaking down a business into its component processes and then subjecting these to thoroughgoing reframing and retooling. Cross-functional and cross-level employee teams typically took responsibility for reengineering basic business processes such as new product development, materials handling, logistics, production and operations, order fulfillment, and managing customer relationships. Reengineering focused efforts beyond optimizing existing ways of managing and proceeded to rethink business processes from the ground up, starting with basic questions: If designing this process now, from scratch and for a new organization, what should it look like? Which activities are essential to perform?

Which among these can be farmed out to partners? How can technology help to streamline and automate this process? At what level should decisions be made? Under what controls?

Reengineering swept across the industrial landscape, leaving smaller and vastly altered organizations it its wake. By 1994, all of the F100 companies had pursued major reengineering initiatives. Although most of them customized the technique and adapted it to local circumstances, generally they achieved significant savings through simplification, automation, and outsourcing. At IBM, for example, reengineers slashed the time to assemble and test a major new product from three weeks to two days. They also hacked away at the company's financial control systems, reducing the number of separate systems from more than three hundred to 36. Many gains from reengineering proved temporary, however, and the technique fell into disfavor after a few years, its benefits eclipsed by memories of the painful nature of the process. Nonetheless, like TQM, reengineering illustrated that executives were coming to understand their organizations as arrays of discrete activities and processes, many of them linked horizontally, rather than as traditional hierarchies under vertical control.[44]

As they evolved from functional U-Form and multidivisional M-Form into network N-Form organizations, companies required new management systems and measurements, which practitioners, consultants, and academics stood ready to supply. One new metric was Economic Value Added (EVA), which top executives used to track overall corporate performance and align decision-making and behavior with shareholder interests. EVA gathered steam in the early 1980s as an alternative to the traditional evaluation criteria of earnings per share, return on equity, or return on assets. The simple definition of EVA is "the profit that remains after deducting the cost of the capital invested to generate that profit."[45] In other words, a company creates value when it pays a return higher than the cost of the money it invests. EVA measures benefited senior executives by providing them with a clearer understanding of how shareholders and investors actually think and behave. Given the need to attract long-term investment capital, companies had to ensure that they were creating real economic wealth. EVA told their leaders at a glance how they were doing. At the same time, EVA metrics provided rank-and-file employees with a sharper sense of how the activities that engaged them affected the company's overall performance and meshed with shareholder expectations. In the 1980s and 1990s, many big industrials adopted EVA metrics for their management control systems and incentive systems—although they sometimes balanced these with nonfinancial measures (see below).

At about the same time, activity-based cost (ABC) accounting began to replace traditional cost accounting in the financial control systems of most manufacturing companies. Du Pont and General Motors had developed traditional cost accounting and control concepts in the 1920s. These were based on traditional hierarchical units:

in factories, costs were calculated by operation, then combined with costs of other operations into a department cost, then combined with other departments into larger cost aggregations, and eventually summed into a total manufacturing cost. TQM and other management techniques of the late 1980s began to challenge this approach to cost measurement. The focus of analysis shifted from individual operations aggregated into vertical units to horizontal activities or business processes that were complete in and of themselves. A manufacturing operation, for example, might be broken down into discrete activities such as set up, machining, receiving, packing, and engineering. ABC accounting would then determine the costs of each activity as well as the factors driving those costs. The result was a much more accurate assessment of the real cost of manufacturing and a much deeper understanding of ways to manage that cost.[46]

Human resource systems also changed in N-Form organizations. Performance appraisal and compensation, for example, shifted from an almost exclusive focus on individual achievement to tracking and rewarding teamwork and collaboration. Many companies adopted "360 degree" appraisals, which incorporated inputs from bosses, peers, subordinates, and even outsiders into individual evaluations. At the same time, incentive systems were modified to take account of team and group performance, although most also retained a significant element based on individual performance.

Another new set of systems and metrics reflected a burgeoning interest in organizational learning and the management of intangible assets. As their companies struggled to grow and competed for fractions of market share points, executives recognized that competitive advantage based on the traditional "hard" assets such as capital, technologies, and factories was fleeting. Rivals could readily copy or counteract such advantages. Intangible assets—such things as intellectual property, brand value, market dominance, experience, training, management best practices, proprietary databases, the knowledge and ideas resident in employees' heads, and the networks of communications that enabled all of this knowledge to be tapped, shared, used, and upgraded—appeared to comprise a more enduring and sustainable source of success.[47] Intangible assets could account for an extraordinarily high fraction of a company's total worth. In the early 1990s, for example, the market value of Microsoft Corporation was about 40 times greater than the book value of its assets and about 30 times greater than its annual revenues. Intangible assets—chiefly market dominance and control of software industry standards—accounted for the difference.

Much as management and control systems reshuffled after TQM, so too did they adapt to the knowledge-based enterprise. Information systems, for example, were no longer used primarily for purposes of control; rather they served to enable employees to apply their intelligence and enhance their personal productivity. Meanwhile, companies accelerated attempts to learn, typically through team-based exercises. Many companies commissioned teams to look outward for examples of management best practices as benchmarks for self-evaluation and learning. Xerox is widely credited with starting the practice, which began with its visits to Japan and its detailed study of manufacturing practices at Fuji-Xerox. Over time, Xerox teams benchmarked a diverse array of companies and processes, identifying, for example, the direct mail retailer L.L.Bean as a paragon of order fulfillment.[48]

In 1992, Harvard Business School professors Robert Kaplan and David Norton developed a new accounting concept that captured the changing dynamics and diverse measurements inside companies.[49] They proposed a "balanced scorecard" that would "maintain a balance between long-term and short-term objectives, financial and nonfinancial measures, lagging and leading indicators, and between internal and external perspectives." The basic scorecard included four components: the financial perspective, which tracked measures such as EVA, growth, and profitability; the customer perspective, which followed such measures as satisfaction and loyalty; an "internal business process view," which measured the efficiency and effectiveness of internal processes and activities; and "the learning and growth perspective," which tracked the ability to learn and capitalize on knowledge assets. The balanced scorecard gained increasing acceptance in large companies as a vehicle to help translate strategy into action. It was no longer a given that financial metrics would point the way. Rather, the balanced scorecard indicated that long-term financial success was predicated on treating employees and customers well and by expanding the capacity to learn. As such, the balanced scorecard provided a sharp contrast to the traditional control metrics of U-Form and M-Form organizations.

By the late 1980s, the internal control systems that had supported the U-Form and M-Form structures of the heyday of the American industrial corporation had changed in fundamental ways. As they reorganized around business processes and teamwork, the big industrials took advantage of new technologies and management concepts to modify their management systems. Such was the case at Xerox in 1992.

THE N-FORM AT XEROX

When Paul Allaire succeeded David Kearns as chairman and CEO of Xerox in 1990, he was not inclined to rest on the laurels the Leadership Through Quality initiative had won. Allaire recognized that the Japanese competitive threat constituted part one of a larger, continuing challenge. Part two was the rapid pace of digitization. Electro-optical and mechanical technologies lay at the heart of Xerox copiers, but new electronic technologies could—and would, sooner or later—render them obsolete. Electronic scanners could translate the information on a piece of paper into digital format, and, once digitized, this information could be used and managed in different ways: it could be reproduced on a laser printer; stored in a memory device; transmitted as a facsimile; or manipulated and enhanced into a different image. Although Xerox had developed significant capabilities in computers, electronics, and software at PARC and in a few other locations, these capabilities were not widespread in, or consistent across, the company.

Xerox responded strategically to the threat of digitization by attempting to reposition itself from a maker of photocopying equipment to a "document company." "By focusing on managing documents and using them more effectively," Allaire claimed, "Xerox can help our customers improve productivity."[50] Competing as a document company entailed two challenges: upgrading and extending its capabilities in electronics, and converting its knowledge of office systems and its capabilities in equipment service into a consulting practice in information and office management systems.

In 1992, Xerox supported its new strategy by abandoning its longstanding U-Form organization in favor of a new N-Form. The goal, said Allaire, was "to make this $17 billion company more entrepreneurial, more innovative, and more responsive to the marketplace. The new structure featured nine business units, each with its own income statement and balance sheet, focused on distinct markets such as small business and individuals, office document systems, and engineering systems. The horizontal dimensions of the new organization structure were most evident. Three layers of management disappeared. The corporate center retained an R&D function, including Xerox PARC, and featured a Customer Operations organization, which managed sales and service for a significant majority of the company's business units, and a Strategic Services organization, which provided support to the business units in areas such as purchasing and specialized manufacturing.

"In a sense," Allaire pointed out,

> we have turned the traditional vertically integrated company on its side. At one end is technology, and we have retained an integrated corporate research and technology organization. At the other end is the customer. We have organized our sales and service people into three geographic customer-operations divisions, so that we can keep a common face to the customer. Between these two poles are the new business divisions. Their purpose is to create some "suction" on technology and pull it into the marketplace.[51]

Teamwork and horizontal systems pervaded Xerox's N-Form. Each of the business units was founded on teams as building blocks—what Allaire called "microenterprise units" and "productive work communities" based around complete work processes or subprocesses. "Our ultimate goal," claimed Allaire, "is to organize the entire company into self-managed work teams. . . . I envision a time when this company will consist of many, many small groups of people who have the technical expertise and the business knowledge and the information tools they need to design their own work process and to improve and adapt that process continuously as business conditions change."[52]

Allaire began pushing decision rights down into the organization, declaring that Xerox would develop common components for equipment sold across the divisions and obliging the general managers to agree among themselves on the optimum designs for the company as a whole. Xerox supported the structural change with new systems, modifying the ways in which managers were selected, trained, and compensated. The business team leader became the new entry-level general management position in the company. Training and incentives were designed to facilitate and encourage collaboration and an ability to balance individual with team and corporate objectives. At the upper levels of management, up to 10 percent of compensation depended on the individual's success in fostering positive change in the company's culture.

THE IMPACT OF THE INTERNET

As Xerox was beginning to test its new strategy and structure, another seismic change rippled through the modern economy. The development of large-scale computer networks, especially the Internet, triggered still more profound changes in the operations and internal systems of the big industrials.[53] During the 1980s, some companies had developed private electronic data interchange (EDI) systems to connect in real time with their suppliers and customers. Such systems, for example, tied the cash registers of leading retailers such as Wal-Mart to the production and logistical systems of vendors such as Procter & Gamble. EDI enabled both partners to reduce their inventories, hasten the replenishment of stock, and reduce costs throughout the supply chain, all the while providing real-time insights into customer preferences and behavior.[54] EDI also wrought significant innovations in supply chain management in the auto industry. Chrysler could now engage its suppliers at every stage of the product development process by transferring design documents back and forth. This not only reduced the time taken to develop new models; it also slashed production costs by improving the manufacturability of the new models.[55]

In software, new "groupware" such as Lotus Notes enabled teams and workgroups to collaborate on projects by sharing databases and electronic documents. The advent of new object-oriented programming languages such as Java made it possible for different applications software packages to run on virtually all computer platforms. Coupled with new protocols (such as hypertext markup language—HTML) and network "browsers" featuring graphical user interfaces (such as Netscape Navigator and Microsoft Internet Explorer), the new software spawned easy-to-use intranets inside companies and stimulated the explosive growth of the Internet, via the World Wide Web, on the outside. The Internet, in turn, hastened new "business-to-business" (B2B) exchanges that delivered benefits well beyond the capability of the early EDI systems. Many companies, for example, centralized purchasing of raw materials online, thereby realizing benefits in reduced inventories, streamlined operations, and significant cost savings.

Inside companies, enterprise information systems (EIS) made it possible to gather and store information electronically and, via online analytical processing (OLAP), analyze, manipulate, and distribute it to decision makers in real time. As Bill Gates, chairman and cofounder of Microsoft, put it in his 1999 book, *Business @ the Speed of Thought,* a company could now operate with an entirely electronic, "digital nervous system" that linked its every thought and action:

> Basic operations such as finance and production, plus feedback from customers, are electronically accessible to a company's knowledge workers, who use digital tools to quickly adapt and respond. The immediate availability of accurate information changes the strategic thinking from a separate, stand-alone activity to an ongoing process integrated with regular business activities.[56]

The digital tools Gates referred to included an array of new systems for such activities as Business Information Collection (BIC), Business Planning and Simulation (BPS), Manufacturing Resources Planning (MRP), and Customer and Stakeholder Relationship Management (CRM and SRM). The rubric for these systems was a meta-system typically labeled Enterprise Resource Planning (ERP). Strictly speaking, ERP relied on relational and shared databases, which permitted "knowledge workers" throughout an organization to obtain real-time information about performance and make appropriate decisions and interventions. An elite set of vendors including SAP, Oracle, Baan, and Peoplesoft promoted ERP with notable success as a tool to guide information flows within a company, automate many routine administrative tasks, and promote collaboration and teamwork.[57]

ERP and other similar systems emerged in tandem with a growing interest in knowledge management (KM)—the cultivation of proprietary knowledge for strategic advantage. The same vendors, as well as a host of "information solutions" providers such as EDS, IBM, Accenture (Andersen Consulting), Price Waterhouse Coopers, and others developed burgeoning consulting practices based on advising companies about systems and tools to promote KM. New tools and techniques included software that took advantage of computer networks to generate, pool, and transfer useful knowledge to decision makers on a timely basis.[58]

The Internet and accompanying software and systems enabled companies to operate according to new "business models." Cisco Systems, which assembled and sold routers and other networking equipment, for example, fed on and fueled the demand for big computers, much as IBM did. But Cisco, working with the benefit of a clean sheet beginning, rapidly internalized the new systems paradigm. Indeed, Cisco seemed an extraordinary type of industrial corporation. Its equipment was technologically complex and had to be individually configured to its customers' specifications. In the late 1990s, Cisco moved this series of transactions onto the Internet. Customers placed their orders through the company's Web site. Meanwhile, on the upstream end, the company outsourced nearly all of its manufacturing; suppliers joined the process via the Web, bidding for contracts and posting quarterly quotes on the company's Web site, as well as joining in Cisco's design and development process there too.

Meanwhile, another young company with an unconventional business model made its mark in the market for personal computers. Dell Computer laid out its business much as Cisco did, staking out and occupying another hub on the emerging metanetwork of post-industrial enterprise. Like Cisco, Dell sold online, inviting retail customers to draw up custom sets of specs. Orders were then relayed directly to components suppliers, in the form of a continuous, real-time stream of data specifying what Dell needed—hard drives, motherboards, and so on—via the company's "extranet" (a proprietary network like an intranet but open to selected outsiders). And information tracking the assembly and delivery of computers, in turn, streamed into the Dell Web site so that customers could follow the progress of their orders as they made their way toward final delivery.

Older "brick-and-mortar" industrial companies, meanwhile, paid close and somewhat uneasy attention. As corporate data loosened and liquidized, and "supply chain management" systems grew more sophisticated, some industrials concluded that they no longer had to be vertically integrated to sustain a steady flow of supplies, raw materials, and component pieces.[59] Under pressure, some of them, including Xerox, eventually concluded that the new systems would allow them to unbundle many of their core business processes.

SYSTEMS MELTDOWN AT XEROX

During the mid-1990s, Xerox's new N-Form strategy, structure, and systems initially appeared to pay off, as the company reported solid earnings and defended its dominant position as a supplier of high-end equipment to corporate copying and document production centers. Xerox achieved some cost savings by abandoning unprofitable lines at the low end of the market and outsourcing management of its internal information technology systems to EDS. At the same time, Xerox sought to build its own outsourcing business and take over management of the document production processes and systems of its major customers.

But the mid-1990s also brought indications that all was not well at Xerox. For one thing, the company was late in embracing the digital revolution. At the low end of the market, the growing popularity and relative low cost of digital equipment combining the functions of fax, printer, and copier made deep inroads into Xerox's business. Although Xerox introduced its own combination machines, Canon, Hewlett-Packard, and Lexmark International surged ahead in this market.

Another problem stemmed from the growing popularity of color printing and copying, technologies in which Xerox lagged its major competitors. Still another problem was the rise of networking and the Internet. Relatively small and inexpensive equipment could be linked in ways that rivaled the capabilities of Xerox's high-end equipment and systems at much lower cost. At the same time, Canon and Germany's Heidelberg Druckmaster, which licensed digital imaging technology from Kodak, offered high-end machines that nearly matched Xerox's at significantly lower prices.

While Xerox contended with these external forces, it also faced a series of internal crises. Under its longstanding U-Form organization, the company had not developed senior executives with general management experience, and several of the new general managers after the 1992 reorganization struggled in their assignments. As a result, when the board looked for Allaire's successor, it ended up hiring an outsider. In 1997, Xerox recruited G. Richard Thoman, as president and chief operating officer. A former consultant and close associate of Louis Gerstner, who had taken over the top job at IBM in 1993, Thoman had rescued and stabilized IBM's personal computer division before becoming the company's chief financial officer. He arrived at Xerox at a difficult time, however. Just months before he came on board, the company announced lay-offs of 9,000 employees worldwide.

Thoman appeared to have the necessary background and skills to guide Xerox along the path to digitization. In September 1998 Xerox entered a strategic alliance with IBM, bundling Big Blue's networking software (Lotus and Domino) into its line of digital copiers and printers. "We're in a world which is drowning with documents," Thoman proclaimed by way of promotion. "What we're talking about today is putting together the best groupware in the world with the best set of document-management hardware." Programmed with Lotus and Domino capability, Xerox's line of digital copiers and printers stood ready to print out documents at any point in a company's LAN. And the process would work in reverse, too: documents scanned through Xerox machines could be converted into electronic files such as Lotus Notes e-mail, for digital distribution. "Xerox," declared Allaire, "is committed to a strategy that transforms its core business, completes the transition to digital and leads our industry in a new direction—rediscovering and reinventing the way people share what they know."[60]

Six months later, on schedule, Thoman succeeded Allaire as CEO. His tenure began in crisis and proceeded downhill from there. In January 1999, the company announced its second major reorganization in less than ten years, this one regrouping operations into four new divisions. The largest and most important group—Industry Solutions Operations—absorbed the company's direct-sales staff, breaking it up into industry-specific groups dedicated to particular kinds of clients (financial services, government, etc.). The move was more than a rearrangement. Xerox was redeploying and in fact recasting its sales force as information systems consultants, versed in the specific dynamics of clients' industries.[61]

For the sales force the transformation was jarring. Performance and bonus structures were overhauled, personnel crowded into retraining sessions, longstanding client relationships were severed. Many sales reps, struggling to learn new industries and taking compensation hits as sales targets grew harder to hit, left Xerox in frustration. More than a quarter of the U.S. salesforce quit in 1999, some to join Xerox's competitors.[62]

Other separate, simultaneous moves made the sense of dislocation even more disorienting. For critically, as things would turn out, at right around the same time as it reorganized its sales force the company consolidated its billing systems. It was the kind of move many corporations were making, folding disparate legacy systems into new configurations, drawing together the various streams of information that coursed through the far reaches and intricate branches of corporate operations, and taking advantage of the new efficiencies to streamline back-office operations. In Xerox's case, the pressure to reduce costs was growing particularly urgent. Thoman pressed to cut the company's general and administrative expenses in half. "I always worry that we're not doing things fast enough," he revealed in an interview. "There has to be a great sense of urgency."[63] In this frame of mind, the company compressed its 36 U.S. administrative offices into three new regional centers, announcing another 5,200 layoffs in the process.

Few outsiders sensed it at the time, but the elements of a catastrophe were building at Xerox. The first ominous signs surfaced when the company began issuing earnings warnings in mid-1999. The numbers continued to slide through the rest of the year; by mid-December Xerox forecast an earnings shortfall of 40 percent. The company blamed Y2K fears (the potential computer glitch resulting from the design of some antiquated software that incorporated a two-digit annual calendar that had to be modified for use after the year 1999), competitive pricing pressures, and deteriorating conditions in global markets. In early 2000, however, word of major internal systems snarls began to leak. Billing snafus were erupting everywhere, paralyzing company finances and frustrating customers, and Xerox, in the throes of reorganization, struggled to smooth out the problem.[64]

The collapse of the company's billing systems created horrible confusion and intense customer disenchantment. Clients squinted at invoices that were indecipherable and riddled with wrong charges. "Every invoice has to be checked—every single one," complained one copy chain executive overseeing over 1,000 stores; his franchises were receiving charges for machines they had traded in years ago. Xerox salespeople waded into the breach, spending inordinate time and energy—typically half and as much as 80 percent of their time, by some accounts—trying to sort out problems. But they were already reeling from reorganization, most were dealing with entirely new customers, and they were growing demoralized. "A customer would be told the price, and then, when our bill came, it would be something completely different," one rep revealed shortly after leaving the company. Not surprisingly, new sales suffered badly. Even more seriously, from a short-term cash-flow perspective, many customers withheld payment altogether until charges were unscrambled. Receivables began rising sharply, by 15 percent over the first half of 2000, to $3 billion.[65]

From there things spiraled downwards precipitously. Thoman was ousted in May 2000, replaced by Allaire, who promoted Anne Mulcahy as president and chief operating officer. Mulcahy had spent much of her Xerox career in staff positions, serving as vice president of human resources and as chief staff officer before a 1999 appointment as president of General Markets Operations, a unit that created and sold products for reseller, dealer, and retail channels. Meanwhile, as word of Xerox's troubles spread, the costs of arranging short-term financing mounted. By the end of 2000, Xerox's credit rating had fallen to junk bond levels, and the stock was trading below $4 a share—down from a high near $63 a year-and-a-half earlier. Rumors circulated that the company might be sold or forced into bankruptcy. In these circumstances, management took drastic measures, arranging to sell Xerox's operations in China and half of its 50 percent interest in Fuji Xerox.

In August 2001, Mulcahy succeeded Allaire as CEO and as chairman and CEO five months later. During 2000 and 2001 Xerox sold off $2.2 billion in assets, slashed more than $1 billion in costs through downsizing and restructuring, and transitioned most of its equipment financing business to GE Capital. The company abandoned the small office/home office market that it had served primarily through retail channels. It moved out of its headquarters building in Stamford, Connecticut, into a smaller space nearby. It announced that Xerox PARC would be reorganized as an independent subsidiary, a move designed to attract alliances and outside investment in the R&D unit. Xerox also arranged with a Singapore-based company to take over some Xerox production facilities and manufacture certain products and components.

By the end of 2001, Xerox had stemmed its losses and escaped from its short-term liquidity crisis. As its stock inched above $10 per share, Mulcahy was "cautiously optimistic" that Xerox would resume profitable growth in 2002. The company expected to capitalize on growing demand for "solutions and services"—a catchall covering the office management, document management, and information management needs of big corporate customers. Xerox's solutions portfolio included customized services such as one-to-one marketing, electronic bill and statement presentment, and print-on-demand. Its services portfolio featured business process consulting, systems support, network integration, and other electronic commerce-related services.[66]

The Xerox of the early twenty-first century had evolved into a vastly different sort of company than it had been during its heyday a quarter of a century before. It had an altogether different strategy and new structure, and it featured numerous new systems. The company operated less as a traditional vertical hierarchy than as a collection of horizontal activities and processes, some of which it outsourced to partners, and nearly all of which were managed by teams. Xerox was clearly moving in the direction of networked companies like Cisco and Dell, pulling apart its functions and operations and putting some of them onto networks.

In making these moves, Xerox typified many other large American industrials, which used information networks to reorganize their operations and redefine task assignments. By 2000, all of the *Fortune* 100 companies had adopted ERP systems and were using corporate intranets and the Internet to manage their operations as collections of horizontal activities and processes rather than as units under vertical control. These companies adopted network technologies rapidly. It took just three years for the entire population to embrace these technologies, in contrast to 14 years for TQM and six years for reengineering.[67]

Like the new strategies and structures that developed along side of them, the management systems of the large, late-twentieth century industrial corporation differed profoundly from those of the heyday of the M-Form. In the N-Form corporation, vital business information no longer resided exclusively at the center, and vital business intelligence was unbound and widely dispersed across the organization. New information technology combined and interacted with new management techniques and systems such as TQM, reingineering, and ERP to revolutionize the way companies functioned in daily life. The result was much more efficient and productive operations, tighter coordination and increasing exchange within and across organizational boundaries, and the constant reshuffling of corporate structures, functions, and processes. The rate of change proved it faster than traditional vertical control systems could accommodate. Accounting systems, in particular, largely failed to keep pace, and companies are rushing to develop new metrics to reflect new ways of making and implementing decisions.[68] Nonetheless, the advantages of the new techniques and systems are overwhelming. In most companies, new information networks and ways of working are proliferating spontaneously, organically, and unpredictably, a pattern that seems destined to persist as the N-Form corporation continues its rapid evolution.

CHAPTER 6

GOVERNANCE: THE TIGHTER LEASH

In the end, the deal went down cleanly and quietly. A conversation on a golf course, some figures jotted on a scrap of paper, a handshake a few days later, and it was done: Andrew Carnegie, the world's largest steel maker, had sold out to J. P. Morgan, the world's preeminent financier. It was a discrete transaction, handled in a disarmingly casual kind of way. Nevertheless it was epochal, marking the beginning of a new century and signifying the arrival of a new era of business. With Carnegie's operations in hand, Morgan promptly forged U.S. Steel, an enormous agglomeration of 41 mines and 213 steel mills, furnaces, coke ovens, railroads, and steamship lines. Along with Carnegie Steel, the new corporation consolidated American Tin Plate, American Steel Hoop, American Sheet Steel, American Bridge, American Steel and Wire, National Tube, National Steel, and Shelby Steel Tube. Together, they formed the world's first billion dollar corporation.

THE STEEL COMPANY AND THE SILVER GIRDLE

Capitalizing such a colossal venture was no small matter in 1901, when Morgan wrapped up the deal and prepared to take U.S. Steel public. The financial market for industrial stocks was still fledgling. Nothing on this scale, in fact, had ever been put in play. "I confess," admitted one Wall Street veteran, "it is enough to take one's breath away." Morgan's imprimatur would draw investors, however, and he knew how to put this kind of thing together. The man known as "Jupiter" collected a syndicate of 300 underwriters and, to buoy the market over the first few days, appointed agents to simultaneously buy and sell shares. With this backing U.S. Steel launched on the Big Board in the Spring of 1901, a package of $550 million in controvertible preferred stock, $550 million in common stock, and $304 million in 5 percent gold bonds. And it floated: the common shares opened at $38 and quickly rose to $55.[1]

It was a new kind of business and a new kind of investment, and contemporaries strained to grasp the vastness of scale, the weight of capital, that had amassed in the enterprise. "No one can conceive how much this great capitalization, $1,404,000,000 is," pronounced Michigan law professor Horace Wilgus, after studying the new creature's financial structure and legal status; "it is only by making comparisons that we can realize anything about it." Investors had lodged one-sixty-seventh of the total wealth of the United States in 1900 in U.S. Steel, Wilgus calculated, a sum amounting to fully two-thirds of the value of all the money then in circulation in the country. Those figures were mind-boggling enough, but then the professor hit upon an even more arresting image: cashed out in the form of silver dollars "fastened edge to edge," the capital comprising U.S. Steel would fashion "a silver girdle around mother earth," tied off with "a double-bow knot, each bow being one thousand miles long, with streamers of over one thousand five hundred miles each."[2]

What this silver girdle was binding together were the thousands of investors who now came into legal possession of U.S. Steel and the body of managers who were actually going to run the business. The arrangement enabled the assembly of a business of immense bulk and power. But it contained at its core a latent tension, an ambiguous if not exactly uneasy set of understandings about authority, control and responsibility. The steelmen who were going to run U.S. Steel would not own "their" company. They would be working on behalf of a widely scattered, otherwise miscellaneous mass of investors. In such an institutional situation, distinct interests, distinct parties, had to be coordinated and brought into alignment. A steel company had to be fitted into a silver girdle. New mechanisms of corporate governance, in short, had to be installed. Thus Morgan and his staff constructed an elaborate apparatus to mediate between the new company's operators and its equity holders. The financiers set up an annually elected board of directors, vested it with broad fiduciary powers and responsibilities, and at the same time removed the shareholders as a body from otherwise governing the corporation's affairs.

It was this basis of organization that established itself as the dominant mechanism of corporate governance in industrial America. Investor-ownership, operational management by salaried executives, and sitting between the two a board of directors—this became the arrangement of corporate ownership, operation, and oversight for the next century, at U.S. Steel and indeed across the industrial landscape.

It did not always prove to be a stable system. Over the next one hundred years, the balance of power shifted back and forth, sometimes subtlely, sometimes sharply, between investors and managers. A complicated interplay of interests was at work here, a continual process of coordination, contest, and recalibration. By the middle of the twentieth century, however, an equilibrium of sorts was reached as managers consolidated their control over the corporation. They enjoyed almost complete autonomy in making the key strategic and resource allocation decisions that affected the fortunes of the enterprises they managed. Even though in most instances they owned negligible amounts of their company's stock, managers acted as if they were owners. Indeed, in managerial circles it became commonplace to assert that it was the CEO's responsibility to protect the firm's long-term interests from the short-term interests of Wall Street investors.

To ensure that they had the latitude to direct the affairs of their companies as they saw fit, managers took control of the process of appointing the members of their boards. Typically, they chose other CEOs or close associates who could be relied upon to support them. It became an unspoken norm that board members did not openly challenge the CEO and deferred to his judgment. Given the increasingly interlocked nature of corporate boards (an elite inner circle of people sat on multiple boards), it was easy to enforce this norm. The implicit contract was simple—"You support me on my board and I'll support you on yours." This is not to say that CEOs failed to consult board members on many matters. They often did, but these conversations typically took place in private rather than in the boardroom. Board meetings were largely routine affairs, with the CEO tightly controlling and orchestrating the agenda and discussion.[3]

In this environment, it was not surprising that board members rarely acted to fulfill their central responsibility—the firing and hiring of CEOs. It was almost unheard of for a CEO to be fired and more often than not, the board approved the CEO's hand-picked choice as successor.

For the most part, this inner circle of senior managers remained firmly in control of the governance of large industrial corporations through the end of the 1970s. Then, over the past two decades of the century, the balance of power shifted. As the large American industrial corporation struggled with the necessities of decline, the inherent tension between managers and investors bubbled to the surface. Eventually, investors reasserted control. The rise of pension funds and other types of institutional investors reconcentrated the ownership of stock in the hands of increasingly powerful money managers. Unlike individual investors who had only one option to deal with the entrenched power of managers—to exit by selling their shares—these new money managers could not exit. They could, however, exercise voice.[4]

And exercise their voice they did, first by supporting raiders who promised to take over underperforming companies and turn them around. Then the institutional investors became even more direct, intervening in the appointment of directors who helped them oust recalcitrant CEOs. Finally, they even joined forces with each other through associations like the Council of Institutional Investors to take on management in proxy fights.

Of course, managers fought back through a variety of devices like "poison pills" and "golden parachutes" to protect their companies' independence and themselves.[5] But in the end, they had to cede some control to investors. Though they remained powerful actors in the American system of corporate governance, by the end of the century they recognized the necessity of coming to terms with their shareholders.

The contest over corporate governance flared up in one form or another in nearly all of the large industrials. It erupted dramatically, for example, in U.S. Steel, the very company that had so prominently woven the original "silver girdle." As U.S. Steel became USX in the 1980s, a succession of dangerous, high-stake struggles broke out for control over the strategy and the very identity of the company. First the company faced and fended off a corporate raid. Then management found itself in a close proxy fight with its largest shareholder, each side trying to pull powerful institutional investors to their side. They were struggling not just for billions, not just for a company, but for a legacy of corporate governance that remained deeply ambiguous.

To fully understand the struggle over USX in the 1980s, though, one needs to set it in the context created back in 1901, when Morgan, his financier-allies, the investors they attracted, and the steelmen they enlisted all coalesced into U.S. Steel. And to grasp the significance of that development, in turn, one has to delve further back, into the history of the new corporation's most important component—Carnegie Steel.

CARNEGIE STEEL: THE PARADIGM OF THE INDUSTRIALIST

Like most nineteenth century industrial entrepreneurs, Carnegie financed his ventures by organizing "corporations" that were in fact not corporations in the modern sense (though they were incorporated), but more precisely partnerships, collecting a few prominent investor-businessmen, perhaps a dozen or so—in effect, accumulating enough reputation to be able to issue bonds and thereby capitalize the venture. The bonds were theoretically convertible into stock. But before 1900 or so, investors tended to prefer bonds, which were considered more reliable than industrial stocks, and Carnegie for his part consistently resisted conversion. When bond holders did try to convert their securities, Carnegie generally offered to buy them out with cash, and at the same time threatened to dispute conversion in court. Meanwhile, as his steel mills prospered, Carnegie worked determinedly to buy his investors out, tighten up his circle of partners, and thus consolidate equity. So, for example, in 1873 he wrote to one partner: "I want to buy Mr. Coleman out & hope to do so.—Kloman will have to give up his interest. These divided between Tom, Harry You and I would make the Concern a close Corporation[.] Mr. Scotts loan is no doubt in some Bankers hands & may also be dealt with after a little then we are right & have only to watch the Bond conversions which will not be great as our foreign friends will want to stick to the sure thing I think."[6]

Carnegie's sense of governance, in short, amounted to securing ownership in the hands of his firm's managers. Since Carnegie himself held or soon managed to acquire majority shares in his most important enterprises, he served as both the weightiest investor and the most important manager. Day-to-day operation, however, he delegated to a series of men he called his "young geniuses"—managers Carnegie culled from the middle ranks, elevated to senior executive positions, and conferred with minor shares of equity. "Every year should be marked by the promotion of one or more of our young men," he advised his partner Henry Frick in 1896. "It is a very good plan to have all your heads of departments interested. . . . We cannot have too many of the right sort interested in profits."[7] Thus the investor-partners owning Carnegie Steel and the managers running it were one and the same. Those partners falling from Carnegie's favor, moreover, were not permitted to hold onto their interests. When an individual quit, or crossed or otherwise disappointed Carnegie (something that happened fairly frequently), the senior partner in one stroke fired him as manager and stripped him of his partnership, forcing him to sell back his equity at book value.[8]

Carnegie, in sum, arranged his financing so as to yield as little control as possible for as short a time as possible. Throughout his industrial career, he remained distinctly suspicious of the concept of corporate ownership. "Individual management will show its superiority in the future as in the past," he insisted to A.I. Findley, editor of *Iron Age,* as large industrial firms began to go public in the late-1890s. "When a concern becomes the football of Wall Street, it is owned by nobody or anybody, nobody knows who—a waif that will wreck at the first storm. . . . [W] here stock is held by a great number, what is anybody's business is nobody's business."[9]

Ironically, though, Carnegie himself was driving his business beyond his bromides. Even as he uttered the conviction, Carnegie Steel was growing too fast, too big, too broad to be contained within the bounds of what he called "individual management." In 1892, Carnegie and his principal partner, Henry Frick, drew their various businesses into tight formation as the Carnegie Steel Company Limited, capitalized at $25 million (with Carnegie holding 58.5 percent). Over the next half dozen years, the return on that capital climbed over 50 percent, then over 100 percent, then over 200 percent. By 1899, Carnegie and Frick were feuding, the firm was preparing to expand into finished steel (tubes, piping, wires, etc.), and Carnegie was thinking seriously about pulling out. He wanted to sell off his interest to his partners, but they preferred selling to a third party. Few buyers, however, were in a position to absorb such a massive enterprise. John D. Rockefeller's Standard Oil group was uninterested, and the only other viable potential buyer, Morgan's Federal Steel Syndicate, was not in a position to make the purchase. Carnegie quashed an effort to assemble a syndicate to put the business on the stock market—a project rank, in his nostrils, with the smell of "speculation." Then in 1900, following a break with Frick, the industrialist reorganized his business, reset the capitalization at $324 million and laid plans for a new round of expansion.

He was reaching a major decision point. Moving into finished steel would mean taking on Federal Steel along with a host of other powerful competitors and, Carnegie figured, also building up a new trunk railroad system to compete with the Pennsylvania. Either venture by itself was ambitious. In tandem, the prospect was downright daunting. Meanwhile, Morgan and his steel associates were alarmed at the threat of competing directly against Carnegie. A monstrous battle loomed, one that would require all sides to mobilize and put vast resources at risk. Carnegie gave every appearance of earnest preparation. Still, when one of his partners, Charles Schwab, quietly brokered a deal with Morgan that would combine the various steel businesses into a single, publicly owned corporation, Carnegie agreed to sell out. Thus Carnegie Steel, the firm founded on the principle proprietary management, gave way to U.S. Steel, a firm governed by a very different set of mechanisms and principles.

U.S. STEEL: THE ARTICULATION OF "THE CORPORATION"

In organizing U.S. Steel and making arrangements for governance of the new enterprise via a board of directors, Morgan applied structures he and his staff had originally developed a dozen years before when they had reorganized the country's sprawling, brawling railroads. In the vocabulary of the period, Morgan "Morganized" U.S. Steel. Specifically, he imposed over the managers of the new corporation a board of twenty-four directors, elected by the shareholders in staggered, three-year terms. An Executive Committee and a Finance Committee, elected by the directors from their own ranks, took up responsibility for regular administrative oversight. As he had in the railroad deals, Morgan himself took a seat on the board and packed it and its committees with close business associates. Thus the financier surrounded the company's industrial managers with powerful instruments of fiduciary supervision. At the same time, he set clear boundaries around the company's investors. Indeed, once they had elected the directors, the shareholders—the people who in fact owned U.S. Steel—were largely removed from effective decision making. They were not even given the right to inspect the company's books.[10]

As the company went into operation, however, it evolved less formal but no less formative balances that implicitly recognized and strengthened the position of its shareholders. Actually, U.S. Steel offered its shareholders what was, for its time (in the days before SEC regulation), an impressive degree of transparency. Elbert Gary, the company's chairman, was closely attuned to the political delicacy of running a concern like U.S. Steel in an era of antitrust suspicion, and he made it clear during his tenure that the enterprise was not in the business of enriching its powerful inside financiers at the expense of its broader community of shareholders. Gary took questions from shareholders at the company's annual meetings. He issued the company's quarterly statements to the directors and the press simultaneously, at 3 P.M., just as the Stock Exchange closed (shutting off lucrative possibilities for insider trading). And the annual reports the company issued were, in the characterization of *Fortune* (1936), "models of complete, detailed information, the admiration of accountants."[11]

So notions of governance coalesced at U.S. Steel. Practices became habits, over the first decades of operation; habits gradually cohered as expectations, and thus experiments in corporate control reinforced themselves. In the natural course of business Morgan's personal stature receded, while at the same time U.S. Steel grew more solid as a concern, a concept, a covenant. What emerged, in effect, was a certain dynamic of governance—a common understanding of boundaries, of balances, of business. Call it a proper sense of the proprietary, one that survived Gary's death in 1927 and the succession of Myron Taylor as chairman and established U.S. Steel as simply "the Corporation" in the American business imagination through midcentury.[12]

While the shareholders strengthened their purchase on their company, the management of U.S. Steel solidified prerogatives of their own. Particularly during the 1930s, as the corporation reorganized under Taylor's leadership and developed a strong headquarters apparatus, its executives effectively asserted control over the enterprise's operation. By the mid-1930s, a tacit working understanding was governing relations between investors, the board, and management. "The control of the corporation is theoretically in the hands of its owners, the stockholders," *Fortune* magazine recognized, but the shareholders were "too scattered to have the interest, the knowledge, or the ability to exercise any effective control." The board of directors, still dominated by "Morgan men," supposedly lent those interests a more focused voice in business affairs. And for good measure, *Fortune*'s profile continued, the company's chairman, Myron Taylor, was "primarily a financial man." Consequently, "If there ever was a case of banker influence on management, for good or evil, the Steel Corporation is it." Still, *Fortune* conceded that "directors mean very much less in a modern corporation than, legally and popularly, they are supposed to mean." Practically speaking, management had secured a large measure of control over U.S. Steel: "The Board of Directors controls the management," but "the management, which has had a majority of proxies at every stockholders' meeting since 1901, in effect appoints the Directors." The result amounted to what *Fortune* aptly characterized as a "charmed circle of self-perpetuation." Ultimately, "as in most corporations, the management runs the company as seems best to it."[13]

THE EMERGENCE OF MANAGERIAL CONTROL

Governance at U.S. Steel thus proved complicated and somewhat ambiguous, much as Andrew Carnegie had warned it would. But it grew firmer over time. By midcentury the balance of governance was tilting decidedly in favor of management within "the Corporation," and indeed throughout industry. U.S. Steel's corporate executives, like their counterparts in other major industrial firms, became accustomed to running their company as they saw fit. What business historian Alfred

Chandler has characterized as the "Visible Hand" of professional management gradually emerged as the dominant force in corporate governance.[14]

Various factors strengthened the grip of the visible hand. Evolutions in both strategy and structure reinforced managerial authority, making the industrial corporation a dauntingly complicated enterprise to run and, in effect, claiming what had been a market function—the allocation of capital—for corporate management. Running multidivisional, multidimensional businesses became an increasingly demanding responsibility, requiring sophisticated skills and talents. Eventually owners of capital were forced to rely on the specific knowledge of professional managers at both the top and middle layers of the corporation. Management in the hands of entrepreneurs like Carnegie had been an intuitive art. His corporate successors made it a profession, buttressed by university education and training in dedicated management programs.[15]

The growing scale of enterprise also bolstered management's hand. Businesses like U.S. Steel required capitalization on a massive scale, across a vast field of owners. Ownership of capital, under the circumstances, was necessarily widely dispersed. Particularly in the context of the financial markets of the mid-twentieth century, no individual or institutional holder was in a position to amass enough of a stake in a concern like U.S. Steel to exert any real influence over corporate strategy. In theory shareholders exercised control through boards of directors; in practice their only real option, if dissatisfied with management, was exit via divestment.[16] Corporate boards, meanwhile, became distinctly cozy affairs, made up more and more by insiders or outsiders who were themselves managers of other large corporations, steeped in the assumptions of the visible hand.[17]

Finally, postwar prosperity within a comfortably stable pattern of oligopolistic domestic competition further reinforced managerial autonomy. By and large, investors had little incentive between 1945 and 1970 to tinker with what seemed after all to be smoothly running machinery. Growth and long runs of profitability vindicated managers' implicit claims of professional expertise. Diversification, and at the extreme end conglomeration, signaled the market's willingness to leave things in visible hands, at least while business was humming nicely along. By 1963, according to a study of the 200 largest industrial firms, fully 85 percent were management-controlled, up from 40 percent in 1929 and 20 percent at the turn of the century.[18]

None of which is to say that the latent tensions within this arrangement of corporate governance had been resolved. As early as 1932, observers were warning that the separation of ownership and control had the potential to create problems. Principals, the owners of capital, needed the specific expertise that managers possessed—that much was inescapably clear. But owners had no effective way of ensuring that their assets would necessarily be employed in ways that would earn maximum returns. It was simply impossible to write complete contracts that would bind managers to proper behavior. Principals had little choice but to assign managers broad discretion over how to spend the capital they turned over.[19] It was a relationship that worked smoothly in an atmosphere of industrial growth, but not an entirely easy one, at bottom. Nevertheless, at U.S. Steel as at most other large industrial corporations, the silver girdle that had originally bound managers loosened considerably by the 1970s, as the company slid by degrees into crisis.

U.S. STEEL, 1973–1987: CRISIS AND CONTEST

Steel imports to the United States began to climb rapidly in the late 1960s, driven by Japanese and European firms employing state-of-the-art technologies and highly efficient production regimens. Like other American steelmakers, U.S. Steel proved poorly equipped to compete. Its mills by this point were running on old and inefficient technologies, its production costs were heavy, its management was bureaucratically bloated, and the company was trying to run far more plant than it could profitably employ. Executives blamed foreign "dumping" for their problems, and environmental regulation, and the energy crisis, and the high price of American organized labor. Meanwhile the company's performance declined year by year, until eventually the need for retrenchment became undeniable. By 1979, the magnitude of the crisis was dawning on the company, and particularly on its board of directors as it weighed candidates to replace retiring CEO Edgar Speer. The time had come, the board decided, for resolute, even ruthless measures at U.S. Steel.

To carry out these measures the board appointed a man from within the company's senior executive circle. (No one yet imagined the situation was so grave as to require outside leadership.) Still, the directors did make a pointed choice. "We wanted something new and different," one of the directors later recalled. "Someone who was willing to take tough actions."[20] They chose David Roderick. He had never managed a steel mill; the new CEO came from the financial side, not the production side of the company. But Roderick was steely-eyed, if not a steelman. A former boxer and U.S. Marine, he held a decidedly unsentimental view of the company over which he was assuming control. He was ready to downsize, ready to dismantle, ready to take the "tough actions" the board expected.[21]

He would be working under pressure, however, and the pressure would increase steadily over Roderick's 10-year tenure, as the shareholders of U.S. Steel grew more impatient with the company's performance. The men who had been running "the Corporation" were awakening to the need for radical restructuring. Now they had to work fast and hard, first to make the changes that would shore up the company's strategic position and then, as the situation continued to deteriorate, to keep control over the process of change.

Roderick began forcefully. Within months of taking over U.S. Steel, he shuttered over a dozen mills, scrapped plans to build a new $4 billion integrated mill on Lake

Erie (a pet project of Speer's), and put everyone who remained on notice that more cuts were coming. He brought in senior managers from outside the company, including Thomas Graham in 1983 from LTV Corporation, who in rapid order replaced most of the company's mill managers, slashed headquarters staff, and redirected capital expenditures to a handful of targeted mills, thereby signaling that the corporation was going to let its less viable mills wind down. Over the first five years of Roderick's administration, U.S. Steel reduced its raw steel capacity from 38 million to 26.2 million tons, sliced total employment nearly in half, from 166,800 to 88,753, and cut 53 percent of its salaried workforce.[22]

Sharp downsizing represented one element of Roderick's master plan for recovery. Strategic redirection represented another. As he shut down steel capacity, Roderick informed his shareholders it had become "essential to direct available funds where they will provide the greatest return." Over the last decade, the new CEO added bluntly in his first annual report in 1979, "U.S. Steel's nonsteel businesses have been profitable and virtually self-sufficient in terms of cash flow. The steel business has not."[23] Over the following year he sold off a string of assets—the Universal Atlas Cement Division, some real estate, coal properties—in preparation to make substantial non-steel acquisitions. Much like their counterparts at Dow, Union Carbide, and Monsanto during the same period, the managers of U.S. Steel were preparing to diversify. Or, as Roderick put it in the next year's letter to shareholders, the company was "converting underutilized assets into cash for more profitable redeployment."[24]

Talk of "asset redeployment" figured heavily in executive communiqués from U.S. Steel headquarters during the early 1980s. The terminology was telling. It indicated that Roderick recognized the need to downsize steelmaking operations. But it also revealed that he was not contemplating shrinking U.S. Steel as an industrial entity. Faced with market contraction, Roderick never contemplated (as William Anders would in an analogous situation at General Dynamics 10 eventful years later) transferring assets back to shareholders. No, as Roderick saw matters, the role of U.S. Steel's corporate managers under the circumstances was to shift assets into other, more profitable businesses.

He soon made his play, and he made it a big one. Late in 1981, as the company struggled through a sharp national recession and particularly bleak conditions within the steel industry, Roderick got the kind of opportunity he had been looking for when Mobil tried to acquire Marathon Oil in a hostile takeover. Offering itself as a white knight, U.S. Steel intervened in the contest and bought the besieged energy firm for $6 billion. The move deeply and dramatically realigned the strategic makeup of "the Corporation." In a single stroke, the managers of U.S. Steel had transformed their company into something much more complicated than a steel company. Steel, in fact, went from 80 percent of the corporation's revenues to something like one-third. Roderick touted the acquisition as both "an energy hedge for our energy-dependent steel business" and a way to even out cyclical performance. "Today," he assured shareholders in 1982, "we are a broader based company with more opportunity for growth and profitability, and we are less vulnerable to a downturn in any one of our business segments."[25]

Actually, the upshot from the Marathon purchase was harder, for awhile, to gauge. At considerable expense, management had added a new business, new assets, and new liabilities. Some of those liabilities were immediate and financial; the firm borrowed heavily to fund the acquisition. Others were less tangible. Analysts on Wall Street, for their part, regarded the move warily. "They're making an immense bet that the oil business is going to be better than the steel business," observed Bruce Lazier, of Paine Webber Mitchell Hutchins. "In fact they're betting the whole ranch with their future financial stability at stake."[26] Roderick had acquired an oil company, as it turned out, just as oil prices peaked and began to decline. Marathon performed fairly well, over the next few years, but not spectacularly. Enough to offset continued woes in the steel sector, but beyond that barely enough to pay off the financing costs the deal had imposed on U.S. Steel.

Meanwhile, on the stock market, the company's fortunes slid backwards. By early 1984, shares of U.S. Steel had fallen to around 30, a figure that put the company's total market value at just over $4 billion—scarcely two-thirds of what it had paid to acquire Marathon two years before. And Marathon was property-rich with readily disposable assets, including a 49 percent stake in the Yates oil fields of West Texas and substantial coal, timberland, and real estate holdings. In other words, U.S. Steel in pieces was starting to look a good deal more valuable than U.S. Steel intact. That was a dangerous perception, in the context of the mid-1980s. For new forces were by then impinging on corporate America, on both management and the financial market that sustained it. Corporate raiders were launching increasingly audacious hostile takeover attempts, making tender offers that were unseating increasingly large and well-established companies. Names like Carl Icahn and T. Boone Pickens were stalking the industrials, eyeing balance sheets like U.S. Steel's.

From the vantage of corporate headquarters at U.S. Steel, now tending a major oil company as well as the steel business, Pickens represented a particularly unsettling specter. He had started his career in 1969, working on a small scale through Mesa Petroleum Company, taking over a series of undervalued lower-tier oil companies. From there, he vaulted into more prominent fields. In 1982, he amassed leading stakes in Cities Service and General American Oil of Texas. Two years later, he lodged tender offers for Gulf and Unocal. Most of these bids fell short of securing outright control over their targets. But they nevertheless made money and a reputation for Pickens, who generally managed to sell off his holdings at healthy profits as he withdrew. And they left survivors seriously destabilized. Cities Service ended up merging with Occidental in the wake of Pickens' campaign. Gulf fell to Chevron.[27]

The suggestion that a company as large and well-established as U.S. Steel might be vulnerable to this kind of financial turbulence would have struck earlier generations of management as preposterous. But by 1984, the threat had grown substantial. Pickens was roiling corporations nearly as large, almost as well-established. And those companies he did manage to acquire he then restructured radically, spinning off domestic oil and gas reserves as royalty trusts and thereby diverting what corporate managers considered as the lifeblood of their companies directly into investors' hands.

Strictly speaking, the dynamics driving Pickens were specific and local to the oil industry. Companies like Cities Service, Gulf, and Unocal had grown vulnerable, Pickens realized, because they were draining their oil and gas reserves faster than they were replacing them. They were burning their way through their foundation assets, in other words, and not putting the proceeds to particularly profitable use. Pickens' alternative proposal, the royalty trust concept, in effect rechanneled the proceeds of the oil drain from the corporations to the investors who owned them. It was a form of financial insurgency, in other words, custom-designed for oil companies. It was also, however, a proposal that revealed deep shifts in market assumptions about industrial equity—part of a general trend, in fact, that was transforming the dynamics of capital markets. Pickens' rise signaled seriously diminished market confidence in the ability of companies like Gulf to work their way out of their troubles. Large industrial corporations were losing their aura of mastery, first individually, but over time collectively. Gradually, inexorably, they came to resemble the oil companies Pickens was targeting—burning their way through economic resources, failing to renew the wealth they consumed. By the middle of the 1980s, they seemed to be not just losing money, but depleting value.

The perception fulfilled its own prophecy as it took hold and tightened, and as it did so the financial turbulence Pickens embodied spread beyond the oil patch. Some of the economy's largest conglomerates began toppling, bought up in highly leveraged transactions by previously obscure figures, then taken apart and sold piecemeal. Carl Icahn, for one, put this scheme to work in 1984 when he bought out ACF Industries, then sold off its oil and gas exploration operations, oil field service equipment, industrial plastics, and auto parts businesses. By the time Icahn was done with ACF, only the company's railroad car manufacturing and leasing unit remained. To run the surviving business, Icahn cut deeply into management, trimming ACF down to a lean, efficient operation. The deal netted him a substantial profit and put a healthy income stream at his disposal—assets he promptly leveraged for a new round of bigger takeovers.[28]

The fact that U.S. Steel was trading far below its bust-up value (not to mention the fact that financial analysts were running numbers on what that bust-up value might be) certainly made the firm vulnerable to the likes of Pickens and Icahn. Now, for good measure, it was sitting on rich oil reserves. On the other side of the balance sheet, though, the heavy debt the company had taken on in order to acquire Marathon weighed against a hostile tender offer. Any raider trying to acquire U.S. Steel would have to swallow the company's $8 billion in debt, $4 billion of which represented the Marathon purchase. Nevertheless, Roderick and his fellow senior managers decided it would be "prudent" to defend against the possibility. In March 1984, management prepared a proxy statement asking shareholders to ratify several antitakeover measures, including staggered board elections (preventing an insurgent from sweeping in a new board on a single slate) and a requirement that any takeover earn a two-thirds vote from the shareholders.[29]

These measures and the company's debt notwithstanding, rumors of possible takeover attempts continued to hover over U.S. Steel through the mid-1980s. In 1985, the *Wall Street Journal* reported that the average steel stock was trading at 73 percent of its book value, the lowest rate among the major industries, and that U.S. Steel in particular was trading at a market value substantially below what the company had paid to acquire Marathon just a few years before. By at least one investment banker's calculations, the company was "ripe for a Boone Pickens." Indeed, Pickens himself was reportedly weighing a move on the company. The idea of restructuring U.S. Steel was not far-fetched, the *Journal* added. Dismantled, the company might be worth as much as $70 per share. It was trading at $29.[30]

Fears of takeover may or may not have contributed to Roderick's next strategic move. In October 1985, U.S. Steel revealed it was negotiating to acquire Texas Oil & Gas Corporation, a major producer of natural gas. It was an awkward disclosure, coming at an awkward time, with the company still straining to digest Marathon. To avoid assuming further debt, executives structured the deal as an all-stock transaction: U.S. Steel issued 133 million new shares, more than doubling the number of outstanding shares to 255 million. "Sometimes you can't control the timing of a good acquisition," explained Roderick. "It was an opportunity we just felt we couldn't pass up."[31] Skeptics saw other motives. Senior management was trying to make the company less attractive, they charged, to repel a potential hostile bid. Corporate spokespeople denied the suggestion.[32]

Nevertheless, shareholders protested sharply against the dilution of their equity. One fund manager holding more than one million common shares of U.S. Steel described his reaction as "surprise, disbelief, and resentment."[33] Kim Schnabel, of the College Retirement Equities Fund (holding 2.3 million shares), complained that the company's stockholders had been "taken to the cleaners."[34] Schnabel was particularly upset because Roderick had recently assured shareholders nothing of this sort was going to be undertaken. The CEO had squandered the company's equity and lost credibility, making an acquisition that would have "a permanent downward effect on the stock for the rest of the current management's tenure," Schnabel grimly predicted.[35] Alan L. Edgar, a Dallas broker, was more succinct. He was "shocked," Edgar declared. "Management has relegated common shareholders to second-class citizenship."[36]

Talk of revolt simmered for awhile. Schnabel and other institutional holders declared they would vote against authorizing the acquisition when management put the question to shareholders at the company's annual meeting. In the event, though, a majority of shareholders ratified the acquisition, in February 1986. Most of the smaller shareholders sided with management while among the company's institutional shareholders, some remained guardedly optimistic about the merger prospects.[37] Still, Roderick's highhanded wheeling and dealing was clearly beginning to alienate important constituencies among his shareholders. Moreover, it failed to generate better operating results. U.S. Steel made the Texas Oil acquisition just as natural gas prices peaked. Over the course of 1986, even as U.S. Steel rechristened itself USX to reflect its new diversified identity, slumping energy prices drove the company's oil and gas operating income down to $42 million (from $1.6 billion in 1985), and Texas Oil & Gas Corp. posted a $31 million loss.[38] As he had with Marathon, Roderick had paid a premium price for a property that almost immediately started to decline in value.

And triggered, in the process, an ominous series of moves in the financial markets. In August 1986, with the company's steel operations stalled in a protracted strike, USX's share price slid down to 15. A month later, word surfaced that Icahn had begun accumulating shares, amassing a stake that was approaching 5 percent. Other "raiders" were also acquiring blocks, and arbitrageurs busily began buying and selling in anticipation of a full-scale takeover bid. Wall Street rumors had Pickens jumping into the fray, then pulling out. By early October, 50 million shares had changed hands, amounting to one-fifth of the common stock. In an effort to calm the market and allay shareholder frustration, Roderick announced the company had hired First Boston and Goldman, Sachs to draw up "a wide range of restructuring alternatives to enhance shareholder value." "No matter what happens," the *Wall Street Journal* concluded, "one thing is clear. Neither USX nor Roderick are masters of their own fates anymore."[39]

The covert activity escalated and broke out into the open on October 6, when Icahn revealed in an SEC filing that he had accumulated just over 25 million shares, 9.8 percent of the total outstanding, and offered $31 per share to acquire the rest. The offer fell just short of a full-fledged takeover attempt. Icahn made his offer contingent on seeing the company's books, and characterized his proposal as "friendly." At the same time, he warned that if USX's managers failed to either accept the offer or otherwise boost the company's share price above $31 per share, he would lodge a formal, hostile bid. It was a "hold-your-feet-to-the-fire tactic," observed one investment banker: Icahn would keep his offer on the table until USX promulgated a restructuring plan of its own later in the month, after the recommendations had come down from First Boston/Goldman, Sachs.[40]

Roderick responded defiantly. Resisting the suggestion that he spin off the company's energy properties—an anonymous former USX executive predicted he would fight "tooth and nail" to keep "his babies"—he girded the corporation for battle. The company accelerated a planned sale of its chemical operations and secured a $3 billion bank credit line, piling up a formidable warchest. And it laid in a further ring of takeover defenses, providing golden parachute clauses for twenty top executives. As October wore on, the rhetoric emerging from USX headquarters grew more confident. The report from First Boston/Goldman Sachs did not arrive on schedule—or if it did, management sat on it. By the end of October, Roderick was stressing that the company would review any restructuring proposals carefully and slowly. "We will take whatever time it takes to do it well," he vowed. "That process will not be rushed." USX, it became clear, was going to wait to see Icahn's next move. "Let him make a tender offer," an anonymous executive challenged. "Carl's a big boy."[41]

Icahn, for his part, was stuck. USX's takeover defenses were daunting, and the company's underlying finances made a potential bust-up extremely difficult. In any event, an SEC investigation was sapping Drexel Burnham, Icahn's principal source of financing. Arbitrageurs sensed the change in momentum and began to pull back. The share price retreated with the speculators, to the mid-20s in early-November, and by the end of the month to below $22.20—the average price Icahn had paid acquiring his stake. Then in December Roderick managed to seal off the West Texas Yates oil assets, the company's most readily saleable property, by tying the unit's revenues to a $1 billion loan from Citibank. Early in January 1987, Icahn conceded the round, announcing he was dropping his bid. To virtually no one's surprise, the company followed this announcement several weeks later with one of its own unveiling a distinctly modest plan of restructuring that retained the company's oil and gas properties. "It's essentially the same thing we've been doing all along," an executive confirmed. "The company, in effect, is concluding that there aren't any better alternatives to the strategy it already had."[42]

USX had managed to stave off Icahn's bear hug. But the firm had not exactly triumphed. In the wake of the contest "the Corporation" stood on uncertain grounds. Several longstanding primary shareholders had pulled out in all the activity, and many of those who had acquired or held onto shares were clamoring for major strategic restructuring. Icahn had emerged as the company's largest shareholder, a force to be reckoned with and a focal point for shareholder activism. Roderick had resisted Icahn's dictates, but he recognized that he had to pay attention, or at least appear to pay attention, to Icahn's advice, and began meeting informally with his adversary to discuss the company's strategy. The silver girdle was tightening again, not yet binding headquarters, but taking up much of the slack. Management no longer held free rein.

Just how constricted the terms of governance had grown at USX became plain several years later, when Roderick retired. He left USX "intact," in June 1989—still holding onto both the steel and the energy properties. But the assemblage was straining. Within months of taking over, Roderick's successor, Charles Corry, put Texas Oil & Gas's energy reserves up for sale, declaring the company would apply the proceeds to debt reduction and stock buy-backs. Analysts predicted the firm would soon sell off the entire unit. Corry felt Roderick had overpaid for the acquisition, the press reported, and the unit's cumulative losses had reached $61 million.[43]

There was still the Icahn factor to deal with, though. If Corry had hoped that selling off the Texas Oil & Gas reserves might placate his largest shareholder, he miscalculated. In October, Icahn revealed he had increased his stake to 13.1 percent and was contemplating another run at a takeover. He was going to take Corry's measure.[44]

Corry's initial response reprised Roderick's tactics. The new CEO called an emergency board meeting to plan a defensive strategy. The board promptly implemented a poison-pill measure, triggered when any single investor amassed a 15 percent stake. Icahn, meanwhile, built up his stake to 13.3 percent in December and began sounding out investment and commercial banks about financing a bid.[45] Another contest loomed. But not a takeover contest, this time. Even as he explored the possibility of renewing his bid for outright control, Icahn intensified his pressure on management. He made repeated phone calls into headquarters, urging management to break apart of the company's steel and energy operations and threatening to stage a proxy fight on the question. Now, with a new CEO in charge, with alterations in strategic outlook at USX headquarters, and with intangible yet distinct new dynamics of governance working on the company, Icahn got a hearing. Corry eventually agreed to let shareholders vote on a proposal to spin off up to 80 percent of the company's steel operations. The vote would be nonbinding, but Corry promised to give careful consideration to the shareholders' verdict. Icahn proclaimed himself satisfied. "USX has said in our agreement that they will give due consideration to the will of the majority voting yea or nay," he reported. "I believe they sincerely will follow the will of the majority."[46]

The two sides campaigned energetically in the proxy fight that ensued. Icahn contended that breaking USX into distinct, pure plays—in steel and energy, respectively—would yield a substantial payoff for investors. He commissioned a study projecting a combined value of $48 for a pair of stocks. And he took to television to make his case, pitching his proposal on the Financial News Network's Institutional Research Network—a first for proxy contests, the *Wall Street Journal* observed. Management disputed Icahn's numbers as "conjectural and speculative": how, Corry demanded, would "tearing paper in half" create "magic value?" The CEO dismissed Icahn's study as "a lightweight analytical job," an assessment some third-party analysts seconded. But Icahn's basic challenge remained potent. "If the company had extra money that it didn't wish to invest in steel," he demanded, "why couldn't that money have been given to shareholders? Why should the company make a decision to go into another business without consulting shareholders?"[47]

The two sides also contended over the anti-takeover provisions the company had adopted over the last few years. Icahn used the opportunity of the strategy referendum to propose the company eliminate its staggered board elections, a poison pill shareholder rights provision, and its golden parachutes. He also urged the company to require its directors to own at least 2,000 shares of company stock. Management, predictably, opposed any restrictions on anti-takeover measures, arguing the tactics helped protect "continuity and stability" of corporate governance.[48]

As the two sides marshaled their forces, it became clear that the vote would be close enough to create serious pressure for USX. Company executives canvassed their institutional holders intensively. They found that a number of primary holders planned to back Icahn's proposal, even though it seemed unlikely to carry, in order to send management a sharp message. "We don't believe he'll get a majority," conceded Richard Hirtle, treasurer of North American Security Trust, who nevertheless planned to back the insurgent in an effort to prod the company into action. Martin Sass, president of M.D. Sass Investors Services, made similar plans for his fund's block of 950,000 shares. "I think they [management] have a mandate to move in a fairly bold fashion, to further enhance shareholder value," Sass declared. Icahn himself sounded much the same note. "The more votes I get," he declared, "the more leverage I will have in dealing with management."[49]

The company carried the vote, once again fending off Icahn. But by now even management was conceding that the time had come for some kind of restructuring. In lobbying the institutional holders, company executives had found themselves arguing not against restructuring per se, but against directing it from the outside. Let management do what needed to be done, Corry and his colleagues in effect pleaded. Their victory thus bought them little more than time. The company had been weighing "strategy . . . to do something will the steel business," an anonymous director affirmed in the wake of the vote. "I think something will happen here." The CEO made vaguer, but essentially similar assurances. "This is a corporation that has changed and will continue to change," Corry declared. "That is inevitable."[50] Indeed, early in 1991, just one year after fending off Icahn's proxy, management put together a proxy proposal of its own to split USX stock into two separate classes, one tracking the steel group (along with a few other businesses) and the other tracking the energy businesses. Icahn endorsed the plan, and in May shareholders ratified it by a large margin.

IN THE RAIDERS' WAKE

So dissident investors eventually forced USX to redefine, if not retreat from, the program of diversification management had launched 10 years before. Corporate executives managed to retain Marathon, at least, but only at the cost of financially restructuring the enterprise. And in the process of working out this understanding, the managers of USX had found themselves implicitly renegotiating the fundamental terms of governance that underpinned "the Corporation." The final shift happened behind the scenes, somewhere in the midst of those tense conferences between management and the company's institutional investors. It was decisive, though. In the larger story of corporate governance, what had transpired was arguably nearly as significant as the pact that had defined the incorporation of U.S. Steel 90 years before. For it marked the emergence of a distinctly new dynamic of ownership and management. The corporate covenant, the silver girdle that bound the enterprise together, had been reforged.

To some extent, the tug of war between the corporate managers and insurgent shareholders of USX can be attributed to local, specific circumstances. Roderick made a couple of questionable plays, by this account—one dubious (Marathon), the other clearly a mistake (Texas Oil & Gas), both fairly expensive, neither well-timed. In response, external market forces intervened, checking and then correcting what turned out to have been strategic miscalculations. This particular company, under this particular CEO, simply blundered, though it was eventually nudged back on course. A morality tale for other errant CEOs, perhaps.

But something more, too: a parable. In calling on USX to decouple its energy acquisitions from its steel operations, Icahn was giving expression to powerful market demands. What was happening here was more complex than an opportunistic grab at a vulnerable set of properties. It was an effort to wrest strategic autonomy from the managers who ran "The Corporation," and the fact that the bid to force USX to deconglomerate came as close as it did to succeeding betrayed a profound loss of faith. As far as the market was concerned, industrial corporate powers that had once seemed masterful had lost command over the course of economic events. Investors had grown weary and wary of diversification—skeptical, by implication, of the ability of an entity like USX to efficiently or profitably invest in and manage new businesses, new industries, new technologies. That was Icahn's message to the corporate management of USX. Investors wanted "pure plays." They wanted to be able to make investment decisions on their own behalf. They were working collectively, in increasingly coordinated fashion, to exert some measure of control over what an earlier generation of corporate planners had handled internally as resource allocation. They were demanding, bidding for, and forcibly acquiring, a strategic autonomy of their own.

The outcome of this tacit struggle was not clear-cut. Industrial executives managed, with increasing skill over the late-1980s, to fend off the most swashbuckling of the raiders. Between five and six *Fortune* 100 firms a year drew tender offers through the mid-1980s, a substantial number of them hostile. But then the number dropped. By the 1990s a hostile offer was a singular event. (See Figure 6.1.)

The managers' victory proved pyrrhic, however. The takeover defenses erected by the industrial corporation proved very expensive, not just at USX, but at many other siege points on the landscape, and even those firms that survived takeovers

Figure 6.1
Tender Offers Received by *Fortune* 100 Firms, 1981–2000

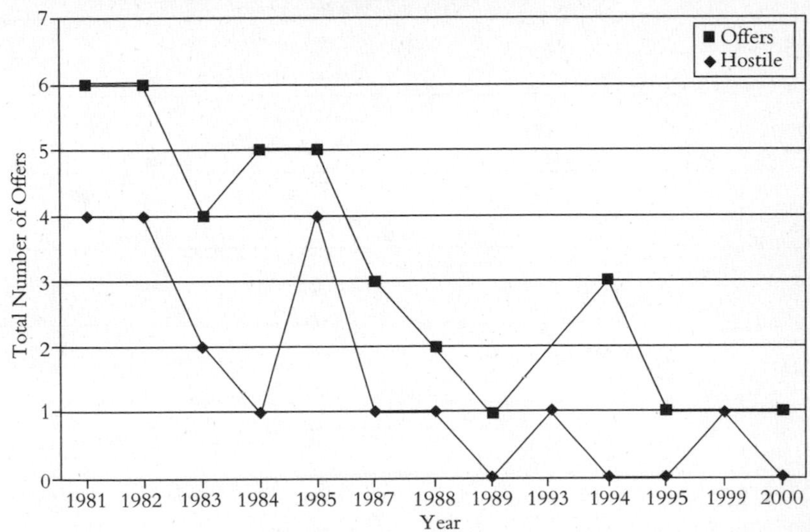

emerged highly leveraged. Indeed, the typical F100 company took on heavy debt over the late 1980s. Through the mid-1980s its debt-to-equity ratio hovered under 40 percent (Figure 6.2). Then the figure began to climb, approaching 100 percent by 1992. The large industrial corporation, in other words, was carrying an average debt load roughly equal to its net worth by 1992—a burden it did not manage to discharge through the remainder of the 1990s.

The raiders may not have managed to wrest outright control over corporate strategy, in other words, but over the course of the contest senior management nevertheless lost a good measure of that control. Or at least, corporate managers' margin for maneuver grew sharply constricted. Corporate debt had to be serviced, of course, and meanwhile corporate earnings were not keeping pace. The ratio between the typical industrial's free cash flow and total market equity slid significantly through the 1980s and early 1990s (Figure 6.3). In other words, American industrial corporations threw off less and less cash, relative to their market values. The latitude for major strategic moves grew inexorably narrower. It became much more difficult to pull of the kinds of major deals that an earlier generation of corporate leadership had come to think of as managerial prerogative.

Encoded in these numbers, in sum, is a significant shift in the balance of power between managers and investors. To fend off the raiders, corporate executives had to come to new financial terms, and by the time they woke up to that necessity they found they were dealing with new kinds of investors.

Figure 6.2
Average Debt-to-Equity Ratio for *Fortune* 100 Firms, 1978–1999

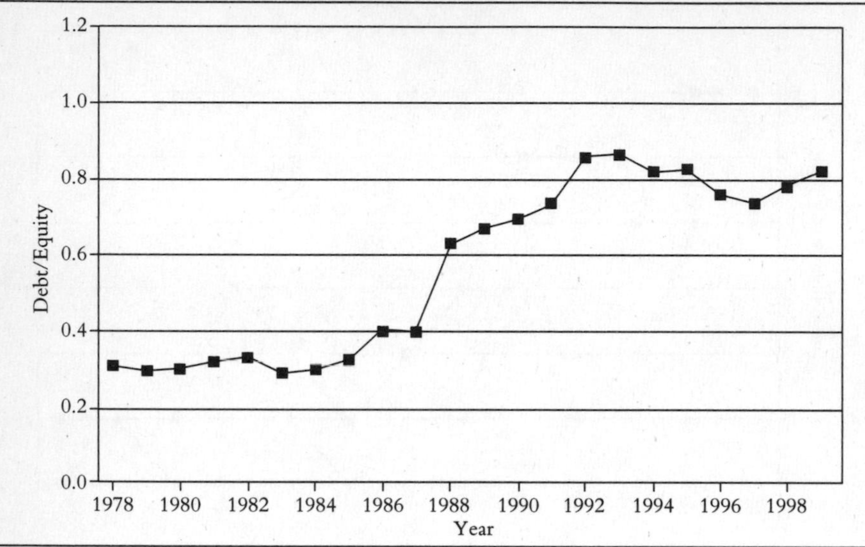

Figure 6.3
Free Cash Flow/Total Equity for the *Fortune* 100 Firms, 1978–1999

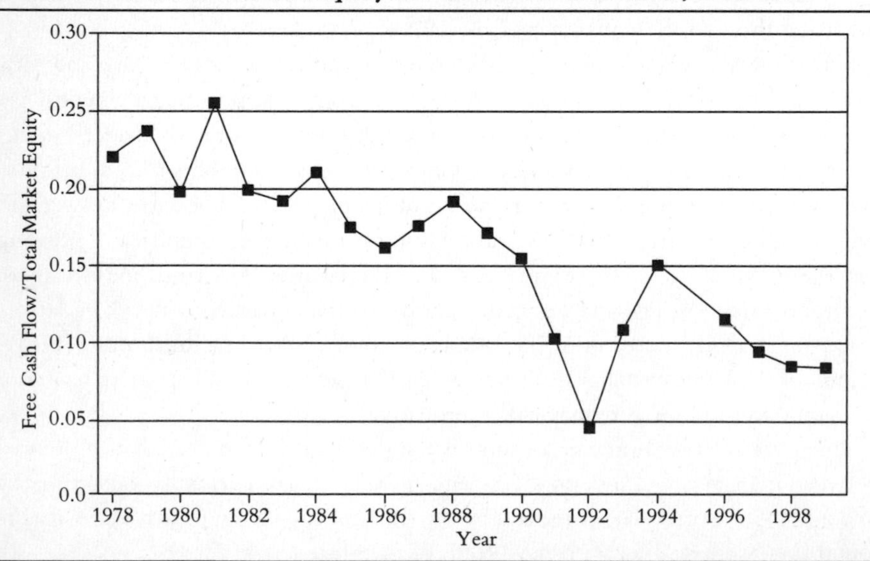

In their struggle with Carl Icahn, USX's managers repeatedly cast their nemesis as a "raider." They contained Icahn in part by labeling him. He was merely a "speculator" according to the company's 1986 annual report (which did not even deign to name him)—an investor seeking only short-term gain, at any price, willing even to dismantle the company for a quick pay-out. The characterization grew somewhat problematic as time went on and Icahn demonstrated that he represented a more complicated force. He publicly proclaimed he would not be bought off with greenmail in 1986, or a special dividend in 1989 and 1990. Against the charge that he was a "raider," Icahn articulated a vocabulary of "shareholder value," contending he was acting benignly on behalf of all of the company's investors. Nonetheless, the raider rhetoric worked powerfully on the contest. Characterizing Icahn as a "raider" implicitly cast management as noble stewards, valiantly defending the institution under their care against pernicious and short-sighted pillage. The various institutional investors he courted in the 1990 proxy contest remained suspicious of his motives and uneasy about the depth of his commitment to the company. When he pulled out just a few weeks after the company split its stock, primary shareholders reacted with relief. Many had supported his efforts to prod management into action, but they had also been waiting nervously for him to unload the shares, apprehensive about the sag in share price his sell-off was bound to create.[51]

Describing Icahn as a raider may or may not have been fair, in the end, but it did highlight one of his critical weaknesses. Whatever his purposes, whatever concessions he managed to extract from management, Icahn remained a freelancer, a rogue element. He set powerful forces in motion, but in the end proved unable to control or exploit them. In any event, over time management, at USX and other large industrial firms, figured out how to defend companies against figures like Icahn and Pickens. The total assets managed by takeover-driven organizational forms reached $70 billion in 1987, and then fell off.[52] Inflammatory headlines and furious controversy aside, the aggregate size of the takeover market amounted, at its peak, to only 2.2 percent of total corporate equity. By 1990, most firms had laid in formidable takeover defenses and the "raiders" were in retreat.[53]

Nevertheless, managers were not resting comfortably within their fortresses. The forces touched off by the raiders continued to reverberate beneath them. It was one thing for a company like USX to keep an investor like Carl Icahn at bay. It was quite another, as it turned out, for a company like Beatrice to contend with a force like Kohlberg Kravis Roberts.

"We're Beatrice"

In broad strategic trajectory, Beatrice's growth through the 1970s tracked the general pattern of American industrial corporate development. Incorporated in 1897, Beatrice first did business as a dairy products firm, growing through a string of acquisitions, dairy by dairy, over the 1920s and 1930s. By the time it was listed on the New York Stock Exchange in 1929, it had expanded to a national scale of operations. In the 1940s and 1950s, the firm began to acquire nondairy food businesses. And in the 1960s, expansion grew yet broader in scope as the firm acquired a string of unrelated businesses, including food service equipment, chemicals, and other products. By 1975, Beatrice was a full-fledged conglomerate, earning less than a third of its total sales, and less than a quarter of its earnings, from dairy products. All of which the company's board and investors presided over with general equanimity. From an investment perspective, the firm added value steadily and healthily; between 1952 and 1976, the stock returned an average 14 percent annually to shareholders.[54]

The firm's performance began to falter in the late-1970s, however, even as management embarked on its most ambitious round of expansion to date. In 1978, a few years after taking over as CEO, Wallace Rasmussen, engineered the acquisition of Tropicana Products Inc. for $490 million in cash, outbidding Kellogg in the process. The move signaled a significant escalation in the firm's growth strategy. It was Beatrice's largest acquisition (by a factor of six), and the first publicly held target the firm had pursued. Several years later, under Rasmussen's successor, James Dutt, Beatrice acquired the Coca Cola Bottling Division of Northwest Industries, paying $580 million, a $450 million premium over the company's book value, and a figure representing 22 times the unit's earnings. And several years after that, the company upped the ante once again, announcing in 1984 it was acquiring Esmark, a holding company formed as part of Swift & Company's restructuring in 1973, for $2.7 billion. With Esmark's grocery-distribution and marketing operations, Dutt proclaimed, Beatrice had positioned itself to become "the world's premier marketer." The financial market, however, was less than impressed. Between 1972 and 1982, the company earned a total return on investment of negative 4.2 percent. Nearly $2 billion in market value evaporated from Beatrice during the combined tenures of Rasmussen and Dutt. Every new acquisition announcement set the stock further back. On the other hand, investors reacted positively to divestiture announcements and news of withdrawals from planned acquisitions.[55]

Evidently the financial market was growing leery of Beatrice's increasingly grandiose strategic strokes. Analysts were also troubled by signs of a rift between management and the firm's board of directors. In 1978, as he approached retirement, Rasmussen had appointed a three-person committee of outside directors to nominate his successor and recommend changes in the composition of the board. At the time Rasmussen had expressed concern to Durwood Varner, the committee chairman, that the board needed to strengthen its outside representation. But then Rasmussen ignored the committee's candidate in favor of his own choice, Dutt. The CEO managed to ram his pick through the board, carrying the firm's inside directors and several outside members. The boardroom confrontation, however, drove Varner and two other outside directors to resign. In the wake of the turmoil, stockholder King

Shwayder initiated a lawsuit denouncing the board as insider-dominated and accusing Rasmussen of reneging on his promise to appoint a majority of outsiders to the board. The suit fizzled, and the slate of directors backing Dutt won election from stockholders. Still, the unseemly affair exposed serious cracks in Beatrice's governance. "The actions being taken today will serve as evidence that some major corporations are indeed controlled by employee directors," Varner had proclaimed as he resigned, in a speech that Shwayder's lawsuit subsequently made public. "It will heighten the anxiety existing in many quarters that self-interest is a factor in vital decisions in corporate affairs. It will serve as a clear warning that outside directors must beware—that unpopular positions may well result in punitive action. . . . I am astounded by the actions taken here today."[56]

The Esmark deal reinforced the growing impression of management running amok at Beatrice. In early 1984 Esmark, itself wheeling and dealing under the aggressive helm of Donald Kelly, had bought up 1.4 million shares of Beatrice stock, triggering speculation that Beatrice was a takeover target. Then KKR had stepped in with an LBO bid for Esmark, for $2.4 billion. Dutt, at this point, seized the opportunity to turn the tables on Kelly, intervening in the KKR negotiations to bid $2.7 billion for Esmark. He got his prize, but the transaction came off looking more like a power play than sober strategizing. "I don't lose," Dutt had grimly declared when asked what he would have done if KKR outbid him; he would "go the mat" to win.[57]

That kind of rhetoric was not serving Dutt well. His autocratic style of management was demoralizing the company's executives and alienating his directors. He had undertaken an expensive, dubious corporate brand marketing campaign, "We're Beatrice," that had failed to check slippage in both sales and earnings, after decades of consecutive growth. His company was acquiring a distinctly sour taste in the market, and his board was growing increasingly concerned. Finally, in August 1985, the directors felt compelled to take action, forcing Dutt to resign as chairman and CEO and installing William Granger, a retired Beatrice vice president, in his place. Investors roundly endorsed the move: over the three days following Dutt's resignation, the firm's market value surged by $300 million.

The turnover in management did not end Beatrice's travails, however. Only a few months after Dutt resigned, rumors of an LBO resurfaced. They were well founded. In October, KKR, backing a management team headed by Donald Kelly, tendered an offer of $45 a share for the firm. Negotiations ensued, the offer was eventually raised to $50 a share—a premium of 53 percent over the share price the day of Dutt's resignation—and the board accepted. In the bargain Beatrice's shareholders managed to recoup nearly all of the value lost over the last dozen years. And KKR pulled off what was at the time the largest leveraged buyout in corporate history.

The dénouement duly followed. Kelly came in as CEO, installed a top management team made up largely of former Esmark executives, and took his seat at a reconstituted board comprising four management seats and six seats controlled by KKR. And promptly began making large-scale divestitures, shearing off major pieces of the company. By 1987, Kelly had pared Beatrice down to its domestic food businesses. This final piece took a few years to divest, but eventually, in 1990 KKR's team completed the bust-up, selling off the food group to Con-Agra.[58]

So Beatrice dispersed into the corporate landscape, reconstituting in 11 components, each mid- to large-sized companies in its own right, five of them structured as management buyouts. As of 1990, the deal represented the largest corporate sell-off in history, chewing apart and swallowing what had been in 1985 number 26 on the *Fortune* 500.[59]

The LBO Phenomenon

The Beatrice deal typified KKR in action. Where Icahn improvised, the LBO firm executed by way of a well-crafted set of tactics—tactics that enabled KKR to take on companies like Beatrice and, in its most audacious (and infamous) strike, RJR-Nabisco. The tactics proved devastatingly successful due to a number of confluent forces, some of them running very deeply in the industrial economy. KKR was taking advantage of specific missteps by senior management, to be sure—at Beatrice and at a string of other companies. And the numbers added up: in financial terms, the LBO firm was exploiting the opportunity created by low market valuations for established businesses earning high revenue streams. That is what the situation looked like on balance sheets. But the psychological dimensions of buyouts like the one that engulfed Beatrice may have been even more telling. Companies like Beatrice were trying to work their way out of stagnant core businesses. Their senior managers were groping and grasping for control. As they did so, they were putting traditional mechanisms of governance under increasing stress. Impressions of overweening managerial ambition and excess were gaining validity and spreading beyond the sometimes inflated rhetoric of the initial raiders. They were taking hold, those impressions, deep in the shareholding base of the corporation.

Icahn and even to an extent KKR may have been freelancers, in other words, but they drew power from deeper sources. More and more investors were becoming convinced that corporations were losing the internal ability to work their way out of their troubles. Icahn would not have been able to mount a serious run at U.S. Steel, nor would KKR have been able to take on companies like Beatrice and RJR-Nabisco, if corporate managers had managed to hold onto the general faith of their shareholders. The popular account of KKR's "raid" on RJR-Nabisco cast the LBO firm as the "Barbarians at the Gate." But the barbarians broke in only because most of the denizens behind the gate decided they were better off in their hands.

What, then, drove the denizens to open the gates?

CALPERS: THE LOGIC OF INVESTOR ACTIVISM

In 1988, *Fortune* magazine reported that pension funds had acquired 50 percent (by value) of the shares trade on the New York Stock Exchange, and fully 65 percent of the Standard & Poor's 500—proportions that were growing greater by the day.[60] The announcement revealed a trend that had in fact been underway for a number of years. Over the last quarter of the twentieth century, institutional investors—pension funds, mutual funds, and the like—gradually amassed a preponderant share of American industrial equity. That central fact was already restructuring not just corporate equity, but the financial markets in which that equity was bought and sold and, ultimately, the industrial corporation itself. It was the institutional investors who had created a financial market for corporate takeovers—the institutional investors, by implication, who had fuelled forces like T. Boone Pickens, Carl Icahn, and KKR (see Figure 6.4). In the grand scheme of things, the "raiders" were agents, propelled by deeper forces.

Corporate managers eventually learned how to contain figures like Icahn. But then, once USX had neutralized Icahn, it still found itself facing its shareholders, simmering with frustration. Somewhere in the train of events between 1982, when U.S. Steel acquired Marathon, and 1991, when USX financially restructured the business as a separate tracking stock, a significant degree of initiative, if not control,

Figure 6.4
Institutional Holdings of Equity in the *Fortune* 100 Firms, 1978–1999

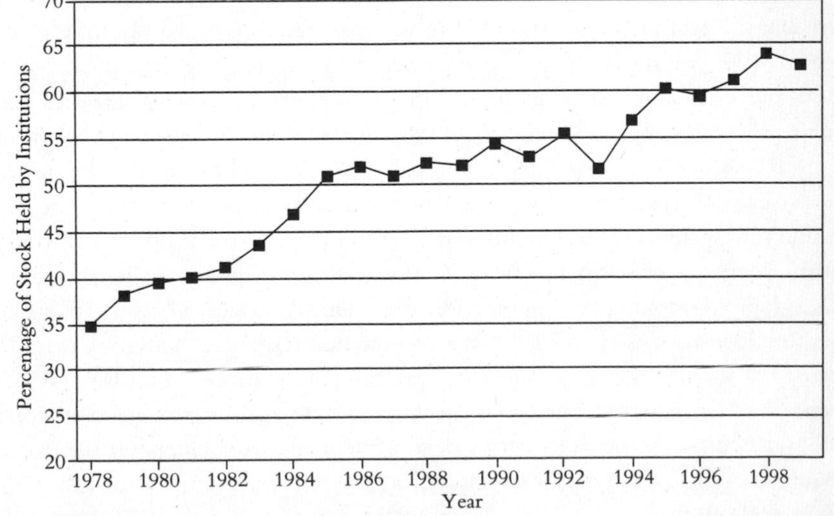

had swung from management to investors. To follow that shift, we need to execute a similar swing. We need to descend from corporate headquarters and boardrooms like USX's and look at the story from the point of view of the institutional investors who were increasingly driving financial markets. We need to inhabit, in other words, the perspective of people like Jesse Unruh and Dale Hanson, who ran the California Public Employees' Retirement System, as they struggled to steer some of the largest investors in the world through the corporate turmoil of post-industrialization.

From the helm of a fund like Calpers, the view on America's large industrial corporations took on very different proportions—disquieting ones. Managing tens of billions of dollars in assets, deployed in blocks of shares typically numbering in the hundreds of thousands if not millions, the fund manager had to be deeply staked in most large American industrial corporations—so deeply that he could not easily or gracefully pull his fund out. Dozens of investments were yielding disappointing returns by the mid-1980s, as corporations struggle to adapt to global competition and the gradual emergence of a post-industrial economy. Institutional investors could not afford to "vote with their feet," though. As one fund manager observed, "The larger pension funds can't just walk away when companies aren't performing well. There'd be no market. Everybody would be on one side of the sale."[61] In short, the fund manager found himself tethered to companies by a silver girdle of his own. That central fact of life was working powerfully on Calpers by the mid-1980s. By necessity as much as anything else, the fund began to search for points of entry, for levers, for ways of effecting or at least accelerating better performance.

The emergence of a takeover battle for Texaco became the turning point. In 1984, parrying a raid by the Bass Brothers, the oil company proffered a greenmail payment of $1.3 billion. That ransom bought off the raiders and rescued Texaco's management, but it also thoroughly incensed those shareholders who had been left out of the deal. "Do you mean these people can elect to buy out one class of shareholder at $55 and leave the rest of us in at $35?" demanded California Treasurer Jesse Unruh, who ran Calpers. "Like hell!"[62] Galvanized, Unruh convened counterparts Harrison Goldin (New York City Comptroller) and Roland Machold (who managed New Jersey's investments) to form the Council of Institutional Investors. The group was thus fully primed several months later when management at Phillips Petroleum, fighting against a takeover bid from T. Boone Pickens, presented its shareholders with a dubious-looking recapitalization plan. Unruh, Machold, and Goldin convened in New York City to map out a coordinated response. "Guys," Unruh later recalled telling the others, "in this room we control the future of Phillips. We need only to vote the proxy." The group decided to vote against management, forcing Phillips executives to devise a better deal.[63] Events pulled Calpers off the sidelines and into the takeover fray, indignant, gathering resolve, though still unsure as to how to exert itself.

Calpers' intervention in the takeover machinations at Phillips underscored how complex governance was growing not just for companies like USX or Phillips, but for investors like Calpers as well. Numerous companies in which Calpers was deeply staked were performing badly. Indeed, industrial corporate America generally was struggling to adapt to new, more exacting conditions. Calpers needed these companies to adapt, to continue growing. But the fund also needed the raiders that were preying on them. An active takeover market was winnowing out the weakest performers and toughening the survivors. Agents like the Bass Brothers and Icahn served Calpers' interest—directly when they drove up certain stock prices, and indirectly as a threat prodding corporate managers to restructure and reengineer more rapidly, more radically. Over the late-1980s Calpers, and other funds, learned to play raiders against underperforming managers. By the time Calpers got an opportunity to revisit the situation at Texaco, things had changed markedly. In 1984, Calpers had fumed impotently while Texaco's management had dealt its way out of trouble. In 1988, when the oil company was again besieged, the fund intervened, determined this time to bring Texaco's managers to some sort of account.

After paying off the Bass Brothers in 1984, Texaco had slid into even deeper financial turmoil. In rapid succession the company had acquired Getty Oil, then been hit with a lawsuit from Penzoil (which had been negotiating to acquire Getty for itself), then suffered a series of adverse legal rulings that forced Texaco into bankruptcy protection and eventually cost the firm a $3 billion damage settlement. In the meantime, Texaco was carrying notoriously inefficient operations and a dismal exploration record. By 1987, the stock was trading at less than half of its $59.40 a share in net worth. On cue, Icahn moved in. The raider built up a 14 percent stake, then made a tender offer to acquire the remaining shares for $12.4 billion. Management turned him down. Icahn countered by launching a proxy fight to remove CEO James Kinnear and install himself and four allies on the board. All of which Calpers watched with mounting concern and a stake of 763,000 shares.[64]

Inevitably, Texaco's deteriorating financial position undercut managerial dominion. Even by industrial standards the company was autocratic. A 1987 missive from headquarters captured the traditional tone of business perfectly: in the midst of its travails the company saw fit to assure its investors, in proxy statement language *Fortune* aptly characterized as "weirdly imperious": "The Company strongly supports the role of corporate democracy and the right of stockholders to have their views submitted to, and considered by, the Company."[65] Even as Texaco issued the utterance, though, the terms of governance were changing markedly. When the company initially resisted settling with Penzoil, a bankruptcy judge put the business in the hands of a special stockholders' committee. By the time Icahn moved in, shareholders were dangerously disaffected and management was truly alarmed. Kinnear knew he was in trouble. He needed the support of his institutional holders to put down Icahn's proxy challenge, and readily agreed to meet with his institutional holders to make management's case. Huddling privately with Dale Hanson (who had replaced Unruh) and Ned Regan (who ran the New York state and local employees' retirement fund), Kinnear promised to accord the funds a greater voice in appointing the company's directors. The concession was vague on details, but an important gesture nonetheless. Hanson and Regan were not looking for concrete results so much as a tone of accommodation and urgency at Texaco. They decided to throw Calpers' 763,000 shares, and New York's 3 million, with Texaco's management.[66]

Hanson and Regan were not keeping perfect formation. They disagreed, in fact, about how to fit their institutions into the board of directors' ongoing governance, and they came away from the Texaco vote with two distinct descriptions of the accord they had hammered out behind the scenes. At Calpers, the feeling was taking hold that the institutional holders needed a formal voice in at least this particular company's governance. "This is a threshold thing," Hanson declared. "I want to be able to say we've gotten a director on the board."[67] But Regan, for his part, was uncomfortable with appearing to dictate board elections. "The current directors should be governing," Regan maintained; "I don't want anybody on the board." And Goldin, for that matter, had decided to cast NYCERS's votes with Icahn. The fund managers remained divided over tactics and ambivalent about their growing clout. They were searching for appropriate ways to intervene, ways to make their proprietary interests known and felt while maintaining their roles as investors rather than managers.[68]

Diffidence marked the Texaco proxy votes, and some uncertainty hovered afterwards. For several months following the vote, Calpers heard nothing from Kinnear. By November, Hanson realized it was going to take further prodding for Texaco to deliver. Feeling he needed to confront the CEO, wanting (as he later put it) "a gut check," Hanson first sounded out his own board. "This is what I want to push for, but I don't want to push for it if you're not behind me," he later recalled telling the board. "They said you're the closest to it, so go for it." He did. Hanson filed a proxy resolution at Texaco calling for the formation of a shareholders advisory committee and giving management a month to respond. In January, the company agreed to appoint a new director from a list of nominees supplied by Calpers. The fund, in exchange, dropped its proxy threat.[69]

Texaco's new director, John Brademas, was not an employee or agent of Calpers. In fact Brademas, who was the president of New York University and a former U.S. congressman, had never even met anyone from Calpers. Hanson's team assembled their list on the basis of nominees' public reputations. Calpers was not trying to call the shots directly at Texaco. Hanson did, however, want to shore up the independent standing of the board of directors. And he wanted above all to send, and receive in return, a strong set of signals.[70] Kinnear got the message. In the months following his narrow escape, he launched a round of sharp restructuring and vigorous managerial shakeup.[71] The CEO also began meeting regularly with Hanson to discuss shareholder rights and governance issues. Texaco implemented a series of bylaw changes to increase shareholder power, including one prohibiting any future greenmail payments. "I have a very warm spot in my heart for Texaco," Hanson would be reminiscing within a few years; Kinnear "was really the first corporate CEO that I had any exposure to, and that relationship has kind of evolved."[72] Even Icahn was impressed. Following Brademas' appointment, Icahn agreed to back off of Texaco for at least seven years. "Why fight," he explained, "when Kinnear's doing the job I want to see done?"[73]

Confrontations like the Texaco imbroglio catapulted investors like Calpers into unaccustomed prominence. Once anonymous background forces, the pension funds and the people who managed them became cover story subjects in the *Wall Street Journal, Fortune,* and *Business Week*—subjects of note and of some controversy. Corporate chieftains sputtered at the unaccustomed interference, which looked like nothing so much as a new form of insurgency in a decade of turmoil and instability. "The guys who run the public funds are accountable to nobody," complained Andrew Sigler, chairman of Champion International.[74] For that matter, the fund managers themselves fretted uneasily about both their rising prominence and their growing importance. "None of us is interested in making the day-to-day decisions that affect corporations," maintained Harrison Goldin, New York City comptroller.[75] "We should not be running around with our dukes up, yelling at [GM CEO] Roger Smith about Perot [then an insurgent investor within the company]," agreed Regan. "The question is how do we act as external proprietors. If we can define that role, then public pension power is not just appropriate but enormously healthy for the country."[76]

For Calpers' part, Dale Hanson was willing to probe the boundaries. By the late-1980s the fund was voicing strong opinions on corporate governance issues in the press and working both behind the scenes and increasingly publicly to make itself heard on dozens of problem cases. When especially dire circumstances attracted takeover efforts, Calpers was carefully weighing its options. "We do not believe all takeovers are good, but we don't believe all takeovers are bad, either," stated California deputy attorney general Susan Henrichsen, speaking for Calpers in the midst of an insurgency within Lockheed; "each takeover must be evaluated on its own merits."[77] Consistent with this position, the fund played a leading role in opposing the erection of takeover defenses. When, for example, the state of Pennsylvania passed a tough anti-takeover law in 1990, Calpers promptly called on companies incorporated in the state to pull out of the law. On a case by case basis, meanwhile, the fund lodged a series of proxies proposing the disgorging of poison pills and the dismantling of devices such as greenmail.[78]

Raiders proved to be unreliable proxy agents, however. By 1990, corporate defenses had grown formidable, takeover activity was waning, and Calpers was casting about for more durable mechanisms of communication and influence. At Occidental, for example, where the fund held 1.7 million shares, Calpers pressed for the establishment of a shareholders' advisory committee, threatening to put the question before the shareholders. Corporate executives resisted, arguing the proposal "impugn[ed] the character of . . . directors." Still, Occidental did agree to set up regular meetings, twice a year, between Calpers officials and four directors. Calpers accepted the compromise, insisting though that two of the corporation's delegation be outside directors. An essentially similar drama played out at Lockheed over the same period. When Dallas investor Harold Simmons assembled a slate of directors to replace management's lineup, he courted Calpers' support by promising to set up a shareholders advisory committee if he carried the vote. Calpers was tempted to throw its lot with Simmons. The fund was feuding with Lockheed's management over whether or not the company should be governed by Delaware anti-takeover law, and growing frustrated with the board's passivity. "We're tired of people who just take the annual retainer and run," Hanson declared. Lockheed chairman Daniel Tellep proved willing at least to give ground on the issue of confidential shareholder voting.[79]

Calpers' public statements about business at Occidental and Lockheed revealed an emerging shift in tactics for Hanson and his staff. By 1990, the fund was starting to focus its energies on boards of directors at underperforming companies. Of course, it was the boards that theoretically offered investors the proper channel of discontent and reform. Under the grand plan laid out by financiers like J.P. Morgan nearly one hundred years before, investors were relegated to the periphery of corporate governance, and the directors established in their stead as fiduciary representatives. By 1990, boards were taking that role a good deal more seriously. Financial turmoil, a run of takeover bids, and in their wake a spate of shareholder lawsuits were exposing outside directors to an unaccustomed degree of vulnerability. They were feeling the heat from institutional investors. At the same time, painful but productive cases of restructuring, reengineering, and restrategizing were emerging by the end of the 1980s, indicating broad possibilities of corporate industrial revivification. In combination, these developments were creating a new tone of business in corporate boardrooms. Dean Richardson, CEO of Manufacturers National Corp. and outside director on four other boards, felt the change acutely. By his account, a typical board meeting when earnings were down used to be a low-key affair: "Management would say, 'Here's why.' Everyone would say, 'Okay, but you're taking care of it?' Management would say, 'Yes, we're taking care of it,' and the board would say, 'Okay, that's it.' " No longer. Now, Richardson reported, board members were grilling management, demanding: "How are you taking care of the problem? When will there be a solution? What will it be?" Directors were interrogating CEOs not just about plans for recovery, but also about what alternatives had been considered. And they were looking much more skeptically at proposals to risk money in new lines of business, asking whether companies should not just increase dividends instead.[80]

In short, outside directors were beginning to ask the same kinds of questions Calpers was asking, or at least burning to have asked. As the trend picked up momentum, Hanson adjusted the fund's rhetoric and tactics accordingly. "Two or three years from now, hopefully what we're raising today won't need to be raised," Hanson declared in 1990 in the immediate wake of the Occidental and Lockheed imbroglios, "because the law of the land or the unwritten law of the land will be that directors on corporate boards are fiduciaries representing the interests of shareholders."[81]

The hope was put to dramatic test at General Motors. Indeed, Calpers' dilemma as it weighed what to do with or through its stake in GM became a defining moment in the intertwined evolution of institutional investment and activist governance. Here was the country's biggest investor, massively staked in the world's biggest corporation. No raider or LBO firm was going to take on a company the size of General Motors. Yet by 1991 the company was sliding into one of the steepest corporate losses in history, and dragging Calpers' 7.2 million shares with it.

The fund began applying pressure on GM publicly in early 1990, when Calpers officials (in conjunction with New York State Comptroller Regan) visited Detroit to request a voice in choosing Roger Smith's successor. GM's directors heard the fund managers out, but resisted conferring them with anything like a formal representation. Meanwhile the board continued to back the company's management, underscoring its support by elevating Robert Stempel to replace Smith and, for good measure, moving up Lloyd Reuss as president. Still, in a gesture to its institutional holders, the board at the same time formalized a requirement that outside directors constitute a board majority (as they already did). Hanson publicly welcomed the reform as "a breath of fresh air" and retreated to see how events played out. Things quickly and dramatically went downhill: GM lost an eye-opening $4 billion in 1990 and then a staggering $9 billion in 1991—by which point Calpers no longer felt it could afford to fret on the sidelines. In coordination with other institutional holders, the fund began openly calling for new management and working behind the scenes on the board. The insurgents found an opening channel in Ira Millstein, a New York corporate attorney whom the company's outside directors had hired several years before.

GM's directors responded somewhat tentatively, at first, but were ultimately prodded to act decisively. In Spring 1992, the board deposed Reuss, elevated Stempel as CEO, and separated the offices of CEO and chairman of the board. The move put GM's management on sharp notice: the board wanted to see radical changes, though it was willing to give the insiders a window of opportunity in which to effect them. From the sidelines (or, depending on how one regarded the situation, from behind the scenes), Calpers endorsed the move. "This sends a great message to other companies," declared Richard Koppes, the fund's general counsel; "For nonperformers, the status quo doesn't do."[82] Six months later, as the financial crisis deepened, the board stepped in again, ousting Stempel and this time installing an outside director, John Smale, as chairman and Jack Smith as CEO.

The decapitations at GM sent shockwaves through corporate America. Not for 70 years, since the DuPonts had jettisoned founder Billy Durant, had board politics been so roiled at GM. The import was unmistakable: no CEO was safe, no matter how large, well-established, or venerable the company. The board of directors was energizing itself as an institution, and not just at GM, but across corporate America. Within the space of a few bloody months in 1992 and 1993, boards forced executive turnovers at GM, IBM, American Express, Westinghouse, and Kodak. In the 1980s, insurgency had come from the outside—from "raiders" on the periphery of industrial corporate America. In the early 1990s, insurgency (if that is the term) came from inside, from up top, from the very heart of the corporation.

Calpers avoided gloating over Stempel's deposing, but the fund must have been satisfied at the result. GM's fortunes began to improve substantially, both in automobile showrooms and in the financial market. Less tangibly but more significantly, the company's directors had created an invaluable demonstration of fiduciary-minded intervention. The traditional mechanisms of governance had creaked into gear, and they had worked.

In 1994, Dale Hanson retired from Calpers and executive management of the fund passed to James Burton. The turnover marked a distinct shift in approach to corporate governance on Calpers' part. Burton had formerly served as an assistant to Jesse Unruh in the state treasury in the mid-1980s, and in that capacity had been one of the original architects of Calpers' corporate governance program. But Burton was temperamentally unlike Hanson, more of a political insider. And circumstances had changed. Over the mid-1990s, Calpers retreated from public pulpits. The fund remained committed to reforming corporate governance, officials insisted, and was still deeply interested in the performance of virtually every company in the American industrial elite. It could not help but be: in 1996 the fund's investment portfolio reached and passed the $100 billion mark. But Calpers was rethinking its confrontational rhetoric, retreating to work more quietly behind the scenes. "Dale spent a lot of time with corporate governance," Burton responded when asked whether Calpers was backing out of the fray. "Now there's a crying need to take care of internal problems, like technology, business processes, software, evaluations." And in any event, Burton added, "To be less visible is not to be less effective."[83]

CONCLUSION: THE SLACKENING GRIP OF THE VISIBLE HAND

The train of events and shift in perspective that carries the story from Andrew Carnegie to J. P. Morgan to David Roderick to Carl Icahn to Dale Hanson is an admittedly tangled one, but these men and the forces they represented were closely and inextricably bound to each other. Corporations must go to public markets to get capital, yet cannot function without managers. The two components have to be brought into some form of alignment, and that process is inevitably fluid and organic. These are not the sorts of relationships that are defined comprehensively in enduring contracts or formulas. They evolve dynamically, in ebbs and flows of influence and authority.

Still, broadly speaking, the end of growth and internal collapse of the M-Form signaled a decisive shift in balance. The "managerial revolution," predicated on the separation of ownership and management, had played an indisputably critical role in the process of industrial growth and expansion over the early and middle years of the twentieth century. As the power and presence of the industrial corporation waned, though, ownership and control fused back together. Strategic and structural redefinition of the industrial corporation was accompanied, then abetted, then appropriated by a wave of investor activism the likes of which corporate managers had not seen since the age of "Jupiter" Morgan. The visible hand, in other words, started losing its grip in the 1980s, in what one authority has termed a shift from managerial capitalism to investor capitalism.[84]

Fusion of ownership and control emerged in stages, in various forms. In its most straightforward and dramatic manifestation, raiders such as Icahn and investment groups such as KKR simply took public firms private. Owners made themselves managers or, in management-driven LBOs, managers made themselves owners. An increasingly large and liquid private equity and high-yield bond market spurred and fueled these bids, putting investment banks such as Drexel, Burnham, and Lambert centerstage in the drama.[85] Even the House of Morgan joined in. In what was either (depending on one's point of view) a rich historical irony or perhaps a return to original principles, Morgan Stanley (the investment banking firm descended from Jupiter) made itself one of the earliest and biggest players in the LBO field.[86]

Whoever the players, buyouts decisively reconfigured governance relations within target firms. Managers became owner-managers, with substantial stakes in the firm's success. So, for example, when Warner-Lambert was taken over, the amount of stock held by the firm's managers swelled from 1 percent to 18.2 percent.[87] Under these much altered circumstances, the combination of strong incentives and the discipline required by high debt levels drastically altered strategic outlooks.

In the event, free agent efforts to re-fuse ownership and management unsettled but failed to unseat corporate managers. Even as executives learned how to fend off the "external" threat, though, the ground beneath them was giving way. The concentration of industrial equity in institutional hands collected ownership, gave it new focus, new instruments for exerting shareholder influence. Fund managers may have carried themselves very differently than their classic financier counterparts. Certainly none of them swaggered so imperiously as Morgan had. But their weight was very real, and it took only a handful of years, roughly from 1985 to 1992, for them to figure out how to bring it to bear on corporate managers.

The results were tangible and sometimes violent. Boards of directors, long slumbering, awoke to their fiduciary responsibilities to their shareholders. Either at the instigation of boards, or in preemptive strikes by management, companies began making unprecedented cuts in their ranks. Even the figureheads at the top were lopped off. Underperforming CEOs were significantly more likely to be fired by the early 1990s, and their replacements far less likely to have been hand-picked by outgoing executives—moves that would rend deep tears in the very fabric of the corporation (see Chapter 7). Whether the shift was actual or symbolic, though, the impact was much the same. The visible hand, once masterful, had relinquished the reins of power.

CHAPTER 7

Fraying Loyalties

Early in Spring 1993, Eastman Kodak rolled out what one executive called "our most aggressive effort" at marketing to date, an ambitious new ad campaign built around the catchphrase "A Kodak Moment." Crafted by J. Walter Thompson USA, to whom the company had transferred its ad account the year before, the new marketing strategy came at a critical point in Kodak's venerable, prosperous, but recently faltering history. Through most of the twentieth century, Kodak dominated its industry, selling a fluctuating share of cameras, but more than 90 percent of the photographic film in the U.S. market. The word "Kodak" had come to signify photography in the American consumer's imagination; experts had identified it as one of the most popular and valuable brands in the world. This was precisely the reflexive association that the "Kodak Moment" campaign meant to fortify. But the association was beginning to weaken. In the 1980s, Fuji had launched a sustained offensive on the U.S. market, and Kodak had given ground. By 1993, Kodak's market share had dwindled to 70 percent—still a commanding figure in other contexts, perhaps, but as far as investment analysts were concerned a deeply troubling number in Kodak's case. The "Kodak Moment" campaign represented an effort to rekindle a brand that seemed to be losing its talismanic power. Consumer loyalty was eroding from under the corporation, and Kodak was struggling to shore it up.[1]

The "Kodak Moment" campaign was too soft a sell, some critics charged. Rather than bathing consumers in a warm, diffuse glow of anticipated nostalgia, the company should be plugging value, or hyping its film's technological merits. Whatever the marketing wisdom, the ads spoke to deep impulses, not just among Kodak's customers but within the company itself. They tapped a distinctive sentimentality. They exuded just a whiff of wistfulness, perhaps. Or maybe it was ambivalence, anxiety about what lay ahead. Kodak seemed to be clinging to an older world, even as it was slipping away.[2]

Kodak was losing its hold on more than just its consumers. Other loyalties were beginning to fray within and around the corporation. Investors, for example, were rapidly losing faith in the company. As recently as 1982, Kodak had enjoyed one of the 10 highest market capitalizations in the world, but over the decade leading up to its "Kodak Moment" the shareprice had not only lagged the market, it had actually lost value, falling 8.4 percent. That was a truly steep fall from grace.[3]

And then there were what the company euphemistically called the "separations." With the company losing its hold on its market and investors clamoring for better results, Kodak had begun letting waves of employees go in the mid-1980s. The company had begun gently, at first, prodding employees to retire or accept early "separation" packages. Eleven thousand had weighed the offer, sniffed the wind and left in 1983, then 13,000 more three years later, another 5,000 in 1989, and then 8,000 between 1991–1992. The early retirement incentives proved expensive, however, and in any event downsizing neither improved the company's performance nor mollified its investors. The company's early retirement packages were actually oversubscribed. By 1993, Kodak's senior managers were coming to feel that they were losing many of their most valuable, highly skilled people. Free agency was beginning to bleed the company, and to make matters worse, Kodak seemed to have lost control of the process. Meanwhile analysts were grumbling that Kodak was downsizing too politely, too expensively, with too little to show for it on the bottom line.[4]

The "Kodak Moment" campaign thus took shape in the midst of disarray and uncertainty in the marketplace, on Wall Street, and within the company itself. Customer loyalties were loosening, investor loyalties were coming under stress, and employee-employer loyalties were beginning to dissolve. A mechanism as highly engineered and intricately interlocked, in its way, as one of Kodak's cameras was breaking down, piece by piece. Wall Street was complaining that "Big Yellow" remained bloated and inefficient. The stock was depressed. Analysts were calling on Kodak's management to spin off its noncore businesses and work what remained down to leaner, more nimble dimensions. The world seemed to be catching up to Kodak and in fact to any number of large industrial American corporations.

Between 1978 and 1999, the *Fortune* 100 companies announced layoffs displacing more than five million employees. The average firm underwent 21 rounds of layoffs, roughly one per year. A new term, euphemistic but no less chilling, entered business discourse: "downsizing" became a regular fact of corporate life. The large American industrial corporation cut its workforce by a third over the last quarter of the twentieth century: employment in the average *Fortune* 100 industrial firm fell from over 90,000 to under 75,000. That is a weighty number, signaling blood and confusion within the firm and profound destabilization all around it. It represented an eventful set of structural and strategic adjustments, and beneath those adjustments a momentous redefinition of the corporation as a social and economic force in the lives of workers and communities. Business sociologists talked of the arrival of "free agency."[5] In an era of downsizing, of fluid "churn," of constant rapid change, employers and employees would have to shed the encumbering alliances that bound them tightly together, it was said. Corporations and the people who worked within them would have to learn to adopt more flexible patterns of association. (See Figure 7.1.)

Figure 7.1
Average Employment and Number of Layoffs, 1978–1999

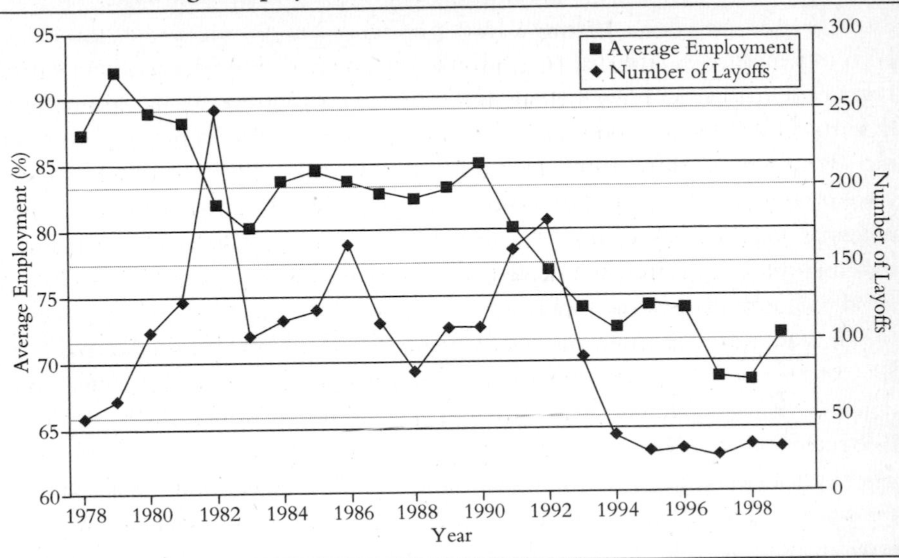

Perhaps the most wrenching social aspect of change was the dislocation of the white-collar elite—the managers, engineers, and administrative staff of the industrial corporation. These were people who had rarely known layoffs in any breadth or depth. Through the middle decades of the twentieth century, they were largely insulated from the ebbs and flows of business cycles. Substantial, well-established industrial firms might be compelled to thin out their factory workforces from time to time, but rarely the people who sat at desks. If you came into a corporation at the "management" level, the assumption ran, or if you reached the management level, and you were basically competent, you had a job for life. You had become an "organization man," part of the lifeblood of the enterprise, too vital to let go.[6]

Nevertheless, in company after company these people *were* let go. The industrial corporation cast its "organization men" adrift. At GE, "Neutron Jack" Welch lopped off entire units, sliced wide swathes of managers out of the company. (See Chapter 1.) In Detroit, engineers and staff personnel suffered recurring rounds of attrition as the once mighty and secure auto manufacturers underwent repeated rounds of restructuring and downsizing. (See Chapter 4.) By 1990, it seemed, only a few bastions of security were holding out: companies like Procter & Gamble, IBM, and Kodak, protecting longstanding traditions of loyalty and lifetime employment. Then, in a final, sharp spasm in the early 1990s, these companies too let go of the traditions.

The passage was painful, but remorseless and relentless, as corporations and their stakeholders adjusted to post-industrialization. Long-term commitments—the bonds of loyalty—that intertwined the fates of customers, employees, and investors of large industrial firms could not be maintained in the absence of growth. When large industrials were growing, its stakeholders participated in a positive-sum game. Everyone benefited in a series of interlinked bonds that formed a virtuous circle. Investors gave managers the capital and the autonomy to grow the enterprise. Firms in turn used these resources to produce an innovative stream of products that materially improved the lives of their customers, who showed their gratitude through loyal patronage. This customer loyalty, in turn, enabled firms to continue to grow revenues and profits, keeping investors happy and creating wonderful opportunities for employees. A growing firm could provide employees with both job security and good prospects for upward mobility.

The end of growth slowly but surely broke these symbiotic bonds. Given the option of buying cheaper imports that were increasingly of equivalent if not better quality, customers were the first to break their bonds of loyalty. Rather than buy Kodak, as they had for so long, they were willing to try Fuji. This first breach set in motion a vicious cycle that ultimately destroyed the long-standing compact among the stakeholders of the large industrial corporation. When customers began to defect, investors became edgy as well, losing confidence in the large American industrials' long-term growth prospects. Compelled to cut costs to win back customers, large industrial firms had no option but to start laying-off employees.

Unfortunately, against all hopes, this pattern of response did not restore the compact of loyalty that the large industrials once enjoyed. With each passing year, it became clearer that their halcyon years of growth were unlikely to return. Confronted with the necessity of adapting to decline, the stakeholders in the large industrial corporation found themselves locked in what had become a zero-sum game. Each stakeholder was pitted against the other. Industrial products became commodities, and customers switched their loyalties to whoever offered the best value for money—and that always meant more for less. Investors simply wanted their cash back as they shifted their attention to newer growing sectors of the economy. Employees eventually recognized that large industrials could no longer promise security or mobility. The plum jobs were no longer in the large industrials and employees too started to look elsewhere—the best and the brightest defecting the most readily. Each stakeholder was now looking after his or her own interests. Since each had other options, their relationship with large industrials changed from long-term commitments to flexible, short-term market-like contracts—undertaken for the moment, but reassessed constantly.

BACKDROP: "THE GREAT YELLOW FATHER"

From the outside, the situation may have looked like a structural exercise. But from within and around the corporation, what was happening was a much more complicated, more anguished, and baffling experience. Corporations were taking themselves apart as social constructs, as communities. They were disassembling themselves and, at the same time, in the midst of the confusion disassembly created, they were trying to reassemble themselves, refooting their people on new foundations and new understandings about what would hold the corporate compact together.

The process of recovenanting the corporation forms a vital dimension of the larger experience of post-industrialization. It is the kind of story that must be understood from both deep inside the corporation and from its periphery, from headquarters and from water coolers throughout the firm, from Wall Street and from Main Street, from the historical vantage point of over a century's worth of business evolution and (since we have scarcely begun the work of reassembly) from a perspective that peers uncertainly into the future. And it is the kind of story that becomes particularly powerful in cases like Kodak's, where loyalty had been painstakingly crafted and protected for so many years, and where its collapse culminated in 1993 in a sharp, dramatic confrontation. This was one of the companies that had invested most heavily, most deeply in loyalty. Here the dismantling of loyalty structures came especially hard, and the work of rebuilding began especially urgently, in a distinctively charged atmosphere.

To grasp what all that meant, one has to first take the measure of this particular company, this particular set of stakeholders, and the unique relationships that they had struck with each other. For what was coming undone had been decades and generations in the making. Eastman Kodak had socially and economically anchored Rochester for generations. Lifetime employment at "Big Yellow" had been a company policy and a community article of faith stretching as far back as the 1920s. Over long decades of growth and prosperity running through most of the twentieth century, Kodak's employees and managers collectively created a highly distinctive sense of the enterprise and the relationships that held it together.

The tradition stretched well back into the corporation's history. Within a few years of launching the firm, founder George Eastman was cultivating community within his company through a series of progressive gestures. First he set up an employee suggestion mechanism, then he installed dining halls, smoking rooms, and reading rooms at Kodak Park, then recreation programs, an assembly hall, and an athletic association; eventually Eastman hired string quartets to play while employees ate their lunches. The company set up an employee welfare fund for sick and injured workers, the Kodak Employees' Association, in 1911. By the 1920s, employees were also enjoying the benefits of the Eastman Savings and Loan Association (for mortgage financing) and the Kodak Employees' Realty Corporation (which sold vacant lots to workers). Thus within a few decades of operation, Kodak was defining itself as what one business historian has called "a paragon of welfare capitalism." Eastman tried conscientiously to avoid paternalistic domination of his employees' lives. The term "family" did not figure heavily in the company's industrial relations rhetoric. But the company nevertheless assumed the outlines of a social organization that went well beyond the business it transacted. Kodak's managers took to referring to the company's people as a "clan." Around Rochester, the company became known as the "Great Yellow Father."[7]

The impulse behind Great Yellow Fatherhood stemmed from several sources. Eastman's individual sense of corporate responsibility played a key role. Material considerations also figured in. Kodak's camera and film-making operations were extremely delicate technological processes, acutely vulnerable (at least in Eastman's thinking) to either sabotage or industrial espionage. And then there was the need to nurture the loyalty of a reliable, trained workforce. Finally, among the highly skilled engineers at Kodak's managerial core, a collective faith in the power of scientific methods of management ran strong. The company came to believe implicitly in its technological prowess, its ability to rationally structure and manage what today goes by the name of human resources. That outlook translated into a set of benefits and a sense of belonging that continued growth seemed to vindicate, or at any rate, ensconce unchallenged.

The ethos of common enterprise extended to profit-sharing of a unique sort. As Kodak went public and Eastman reaped lucrative financial rewards he distributed several "divvies" to the workers, offering stock at prices well below market value. In 1912, the company institutionalized the policy in the form of a profit-sharing "Wage Dividend Plan." The benefit, for which all Kodak workers were eligible, paid out substantial annual sums, averaging roughly a month's wages, in a formula keyed to the company's dividend payments. He implemented the wage dividends, Eastman explained, in order to "make the worker feel that he belongs to the success of the plant."[8] It was a striking measure, not just as an effort to deepen his workers' commitment to the enterprise, but more basically as an implicit affirmation that Kodak could and would be made to serve the interests of both its employees and its investors simultaneously, on something like an equal footing. Kodak in effect was trying not merely to adjudicate or broker, but more fundamentally to interlock and equalize standing of the corporation's various stakeholders.

Robust performance over the decades that followed fortified the benefit and, implicitly, bore out its underlying belief in mutual obligation. For a string of years rarely broken, Kodak's workers and shareholders received their regular, parallel payouts. "Dividend Day" became an annual event in Rochester, ritualistically reaffirming the collectivity of the enterprise's constituent parts. And in the meantime, the company worked to smooth out its production cycles and tighten up its strategic planning so as to create remarkably stable employment patterns. Generations of Kodak workers never experienced layoffs to any depth, even in the years of the Great Depression. Jobs within "Kodak Park," where the company manufactured its film, remained especially secure.[9]

So by the middle of the twentieth century, Kodak was solidifying a sense of itself as an organic union of interlocking interests. Which is not to say the corporate mechanism was seamless or frictionless. Investors, for example, regarded Kodak somewhat warily in the early years. Initially they fretted over the disproportionate share of equity held by the founder himself, fearing that any misfortune on Eastman's part would throw the company into chaos. In fact, this fear had been one of the key factors behind Eastman's early "divvies," which had the effect of distributing the stock more widely while at the same time keeping it under the company's control. The wage dividend arrangement, when it became part of the picture, also provoked some qualms among potential investors, cutting in as it did on shareholder returns.

The company stuck by the wage dividends, though it did reconfigure the system in subtle but significant ways in the 1950s. The program's original underlying formula basically split all corporate earnings over $3.50 per share evenly between employees and stockholders. Inflation, coupled with the benefit's specific formula, gradually created a more lopsided ratio, however, weighting increasingly heavily in favor of workers. Eventually brokers balked and started to recommend against buying the stock. The company resisted revising the formula, fearing that employees would protest. But it did take steps to mollify the brokers, first by paying extra dividends in the form of stock rather than cash, and then a few years later declaring a five-for-one stock split. Finally, in 1953, Kodak executives held their collective breath and capped wage dividend payout rates. Corporate managers kept an anxious eye on its workers as they did so, but they found that employees did not complain too loudly. The workers, it turned out, were measuring their wage dividends against their earnings, not against the company's dividend payments. In other words, the benefit had, at least by mid-century, drifted a bit into something less symbolic, something more substantial than what its founder had intended. Eastman had hoped that the wage dividends would foster a sense of ownership among his workers, by implication tying together the interests and outlooks of his employees and his investors. His workers, for their part, took a simpler view of the situation. As far as they were concerned, the wage dividend represented a bonus, a part of their earnings. Everyone had grown comfortable with the idea, it seemed: the company capped the payout again in 1956, and once more in 1960.[10]

THE IMPERATIVE OF STABILITY, THE ONSLAUGHT OF DESTABILIZATION

Kodak's effort to align the fortunes of its investors with those of its employees was highly distinctive, and the company's commitment to loyalty especially intense. The underlying logic, however, was widely felt across American industry. One way or another through the early and middle decades of the twentieth century, virtually every major American corporation learned to cultivate and came to depend on stability. The traditional industrial firm needed stability in all kinds of markets—financial, consumer, labor—in order to collect and coordinate the enormous resources these massive economic engines consumed.[11] They needed predictable customers, patient investors, reliable workforces and steady managerial talent, to tool up plants that consumed fortunes, to undertake product cycles that took years, to make and sell batches that numbered in the millions and higher.[12] Firms developed different ways of achieving and then sustaining that stability. But however they did it, it became an absolutely vital corporate skill.

Managerial loyalties became particularly deeply entrenched. As both the strategic and structural articulations of managerial capitalism grew more elaborate over the mid-1900s, the growth and prosperity of the multidivisional corporation depended increasingly heavily on its ability to nurture a loyal staff of professional managers. An implicit social contract emerged: Expectations of permanent employment and upward mobility came to define white-collar participation in the corporate enterprise. Kodak was somewhat unusual in extending the contract to its blue-collar workforce. But nearly all of its industrial peers recognized the usefulness—indeed the necessity—of maintaining cohesion and stability within its managerial "core." So long as stability was needed, and so long as business seemed clearly manageable, the organization man represented the heart and soul of the corporation.[13]

He, and, by the 1980s, she were in for a series of shocks at Kodak and everywhere else, as the vexing challenges and hard business realities of post-industrialization hit the industrial corporation. For by the 1980s, firms were no longer laboring to preserve stability. They were struggling to adapt, pressing to speed up, straining to operate more elastically. Strategic refocusing, structural overhaul, systems rewiring, and investor activism all took their toll. By the late 1980s, white-collar layoffs were roiling the corporate landscape.

What made business in the last quarter of the twentieth century so devastating was that all of it seemed to come apart at once. Churn unsettled an intricate overlay of loyalties. Customers began to dislodge themselves from brands, capital grew impatient, companies and their employees began to disengage from each other. And it all happened simultaneously. Flexibility emerged as the new corporate dictum, the new condition for doing business in the new economy. Businesses found themselves hurtling into an era of "fast history" in which product cycles accelerated from decades to years to (in extreme cases) months, markets and entire industries bloomed and matured in dizzying succession, and everybody had to cope with much more fluid business conditions.[14]

THE DRAMA OF DECLENSION: KODAK, 1992–1993

The sense of dislocation made itself felt everywhere. But it unsettled companies like Kodak and communities like Rochester particularly violently. For here the implicit contract had been especially widely extended and understood with a distinctive confidence. Here the whole assembly had worked: here the interests of workers and investors had been explicitly bound together. The fact that Kodak's wage dividend program settled into something like bonus status, despite the grander intentions of its implementers, might have indicated that Great Yellow Fatherhood was always, perhaps inevitably, a somewhat strained effort. The early retirements, layoffs, and downsizings of the 1980s certainly put new stresses on Kodak's corporate sense of loyalty as an organizing principle. Even so, Kodak managed to preserve at least a vestige of corporate paternalism and carry at least its habits and assumptions into the 1990s. Then they ruptured altogether, in what became a powerful drama of declension.

By the end of 1992, affairs at Kodak seemed to be sliding toward something like a crisis. Not that business was collapsing. The financials shaping up for the year indicated modest gains, certainly nothing calamitous. Still, pressure was building on the company. Kodak's market share was deteriorating, its share price was mired in the low 40s, earnings from operations in the core film business were slipping, and Wall Street analysts were growing increasingly pessimistic about the company's outlook and attitude. "After $1.8 billion worth of restructuring charges and double-digit currency translations, the company managed to post flat earnings," intoned B. Alex Henderson (Prudential Securities), in October in response to the company's third quarter earnings announcement. "It's hard to get excited about. It's kind of pathetic. We've gotten so jaded on this company that flat numbers are viewed as okay." In private meetings with Kodak executives, meanwhile, Henderson's peers were calling on the company to unload expensive diversification ventures and reduce operating expenses. The company's directors were also growing impatient. Early in January 1993, word broke that the board was setting up a committee of outside directors to monitor the company's operation.[15]

Ominous external events, meanwhile, loomed in the background. IBM was facing serious financial crisis and beginning to dismantle a long company tradition of lifetime employment. And over at General Motors, the board of directors was forcing out chairman and CEO Robert Stempel in an effort to force radical retrenchment there. The portents spread disquietingly through Rochester. Layoffs at Big Blue? Board intervention at General Motors, once the biggest and most powerful corporation in the world? What, then, lay in store for Kodak?

Signs from the top of Kodak Tower were not encouraging. For a decade, Big Yellow had been trying to downsize gently and gracefully, and for a decade the company had been slowly losing ground. Feeling the pressure, Kodak's executive management was preparing to retrench. Late in December 1992, CEO Kay Whitmore brought in an outsider, Christopher Steffen, to take up position as Kodak's new chief financial officer. Steffen came into Kodak's executive suites by way of Chrysler and Honeywell, where he had earned a reputation as a no-nonsense, results-oriented manager and a ruthless restructurer. Observers began predicting Kodak was in for sizeable layoffs.[16]

It was. On January 19, Kodak's workers assembled at Kodak Park, Elmgrove, and the company's corporate offices on State Street to learn the company would be letting 2,000 Rochester-area employees go from its Imaging Group, a third of them from the R&D staff, the remainder from administrative ranks. The cuts were not as deep as many outsiders had hoped (later a report would surface that some executives had pressed for twice as big a cut, though Whitmore had balked), but they were slicing into the heart of the company, excising engineers, middle managers, and support staff from its core film unit. "The people that are going to wind up being separated from Kodak are good status employees," lamented Leo "Jack" Thomas, president of the Imaging Group, "but we have got to reduce the amount of administrative activity in this company."[17]

What lay ahead was more complicated than just another round of layoffs at yet another old economy industrial. A struggle was emerging for the soul of Kodak. On one side, the company's investors were demanding downsizing and strategic refocusing. "Kodak Layoffs Satisfy Wall Street," announced one telling headline in the local *Rochester Democrat & Chronicle* on the day the news broke. Indeed, voices from the Street did chorus approbation. Henderson (Prudential Securities), for example, read the downsizing as an encouraging indication that Kodak was finally recognizing the low-growth prospects of the film business.

From the factory floor in Kodak Park, and for that matter from the offices on the middle floors of Kodak Tower, the situation naturally took on a different aspect. In the immediate aftermath of the January layoffs, anxiety prevailed, tempered by a sense that what was happening was bound to happen, was happening everywhere, represented only the beginning of change at Kodak. "All of us have been very stressed out for the last few weeks," reported Mae Dupree, from the company's financial services group; "I've been at Kodak 20 years. . . . I'm just hoping Kodak is able to turn around again—we've done it before. It has affected our work because we've been very busy and had a very heavy workload, but we are all positive and all have faith."[18] Other employees contacted by the local press sounded much the same notes: not of shock or despair, so much as resignation mingled with a measure of disillusionment. "People always thought that because the company was so big it could stay big," observed Ross Koenig, whose position as a financial analyst in the corporate staff afforded him a certain macroeconomic perspective as well as an internal view. "We're subject to the same competition as everybody else. It hit the chemical industry, it hit manufacturing—now it's the photographic industry's turn."[19]

Official rhetoric from the top of the company confirmed the hard truth of that assessment, assuring shareholders and warning employees that Kodak would be tightening up its operations. "We are going to look at the world as it is, not as we would like it to be," a company spokesperson promised.[20] In the press in January, the quote was unattributed, but a few months later Whitmore himself publicly attached his name to the phrasing, reiterating to his restless shareholders that the company was committed to "right-sizing" itself. With an eye on the company's increasingly impatient board, Whitmore was talking tough.[21]

An unsentimental view of Kodak's growth prospects implied, naturally, an unsentimental view of any obligations it might have towards its workforce. Yet Kodak's people had come to think of their company as something special, a community bound together by close ties of mutual loyalty. Now, as Kodak faced what Whitmore was describing as "a year for anything but business as usual," people in the ranks were waiting to see whether and how Kodak proposed to keep faith with its people.[22]

Events at Kodak were taking on an air of high drama, and the two principal players of that drama's opening act were clearly Whitmore and Steffen. The two stood for very different styles of corporate leadership—stewardship, in fact, of two distinct corporate aspects of Kodak. Steffen clearly came in as the shareholders' champion. News that he was entering Kodak's executive suites sent the stock up $3.25 in early-January 1993; he "hasn't even started yet and he's added a billion dollars to the company's value," one analyst enthused.[23]

In Rochester, meanwhile, Kodak employees were soon calling Steffen "Cut and Slash." The new CFO had not participated in the January layoffs, but his arrival coincided closely with the downsizing and the two events were unmistakably related: both were intended as signals to the board and to investors that Kodak was resolved to restructure rationally and, if need be, ruthlessly. Steffen himself confirmed what he stood for and what he hoped to accomplish at Kodak, stating as he came in that the company needed a "definite change."[24] The *Wall Street Journal* caught the character of the man, the symbolic role he was playing in this corporate drama, in his costume and his bearing. "Mr. Steffen," a profile observed, "favors limited-edition Trafalgar suspenders and matching tie and kerchief sets. He relishes confrontation. Referring to his earlier experience at Chrysler Corp., he says that when half the workers at a troubled company must be laid off, 'the other half buy in pretty quickly.' "[25]

Whitmore, for his part, was also talking tough, but he seemed uncomfortable in that role. Kodak's chairman and CEO had been with Big Yellow for 33 years when he assumed leadership (in 1990), having risen through the managerial ranks, attended MIT's Sloan School of Management at Kodak's expense midway through his career, and deeply imbibed the company's distinctive ethos of community. In a phrase that seemed to characterize Kodak itself, *Forbes* described Whitmore as "a gentlemanly engineer." The same *Journal* report that depicted Steffen in his Trafalgar suspenders, itching for confrontation, profiled Whitmore as "the sort of boss most people would want: Kind, generous, collegial. Sure, he's chairman of Eastman Kodak Co., but Mr. Whitmore, 60 years old, often wears his name tag on his shirt just like the regular Joes." He was a Morman and a boy scout, by all accounts an honorable man. Not particularly adept at corporate politics, Whitmore managed by consensus, spoke his mind, felt the responsibilities of his office deeply. A leader, in sum, shaped by the system of loyalty he was now called upon to put aside. Certainly he enjoyed a profound rapport with his company and his people. "The question," as the *Journal* put it, "is whether Mr. Whitmore is a charming anachronism in an age that requires Christopher Steffen."[26]

The question pressed in on Kodak. By the time the *Journal* was uttering the suggestion, it had become clear on Wall Street and in Rochester that the chairman and the CFO were at odds. The struggle happened largely behind-the-scenes—offstage, as it were, out of hearing up in the high reaches of Kodak Tower. But the outcome emerged quickly enough. In late-April, Steffen abruptly resigned—news that "sent shock waves from State Street to Wall Street," according to the *Rochester Business Journal.*[27]

His explanation was carefully bland. "The company and I," he stated for the record, "disagree on the approach to solving its problems."[28] Whitmore's account was a little more forthcoming. Steffen "wasn't fully comfortable with the methodology I was using, with how much management buy-in [we needed] to go forward," Whitmore reported. Indeed, by several accounts Steffen had quickly grown frustrated at the company's ambivalence about doing what needed to be done (he felt) to turn things around. And he freely expressed his frustration to investment analysts, an indiscretion that reportedly peeved Whitmore. The CEO himself indicated as much in a veiled comment: "I said to Mr. Steffen I'm the chief executive, this is how I want to do it. Let me make a stab at making my process work."[29]

These kinds of details emerged in various accounts over the next few days, as investors and employees absorbed the news and weighed its import. For a company and a city beginning to confront hard realities, Steffen's departure may have removed a threatening outsider, but it did not create anything like a sense of relief. If anything, it intensified the building pressure. The stock plunged more than \$5, to under \$48, in the immediate aftermath of Steffen's resignation, and only partially recovered over the next few days.[30] "A Whitmore under so much pressure," warned the *Rochester Democrat & Chronicle,* "may not have the ability to soften the blow for workers or for Rochester. Maybe Steffen is not a part of Eastman Kodak, but the expectations that went with him still are. It may be too late to push the genie back into the bottle."[31]

Indeed, Steffen's exit galvanized investor frustrations with Kodak. B. Alex Henderson described himself as "stunned, dismayed, disheartened" to hear the news. R. Jackson Blackstock (First Boston) warned that repercussions were in store: "Either board members get Whitmore to deliver results or they deliver Whitmore's head."[32] Within Kodak's executive circle, the mood was reported to be sober. "When the stock drops 12 percent in one day and you've got Goldman Sachs and Morgan Stanley going from a buy to a sell," an anonymous executive conceded, "you've got to hold someone responsible—and that's Kay [Whitmore]."[33]

Whitmore realized he was facing a serious crisis. Whether intentionally or not, Steffen had timed his exit for maximum dramatic effect, pulling out only a few weeks before the company's annual meeting with its shareholders—just enough time to bring investor discontent to a high boil. To calm or at any rate test the waters, the CEO hurriedly arranged a series of meetings with analysts in the days leading up to the meeting. In these private sessions (according to press accounts), Whitmore forcefully affirmed that he appreciated the urgency of the situation and promised to sell off a major asset. Investors came away guardedly reassured, conditionally supportive. "Things will get resolved because there's going to be tremendous pressure," decided Richard Rosen (Bear Stearns); "I think Kay probably saw his own mortality at this morning's meeting."[34] Calpers fund managers also let themselves be persuaded by Whitmore's pitch, in part because the CEO agreed to let Calpers set up "close and active" monitoring of the company's performance.[35]

Now Kodak's board of directors began to emerge from the background of the drama. Whitmore depended on their support. In earlier, happier times management could have counted on it more-or-less automatically. But in an age of investor activism, when the understandings that traditionally underpinned corporate governance were giving way (another band of loyalties, once wrapped tightly around Kodak, now coming undone)—in such a climate, the board could not afford unconditional support. The company's financial performance was mediocre, and now it appeared to be shrinking from the kind of remedies that other companies were adopting. The board needed to see performance in several senses of the term, by this point. The company was just not playing well in the market, and to that extent it no longer mattered all that much whether Whitmore's turnaround tactics were workable or not. The situation's symbolic dimension—its meanings as a drama—was assuming paramount importance. And on this count, the board was nervous. A few days before the annual meeting, all nine outside directors affirmed they "fully support[ed]" Whitmore. That was for public consumption. But they, like analysts, were losing patience, and they made it clear they expected Whitmore to find a new CFO, preferably an outsider. They wanted to see better numbers, quickly.[36]

The scene now shifted down to Ft. Lauderdale, Florida, where some 400 stockholders gathered to hear company executives account for their performance over the last year of operation. Annual meetings tend to be highly staged, often largely ceremonial affairs, but Kodak's 1993 session took place in a highly charged atmosphere and provided more drama than usual. Whitmore was in damage control mode, fully aware that his shareholders were aroused and his board impatient. "Shareholders have been an underserved community in recent years," the chairman conceded in his speech to the assembly. "You've raised the question of whether we have the stomach for change. We will all find out as this rolls out. It is our 100 percent intention to deliver." He was vague on specifics, reiterating his promise to sell-off at least one major business. But he did stress he would not balk at further downsizing. "Part of my commitment," he declared (in remarks that must have stirred apprehension in Rochester, when they were read in the local paper the following day) "is not to be held captive to Rochester."[37]

Shareholders took in the performance, presumably measuring the man before them. Some were wavering. At least one was fed up. Texas shareholder John Ragusa had driven from Texas all the way to Ft. Lauderdale to confront Whitmore, and when the time for questions from the floor arrived he stood up to complain bluntly about the company's performance, adding "the people directly responsible for this mess are sitting right up front." As Ragusa continued, running over his three minutes, Whitmore interrupted to ask him to wrap up his remarks. Ragusa demurred. "You're going to force me to ask you to leave," Whitmore warned. "I would remind you," Ragusa shot back, "that you are an employee here." The line reportedly drew scattered applause. Ragusa promised to summarize the rest of his remarks. Whitmore let him finish.[38]

In the end, Whitmore escaped more damaging censure—sort of. In the wake of the meeting, Goldman Sachs upgraded Kodak stock to "buy" and the share price promptly rose $1.625 to $53 in heavy trading.[39] But the result hardly amounted to an endorsement of management. In fact what was happening, judging from the analyst commentary emerging from Florida, was that investors were growing confident that they would be able to force the board of directors to do what needed to be done. They were taking their measure of the board, not of Whitmore. "The dynamics have gone beyond the company," Goldman's Jack Kelly declared, "to shareholder activism and the outside board." He and his peers took particular heart in the voting on a proposal to unstagger the board elections. The proposal fell short of passage, but nonetheless attracted an eye-opening 42 percent of the vote. "That's a message," Whitmore conceded. "The board of directors has got to look at that." As, of course, did Whitmore himself.[40]

Back in Rochester, where the Florida proceedings received front-page coverage, reaction coalesced into a spirit of resolute acceptance. A team of community leaders had traveled down to the meeting to register their support for Whitmore, his management team, and their plans for cost-cutting. Rochester's business community recognized that Kodak had to tighten up, declared Thomas Mooney, president of the Greater Rochester Metro Chamber of Commerce; everybody was "ready to get on with it."[41] Monroe County Executive Robert King struck the same note, urging Kodak to do whatever needed to be done to keep itself viable. If that meant accepting short-term pain in the form of layoffs, so be it; "it will strengthen Kodak so they won't have to go through this again in the future," King stated.[42] And the *Rochester Democrat & Chronicle* echoed the sentiment. "In the long run, a restructured, healthier Kodak will be good for the entire community," a lead editorial declared. If that meant the company could no longer "be held hostage to Rochester," then "neither can Rochester be hostage to Kodak. This community has to get ready." In short, the local paper declared, a "new era" was upon everybody. "We've got to recognize that the Great Yellow Father can't take care of all of us any longer. We've got to grow up and take care of ourselves."[43]

Bracing words, describing a daunting prospect. Disentangling an entity like Kodak from a community like Rochester was bound to be profoundly dislocating. In one sense the process was already well underway. Local economists indicated that over the last decade or so the region's employment base had diversified significantly. While Kodak's payroll had shrunk, thousands of small-scale firms had taken root in the area, many of them planted by former Kodak engineers and managers who had been coaxed into voluntary "separation." Kodak's share of the regional nonagricultural workforce had fallen from close to 25 percent a decade before to less than 15 percent in 1992.[44] "Restructuring at Kodak hardly means the lights are going out on Rochester," the *Democrat & Chronicle* concluded.[45] But then, the wider dimensions of corporate involvement were harder to assess. Kodak was, for example, one of the largest sources of charitable donations in the region. Local charities were already trying to gauge how the company's belt-tightening would affect them.[46]

In any event, Kodak had long figured as more than an employer in Rochester's collective imagination. The company had been a touchstone for more than a century, a fixed point on the map and, more widely, an orienting emblem of the community's participation in the wider business world. If its economic role was diminishing, its symbolic role lingered. The unmistakable signs of instability within Kodak revealed and refracted a wider, deeper sense of a world unmooring.

"Overhaul Starts": The Sense Making

By the time the annual meeting had dispersed, it was clear that Whitmore's position was growing precarious. Still, the axe seemed to drop suddenly. On August 7, the front page of the *Rochester Democrat & Chronicle* ran a grainy picture of Whitmore, grim-faced, driving away from Kodak headquarters. Above that image loomed a stark headline: "Overhaul starts."[47]

In fact, it was already well underway, though the news had been kept under wraps for several weeks. Late in July the board had met, asked its inside directors to leave the room, and deposed Whitmore on a unanimous vote. Subsequent accounts revealed that the outside directors had been trying for several years to prod Whitmore to more vigorous action, including deeper, sharper cuts in personnel. (Institutional investors were calling for layoffs of 20,000, 10 times the number Whitmore had reluctantly signed off on in January.) Board members also wanted the CEO to start benchmarking Kodak against leading competitors. Apparently the last straw had been Whitmore's choice for Steffen's replacement, an (unnamed) candidate the board had soundly rejected.[48]

Predictably, investment analysts cheered the board's move. Whitmore, they had become convinced, simply was not up to the job of revamping Kodak. He "didn't have the stomach to take the steps necessary to turn around the company," concluded Alex Henderson.[49] J. Robert Maney (Prudential Bache) sounded a little less macho, a little more ambivalent, but essentially he agreed: "Kay Whitmore is a decent human being. He grew up with these people. He did not have it in his heart to throw them out in the street. And he was never going to be successful until he did that."[50]

Within the company's ranks, the reaction was more complicated. People understood the occasion as marking the passing of an era for Kodak. Whitmore had come to embody the old corporation. His exit stirred up deeply conflicted responses. He was mourned. "I'm afraid of the company losing its human element," admitted Patricia Papa, who had been secretary with Kodak for 25 years and who had recently retired.[51] "I don't think an outside person will have as much care for the employees," added a Kodak machinist who had worked with the company for 24 years; "I think that some of these stockholders that are so concerned about their dividends should be happy that they don't have stock in IBM."[52] Anxiety, tinged with an indefinite but strong sense of betrayal, colored the response recorded by another employee, anonymous, 17 years with the company: "I've worked extremely hard to earn a good reputation. I've worked long hours, and never asked for any extra compensation. I feel like it's all for naught. It's frightening. I've got four children, a single income. It looks extremely bleak. . . . My greatest fear is for the children, their education. This shakes my faith to pieces—my faith that education, hard work will pay off. . . . I want to demonstrate now that I'm a good worker but the stress of the announcement is paralyzing me. I feel like my children are betrayed. That's the bottom line. All of us are betrayed."[53]

Other voices from within Kodak, however, expressed the hope that the company would now be able to move more forcefully toward recovery. "A lot of people have been talking that it's a good thing he resigned, or stepped down," commented Kathy Jason, a secretary working in Kodak Park. "A lot of people think it's a good thing they're looking outside rather than within. . . . Maybe we need to change and go outside and bring someone in. We know they'll be more layoffs. Maybe it's just best to get it over with."[54] It all came down to where you stood within the company, according to one employee within headquarters (who declined to be named but who did relate being "redeployed" 12 times over the last 18 years): "I find it interesting how people at Kodak see this. From midmanagement up, they see it as a death in the family like, 'Oh my god, I can't believe this is happening.' They're very sorrowful, upset. But people under that level were jumping for joy in the hallways. . . . The rest of us want a leader, someone with a clear vision."[55]

Another response was even more telling. Kevin Hurley, who worked on the motion picture staff at Kodak Park, recognized that events were unraveling the company's traditional loyalty structures. "A lot of people feel Kay is like a parental figure at Kodak. A lot of people are nervous they'll bring in someone else who'll make wide cuts," Hurley observed. But then, he was also watching the share-price, and part of him felt compelled to add, "I'm surprised to see the stock market went up like that. I wish I'd gotten into it." All of which he capped with, "a lot of people feel we needed a change."[56]

Hurley was all over the map. But then, so was everybody. It was hard to let go. It was time to let go. It was hard to know how to let go. People pined for loyalty while they primed themselves for free agency.

It fell to the *Democrat & Chronicle* to editorially encapsulate the situation and its meanings for the community. Which proved profoundly difficult. There seemed to be several meanings here, and the paper's editors struggled to come to terms with them. "The most dismal view" of the news was "to see it as a coup." Whitmore's dismissal, unprecedented for Kodak, "was engineered by outside directors who have no particular loyalty to the community the company has nurtured for so many years. In this view, Kodak is no longer the company George Eastman built." But the situation was complicated, the editors recognized. The company's shareholders had legitimate interests at stake here, interests certainly underserved by Whitmore's leadership. So who had the stronger claim on the company? "There's got to be some middle ground," the editorial pleaded. "Let's hope that the committee also remembers Whitmore's strengths. . . . He cares deeply about his workers, and about the people of his community. And thousands of them are Kodak shareholders, too."[57]

Ultimately the situation confronting Kodak and Rochester was bigger than either the company or the city. "Everybody understands that Kodak is in need of the same kind of reshaping that faces so much of the rest of American industry," the editorial recognized. "New blood and new ideas are desperately needed. But all this downsizing and streamlining is costing the American people in other ways. Laid-off workers can't be customers for anybody's products. . . . So yes, find a new chief executive officer who can take Kodak into the twenty-first century. But find someone who will let the company keep its human face too."[58]

In the wake of Whitmore's dismissal, Kodak fell under interim management while the board searched for a replacement. Meanwhile, plans went forward for implementing a preliminary restructuring along the lines that the investment community was so clearly demanding. On August 18, with Whitmore still standing in and his succession still undecided, the company announced it would layoff 10,000 employees, 10 percent of the total workforce, by the end of 1995. "Despite these reductions," Whitmore stated in a letter to employees, "the overwhelming number of you will not only be around tomorrow, but will be responsible for making this company more competitive and successful."[59] To this bracing sentiment other company spokespeople added, in comments to the press, that most of the coming layoffs would be "involuntary separations." And several investment analysts contributed predictions that further rounds of layoffs would probably follow on the appointment of a new CEO.[60]

There matters stood, suspended, ominous, for several months. Finally, in late October, word came down that the board had chosen George Fisher, head of Motorola, as Kodak's next leader. It was a bold choice, one that took nearly everybody by surprise. Given the company's circumstances, most analysts had expected the board to bring in a restructuring artist, someone like Steffen, to do the sharp cutting and rigorous streamlining that Kodak seemed to require. Fisher represented a very different strategic direction. He was a builder, not a cutter, "a professorial type," as the *Wall Street Journal* characterized him, "with no experience in, or appetite for, messy corporate retrenchment."[61] Yet the match was intriguing. Fisher had worked magic at old-line Motorola, reviving the company and repositioning it in the New Economy vanguard by shrewdly picking new technologies and overhauling its development and manufacturing methods. It was the same kind of magic Kodak had been trying to work itself. Fisher's stature as a high-tech strategist boded well for the next round.

It also became clear the appointment would provide a measure of relief, at least temporarily, for the company's workforce. As he took his bearings at Kodak, the new CEO braked downsizing plans and began issuing very different rhetoric from the executive office. Thus, one year after Whitmore had promised shareholders to apply a hard-edged realism in "right-sizing" the company, Fisher in his first annual report declared: "The people of this company really are its greatest asset. They are the heart of Kodak, and together we will build this company to be, once again, one of the finest companies in the world."[62]

Though a company outsider, Fisher was powerfully impressed with Kodak's people and with the spirit of mutual enterprise that bound them together. "Ultimately, we will be measured by our publics: our customers, our employees, our shareholders, our suppliers, and the communities in which we live. . . . Certainly there will be a short-term focus on some of the financial issues, but longer term, you will see a greater focus on total customer satisfaction and employee satisfaction—both of which will lead us to higher quality, better growth, and improved profitability."

So Kodak's dramatic year of definition closed in suspense, not resolution. Or, if the company's drama had concluded, it was conclusion of a muddy sort—an effort to recapture or redefine tenets that had seemed to have both remained vital yet somehow become unworkable. First the analysts' champion, Steffen, had been forced out, then the company's champion, Whitmore, was unseated. A new figure, Fisher, appeared on the scene, collected up the pieces . . . and started trying to fit them all together again. "This guy is going to do the cost cuts," B. Alex Henderson (Prudential Securities) remained confident, "but he's going to do it at his pace. The time horizon has been pushed out from two years to five years."[63] Kodak's year of decision had become, by the end, little more than a year of agonized *indecision*.

Fisher's arrival had in effect created a window of opportunity for the company, and the new CEO worked busily to make the most of it, redefining the company's strategic core as imaging, buying down debt, selling or spinning off various businesses (Sterling Winthrop, Clinical Diagnostics, Eastman Chemical) that fell outside the core. All of which created, for core employees, an atmosphere of growth and possibility, an invigorating buzz that held off anxieties over retrenchment. The new

CEO was pressing the company to streamline its processes and accelerate its cycle times, but he also articulated an inspiring vision of the company's prospects. "Digital imaging is going to be like the cellular phone business," Fisher predicted in *Forbes:* "highly competitive, very high growth, good profits for the leader, but not for the followers."[64]

The respite, however, was short. In 1997, competition from Fuji heated up once again. The Japanese firm cut its film prices sharply, dug back into Kodak's market share (which dropped from 80 percent to 75 percent), and launched a major initiative to shift film and paper production from Japanese over to American plants. Under this onslaught, Kodak's earnings slumped badly, prompting analysts once again to call for restructuring. By October, the mainstream business press was weighing in on the issue, reporting that Big Yellow's overhead was heavy and observing that the number of employees working in the company's continuing operations had actually swollen by 3,000 during Fisher's tenure.[65]

Now Fisher, like Whitmore before him, began to send out the warning signals that had to be sent. In September 1997, he issued a letter to employees warning that the company was facing another round of cost-cutting. Earnings were falling short, the shareprice was plunging, Kodak was "under siege," Fisher related, "to win this fight will require some sacrifice for us all."[66]

Reworking the Terms of Employment

The 1997 layoffs marked a decade and a half of downsizing at Kodak. Initially the "separations" were voluntary, but not for long. Some relatively stable stretches stanched the flow temporarily, but then the layoffs resumed again. Round by round, the number of Kodak jobs in the Rochester area shrank, from a peak of 60,400 in 1982 to 34,000 by 1998, with a target figure of 27,700 scheduled by the end of the century (see Figure 7.2).[67] Uneasily, under evident duress, Kodak was redefining what it meant to be an employee of the company. And Rochester, too, was redefining its sense of the corporation and its role in the community.

The process had certainly made Kodak more efficient, if not necessarily more profitable. The ratio of sales per employee climbed steadily between 1987 and 1999. In terms of profit per employee, on the other hand, Kodak's performance was more erratic. Kodak's people, the numbers indicate, were running harder to stay in place (Figure 7.3).

Fisher had entered the process from the outside, after it had already been set underway. He sensed its meanings and implications, though, for both the company and the community. He recognized that the work before him consisted not just of improving Kodak's financial performance, but more fundamentally of reconstituting the ties that bound the company to its employees. Battered by years of departures and downsizing, the company's sense of its social contract with its workers needed to be

Figure 7.2
Total Employment for Eastman Kodak, 1978–1999

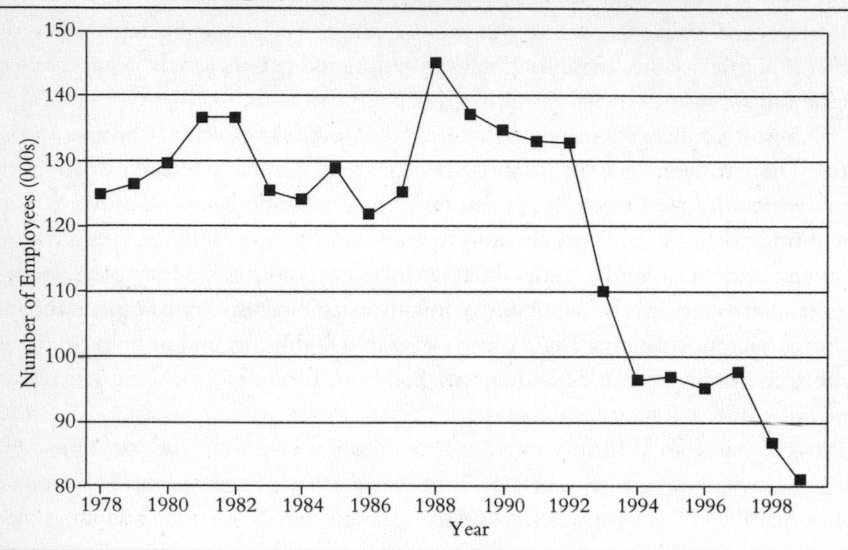

Figure 7.3
Sales/Employee and Profits/Employee, 1978–1999

not just repaired, but rebuilt on new foundations. To lead Kodak through that transformation, Fisher tapped Michael Morley.

It was a telling choice. Morley came from deep within the company, deep within the community. Born and raised in Rochester, he had spent his entire career at Kodak, rising from shift work on the floor at Kodak Park, via night classes in business administration at Rochester Institute of Technology (reinforced later with a masters in management from MIT), to become general manager of the North American operations in the Consumer Imaging Division. He represented, in other words, something like an object lesson of the Organization Man, the kind of figure who had built and been built by the company. Initially drawn to Kodak by the promise of secure employment and the opportunity for advancement, Morley had made the most of both, establishing himself as one of Kodak's highly promising managers, earmarked for important things. "Michael had been identified early in his career as someone with extraordinary potential in the field of human relations," a retired Kodak executive affirmed in a profile in the *Rochester Business Journal,* "and he had been groomed through a variety of management experiences to prepare him for that role." At first he regarded Fisher's offer to move from Consumer Imaging over to Human Resources warily. But Fisher prevailed, persuading Morley that, in Kodak's situation, Human Resources had become something much more important, more strategic, than an administrative function.[68]

In choosing Morley, Fisher sent a strong signal through the organization, implicitly recognizing and promising to salvage what was essential in the relationship that had traditionally bound up Kodak with its people. But not to keep the old covenant entirely intact. Kodak's workforce had to become more performance-oriented, Fisher warned, even as people carried forward the spirit of mutual commitment that had traditionally vitalized the company as a corporate collective. In short, Kodak's new senior management was looking for a way to combine the virtues of loyalty with the entrepreneurial drive of free agency. The company needed to re-strike terms with its people. In 1996, Human Resources under Morley set up focus groups gathering employee input on how to make Kodak a high-performance company. These sessions laid the groundwork for reformulating what company executives called a "social contract" with Kodak's workforce. That contract bound Kodak's workers to pledge their effort, commitment, and willingness to adapt to change; and pledged the corporation to offer at least 40 hours of training to help each employee reach individual development goals. The success of subordinate employees in achieving their objectives became part of performance criteria for their managers. In effect, the company was going to try to craft an understanding that folded loyalty and performance together. The resulting adjustments, Morley admitted a few years into the transformation, proved "traumatic and gratifying," particularly for the company's middle management. "Some were taken aback by the criticism."[69]

New rhetoric about respect for individuals, integrity, trust, and so on was all well and good—even vital. But the work also had to be extended to the company's traditional symbols of collective purpose. To instill a new sense of belonging in Kodak, the terms of the company's wage dividend plan had to be redrawn.

By the late-1990s, the wage dividend had evolved into what amounted essentially to a guaranteed bonus, fluctuating between 5 percent to 15 percent of employees' base wages, irrespective of the company's share performance. The company reformulated the plan beginning in 1995, eliminating both minimum and maximum dividend rates and establishing return on assets targets that had to be hit in order to trigger the benefit. Thus, for example, in 1995 employees received an 8.2 percent wage dividend payment, based on a return on net assets level that grew five basis points. The reformulated plan, Fisher explained, represented an effort on Kodak's part "to drive continuous improvement."[70]

Several years later, in the wake of the 1997 layoffs, Fisher and his executive team again retooled the wage dividend plan, this time pegging it to the company's calculation of "economic value added" over the previous year. The EVA metric, one Fisher was trying to embed in Kodak's managerial consciousness, calculated the company's after-tax operating profit, minus the total annual cost of the capital it consumed. It was a metric, in other words, shaped by the conviction that the corporation's ultimate responsibility was to create wealth for its investors, and guard vigilantly against destroying capital. Retrospective internal calculations indicated Kodak had been earning a return of about 6 percent on capital that had cost more than 14 percent over the six years between 1988 and 1993.[71]

Kodak was feeling its way into the era of free agency, fighting in the marketplace, struggling to hold on to investor confidence, and within its own ranks forging a new kind of covenant with its people.

CONCLUSION: KODAK AS CAMERA LENS

As the American industrial corporation amassed bulk and gathered momentum over the late nineteenth and early twentieth centuries, it pulled vast social forces into its orbit. It assembled workforces numbering in the tens and hundreds of thousands; collectively it became the principal means of livelihood for thousands of American communities. It created a vital capital market, drawing investors into what rapidly established itself as the economy's central engine of wealth creation. And it built the consumer marketplace, imposing patterns of mass production and mass distribution that predominantly shaped modern material life. What made everything work was that it all worked in concert. Arguably the dominant form of social organization in twentieth century America, the industrial corporation sustained and was in turn sustained by a highly complex series of extended, nested relationships, each organically bound up with the other. Employees and employers bound themselves together, investors and managers pledged a mutual faith, consumers and companies came to terms. Each of these affiliations enmeshed themselves deeply in the corporate enterprise.

All of which has made the decline of the industrial corporation a wrenching transformation, the impact of which has reached far beyond the boundaries of the firms themselves. Consider the case of Kodak and Rochester. In 1997, even after successive waves of downsizing, the company remained the region's largest employer. Art Aspengren, president of Rochester's Industrial Management Council, affirmed, "Kodak is the strength of the fabric of this community. It is in everything. If there is such a thing as a company town, this is a company town."[72]

But if Rochester remained a "company town," it was nevertheless a fundamentally altered landscape. Over the last two decades of the twentieth century, Kodak's Rochester-area employment fell from just over 60,000 to under 28,000. In 1982, Kodak accounted for 14 percent of the region's workforce; by 1998, the share had dropped to 7 percent. Rochester had not collapsed altogether, nor had it necessarily de-industrialized. In the place of Kodak (and several other major industrial firms), some 1,500 smaller manufacturers had established themselves in the region—many of them set up by downsized Kodak engineers and managers. As employment dispersed, so too did the demographic picture of the region: Rochester's city population shrank from 330,000 in the 1960s to 220,000 in the late 1990s. And if the region was still faring fairly well, Downtown Rochester was decaying noticeably. By the end of the 1990s, some 39,000 residents were living on welfare, a figure well over the 27,700 area people Kodak employed.[73]

Those were some of the tangible ramifications. The intangible ones defy quantification, of course, but they were even more disorienting. Kodak had anchored Rochester culturally as well as economically. Kodak Tower was still standing, in the wake of Whitmore's overthrow and Fisher's failing effort to shore up the walls, but no longer looming so dominantly in the public imagination, no longer lording masterfully and beneficently over the city or the wider reaches of the company.

Consider, for example, the deeply ambivalent reaction of Jim Sharlow, one of the casualties of the 1993 layoffs. Sharlow had started with Kodak as a machinist at the age of 23, and eventually moved into the managerial ranks. "Kodak was everything. How far I could go seemed to depend on my own ambition," he recalled feeling, neatly articulating the social contract that had governed corporate managerial employment. A Rochester native, he moved to California in the 1980s to run a plant for the company. When Kodak closed the plant down, it did not offer to bring Sharlow back to Rochester. "I knew there were hundreds and even thousands being laid off. I guess I thought I was special," he conceded. "Then the day came when they made a business decision to let me go. It was, 'Bye, and don't let the door hit you.'" The event was a deeply wounding blow for Sharlow, and a lesson for his (grown) daughter, Karen: "We've been taught our whole lives that if you give your loyalty to someone or something, it gives you something back. In our house, we didn't even use anything that wasn't Kodak, Kodak film, Kodak cameras. No one will take care of you. We know."

He had been a loyal employee and manager. He was also an investor and an increasingly active one as the layoff ate into his retirement savings. Most of the Sharlow nest egg resided in a 401(k), invested in mutual funds, stocks, bonds. Sharlow kept a close and demanding eye on his portfolio, according to a newspaper reporter. "He only gambles in the stock market when he is almost sure he will win. Two winters ago, when the market dropped sharply, he sold and put the money elsewhere. He knows the key to the market is long-term investment, but he could not afford to watch their savings vanish."[74] It was just that kind of thinking on the market end that had driven Kodak to let him go.

All kinds of "investments" in the company were surfacing, it appears, all kinds of currents pushing and pulling, as the industrial economy receded and the contours of a post-industrial landscape emerged. As individuals, we stand in complicated, multifaceted relation to the industrial corporation. As consumers, we demand value, driving corporations to maximize quality and pare down prices. As investors, we demand performance, driving corporations to increase growth and optimize earnings. While as employees, we try to ride out the episodes of restructuring, downsizing, consolidating, and general dislocation that corporations undergo as they strain to maximize quality, pare down prices, increase growth, and optimize earnings. We are all, it turns out, swimming simultaneously in multiple markets.

CHAPTER 8

THE CHURNING MIX: THE CHANGING NATURE OF THE LARGEST AMERICAN COMPANIES

In the 1990s, the biggest American industrial corporations benefited from the U.S. economy's sustained expansion. Between 1992 and 2000, macroeconomic growth rates and annual productivity increases rivaled those of the golden post-World War II years, while unemployment and inflation rates tumbled to low levels. At the same time, the big American industrials also benefited from macroeconomic woes that beset their foreign rivals, which themselves now struggled with the logic of industrial decline. These benign external conditions, combined with the sweeping changes the American industrials had made in strategy, structure, systems, and governance, produced more efficient and productive companies, as well as fatter margins and higher stock prices. But the *Fortune* 100 industrials remained frustrated in their ongoing quest for significant growth. Large-scale mergers and acquisitions continued to roil the industrial sector.

The frustrations of the big industrials remained rooted in the steady migration of the modern economy from production of traditional goods toward services and high technology, knowledge-intensive products. The rise of the post-industrial economy is evident in the churning mix of companies on the *Fortune* 100 lists from 1955 to 2000 (see Tables 2.2 to 2.6 in Chapter 2). Over time, the lists contained fewer names of older industrial corporations and many more of those born in the last quarter of the twentieth century. A careful examination of the lists shows the clear decline of the industrial sector and the rise of new sectors of the economy. Only 20 percent of the companies on the 1974 list were still ranked in the top 100 a quarter century later. Worse yet, only 10 percent made it to the top 100 ranked by market value. To the extent that market value is a leading indicator of future performance, these data suggest that financial markets no longer expected industrial corporations to deliver superior long-term earnings growth. This decline is even more telling when the 1974 list is compared with the 1954 list, when *Fortune* first started its annual ranking of America's largest corporations based on revenues. Over 75 percent of the companies on the 1974 list had appeared on the 1954 list. The last quarter of the twentieth century was truly a period of fading fortunes for America's biggest industrial corporations.

THE OLD AND THE NEW: EXITS AND ENTRIES FROM THE LISTS OF THE BIGGEST COMPANIES

One might argue as Heraclitus did two millennia ago that "nothing stays still—all is flux." Indeed, the composition of the *Fortune* and *Forbes* 100 has always been changing. But during the first three-quarters of this century, the change was gradual and primarily consisted of some new industrial companies replacing older ones. For instance, a comparison of the 1954 and 1974 lists shows that competitors in the pharmaceutical (e.g., J&J and American Hospital Supply) and office equipment sectors (e.g., Xerox) were more likely to be on the 1974 list. So were diversified conglomerates like ITT and Litton that grew by unrelated diversification during the 1960s. Yet the 1974 list has fundamentally the same character as the 1954 list. Manufacturing companies dominate both lists. By the end of the twentieth century, the *Fortune* 100 list looks vastly different. Only a quarter of the companies represent the manufacturing sector (see Table 8.1).

The drift of industrial companies from the center of the U.S. economy led *Fortune* in 1995 to itself abandon its practice of considering only the largest industrial corporations in defining and tracking its biggest companies. The new list included

Table 8.1
Composition of the 100 Largest Companies by Sales and Market Capitalization: 1955, 1974, 1999

Sector	*Sales 1955*	*Sales 1974*	*Sales 1999*	*Market Value 1955*	*Market Value 1974*	*Market Value 1999*
Manufacturing	75	64	25	63	61	14
Retailing	14	15	17	4	4	4
Financial services	1	7	23	3	7	15
Telecommunications/media	3	5	10	3	3	24
Information technologies	2	5	11	1	7	29
Pharmaceuticals/health care	0	2	8	2	13	12
Utilities	2	0	3	21	4	1
Transport & other services	3	2	3	3	1	1

Note: The 1955 and 1974 lists are reconstructed to include the largest companies in all sectors, not just the industrial sector which formed the basis of the actual *Fortune* lists for those years.

many new entrants.[1] The editors used examples from a variety of sectors to illustrate the blurring of boundaries between manufacturing and services. They noted the difficulty of classifying even a quintessential manufacturing company like General Motors, which derived substantial revenues from its financial services subsidiary GMAC. Indeed, if we broke down the value of a typical GM car, more than 50 percent could be attributed to IT hardware and software that had gone into the production of the car, including sophisticated computerized systems (like ABS or electronic ignition systems) in the car itself.

Equally, *Fortune*'s editors wondered how to classify a software company like Computer Associates (CA). Initially, it was properly considered a services company because it wrote custom software to order for large corporate clients. But then it started selling shrink-wrapped software products in boxes, making it better suited to be considered a manufacturing company. Now that the Internet is making shrink-wrapped software obsolete and CA is attempting to reposition itself as an application services provider for Internet-based software applications, it is perhaps again best considered a services company. Or more simply, as the editors of *Fortune* suggested, perhaps these distinctions are useless in the post-industrial economy.

Equally useless is the previous distinction between regulated and unregulated businesses. Electric and gas utilities, railroads, airlines, financial services, telecommunications—all highly regulated businesses until the 1970s—have all been transformed in the last quarter century by the gale forces of deregulation and digitization. Competition and free entry by new players has blurred the boundaries of each of these industries. Nowhere is this more evident than in financial services, which pits players as diverse as GE, GM, Microsoft, Citibank, AIG, Morgan Stanley Dean Witter, AT&T, and EDS in competition with each other. With the dismantling of the Glass-Steagall Act, the boundaries of this industry are being redrawn every day.[2]

The break-up of AT&T in 1984 and the progressive deregulation of the telecommunications industry had equally profound consequences. Almost a quarter of the companies on the 1999 *Forbes* 100 list competed in the telecommunications industry. The explosive growth in voice and data traffic, be it through wire, fiber-optic, wireless, or satellite, caused revenues and market value of the companies in this sector to surge. Upstarts like WorldCom and JDS Uniphase rapidly became giants within the industry. The industry also attracted entry from unlikely competitors like Williams, who previously operated in the regulated gas and electricity business, but aggressively moved in new directions once unshackled by deregulation.

The churning mix that defines the new center of the economy is also reflected in the composition of major stock indices such as the Dow Jones Industrial Average and the S&P 500. A close examination shows how much these indices changed over time (see Table 8.2). Companies such as U.S. Steel, Westinghouse, and Chrysler, to name a few, once enjoyed a pride of place on the Dow Jones Industrial Index but no longer appear. Companies such as American Express, Home Depot, Intel, Microsoft,

Table 8.2
Changing Composition of the Dow Jones Industrial Average, 1955, 1974, 1999

	1955	*1974*	*1999*
1	Allied Chemical	Allied Chemical	Alcoa
2	American Can	Alcoa	American Express
3	American Smelting and Refining	American Brands	AT&T
4	AT&T	American Can	Boeing
5	American Tobacco	AT&T	Caterpillar
6	Bethlehem Steel	Anaconda Copper Mining	Citigroup
7	Chrysler Corporation	Bethlehem Steel	CocaCola
8	Corn Products Refining	Chrysler Corporation	Du Pont
9	Distilling &	Du Pont	Eastman Kodak
10	Du Pont	Eastman Kodak	Exxon Mobil
11	Eastman Kodak	Esmark	General Electric
12	FW Woolworth	Exxon	General Motors
13	General Electric	FW Woolworth	Home Depot
14	General Foods	General Electric	Honeywell
15	General Motors	General Foods	Hewlett-Packard
16	Goodyear Tire	General Motor	IBM
17	International Harvester	Goodyear Tire	Intel
18	International Nickel	International Harvester	International Paper
19	Johns Manville Corporation	International Nickel	J.P. Morgan
20	Loews Corporation	International Paper	J&J
21	National Steel	Johns Manville	McDonalds
22	Procter & Gamble	Owens-Illinois	Merck & Company
23	Sears Roebuck	Procter & Gamble	Microsoft
24	Standard Oil (New Jersey)	Sears	3M
25	Standard Oil (California)	Standard Oil of California	Philip Morris
26	Texas Company	Texaco	Procter & Gamble
27	U.S. Steel	U.S. Steel	SBC Communications
28	Union Carbide	Union Carbide	United Technologies
29	United Aircraft	United Aircraft	WalMart
30	Westinghouse Electric	Westinghouse	Walt Disney

SBC Communications, and Wal-Mart—hardly our image of industrial corporations—replaced them, even though the index is still called the Dow Jones "Industrial" average. (One can barely fault the creators of the index, though. Better to stretch the definition of industrial than be irrelevant. It is perhaps only a matter of time before the term industrial will be dropped from the nomenclature.)

Who then are these new entrants to the ranks of America's largest companies? What made them succeed in displacing the traditional industrial company from its vaulted place atop the American economy? To answer this question, we must look at competitors in retail, financial services, health care, information technology, and telecommunications—sectors that account for the largest number of new entrants on the *Fortune* 100 list at the end of the century (see Table 8.1).

Our review of companies in the nonindustrial sectors of the American economy must necessarily be brief. Yet this analysis offers a useful and pointed contrast to the ordeal of the big industrials and the patterns of change that emerged among them.

RETAILING: CHANGING THE RULES OF THE GAME

At first glance at Table 8.1, indicates that the retailing industry has been relatively stable from 1974 to 1999. The number of retailing organizations that appear on the list increased slightly from 15 in 1974 to 17 in 1999. But a closer look at the companies that comprise these lists reveals a very different and meaningful shift in the retail economy. Department store giants like Sears, Roebuck & Company, JC Penney & Company, and Marcor, Incorporated (the former holding company of Montgomery Ward & Company) dominated *Fortune*'s list of top retailers in 1974. While Sears and JC Penney still appear on the 1999 list, they have been challenged on several fronts, from discount retailers such as Wal-Mart Stores and Target Corporation and from "category killer" retail chains like Home Depot, Inc. Once the mainstay of retailing, the traditional department store has been eclipsed by three fundamental developments:[3]

1. The rise in the value and importance of the value-oriented (discount) shopper that has been captured by companies like Wal-Mart, Target, and Costco.
2. The explosive growth of "category killers"—retail establishments like Home Depot, Office Depot, and Circuit City that provide deep selection and focus on a particular product or associated set of products.
3. The growth of the specialty retailer like The Gap with a laser focus on exploiting specific, identifiable, and highly targeted niche markets.

In the last quarter of the twentieth century, the rules of the retail game changed—permanently.

The demise of the traditional department store has not been one of rapid deterioration, but one that has been slow and, in many ways, extremely painful. Traditional department stores became a victim of the tenets that fundamentally guaranteed their early success in the middle decades of the twentieth century. The early success formula entailed five basic components:[4]

1. Downtown urban locations.
2. Floor plans designed to demonstrate style and grace.

3. Decentralized buying with local management control (to accommodate regional tastes and customs).
4. Broad and diverse product selection at moderate prices.
5. Dedicated in-store customer service.

This formula worked well for many years. In both 1955 and 1974, Sears was heralded as the number one retailer by *Fortune*. The success of Sears and other department stores following this "prescribed retail formula" led to a level of complacency and resistance to change which, in turn, made them a target for a new breed of retailer: Retailers who were not afraid to turn these basic business tenets upside down.

The first attack on the retail establishment came from the specialty stores. Specialty retailers shunned the "jack-of-all-trades" approach to product selection and buying. Instead, specialty retailers focused on a limited selection of products that were often highly targeted to a specific audience demographic, one that was typically narrow and easy to appeal to. By doing so, these retailers severely limited the amount of inventory that they need to manage. In addition, specialty retailers have been instrumental in the use of information technology at the point-of-sale. This enables them to more fully understand targeted consumer buying habits. With this data, they can continually stay abreast of new trends and manage inventory accordingly. This investment in real-time information has streamlined the buying function and in essence, eliminated the need for decentralized buying. By turning the inventory management component upside down, specialty retailers have been able to achieve even greater economies of scale, despite their relatively small size.

Even though specialty retailers like The Gap and The Limited were making inroads in specific market segments, many traditional department stores chose not to view them as true competitors. Instead, department stores chose to compete among themselves—often increasing their advertising spending to drive store traffic. With the movement of downtown department stores to suburban malls, this advertising often did drive traffic—to the mall where the specialty retailer reigned. Benefiting from the residual impact of the advertising, the specialty retailer was able to nibble away at many of the core product offerings of traditional department stores. For the most part, they were not considered a serious threat. It was only by the middle of the 1990s that department stores mounted a concerted response, as evidenced by Sears' "softer side" campaign that attempted to compete with the specialty woman's apparel retailer.

Like the specialty retailers, category killers have created a new formula for success in retailing. While traditional department stores prided themselves on the breadth of their product selection, the category killers have focused on depth—offering a wide selection of products within a particular category as Home Depot has done with hardware and building supplies, Toys 'R Us has done with toys, and Circuit City has done with electronics and appliances. By focusing on specific deep product lines, category killers are able to offer wide selection, low pricing, and specialized, tailored service. In many ways, the category killer segment has taken the department store concept to a new level, very personal service on very specific products. As with the specialty retailers, the category killers have been quick to adopt information technology to manage their inventory. In addition, the depth of their product lines enables them to negotiate better prices that they can, in turn, pass along to the consumer.

The traditional department store response to this new breed of retailer has been characterized as one of tacit acceptance. In fact, many department stores "trying to be all things to all people" were unable to adequately service consumers within specific product categories. As such, they willingly abandoned specific categories like electronics or toys, expanding the opportunity for the new retailer to make a killing.

The biggest threat to department stores, however, came from discount chain stores, headed by Wal-Mart. In 1974, Wal-Mart was an insignificant competitor to Sears, which sat atop *Fortune*'s list of retailers. Twenty-five years later, Sears' revenues were one-third of Wal-Mart's. Even the combination of Sears and JC Penney's revenues represented just 53 percent of Wal-Mart sales. In 1999, Wal-Mart sat at number 2 on the *Fortune* 500 list—second only to General Motors as the largest corporation in terms of sales revenues, and by far the largest corporate employer. Commenting on Wal-Mart's meteoric rise, the editors of the *Fortune* 2000 list forecast that "barring some megamerger that remakes the top tier, Wal-Mart will surely rank No. 1 next year."[5]

Wal-Mart in many ways epitomizes that new breed of discount retailers. It has systematically broken all the conventional rules of the business. Its locations are geographically dispersed with a heavy concentration in rural areas, its stores are clean with no frills, its buying function is highly centralized in Arkansas, its product selection is wide and cheap, but not deep, and its service is impeccable. This approach is truly the antithesis of traditional department stores.

Since founding Wal-Mart in 1962, Sam Walton charted his own course. He chose to locate his original stores in rural areas that, heretofore, had not been serviced by traditional department stores. In fact, with the exception of mail order catalogs, the retail establishment had ignored rural locations. By choosing to concentrate on rural America, Walton was exploiting an untapped market potential—essentially becoming the only game in town. From the 1960s to the mid-1980s, Wal-Mart was largely unchallenged in rural America. That changed in the late 1980s, as Target and Kmart adopted a similar strategy.[6]

At its core, the Wal-Mart formula is centered on value. This value is displayed both through the simple design and no-frills layout of their stores and, most importantly, through the prices of its products. A study in the mid-1980s revealed that when Wal-Mart and Kmart were located next to each other, Wal-Mart's prices were roughly 1 percent lower, and when Wal-Mart, Kmart, and Target were separated by 4 to 6 miles, Wal-Mart's average prices were 10.4 percent and 7.6 percent lower, respectively.[7]

Early on, Walton decided to compromise on product variety and depth in exchange for name brand product breadth and low price. Wal-Mart's investment in distribution and logistics systems combined with a strong central purchasing approach has been key to its ability to deliver on its promise of the lowest prices for brand name staple products. With its initial focus on rural America, Wal-Mart had little choice but to develop its own distribution network. This was the impetus for taking the company public in 1972. As Walton said, "Here we were in the boondocks, so we didn't have distributors falling over themselves to serve us like competitors in bigger towns. Our only alternative was to build our own warehouse so we could buy in volume at attractive prices and store the merchandise."[8]

In conjunction with its investment in distribution and logistics, Wal-Mart made a comparable investment in information technology. This information technology enabled local store managers to customize their product offerings for regional tastes while still benefiting from dramatic economies of scale. In addition, Wal-Mart's investment in EDI systems enabled it to electronically interact with its supplier network, saving both time and money in managing the inventory replenishment process. In managing its suppliers, Wal-Mart focused exclusively on centralized buying. Its extensive distribution network enabled Wal-Mart to bargain with its suppliers wielding unparalleled clout. As an example, in 1993 Procter & Gamble generated 10 percent of its revenues through Wal-Mart.[9]

Despite its elaborate distribution network, incredible supplier partnerships, and state-of-the-art technology, Wal-Mart did not lose sight of its first line of business, serving the customer. Richard Tedlow, who has profiled Sam Walton, describes Wal-Mart's uniqueness among discounters as follows: "The problem with discounters, the reason that the early success so many enjoyed turned to failure later on, is that they lost their focus on the customer. When they did, they lost their discipline. Discipline is the key to success in discount merchandising. When cost savings are achieved, the savings have to be passed along to the customer. This formula must become a religion."[10] Wal-Mart succeeded because it created a new set of retailing tenets, a new retailing religion. Walton shattered the conventional wisdom in retailing, and by doing so, created a retail giant.

In 1988, Sam Walton passed the CEO baton to David Glass, who shepherded Wal-Mart to its No. 2 position on the 2000 *Fortune* 500 list. Glass continued Wal-Mart's investments in technology and distribution and created an even larger discount format, the Wal-Mart supercenter—designed to offer more staple household products (including food and groceries) at low prices. In 2000, Wal-Mart generated sales of $191 billion from over 4,000 retail locations employing over 1.2 million "associates."

As Sears and JC Penney attempt to regain some of their former glory, they are no longer looking at each other for clues to success; they are looking at the new competitive landscape. Taking the lead from specialty retailers like The Gap and discount mavericks like Wal-Mart, Sears and other department stores are reevaluating their product mix, investing in information technology, and restructuring their approach to the consumer. While traditional department stores attempt to survive in the new retailing environment, they must also come to grips with the emergence of online retailing, more discount chains, expanded category killers, and fresh niche retailers. The rules of retailing have not only changed forever, they are continuing to be rewritten in real time.

FINANCIAL SERVICES: THE EMERGENCE OF THE "ONE-STOP" FINANCIAL CENTER

It may not surprise many people that financial service companies comprised roughly 25 percent of the *Fortune* 100 list in 1999. For the last two decades, bank mergers and consolidations have been a constant reality. What might be surprising is that in 1974, only seven financial services organizations were ranked among the 100 largest U.S. companies. Why were there only seven on the 1974 *Fortune* 100 list, and, more importantly, how has that number grown threefold in 25 years? Both answers lie in an understanding of banking regulations and how they have been dismantled over this period.

The Banking Act of 1933, also called the Glass-Steagall Act, was enacted as a consequence of many bank failures during the Great Depression. It was commonly believed that, in large part, bank failures during this period were a direct result of overly speculative stock market investments. With this Act, Congress decided that commercial banks could no longer underwrite or broker securities. These services would be strictly relegated to investment banks and security traders. The largest bank at that time, J.P. Morgan and Company, was split into a commercial bank (J.P. Morgan) and an investment bank (Morgan Stanley). For the better part of five decades, these distinct financial service providers co-existed peacefully.

With increasing inflationary pressures in the late 1970s and early 1980s, bankers were forced to identify new sources of income to offset reductions in interest income. In 1983, the Federal Reserve, anxious about potential bank failures, allowed BankAmerica to acquire Charles Schwab, a leading discount broker. This hallmark decision by the Federal Reserve opened the floodgates on merger activity. Both commercial banks and investment houses began creating holding companies to offer additional financial services to their institutional and individual consumers. The "one-stop" financial center was again taking shape. The United States had not experienced this phenomenon since before the Great Depression.

Bank regulations further loosened in the early 1990s as American institutions attempted to compete with global financial service providers that were not bound by the restrictions imposed on U.S. corporations. Though its merits were hotly debated for 10 years, the Glass-Steagall Act was finally repealed in 1999. While this was a landmark decision, the impact of the Glass-Steagall Act had ceased to be of any real consequence by the early 1990s. Consolidation within the financial services sector was in full swing, 20 years before the repeal of the banking act.

Even old guard companies were not immune to being acquired. In what was heralded as a "changing of the guard," Chase Manhattan Corporation acquired J.P. Morgan in the fall of 2000. "How the mighty have fallen!" exclaimed *The Economist*. "J.P. Morgan, once the dominant financial power in America, and arguably the world, swallowed up by Chase Manhattan, a big, old—but not terribly distinguished—rival. Even five years ago, that J.P. Morgan's blue-blooded bank should taint its aristocratic culture by merging with any other institution would have seemed inconceivable. But such has been the pace of change in global finance that nothing seems unthinkable anymore. Certainly, nobody was surprised this week that J.P. Morgan had given up its prized independence. But its choice of partner was a little unexpected."[11]

While Chase's acquisition of J.P. Morgan might have been a surprise to many, it should not have been. Chase actually tried to acquire J.P. Morgan almost 50 years ago after its initial failure to merge with the Bank of Manhattan Company (they subsequently succeeded in acquiring the Manhattan in 1955). Having been initially rebuffed by the Bank of Manhattan Company, John J. McCloy, CEO of Chase, approached George Whitney, J.P. Morgan's chairman, in 1951 about a potential merger. McCloy believed that sooner or later Morgan would need to merge, and its prestige, management, and customer base would benefit Chase.[12] While McCloy and Whitney were ready to seriously consider a merger, senior officers at Morgan voiced strong opposition to it and the discussions were terminated. According to John Wilson's history of Chase, the senior officers of Morgan were adamantly opposed to any merger discussions, "least of all with Chase."[13]

Until their next merger conversation 49 years later, Chase and J.P. Morgan would pursue very different paths. J.P. Morgan remained very insular. With the exception of its merger with Guaranty Trust Company in 1959, J.P. Morgan failed to jump on the merger bandwagon. Instead, it concentrated on the organic growth of its wholesale banking business.

Chase, on the other hand, has been a maverick in the banking acquisition market. By the time it resurfaced merger discussions with J.P. Morgan, Chase had become Chase Manhattan Corporation (an amalgamation of many banks including Chase Manhattan National Bank, Bank of Manhattan, Chemical Bank (itself a product of several acquisitions), and many others).[14] Through this process, Chase and its executives, most notably David Rockefeller in the 1970s and Walter Shipley (formerly of Chemical Banking Corporation) in the 1990s, developed a reputation for achieving aggressive fiscal management objectives. These objectives were achieved, in large part, by smooth, orderly, and dispassionate management of banking mergers.

Despite its depth of acquisition experience, Chase's merger with J.P. Morgan entailed a new level of challenges, and correspondingly a new level of opportunities. As noted in *The Economist:* "The integration of J.P. Morgan will be a huge challenge. Over the past decade, its transformation from a snooty commercial bank into a market-oriented investment bank has fostered a more outward-looking and less separatist culture. But J.P. Morgan employees still regard themselves as a cut above most peers, including those working for Chase."[15]

It appeared that attitudes had changed little in 50 years. Unlike many of its previous acquisitions, Chase's primary goal in acquiring J.P. Morgan was not focused on anticipated cost savings, but instead, it was an opportunity to tap an investment market that had eluded them. "The creation of J.P. Morgan Chase is also a bet that more and more corporate clients will demand full-service relationships with their bankers, rather than product-driven dealings."[16]

Banking deregulation has made the one-stop financial center a reality for consumers. Increasingly, individuals, if they so choose, can meet all their financial service needs (banking, insurance, investing, home mortgage, etc) with one institution. Banks like Chase were hoping for much of the same in the commercial and institutional market. The acquisition of J.P. Morgan brought them closer to that goal.[17]

Shortly after the merger announcement, J.P. Morgan Chase received a call from Jack Welch, CEO of General Electric. Welch was attempting to acquire Honeywell before its planned merger with United Technologies. "But there was another reason for choosing Chase as his M&A advisor. The bank had recently announced it was to merge its investment banking operations with J.P. Morgan, and Morgan had long been the relationship bank for AlliedSignal, which had merged with Honeywell at the end of 1999. . . . This is just the kind of mandate the two banks were hoping they could clinch by merging. Chase would never have won it on its own . . . getting the call from Jack Welch was a huge vote of confidence."[18]

The J.P. Morgan acquisition by Chase was, in many ways, a continuation of the competitive dynamics that existed for over six decades with its crosstown New York rival, Citicorp, now Citigroup, formed by the merger of Citicorp and Travelers Corporation. Chase's aggressiveness in mergers and acquisitions is rivaled only by Citicorp and Bank of America. For decades Chase and Citicorp (formerly known as Citibank, National City Bank, and First National City Bank) tried to outdo each other in size and market reach. For a short period in the mid-1950s, Chase held the number one banking position. This was short-lived, however, as Citicorp outpaced Chase's spending in both domestic and global markets. The frenzy to compete against each other sometimes led to acquisitions and investments that were perilous—especially during the inflationary period of the 1970s. As noted by John Wilson, "But this emphasis on size was to prove a mixed blessing. It fueled a contest between the banks in which size became an end in itself."[19]

The J.P. Morgan Chase merger would have rivaled, even surpassed Citicorp's size, but once again, Citicorp stayed one step ahead by merging with Travelers Corporation. Through this mega-merger, Citigroup, with revenues in excess of $111 billion is, for now, the largest financial organization in America.

The reach and depth of Citigroup's or J.P. Morgan Chase's services could not have been foreseen in 1974. The consolidation within the financial services sector has been both dramatic and rapid. And it isn't confined to pure financial institutions. The lines have been blurred. As noted earlier, both General Motors and General Electric (former bastions of the industrial economy) derive substantial percentages of their revenues from diversified financial services. Deregulation left the door open for massive diversification and consolidation both inside and outside the traditional banking circles. Citigroup, J.P. Morgan Chase, and even General Electric stand as examples of this new world order in financial services.

Health Care: Big Bets on Big Drugs

In 1960, Americans spent only 5 percent of GDP on health care. By 1980, they were spending 8.9 percent, by 1990 this rose to 12.2 percent, and by 1999 it had grown to 14.3 percent.[20] Given this spending pattern, it is not surprising that this industry segment has seen dramatic growth on the *Fortune* 100 list. The dramatic rise in spending over the last 25 years has created phenomenal changes in the health care landscape. A growing U.S. and global population was only one of the factors that fueled this growth. The increasing need to expand health care while simultaneously controlling costs has fostered two major developments. One, health maintenance organizations (HMOs) were formed to deliver quality care less expensively than traditional fee-for-service or indemnity plans. Second, the U.S. Congress significantly altered the medical profitability equation by setting fixed payment schedules for specific diagnoses (commonly known as DRGs, or diagnosis-related groups) in government-funded programs for the poor and elderly (Medicaid and Medicare). These cost containment developments led to companies like Aetna, Cigna, and UnitedHealthcare becoming players within the *Fortune* 100.

While HMOs and other health care insurers have tried to capitalize on the cost management component of health care spending, pharmaceutical companies have focused on the investment side, pouring huge sums of money into research and development (R&D) efforts designed to develop new breakthroughs in the treatment of all kinds of ailments. In 1955, there was no pharmaceutical company among the 100 largest U.S. corporations, even though the industry was about 30 years old, having emerged in the 1920s and 1930s with the discovery and synthesis of sulfur-based antibacterials, penicillin, and other antibiotics and compounds.[21] World War II led to increased investments in government sponsored R&D to provide penicillin and other anti-infection drugs. This increased emphasis on R&D continued after the war and led to the discovery of several important new drugs and vaccines. By 1974, a few pharmaceutical companies were knocking on the door of the elite club of the *Fortune* 100, but none had yet gained entry.

Over the next 25 years, the growth of the industry further accelerated. R&D outlays were 11.9 percent of the total pharmaceutical industry's sales and exports in 1980. They climbed to 16.2 percent in 1990 and reached 20.3 percent by the year 2000.[22] Riding on the medical products and drugs that resulted from this massive investment in R&D, eight companies in the health care sector joined the ranks of the *Fortune* 100 by the year 2000, with many more in the *Fortune* 500.

At the vanguard of this group was Merck, established in 1887 when Theodore Weicker came to America to set up a branch of the German company AG Merck.[23] George Merck, a grandson of the German company's founder, followed him to the United States in 1891. Initially, Merck merely imported products from its German parents and sold them in the expanding U.S. market. In 1904, Merck opened its first production facility in the United States. That began its transformation to a truly American company. Weicker left Merck a year later to establish E. R. Squibb & Sons. When World War I broke out, it became difficult for Merck to operate in the United States as a German company. George Merck wisely decided to hand over the 80 percent stake in the company held by its German parent to the U.S. government. Merck retained his 20 percent share, giving the Merck family a controlling voice in the company for many years to come.

Merck's son, George W. Merck, took over the active management of the company from his father in the 1930s. From the start, his mission was to build a scientific foundation for the discovery of new drugs. This was a lofty goal considering the prevailing public opinion that the U.S. drug industry was essentially comprised of snake oil peddlers. Determined to change this reputation, in 1933 Merck established its first research lab in Rahway, NJ. Here Merck dreamed of creating a place where brilliant minds could be "so protected that their mental powers of thought, study, and imagination could concentrate on problems of great difficulty."[24]

Despite the efforts of Merck and others to give the industry a respectable face, the U.S. pharmaceutical industry remained an industry of carpetbaggers until the 1940s. It was highly fragmented and unstable, with companies going bankrupt on a regular basis. In 1939, the industry had total revenues of $150 million, fragmented across more than 1,000 competitors.

On November 28, 1942, a terrible tragedy occurred in Boston, which forever changed the course of Merck and the pharmaceutical industry.[25] After a football game between Boston College and Holy Cross, many fans crowded into the Coconut Grove, a popular Boston nightclub. Later that night, their revelry turned into misery as a raging fire engulfed the nightclub. Over the next two days, the death toll from the deadly fire rose to 500 and more than 200 people were still fighting for their lives. The situation provoked a national alarm. Hitler was bombing Britain mercilessly and it was looking like the United States was eventually going to be dragged into the war. The Boston incident made painfully clear the potential human toll and the lack of U.S. preparedness for such bomb attacks.

At the time of the tragedy, Vannevar Bush, a former president of MIT, was the informal scientific advisor to U.S. President Franklin Delanor Roosevelt and head of the Office of Scientific Research and Development (OSRD), an organization that had been set up to promote new technologies that might assist the United States in the event it entered the war. Two years earlier, he had brought together four of the nations leading drug companies, Merck, Squibb, Pfizer, and Lederle to encourage them to develop a process to produce penicillin. Even though Alexander Fleming had discovered penicillin in 1928, the compound was highly unstable and had proved notoriously difficult to isolate and produce in large quantities. The first breakthrough came in 1940 when it was isolated by a group at Oxford University and shown to be efficacious in human trials. Ravaged by the war in Britain and short on resources, two members of this Oxford group, Howard Flory and Ernst Chain flew to America hoping to interest someone to help them produce the drug in larger quantities. They found an ally in A. N. Richards, then chair of the OSRD, who encouraged Bush to pursue this project. Though Bush approached all four companies he thought could help with this effort, he found his champion in Max Tishler, who headed a research team at Merck.

Tishler dedicated himself to the penicillin project and through sheer will and energy led his Merck team to isolate enough penicillin to successfully test it in a human patient in March, 1942. When the Boston tragedy struck, Tishler got the call from Bush. Working nonstop for two days, Tishler delivered 32 liters of injectable penicillin to Boston. The drug saved dozens of lives and Merck earned national acclaim. Soaring demand during the war made penicillin the first blockbuster drug—the first of many on which the fortunes and reputations of pharmaceutical companies were built.

Ironically, Merck itself did not prosper from penicillin. The path it had chosen to produce the drug proved inferior to others. But the penicillin breakthrough vindicated the scientific ethos that George Merck and Max Tishler had instilled in the Merck labs. In the years immediately following the manufacture of penicillin, Merck introduced two new blockbuster drugs: Streptomycin, a potent antibiotic that proved effective in treating meningitis, pneumonia, and tuberculosis, was discovered in 1942, and cortisone, an anti-inflammatory agent useful for the treatment of arthritis was discovered in 1944. For the next two decades, under Max Tishler's able leadership of its labs, Merck continued to discover important new drugs for the treatment of heart disease, hypertension, and arthritis and new vaccines for the prevention of measles, mumps, and German measles. Tishler himself held over one hundred patents and was involved in the discovery of 10 of the top selling drugs in history.[26]

With its 1953 merger with Sharp and Dohme, Merck acquired a formidable national and international marketing and sales capability that further propelled its growth. The combination of Merck's remarkable scientists and aggressive salespeople produced many blockbuster drugs, notably Indocine (an anti-inflammatory agent that followed cortisone), and Aldomet (for high blood pressure).

Merck's fortunes soared in the 1960s, but by the end of the decade the engine that had driven Merck's growth began to sputter. Innovation slowed not just at Merck, but in the industry as a whole. In 1959, 65 patents were filed for new drugs. By 1969, this number had dwindled to nine. Lewis Sarret, who replaced Tishler as head of the Merck labs, was unable to match his predecessor's genius. Disheartened by the lack of good news from its labs, Merck, like so many other industrial corporations during that period, tried to revive its growth through unrelated acquisitions, which, for the most part, proved disastrous. But Roy Vagelos, a new head of R&D that Merck had brought in from his post as professor at Washington University, persuaded his colleagues to stay the course and continue to invest in drug discovery.

Vagelos joined Merck in 1976 at a time when its labs and its confidence were at a nadir. He quickly breathed new life into Merck—a company he had long dreamed of working for when he was helping his father run a diner that was located across from Merck's labs. Vagelos was trained in the emerging field of biochemistry and introduced Merck to a new, more rational way of discovering drugs. To promote this new way of thinking, Vagelos recruited a lot of new blood, including Ed Scolnick, who succeeded him as head of research when Vagelos became president and chief executive officer in 1985, and Al Alberts, who discovered Mevacor, a blockbuster drug that helps reduce cholesterol. Over his 20-year tenure, first as the head of Merck's labs and then as its CEO, Vagelos revived the R&D engine that George Merck and Max Tishler had built. During Vagelos's tenure, Merck introduced more than 10 major new drugs and became one of America's most admired and valuable companies.

Vagelos led Merck to great heights. Yet, by the end of the century, Ray Gilmartin, his successor as CEO of Merck was facing a tough challenge. Several of Merck's blockbuster drug patents were scheduled to expire and analysts wondered whether its drug discovery pipeline was full or strong enough to continue to consistently produce new blockbusters. Several of Merck's competitors had merged to bolster the quality of their R&D pipelines and to reduce costs. Historically, the only thing that mattered for drug companies was their ability to discover and market new drugs.

For the last 25 years, pharmaceutical companies were able to enjoy high growth and earnings rates by discovering blockbuster drugs for which they could charge high prices. The industry claims its high returns provide a necessary incentive to continue the enormous R&D investments that are required to play in the high-risk game of drug discovery. Industry leaders emphasize that it takes $500 million to develop a viable drug, which must then go through a long and arduous clinical testing process before it obtains FDA approval to be marketed.[27] This process can take 5 to 7 years and even then only 1 in 20 drugs entering the clinical testing process is approved for sale. Thus, 10 years can elapse from the time a patent is filed to when a drug comes to market, leaving only 10 years of patent protection for a company to earn a decent return on its investment. Even during the patent protection period, companies must often compete with similar products introduced by competitors. After the patent expires, R&D-led pharmaceutical companies must compete with manufacturers of generic drugs that are sometimes priced at 10 percent of the drug's original price. Given all these risks, pharmaceutical companies feel justified in keeping the extraordinary profits they earn when they introduce a new drug that becomes a blockbuster in the marketplace.

Notwithstanding the merits of this risk-reward argument, pharmaceutical companies are facing increasing pressure to reduce the prices of prescription drugs. HMOs and hospitals are applying some pressure, as they consolidate and flex their buying power. Governments of developing countries faced with national epidemics due to diseases like AIDs are putting pressure on pharmaceutical companies to reduce the prices of drugs in these important disease areas. After legally fighting the South African government that had granted permission to generics manufacturers to supply AIDs drugs still under patent, the pharmaceutical industry finally agreed to drop its case and supply their products at significantly reduced prices. Because over a third of the industry's sales come from exports, this incident has caused considerable concern in the industry. The U.S. government is also considering adding prescription drug coverage to Medicare, which if passed through Congress will create further pricing pressure on pharmaceutical companies.[28]

Despite all these cost containment pressures, the prices of prescription drugs outpaced general inflation during the last 25 years. While that gap may narrow in the future, it is unlikely to go away. As the baby boom generation matures, the demand for health care and new drugs will only increase in the coming years. Continuing advances in biotechnology, genomics, and other medical sciences promise exciting new remedies for ailments that still afflict millions of people globally. The main challenge for companies like Merck will continue to be to use their intellectual resources to repeatedly discover and market blockbuster drugs. The quality and yield of their R&D pipelines will determine their fate in the future. Simultaneously, pharmaceutical companies are increasing their efforts to protect the investments that they have made in their existing prescription drugs. As many of these drugs approach the end of their patent-protection period, pharmaceutical companies are turning to general advertising to stimulate consumer awareness, called direct-to-consumer (DTC) marketing. The concept of bypassing the physician and speaking directly to the consumer through DTC marketing is fundamentally changing the playing field. But, in many ways, pharmaceutical companies have no choice. By doing so, they are attempting to create a post-patent demand; one they hope will be strong enough to combat generics and over-the-counter products.

If they fall behind, they may be forced to merge with larger, more successful companies to continue to play the high-stakes drug discovery game. The mega-mergers and consolidation that the industry has witnessed in the last decade may continue. So may partnerships between the established pharmaceutical companies and new biotechnology companies that are often the source of promising new medical discoveries. Indeed, the biotechnology industry has attracted a great deal of venture capital in the last two decades. Some of these well-funded startups may challenge the dominance of the established pharmaceutical companies, as Amgen, Biogen, and Genzyme, three of the biotechnology industry's pioneers already have.

In sum, companies in the health care sector have been some of the strongest new entrants into the ranks of the U.S. economy's largest corporations and this trend is likely to continue in the years ahead.

TELECOMMUNICATIONS: THE INFRASTRUCTURE OF THE NEW ECONOMY

The phrase "what's old is new again" can aptly be applied to the telecommunications industry. During the early part of the twentieth century, AT&T capitalized on the fragmented nature of the telecommunications industry by pursuing an aggressive consolidation path. The lack of subsequent competition that ensued from this effort gave way to the deregulation policies of the 1980s. After several decades of monopolistic reign, AT&T was open to competition on all fronts. Deregulation spawned several new providers and business ventures resulting in the "commoditization" of the industry. The net result—lots of competition in a very price-sensitive market. The opportunity—reaggregate services and capture market share. The consolidation move within the telecommunications industry was back in vogue in the 1990s. AT&T was back in the game, but not without stiff competition even from companies with such inauspicious beginnings as WorldCom.[29]

WorldCom was born out of the deregulation of the telecommunications industry and the break-up of AT&T. Conceived on a napkin in a diner, WorldCom started as Long Distance Discount Services (LDDS) in Hattiesburg, Mississippi. Among the founders was Bernie Ebbers, who owned and operated a chain of Best Western motels. The original business model was straightforward. Lease a Wide Area Telecommunication Services (WATS) line and resell the time to local businesses. Within a year, the company had revenues greater than a million dollars and was profitable as well. Then the prices of WATS lines went up. All of a sudden, the company was in debt and facing the prospect of making significant losses. The board convinced Ebbers to become CEO. Based on his motel experience, he immediately instituted strict operating and cost-control measures. Moreover, he devised a new sales and marketing strategy. He employed a direct sales force geared to satisfying specific customer needs rather than relying on the telemarketing strategy that LDDS and most other long distance resellers had earlier employed. Within six months, this strategy had paid handsome dividends. LDDS was back in the black and growing rapidly as well.

Between 1986 and 1989, LDDS engaged in a roll-up strategy, spending $35 million to acquire small companies that were similarly distressed. Ebbers successfully applied the same formula he had used at LDDS to bring these acquisitions back to health. In 1989, LDDS merged with Nashville based Advantage Company, a publicly traded long-distance telephone company. The merged company was able to provide services in 11 states in the South and Midwest. More importantly, it gave LDDS access to public equity markets to finance its continuing acquisition spree.

Over the next two years, the company spent $100 million acquiring five more companies, expanding its coverage to 27 states. In 1992, it merged with Atlanta-based Advance Telecommunications, making it the fourth largest long-distance carrier in the United States. The next year it merged yet again with MetroMedia Communications and Resurgens Communications Group. The merged entity was renamed LDDS Communications Group and was headquartered in Jackson, Mississippi.

LDDS now began expanding into arenas outside its traditional focus on long distance telephone services. In 1994, it acquired IDB Communications, a satellite communications company. In 1995, for $2.2 billion, it bought the fiber-optic cable network built by Wiltel, a subsidiary of the Williams Company. In keeping with its growing ambition, the company renamed itself WorldCom in 1995.

In 1996, WorldCom bought MFS, a provider of local phone services, which owned fiber-optic networks in several U.S. and European cities. With this acquisition, WorldCom became the first company since AT&T's breakup to offer both local and long distance services. WorldCom further expanded its local service capability in 1998 by paying $2.9 billion to acquire Brooks Fiber, another fiber-optic based provider of local phone services.

The company also expanded its presence in the Internet access market by investing heavily in its subsidiary UUNet Technologies. By 1998, UUNet had become the leading provider of Internet access when it gained control of the network services units of America Online (ANS Communications) and CompuServe (CompuServe Network Services).

WorldCom even expanded abroad, teaming with MCI and Telefonica to enter European and Latin American markets. From an idea on a napkin, Ebbers had made WorldCom a global player to reckon with. Yet, the world gasped at his audacity when he entered a bidding war with British Telecom and GTE to acquire MCI. As the second largest long distance carrier in the United States, MCI's revenues were almost four times that of WorldCom. This was a case of David swallowing Goliath. The final price tag, $37 billion. However, Ebbers had the Midas touch and Wall Street was willing to back him in his audacious bid.

The combined company, briefly named MCI WorldCom before the MCI name was dropped, instantly became the second largest telecommunications company in the world, behind AT&T. The MCI deal also expanded WorldCom's global footprint, enabling it to offer a variety of services in over 65 countries. However, Ebber's ambitions were still not satiated. Recognizing the emerging importance of wireless communications, Ebbers made another bold bid. He offered $120 billion to acquire Sprint Communications, the third largest telecommunications service provider in the United States, and a leading global player in the wireless arena. This is when the Justice Department stepped in, thwarting Ebbers' ambitions. The result was that WorldCom fell behind other telecommunications giants like SBC Communications and Verizon, which continued to grow through acquisition. It is remarkable that the break-up of AT&T and the concomitant rise of the information economy fueled such an explosive growth in telecommunications that by the end of the century there were so many competitors vying with AT&T to occupy a higher rung on the *Fortune* 100 rankings.

If companies like AT&T, SBC, Verizon, and WorldCom have prospered from the traffic in voice and data, companies like AOL have prospered from the increasing traffic in information content that flows across this networked infrastructure. By the year 2000, AOL was the world's number one online service provider, with more than 23 million Web-surfing subscribers.

Like other giants of the information economy, AOL grew from improbable beginnings.[30] In 1983, Stephen Case, the current CEO of AOL took a marketing job with Control Video, which ran an online service for users of the popular Atari computer games. Case became a believer in the future potential of online services based on his experience with one of the first such services called The Source while he was still a marketing executive at Pizza Hut (a division of PepsiCo). His conviction led him to leave a promising career at PepsiCo to join Control Video. When Control Video ran into trouble, Case helped new CEO Jim Kinsey raise venture capital to resurrect the company.

In 1985, Control Video, now renamed Quantum Computer Services, launched the Q-link online service targeted to the general computer user, rather than the computer game enthusiast. By 1989, the company had launched a nationwide service called America Online. The success of this new service led the company to change its name again in 1991 to America Online (AOL).

AOL went public the next year and Case became CEO in 1993. Owing perhaps to his marketing background, Case invested heavily on marketing in an effort to surpass rivals Prodigy and CompuServe. AOL gained considerable momentum in 1993 when it launched a Windows-based version of its online software. Despite a tiff with Microsoft cofounder Paul Allen, who sold his 24.9 percent stake in AOL in 1994 when denied a board seat, AOL reached the magic milestone of 1 million subscribers before the end of 1994.

Capitalizing on its U.S. success, AOL aggressively expanded abroad in 1995. It teamed with the German media company Bertelsmann to launch AOL Europe. Soon thereafter, it launched AOL Japan in partnership with Mitsui and Nikkei. It also created a subsidiary AOL Canada to penetrate that market. AOL's rapid global expansion typifies a pattern common to many other information technology companies including Intel, Dell, Compaq, and Microsoft. They all expanded globally early in their history, rather than wait until later in their life cycle as tended to be the case for industrial corporations. Part of what enabled their earlier global expansion was their lower cost of entry. Moving abroad did not require a massive investment in plant and equipment; as it did for an automobile or chemical manufacturer. By virtue of going global early, many information technology and telecommunications leaders have been able to establish a dominant position not only in domestic, but also in global markets. They often derive over 40 percent of their revenues from international sales as compared to the 20 percent more commonly observed for leading industrial corporations.

To further boost growth and usage, AOL started charging its members a flat rate in 1996, abolishing previous rate structures wherein subscribers were charged per minute they spent online. This new subscription model proved very popular and greatly accelerated AOL's growth. From 1997 onward, AOL sustained its expansion principally through imaginative acquisitions and marketing alliances. In 1998, it acquired CompuServe, one of its main rivals, from WorldCom. It also bought Net Channel, gaining a foothold in interactive TV. In 1999, it acquired Movie Fone, an online provider of movie times and tickets. AOL's biggest and most daring acquisition came later that year when it spent about $10 billion to acquire Netscape. This acquisition dramatically boosted AOL's profile. It was, however, a bitter end for Netscape, the company most instrumental in bringing the Internet (and the World Wide Web) into the lives of people around the world.

Netscape originated in the computer labs of the University of Illinois, Urbana-Champaign.[31] There, Marc Andreesen, a graduate student, helped develop Mosaic, an easy-to-use browser for the UNIX-based computer networks popular among academics. In 1994, Andreesen licensed the rights to Mosaic from the University of Illinois. With the help of Jim Clark, who had earlier founded Silicon Graphics, he launched Mosaic Communications to commercialize the product he had developed as a student. Here we see a pattern commonplace in the post-industrial economy: the fluidity of the movement of talent across institutional boundaries—as entrepreneurial teams form and disband with the rise and fall of new ventures. This fluidity of human capital combined with the fluidity of venture capital is one of the vital drivers of the new economy.

Mosaic quickly gained popularity, owing to the efforts of several companies to whom the University of Illinois had licensed the software. Facing legal action by the university, Andreesen and Clark were forced to change the name of their company. They renamed it Netscape Communications in November 1994 and introduced their own version of Mosaic, called Navigator. Having learned the importance of establishing a standard from Microsoft, Netscape took the bold decision to distribute Navigator free. The gamble paid off as Navigator quickly became the dominant Web browser. By the end of 1996, Netscape enjoyed an 85 percent market share in the browser market.

When Navigator took off, Microsoft retaliated by licensing Mosaic from Spyglass and bundling it in its new Windows 95 operating system.[32] Despite Microsoft's entry, or the fact that it had never made a profit and had an uncertain revenue stream, Netscape went public in 1996 and became one of the hottest IPOs in history. Its first day market capitalization was $2.3 billion. Netscape established a precedent for a wave of later Internet IPOs. It no longer appeared necessary to demonstrate a track record of revenues and profits to go public. It seemed sufficient to have a "cool idea" with the promise of achieving dominance through a first mover advantage on the Internet.[33]

Yet, as Netscape and many other Internet upstarts rudely learned, early victories do not necessarily translate into durable competitive positions. By 1997, Netscape was reeling from losses resulting from failed acquisitions it had undertaken to accelerate growth in the face of competition from Microsoft. Its organic growth also slowed as Microsoft began to wrest market share away from Netscape.

Over the next two years, the browser wars between Netscape and Microsoft intensified. Netscape appeared to have won a major battle when several Baby Bells, Ameritech, Bell Atlantic, Bell South, and SBC Communications, agreed to adopt Navigator as their primary Internet browser. However, Netscape was dealt a huge blow when AOL chose Microsoft's browser as its interface to the Internet.

In 1998, Netscape tried to stem its declining market share by teaming up with Excite to create a portal to compete against Yahoo!, which had emerged as the number one Web site on the Internet. Netscape also formed a joint venture with Qwest Communications to develop an integrated Web interface to handle all forms of communications such as phone calls, e-mails, and faxes. Finally, it launched Communicator 4.5 with a $10 million ad campaign in an effort to destroy Internet Explorer. Yet, Microsoft continued to gain share.

When AOL offered to acquire them in March 1999, Netscape executives recognized that to fight Microsoft they were better off joining their earlier rival than continuing alone. The combined company did prove to be a more formidable competitor. By the end of 1999, AOL had entered agreements with several companies to be their preferred browser. Gateway and Dell, two of the major PC manufacturers had both agreed to market AOL's services on select personal computers. Wal-Mart reached an agreement with AOL to launch a cobranded Internet access service. Under the strategic banner "AOL Anywhere," AOL had also moved to establish a significant presence in the converging entertainment and Internet arena. It had partnered with Hughes Electronics to create a combination set-top box for DirecTV and AOLTV, and to offer a satellite Internet service DirectPC. This network of alliances and marketing agreements established AOL as the leading provider of online services and boosted its stock to stratospheric levels.

Taking advantage of its highly valued stock, early in the year 2000, AOL proposed a merger with Time Warner for roughly $182 billion in stock and debt, creating a digital media powerhouse with the potential to reach every American in one form or another. With dominating positions in the music, publishing, news, entertainment, cable, and Internet industries, the combined company, called AOL Time Warner, boasted unrivaled assets among other media and online companies. The merger combined the nation's top Internet service provider with the world's top media conglomerate. Companies like AOL-Time Warner and Viacom, perched high on the list of the country's 100 largest corporations are redefining what the next generation of telecommunications and media companies might look like.

THE INFORMATION TECHNOLOGY REVOLUTION: OF CHIPS, COMPUTERS, AND SOFTWARE

No other industry sector has seen more dramatic rises and falls than that of information technology. Fortunes are made virtually overnight . . . and they fade just as quickly. The evolution of the information technology sector, in many ways, represents a microcosm of the changes that have categorized the transformation of the old industrial economy. The major difference, however, has been the speed with which those changes have occurred. A quick look at this sector's brief, but dramatic history, demonstrates the manner in which fortunes changed during the last decades of the twentieth century.

No one deserves more credit for the creation of what we have come to call the information economy than William Shockley.[34] He was, after all, one of the three inventors (the others were John Bardeen and Walter Brattain) honored with the Nobel Prize for the invention of the transistor. Developed at Bell Labs in 1947, the transistor has been for the Information Revolution what the steam engine was for the Industrial Revolution—a foundational invention that set in motion a series of remarkable changes in every sphere of human activity.

Within a year of its discovery, the transistor had been commercially introduced. By 1954, nearly a million transistors were being sold to companies such as GE, RCA, Texas Instruments, and AT&T-finding their way into consumer applications like the transistor radio and industrial applications like control systems. In time, the transistor would become the ubiquitous building block of anything electronic. As applications for the transistor grew, so did the manufacturing complexity of connecting hundreds of them with other electronic components such as resistors and capacitors in tighter and tighter spaces. Then came the next breakthrough, engineered in September 1958 by Jack Kilby at Texas Instruments and independently four months later by Robert Noyce at Fairchild Semiconductors.[35] The breakthrough was to construct all the components and their interconnections directly on the same thin wafer of semiconductor material—what came to be called an *integrated circuit*. The integrated circuit and the related techniques to manufacture them pushed the possibilities of miniaturization to an entirely new level, accelerating the information revolution just as the techniques of mass production pioneered by Henry Ford accelerated the industrial revolution.

The next quantum jump came when Noyce left Fairchild with Moore to found Intel in 1968. They were funded to the tune of $2.5 million by Arthur Rock, all on the basis of a one-page business plan written by Noyce, which can still be viewed by logging on to Intel's corporate Web site at (www.intel.com). Rock had previously funded them when they had left Shockley to start Fairchild, pioneering in the process the venture capital industry in Silicon Valley, which became the financial engine of innovation in the information technology sector.

Intel's first product was the 3101 Schottky bipolar static random access memory (or SRAM chip) based on which the company achieved sales of just $2,672 in 1969, its first year of operation. In the summer of 1969, Intel was approached by Busicom, a Japanese electronics company that wanted a set of 12 chips, each to handle a different function, to be designed and manufactured for a calculator. Ted Hoff, a young engineer at Intel had the idea that rather than design 12 separate chips one could design a single general-purpose logic chip that was programmable to take instructions. It took Hoff almost two years to come up with the first prototype—by which time even the Japanese client had given up. Yet, by early 1971, with the help of Federico Faggin and Stan Mazor (two ex-Fairchild engineers), Hoff was able to produce Intel's first microprocessor, the 4004. It measured one-eighth of an inch wide by one-sixteenth of an inch long and consisted of 2,300 MOS transistors. The little microprocessor had as much computing power as the ENIAC, the first digital computer, which had filled 3,000 cubic feet of space and employed 18,000 vacuum tubes. Here was truly a microcomputer on a chip. It could perform 60,000 instructions per second and could be programmed by a user with different types of software to perform all types of functions. Moore declared it "one of the most revolutionary products in the history of mankind."

A year later, Intel came out with the 8008, a chip that incorporated all the essential parts of a computer. It featured not only the CPU, but also the input and output circuits. In keeping with Moore's Law, the 8008 was twice as fast as the 4004, the second in the continuing line of Intel microprocessors that by the year 2002 had led to the Pentium IV 1.4 GHz chip (gigahertz or 1,000 megahertz), the world's highest performance microprocessor for PCs.[36] With this latest product introduction, Intel continued to prove Gordon Moore's now famous law that the performance of semiconductor chips will double every 18 to 24 months.[37] The idea that a single chip could process 1 trillion instructions per second was inconceivable in 1968 when Intel was cofounded by Robert Noyce and Gordon Moore. At the time there were only about 30,000 computers in the world, mostly mainframes that occupied entire rooms and minicomputers the size of large refrigerators. Moore's Law, which predicted the constant doubling of computing power at ever-lower prices has led to the ubiquitous use of microprocessors, from cars to computers to cellphones. Microprocessors can now be found in nearly every material object, be it at home, at work, at the shopping mall, or on the factory floor.

Despite the microprocessor's revolutionary significance, it was not the mainstay of Intel's growth during the 1970s. Till the late 1970s, memory chips remained Intel's dominant line of business. It was the advent of the personal computer that truly catapulted the company into becoming one of the world's best-known brands and most valuable corporations. By the turn of the century, Intel dominated the market for the microprocessors inside personal computers. Based on this dominant position, Intel ranked number 39 on the *Fortune* 2000 list.

A few months after Intel introduced its 1-gigahertz chip, Dell announced that it had taken the number one market share position for unit shipments in the U.S. total branded workstation market, according to estimates by IDC. Dell achieved this distinction by selling over $27 billion worth of computer equipment and services in the 1999 fiscal year. It was the fastest growing company during the 1990s and delivered the highest total return to shareholders compared to any other company during this period. Dell was included in the ranks of the *Fortune* 500 for the first time in 1992. By the end of the decade, it was ranked 56 on the *Fortune* list. What a remarkable achievement by a 22-year-old named Michael Dell who dropped out of the University of Texas at Austin during his sophomore year to found the company.

Dell started college as a pre-med student but found time to establish a business selling RAM (random-access memory) chips and disk drives for IBM PCs.[38] Dell bought products at cost from IBM dealers, who, at the time, were required to order from IBM large monthly quotas of PCs, which frequently exceeded demand. Dell resold his stock through newspapers and computer magazines at 10 percent to 15 percent below retail.

By April 1984, Dell's dorm room computer components business was grossing about $80,000 a month, enough to persuade him to drop out of college. At about that time, Dell started making and selling IBM clones under the brand name PC's Limited. Dell sold his machines directly to end-users rather than through retail outlets, as most manufacturers did. By eliminating the retail markup, Dell could sell PCs at about 40 percent of the price of an IBM.

Dell's idea to sell direct to the consumer was a simple stroke of marketing genius. He recognized that PCs were becoming a commodity product and that customers were increasingly able to specify the type of computer they wanted and buy it directly from a reliable vendor rather than go through a retail channel where they could be handheld through the process. What Dell offered was mass customization—a PC that an individual could configure as he or she chose which Dell would assemble and deliver to their doorstep within two to three days. To assure customers that they would not be left in the lurch if anything were to go wrong after their purchase, Dell was the first PC manufacturer to offer next-day onsite product service. Dell made the process of buying a PC as easy as it could possibly be.

The idea of selling direct was soon embraced by other PC vendors as well. But Dell continued to grow faster than its competition by maintaining its focus and its first-mover advantage. In 1996, the company was the first to started selling PCs through its Web site.[39] By 1997, when the Internet was still in its infancy, the company was selling $4 million worth of computers through its Web site very day. By 1999, that number had jumped to $40 million per day. Dell had been among the first to exploit this new direct channel to the customer and had become one of the largest e-retailers in the world. It even started to offer its technical support services online through "E-Support Direct from Dell." Continuing to exploit the economic efficiencies of the direct model, Dell was the first to introduce a PC under a thousand dollars in 1999, despite a history of avoiding low-cost markets.

Remarkably, Dell had achieved its astonishing growth organically. The company made its first acquisition in 1999 with the purchase of ConvergeNet (storage area network equipment) as it broadened its focus into high-end network servers and Internet-related services.

Dell's successes hinged on his ability to directly serve an increasingly self-assured customer's demand for a personal computer. Yet, he was not the first to popularize PCs and make them the life-defining consumer product of the 1990s, just as the automobile was the life-defining consumer product of the 1920s. That distinction properly belongs to another pair of college dropouts, Steve Jobs and Steve Wozniak, who founded Apple Computer in 1976.[40]

Intel's third-generation microprocessor, the 8080 led to the development of the first personal computer, the Altair 8800. The Altair was offered as a mail-order kit in the January 1975 issue of *Popular Mechanics*. A rudimentary computer, it had to be assembled by the user and could do almost nothing useful because no software had yet been developed for it. As David Kaplan describes, "It was a parody of a computer by modern standards. Fully assembled, it was a rectangular teal box about the size of a microwave oven, with no keyboard or screen or even a joystick. It could be programmed only by flipping a row of eight toggle switches in the correct sequence, each one representing a digital yes or no; its only program made a bunch of lights blink on the front of the box."[41] But it had one huge advantage that quickly stimulated demand. It cost only $400 and could be assembled by any electronic hobbyist. The allure to the hobbyist was irresistible. Here was a chance to build a personal computer, to wrest control from the scientists in white coats that were in charge of the mainframes and minicomputers in the vaultlike computer centers of large organizations.

In Menlo Park, just north of Palo Alto (home to Stanford), a group of hobbyists formed around the Altair. They called themselves the Homebrew Computer Club.

They met every other Wednesday in the auditorium of the Stanford Linear Accelerator to share their latest trials and tribulations in finding applications and enhancements for the Altair.[42] Steve Wozniak, a self-proclaimed "hacker" and a long-time friend of Steve Jobs, was an active member of this group. Motivated more by a hacker's pride to outdo his peers rather than any commercial interest, Wozniak built a computer that would serve as the prototype for the first Apple machine—the Apple I as it came to be known. Interestingly, the computer was not built around an Intel 8080 chip, but a MOS technology 6502 chip that Wozniak had been able to buy at a computer show for $20 each. The blueprint for the new computer Wozniak had designed was a huge hit at the Homebrew Club.

That might have been enough for Wozniak but it wasn't enough for Steve Jobs, who saw the commercial potential of the new computer and was keen to exploit it. In early 1976, working from their garage, using parts bought on credit from local stores, Jobs and Wozniak began offering the Apple I through computer stores around Silicon Valley and by mail order at a price of $666.66. They sold about 175 of them, a number that was more a reflection of their capability to supply rather than the underlying demand. At the same time, Wozniak started working on the Apple II, the next generation computer.

By the end of 1976, the Apple II was ready. A computer for the first time looked like a consumer appliance. It weighed about 12 pounds, it had a regular keyboard, a power supply, and in due course a floppy drive to save data. It was fully assembled and encased in a nice plastic casing with the Apple logo on top. It was easy to program and could display color images on a TV set or other monitor to which it could be easily hooked up.

The creation of the Apple broke another tradition of the industrial economy. The mainstay of new product innovation was until now the heavily funded corporate R&D lab staffed by Ph.Ds. By the end of World War II, large industrial corporations dominated new product innovation. Even Joseph Schumpeter, who proclaimed the importance of entrepreneurs in enabling progress through creative destruction, came to fear that innovation would be so routinized by large companies that the role of the individual entrepreneur would cease to be meaningful. Jobs and Wozniak rekindled the entrepreneurial flame. They became an inspiration for anyone with an idea and a garage. If the heroes of the industrial economy were corporate managers like Alfred P. Sloan, celebrated in accounts such as Alfred Chandler's *The Visible Hand,* the heroes of the information economy were quirky entrepreneurs like Jobs and Wozniak.

Despite its obvious appeal, Jobs and Wozniak had a hard time finding financial backing for the Apple II. Both HP (for whom Wozniak worked) and Atari (for whom Jobs worked) turned them down. So did Moore and Noyce at Intel. Finally, Mike Markkula, who had recently retired at age 34 after making millions running marketing at Intel agreed to step in and put up his own money as well as raise additional funds for Apple. With Markkula's backing, Jobs and Wozniak were able to quit their jobs and Apple was able to move out of the garage into real offices in Cupertino in 1977.

They turned a profit of $ 2 million in their first year. Sales jumped from $7.8 million in 1978 to $117 million in 1980, the year Apple went public. By the end of 1981, sales stood at $335 million. Apple had entered the *Fortune* 500 faster than any other company. It had sold over 300,000 units and had cornered more than a third of the total personal computer market. Within a decade of its founding, Apple sales would top $1 billion, only the second company after Xerox, which had launched the copying machine in 1959, to achieve this milestone so quickly. Despite Apple's early success, this record would soon be overtaken, first by Compaq Computer and then by Dell. Both crossed the $ 1 billion sales mark in less than five years.

Ironically, Compaq and Dell's success would be based on some critical decisions IBM made when it finally entered the PC market in late 1981 and some equally critical choices Apple made in response to IBM's entry. All the established computer companies, including IBM, initially ignored the development of the PC. Apple's early competition came from companies like Radio Shack, Commodore, and Atari that started selling personal computers based on Intel's 8080 microprocessor. Finally, IBM took notice. Recognizing that it needed to catch-up fast, IBM developed its personal computer in a crash development effort lasting less than a year using a skunkworks team based in Boca Raton, Florida. Free from IBM's bureaucratic decision-making process, the team had the liberty to make some critical choices that would forever change the landscape of the computer industry.

Unlike Apple, the IBM PC had an open design that anyone could copy. The design of the central processing unit (CPU), the central hardware element of the computer, was built around the Intel chip and the operating system, the main layer of software on which all other applications ran, was built around Microsoft's operating system. IBM chose an open architecture because it wanted to make its computer the industry standard—just as it had done with mainframes before. IBM reasoned that by setting the standard it could play a central role in shaping the future evolution of the PC market and capitalize on its traditional dominance in the computer industry. IBM's early success appeared to vindicate this view. Despite its clunky appearance and inferior operating system relative to Apple computers, the IBM PC quickly captured market share due to IBM's loyal customer base in large corporations around the world.

But IBM quickly lost control. The IBM PC's modular open architecture meant that anyone who could source components from Intel and other semiconductor manufacturers and license Microsoft's operating system could make an "IBM-compatible" PC.[43] It could then compete with IBM on the basis of price and/or performance. This was precisely the logic Joseph "Rod" Canion and two other ex-Texas Instruments engineers employed when they started Compaq Computer in Houston in 1982 to manufacture and sell portable IBM-compatible computers. Compaq's first portable was developed from a prototype the three sketched on a paper placemat when they first discussed the idea.

Compaq began selling computers in 1982. By the time it went public the following year, sales had climbed to $111 million, a record figure for a computer startup.[44] This success was partly due to the timing with which Compaq released its first portable—beating IBM's release of its portable by almost a year and a half—and becoming the first computer company to release a product based on Intel's revolutionary 386 chip. Another factor that contributed to the meteoric rise of the company was the marketing strategy it employed. Compaq used a wide spread base of dealers and suppliers (spanning 152 countries by 1990) who specialized in IBM PC technology, circumventing the need to train and maintain a large salesforce of its own. And by giving the dealers exclusive rights to the sales and service of its products, Compaq exceeded the $2 billion sales mark by 1988, only six years after the introduction of its first product. The strategy was hugely successful, making Compaq one of the top sellers of PCs going into the twenty-first century.

Despite the success of IBM's open standard, Apple resisted licensing the architecture of its hardware or its operating system. Apple executives continued to believe that the inherent superiority of their product would eventually lead to victory in the marketplace. In 1983, Wozniak left the company and Jobs hired PepsiCo's John Sculley as president. In 1984, they launched a product that represented a real leap forward in the PC market—the Apple Macintosh. The genius of the Macintosh was an operating system with a graphical user interface that enabled the user to navigate using a point-and-click device called a mouse rather than typing in operating instructions. Despite its obvious user appeal, the Macintosh did not stem Apple's declining market share. After tumultuous struggles with Sculley, Jobs left in 1985 and founded NeXT Software, a designer of applications for developing software. That year Sculley ignored Microsoft founder Bill Gates' appeal for Apple to license its products and make its platform an industry standard. This decision almost killed Apple as Microsoft eventually introduced the Windows operating system, which employed a graphical user interface very similar to the Macintosh, eliminating one of the major advantages that Apple enjoyed. From a market share of 20 percent in 1983, Apple's market share declined to below 5 percent in 1993, leading to Sculley's ouster and a revolving door for a string of CEOs, until Steve Jobs was called back in the summer of 1997 to head the company once again. To his credit, Jobs resuscitated a company many had given up on. His introduction of the low-priced iMac, a futuristic looking computer-and-monitor-in-one, available in five bright colors, revived Apple's fortunes. By the end of 1999, Apple's market share had climbed back to 10 percent.

The choices made by Apple and IBM not only shaped the competitive dynamics of the personal computer hardware market. They had an equally profound effect on the nature of the software market and the dominance that Microsoft enjoys in that space.

Microsoft demonstrates the remarkable rise to power of a company that did not even exist when the oil shocks jolted the U.S. industrial economy.[45] Bill Gates founded Microsoft (originally Micro-soft) in 1975 after dropping out of Harvard at age 19 and teaming with high school friend Paul Allen to sell a version of the programming language BASIC. While Gates was at Harvard, the pair wrote the language for Altair, the first commercial personal computer. Like Dell, Apple, and scores of other companies that have come to characterize the new information economy, Microsoft was not born in a corporate R&D lab.

Initially, Microsoft grew by modifying BASIC for other computers such as the Apple. In 1979, Gates moved Microsoft to his native Seattle and began developing a broader suite of programming languages. Microsoft's breakthrough came in 1980 when it was chosen by IBM to write the operating system for its new machines. Interestingly, this storied deal, the very foundation of Microsoft's future success, may never have happened.[46] When IBM first approached Microsoft, Gates referred them to Gary Kildall, the founder of Decision Resources International (DRI). Kildall had written CP/M, the then dominant operating system for personal computers based on the Intel microprocessor. However, the meetings between Kildall and IBM did not go well and they were unable to strike a deal. Besides the lack of chemistry between Kildall, the prototype of the hobbyist turned entrepreneur, and the "suits" from IBM, there were two main sticking points. One, IBM wanted to pay a lump-sum licensing fee, whereas Kildall wanted a royalty for each copy of CP/M sold. Two, IBM wanted the right to rename the product IBM-DOS, while Kildall was insistent on retaining the CP/M name.

IBM approached Gates again to see if he could help broker their differences with Kildall. It was at this stage that Gates made his masterstroke. He cut a deal with IBM to provide them with an operating system compatible with CP-M. To do so, Gates bought QDOS, short for "quick and dirty operating system," for $50,000 from a Seattle programmer, renaming it the Microsoft Disk Operating System (MS-DOS).

When Kildall learned about Microsoft's deal with IBM, he was furious. He felt Gates had reneged on an earlier handshake agreement between them, whereby Microsoft would focus on programming languages such as BASIC, leaving DRI the field of operating systems. Yet, Kildall was hopeful that there would be a market for two operating systems. After all, in every other business there were multiple dominant vendors. However, Kildall had not recognized that operating systems have what economist Brian Arthur has called increasing returns to scale. Because other PC makers wanted to be compatible with IBM, MS-DOS became standard on PCs. Microsoft retained licensing rights and began making compatible software. Soon, there was no incentive for anyone to use CP-M. The range of software available that could only be run on the MS-DOS platform outstripped the programs that were compatible with CP-M. The decline of CP-M relative to MS-DOS left Kildall a broken man and DRI a company with no future. Meanwhile, Microsoft soared to ever-greater heights and Bill Gates became the richest man on the planet.

What helped Microsoft become one of the most valuable corporations was its dominance of the PC operating system market, which further allowed it to market a host of basic software applications such as Word (for word-processing), Excel (for spreadsheets) and PowerPoint (for presentation). Bundled as a package, these applications were optimized to run on the Microsoft operating system, making them a natural complementary purchase. After Apple refused to license its Macintosh operating system, Microsoft introduced Windows in the mid-1980s. Windows incorporated a graphical user interface similar to the Macintosh, neutralizing the one big advantage enjoyed by Apple and the other competing operating systems. Once Windows was introduced, there was no looking back for Microsoft.

In 1986, Microsoft went public and Bill Gates became the industry's first billionaire. The company's stock and Gate's personal wealth continued to soar as the widespread acceptance of Windows and supporting applications made it an industry standard. By the early 1990s, most personal computers shipped had the Windows operating system and application suite already loaded on the system—the user just had to plug the computer in and it was ready to perform the most desired applications. The bundling of applications with the operating system, and with the hardware itself led to cries of foul play and monopoly charges inside and outside the software industry. These cries intensified when Microsoft introduced Windows NT in 1993 to compete with the UNIX operating system, popular on higher end workstations and larger computer networks.

Those who criticized Microsoft's alleged monopolistic practices won their first victory in 1999 when the Justice Department rebuffed Microsoft's planned acquisition of personal software maker Intuit for $1.5 billion. Stymied but not defeated Microsoft embarked on an aggressive strategy of investing in startups and allying with or buying out companies that had promising applications for the Windows platform.

Just when Microsoft appeared to have become the juggernaut that would sweep over the entire software industry, the rise of Netscape and the explosive growth of the Internet almost caught the company napping. Despite being a skeptic of the Internet in its early years, Gates responded quickly and aggressively once the Internet's popularity was established, and he refocused Microsoft's energies to compete on new terrain.

The Microsoft Network (MSN) made its debut in 1995. The same year, Microsoft swallowed its pride and licensed rival Sun's Java Web programming language. Later in the year, Microsoft introduced Microsoft Internet Explorer (MIE), a Web browser pitted to compete against Netscape's Navigator. It also launched Expedia, an online travel site, to help build traffic on MSN.

The speed and intensity of Microsoft's response to the Internet challenge surprised those who felt that Gates' skepticism would inhibit Microsoft. However, Gates proved yet again to be a formidable competitor. And by doing so, he demonstrated one of the key necessities in the new economy, the ability to not only embrace change, but to exploit it. By 1997, Microsoft had begun to turn the tide on Netscape and Sun, the Internet's early leaders. Part of its success lay in bundling MIE with its operating system. This meant that buyers of new personal computers could easily prefer MIE over Netscape Navigator. Microsoft's success with this strategy again invoked cries of monopolistic abuses. In 1997, Sun sued Microsoft for allegedly creating an incompatible version of Java. Microsoft countersued. The next year, in 1998, the U.S. Justice Department finally filed antitrust charges against Microsoft, claiming that it stifled Internet Browser access and limited consumer choice.

The Justice Department's case against Microsoft took its usual twists and turns. As Gates found himself dragged deeper into the lawsuit, he made Steve Ballmer, a long-time Microsoft executive, president of the company, charged with overseeing all Microsoft operations. In 1999, Microsoft reorganized along consumer groups instead of product lines and streamlined its Internet activities around MSN.com. These actions enabled Microsoft to maintain its competitive intensity even as it was embroiled in a distracting lawsuit that threatened the very future of the company. In January 2000, Gates named Ballmer CEO, though he remained chairman and assumed the additional title of Chief Software Architect.

When a federal judge finally ruled against Microsoft in June 2000, Gates vowed to fight back. Whether Microsoft will be broken up remains uncertain until the appeals process concludes. Yet, one thing is certain. Few companies have dominated an era and an industry as completely as Microsoft. Bill Gates stands, without doubt, along side of Andrew Carnegie and John D. Rockefeller, who dominated the steel and oil industries, central to the rise of the industrial economy. Gates has done the same in the software industry, which has been equally central to the rise of the information economy.

NEW ENTRANTS, NEW PATTERNS

If we step back and take a wide-angle view of the new entrants into the *Fortune* 100 over the last 25 years, we begin to see several patterns. First, we see the emergence and growth of the essential elements of a new, knowledge-intensive, information economy. These elements include computer equipment and peripherals, semiconductor chips, software and services, Internet service and content providers, and the telecommunications service providers that build and operate the infrastructure on which all this information flows. Together these elements have shaped an Information Revolution just like the earlier Industrial Revolution that triggered the growth of the industrial economy. Businesses in the information economy all have their counterparts in the industrial economy. Computer manufacturers are analogous to the makers of products like cars and appliances. Chip manufacturers are analogous to the makers of basic materials like metals and plastics. Software companies are analogous to the makers of electromechanical and process control systems. Telecommunications infrastructure and service providers are analogous to transportation infrastructure and service providers. Much like their industrial economy analogues, these information economy companies have grown dramatically as information technology has diffused and been adopted throughout the economy.

Companies in the information technology sector have prospered because they have significantly influenced all other sectors of the economy. In the retail and financial services sectors, the new entrants into the *Fortune* 100 are companies like Wal-Mart and Citigroup that have exploited these new information technologies to deliver greater value to their customers. Healthcare companies have embraced information technologies to speed up the drug discovery process and to help contain costs. Indeed, the human genome project could not have even been conceived without advances in information technology. Even old industrial companies have greatly boosted their productivity by embracing information technologies.

A second pattern that emerges is the increasing importance of intellectual assets relative to physical assets. The heart and soul of industrial corporations lay in their physical plants and factories. The heart and soul of these new corporations is the intellectual capability of their employees. Nowhere is this more clearly seen than in the pharmaceutical and information technology sectors where everything depends on the intellectual prowess of a company's scientists or engineers. A major drug discovery or a brilliant new piece of software can completely alter a company's fortunes. Human capital is no less important in the financial services industry, which has grown on the backs of the new products and services created by the professionals in the field. Even in more mundane services like retailing, the quality of a company's human assets is critical because they directly influence the quality of the consumer's experience with the company. Little wonder that Sam Walton chose to call his employees "associates," instead of the industrial label "workers." His nomenclature highlights that employees can no longer be valued simply for their labor; they must be seen as important intellectual partners in the business.

A third feature of these new entrants is that many were financed quite differently than their industrial forbears. Businesses have often been started by entrepreneurs and financed by venture capital. This risk capital has been a vital force in the rise of the new information technology and biotechnology companies that often can be launched with a small amount of initial capital. Despite the extraordinary growth in venture capital, the public markets remain the main source of growth capital.

Table 8.3
Markets for Equity, Venture Capital, Debt, and M&A (1970–2000)

Year	Total Market Value of Corporate Equity ($ Bil.)	Venture Capital Disbursements ($ Mil.)	IPOs No. of Issues	IPO Proceeds ($ Mil.)	New Equity Issues No.	New Equity Issues ($ Mil.)	New Debt Issues No.	New Debt Issues ($ Mil.)	M&A Total Price Paid ($ Bil.)
1970	906	98	236	567	704	6,662	555	25,080	16
1971	1,059	132	252	1,071	1,117	14,189	607	27,358	13
1972	1,197	130	494	2,186	1,340	13,249	474	20,707	17
1973	948	205	81	281	286	5,455	273	15,751	17
1974	677	96	8	31	123	2,782	374	27,707	13
1975	892	85	5	176	220	7,949	528	36,976	12
1976	1,052	95	40	337	277	8,772	411	28,086	20
1977	996	150	31	221	208	6,651	409	26,030	22
1978	1,029	284	38	225	274	6,229	343	22,791	34
1979	1,206	489	61	388	291	6,509	334	27,696	44
1980	1,569	676	148	1,357	652	18,468	516	40,764	44
1981	1,456	1,358	347	3,055	860	19,596	465	39,406	73
1982	1,642	1,821	121	1,320	634	19,993	572	42,179	62
1983	1,956	3,262	681	13,299	1,650	48,963	594	51,623	66
1984	1,887	3,472	351	3,850	690	14,761	615	66,092	143
1985	2,404	3,546	290	6,185	729	26,765	928	97,991	148
1986	2,794	4,282	692	19,335	1,306	46,533	1,493	207,974	232
1987	2,792	4,721	514	14,814	980	43,447	1,441	211,161	196
1988	3,105	5,298	220	5,749	406	16,281	1,332	220,895	281
1989	3,813	5,135	209	6,485	516	22,456	1,223	256,331	271
1990	3,544	3,698	173	4,734	419	20,539	1,214	275,971	176
1991	4,864	3,115	365	17,057	978	71,075	2,450	491,785	125
1992	5,463	5,782	513	25,464	1,157	82,284	3,503	732,886	112
1993	5,714	5,734	660	35,762	1,608	118,273	4,890	911,106	168
1994	5,539	6,258	567	23,514	1,175	81,696	3,890	559,607	271
1995	7,508	6,711	568	31,674	1,276	105,016	4,145	487,314	384
1996	9,016	13,493	865	53,587	1,822	159,182	5,736	675,891	596
1997	11,702	19,316	601	40,681	1,557	164,441	8,285	1,006,009	723
1998	13,649	26,666	353	37,968	1,076	138,702	9,373	1,461,952	1,325
1999	17,202	72,644	508	62,184	1,047	188,000	8,575	1,378,586	1,281
2000	15,067	132,368	384	58,271	933	216,095	8,785	1,383,934	1,697

Sources: M&A data for 1967–1980 from Mergerstat Review; from 1981–1999 from Securities Data Corp. Equity, Debt, and Venture Capital data from Board of Governors of the Federal Reserve System.

Mergers and acquisitions remain important growth vehicles, as seen in the histories of companies like WorldCom. The flurry of such deals has been another source of growth for the financial services sector. (See Table 8.3.)

The heroes of the new economy are entrepreneurs not managers. Notwithstanding CEOs like Jack Welch and Roy Vagelos, the public imagination was captured more by corporate founders like Robert Noyce, Steve Jobs, Bill Gates,

Michael Dell, and Sam Walton. The fascination with entrepreneurship is reflected in the rise of courses devoted to this topic in business school curricula and the number of newspaper columns and business magazines that are focused on entrepreneurs.

Another important pattern is that many of the new entrants achieved their success by introducing innovative new business models that upturned the existing rules of the game. Wal-Mart changed the prevailing retailing business model by targeting previously underserved rural markets and developing a new value proposition for its customers. In a different way so did category killers like Home Depot and Best Buy and niche retailers like The Gap. Citigroup redefined the financial services industry by creating a mega one-stop financial services center capable of meeting all the needs of both retail and institutional customers. Companies like Merck redefined pharmaceuticals by creating an R&D-led drug discovery engine, boosting research spending (as a percentage of total sales) by a factor of three, compared to other competitors in the industry. The Dell-direct model redefined how companies can reach their customers by circumventing all intermediaries, a model that has also been instrumental to the success of companies like Cisco. New business models enabled by new technologies were a formula for the success of many of the companies that broke into the ranks of the largest companies in the economy.

Finally, we can also discern a new economic logic at work. Economies of scale and scope—the main drivers of industrial growth—remain important for market dominance. But equally important are what may be called network economics—winning the battle for standards, positioning oneself advantageously in webs of alliances, and taking advantage of increasing returns to scale. Microsoft and Intel exemplify these new economic imperatives. Also critical are the economics of time, including speed and flexibility. Nowhere is this truer than in pharmaceuticals where what matters most is to be the first to discover, patent, and market a new drug. But speed and flexibility are increasingly important in all sectors of the economy in order to cope with the greater rate of change in every business environment.

THE LARGE INDUSTRIAL CORPORATION AS DOG AND CASH COW IN THE NEW ECONOMY

Where does all the churning we have witnessed in the composition of the largest American companies leave the industrial corporations that once dominated these ranks? Ironically, the current situation of the large industrial corporation is best understood in terms of a now-discredited strategic planning tool from its heyday. In the late 1960s and early 1970s, the Boston Consulting Group (BCG) developed a portfolio-planning matrix to aid the management of diversified companies. The BCG model distinguished between businesses that might be considered "dogs" (low growth, low market share), "cash cows" (low growth, high market share), "stars" (high growth, high market share), and "question marks" (high growth, low market share). Companies were encouraged to divest their dogs and milk their cash cows for resources to invest in their stars and question marks. By the end of the century, large industrial corporations, such as Union Carbide and Dow had abandoned the idea of trying to manage such a portfolio of businesses, focusing instead on their core business. Ironically, though, even as they abandoned diversification, they found themselves being put into the dog and cash cow quadrants of the economy as a whole. The new stars and questions marks were a different set of companies in growth sectors such as information technology, financial services, and life sciences.

Table 8.4 shows the performance record of different sectors of the economy during the decade 1989 to 1999. Notice that sectors such as aerospace, chemicals, food, metals, motor vehicles, and petroleum refining, all prominent in the *Fortune* 1974 list, are no longer the growth sectors of the economy.

Moreover, as can be seen in Table 8.5, not one of the companies in the list of 50 fastest growing companies during the last decade was on the *Fortune* 1974 list. Only two companies, Lockheed Martin and Textron, which were on the *Fortune* 1974 list, were on the list of the top 50 companies in terms of earnings growth over the decade. Both achieved this position through a decade of vigorous consolidation and cost cutting in their respective industries.

As the dogs and cash cows of the new economy, the large industrial corporation is being milked to extract resources that are being reallocated to stars (companies like Wal-Mart, J.P. Morgan-Chase, Merck, Intel, and Microsoft) and question marks (companies in areas like the Internet, biotechnology, and telecommunications). The flow of resources out of the industrial sector and into other sectors is most clearly evident in the financial markets. Even the recent market correction, which has brought down the inflated expectations from companies in the star and question mark cells, has still not revived the fortunes of the traditional industrial corporation. They continue to languish as dogs and cash cows.

The same pattern of flows can be observed in labor markets, where the best and the brightest no longer dream of jobs in the *Fortune* 100. Graduates of premier institutions of higher education are increasingly looking for opportunities in the new economy. An interesting (albeit limited) indicator is the placement of the Harvard Business School class of 2000. Less than 5 percent of the graduating class of about 900 students took jobs in companies that were on the 1974 *Fortune* 100 list.

Table 8.4
Growth Rates of Different Industries, 1989–1999

Rank	*Industry*	*Average Annual Rate of Return, 1989–1999*
1	Computer peripherals	57.7
2	Securities	28.6
3	Computer and data services	24.3
4	Computer, office equipment	22.8
5	Diversified financials	22.6
6	Soaps, cosmetics	21.4
7	Pharmaceuticals	20.6
8	Pipelines	20.5
9	Specialty retailers	20.5
10	Insurance: Life, health (stock)	20.1
11	Commercial banks	19.5
12	Telecommunications	18.2
13	Food services	17.6
14	Publishing, printing	16.5
15	Aerospace	16.0
16	Beverages	16.0
17	Chemicals	15.0
18	Industrial and farm equipment	14.6
19	Electronics, electrical equipment	13.6
20	Entertainment	12.8
21	Mail, package, freight delivery	12.2
22	Scientific, photo, control equipment	11.9
23	Food	11.4
24	Insurance: P&C (stock)	11.3
25	General merchandisers	11.3
26	Metal products	11.0
27	Forest and paper products	10.7
28	Food and drug stores	10.2
29	Wholesalers	9.7
30	Engineering, construction	9.4
31	Motor vehicles and parts	9.4
32	Metals	9.4
33	Petroleum refining	9.3
34	Airlines	8.7
35	Railroads	8.4
36	Utilities: Gas and electric	8.2
37	Healthcare	6.5
38	Automotive retailing, services	5.8
39	Temporary help	3.0
40	Building materials, glass	2.2
41	Hotels, casinos, resorts	2.0
	Median	12.8

Source: Fortune, April 17, 2000.

Table 8.5
50 Fastest Growing Companies by Annual Revenue and EPS, 1989–1999

Rank	*Fastest Growing Companies (1989–1999 Annual Revenues)*	*Growth Rate (%)*	*Rank*	*Fastest Growing Companies (1989–1999 Annual EPS)*	*Growth Rate (%)*
1	Dell Computer	51.8	1	MCI Worldcom	97.7
2	Microsoft	37.4	2	Seagate Technology	97.6
3	Citigroup	30.6	3	Dell Computers	71.2
4	Home Depot	30.1	4	Lockheed Martin	59.7
5	Compaq Computer	29.6	5	Bank of New York Company	54.1
6	Lear	28.5	6	Campbell Soup	51.9
7	Arrow Electronics	26.0	7	Best Buy	48.3
8	Tosco	25.9	8	Microsoft	42.2
9	Berkshire Hathaway	25.5	9	Charles Schwab	41.1
10	Applied Materials	25.3	10	Unitedhealth Group	34.9
11	Intel	24.5	11	Tech Data	34.3
12	Viacom	24.5	12	Intel	32.2
13	Charles Schwab	23.9	13	Dollar General	31.3
14	Micron Technology	23.8	14	Oracle	30.6
15	Gap	22.1	15	Home Depot	30.4
16	Thermo Electron	21.9	16	Avon Products	30.0
17	Sci Systems	21.1	17	Sun Microsystems	29.6
18	Sun Microsystems	20.8	18	Pacificare Health Systems	29.2
19	Freddie Mac	20.5	19	Gap	28.5
20	Wal-Mart Stores	20.5	20	Ryder System	28.4
21	Circuit City Group	20.2	21	Saks	28.0
22	Lowe's	19.6	22	Paine Webber Group	27.6
23	Federal-Mogul	19.6	23	Office Depot	26.9
24	Duke Energy	19.5	24	Countrywide Credit Industries	26.1
25	Computer Sciences	19.3	25	CNF Transportation	26.1
26	Newell Rubbermaid	19.0	26	Textron	25.8
27	SBC Communications	19.0	27	Applied Materials	25.7
28	Medtronic	18.7	28	Owen & Minor	24.9
29	Costco Wholesale	18.5	29	IBP	24.7
30	Bindley Western	18.4	30	Citigroup	24.4
31	Flowers Industries	18.3	31	McGraw-Hill	24.2
32	Nike	17.7	32	Washington Mutual	24.1
33	Computer Associates International	17.7	33	Tribune	24.1
34	Albertson's	17.6	34	Chevron	24.0
35	Omnicom Group	17.5	35	AFLAC	22.7
36	Walt Disney	17.5	36	Dover	22.7
37	Seagate Technology	17.3	37	Smithfield Foods	21.5
38	Merck	17.2	38	Lowe's	21.4
39	Smithfield Foods	17.2	39	Midamerican Energy Holdings	21.0
40	Williams	17.2	40	Black & Decker	20.9
41	Southwest Airlines	16.5	41	Conseco	20.8
42	Mattel	16.1	42	Aramark	20.5
43	Rite Aid	16.1	43	United Stationers	19.5
44	Progressive	16.0	44	Arvin Industries	19.4
45	Bergen Brunswig	15.9	45	Bristol-Myer Squibb	19.1
46	Johnson Controls	15.9	46	Southwest Airlines	19.0
47	Illinois Tool Works	15.7	47	Centrix	19.0
48	Amerisource Health	15.6	48	Schering-Plogh	18.4
49	Danaher	15.5	49	Freddie Mac	18.4
50	TJX	15.1	50	State Street Corporation	18.2

Source: Fortune, April 17, 2000.

Let there be no mistake. The fulcrum of the market (whether we think of product markets, capital markets, or labor markets) no longer consists of the biggest industrial companies. Although General Motors is still one of the largest industrial corporations in the United States, it can no longer be said that "as GM goes, so goes the nation." Companies like GM, Du Pont, Standard Oil, and U.S. Steel have lost their place not only at the forefront of the global economy, but also at the center of the modern business imagination.

CHAPTER 9

THE INDUSTRIAL CORPORATION IN A POST-INDUSTRIAL AGE

The decline of high-tech stocks at the start of the twenty-first century has raised grave doubts in some minds about the future of what some had been calling the *new economy*. These concerns are understandable. It is hard to remain bullish when the market value of high flying Internet start ups like Amazon.com and Priceline.com have dropped more than 90 percent from their all-time highs. Large scale layoffs, until now associated only with the old economy, have rudely and suddenly ended the hopes of thousands who had giddily embraced the promise of the new economy. What has most shaken the faith of the faithful is the steep decline in the market value and growth prospects of stars like Microsoft, Intel, Dell, AOL, Cisco, and WorldCom that had seemed invincible.

Despite these ominous signs, it would be unfortunate if the pendulum were to swing too far from what was characterized as "irrational exuberance" to what might be called "irrational panic."[1] No doubt, the Internet revolution was overhyped. So too were claims that the new economy would usher in an unprecedented long boom during which the economy would keep growing while inflation and unemployment would remain low. As the high-tech crash dragged the larger economy down in 2001, it became clear we remain vulnerable to business cycles and periodic recessions.[2]

Yet, let there be no confusion. The current setback to the high technology sector does not imply that the industrial economy is going to return to its halcyon days. The world will continue to demand products and services supplied by industrial companies. For the foreseeable future, we will need cars, tires, steel, plastics, petrochemicals, food and consumer packaged goods, paper and allied products, defense, aerospace and farm equipment, machinery and tools for industrial automation, and office equipment. But demand for industrial products will continue to decline relative to the growth in demand for products and services associated with the new economy such as computers, telecommunications, media, health care, software, and other information, financial and professional services.

This relative decline will continue because there has been a fundamental shift in the structure of production and consumption in the U.S. economy during the past 25 years. This structural change is readily apparent when we examine input-output tables that describe the flows of goods and services among different sectors of the economy. The authors of the Commerce Department's 1997 input-output table highlight that the fastest growing input commodities between 1992 (the previous complete input-output table) and 1997 were computers, electronics, and data processing services (including software). Moreover, this growth reflects increased demand by both intermediaries and final users. From 1980 to 1999, information technology's share of the total capital spending by U.S. companies has increased from over 15 percent to just under 40 percent. The other sectors that grew substantially were financial services and health care. Over the same period, the share of durable goods in the total consumption of individual households has decreased from 30 percent to about 16 percent.[3]

These changes are unlikely to be reversed. It is hard to imagine a future in which the share of information technology or financial and professional services in corporate inputs will decline relative to energy, steel, or other industrial inputs. Individual consumers are also unlikely to return to spending a great deal more on cars or food. Industrial corporations must necessarily confront this reality. They have no choice but to continue to adapt to the new economy—for it is here to stay. In the years ahead, sectors of the new economy may grow less slowly than they did during the past decade. They may not attract as much capital or investor interest. Yet, they will surely increase in scale and scope, penetrating deeper and broader into the lives of individuals and companies.

The new economy, and even the Internet, is not like Tulip-mania or the Gold Rush. It is, as Peter Drucker observes, more like the railroad-boom of the late 1820s.[4] The railroads were an extraordinary catalyst for the industrial revolution. However, the development of the railroads took 30 to 50 years, and was punctuated by spectacular booms and busts. Drucker believes that the new economy may be analogous to the railroads because it changes the "mental geography" of commerce, eliminating distances, opening up new markets. As we have recently seen, not all new business models are viable. But some are and others yet to come will be—and these will continue our ongoing transition from an old industrial to a new post-industrial economy.

OPTIONS FOR INDUSTRIAL CORPORATIONS

What is the future of the industrial corporation in this new economy? Close examinations of the behavior of the industrial corporations we have studied indicate four main trajectories: (1) consolidation, (2) growth through innovation and acquisition, (3) metamorphosis, and (4) combination of industrial and post-industrial businesses.

Table 9.1 shows the distribution of the paths taken by the panel of 1974 *Fortune* 100 companies we studied.

Table 9.1
Industrial Trajectories 1974–2000

Trajectory	*Consolidation*	*Growth*	*Metamorphosis*	*Combination*
Percent of companies	81	9	4	6

Notes:
1. The consolidation category includes companies that were part of major mergers as well as those that retreated into a niche.
2. The growth category consists of companies that focused on growing revenues by introducing a steady stream of new products and services.
3. Metamorphosis signifies companies that totally abandoned their industrial roots and moved into a different sector of the economy.
4. Combination signifies companies that attempted to build a substantial presence in emerging sectors of the economy (such as services or high technology) as a complement to their traditional industrial core.

Consolidation

One of the first industries to undergo consolidation—to grapple with it as necessity and sort it out as a set of strategic choices—was the aerospace-defense sector. When the Soviet Empire fell apart in 1989, the foundation of business for General Dynamics, McDonnell Douglas, Martin Marietta, and dozens of other major industrial corporations collapsed with it. Between 1987 and 1994, the total level of spending by "the Customer" (as the Defense Department was known within General Dynamics) melted by more than half (55.5 percent). It was a stark strategic crisis. Clearly, federal defense spending was no longer to support the same level of industrial activity. Some form of consolidation was coming.[5]

The industry's impending crisis seemed inevitable, but its grip tightened slowly. Major firms like McDonnell Douglas and General Dynamics were still working on huge, multibillion dollar contract backlogs in 1990—backlogs that would take years to complete. Companies could try to adapt slowly, bit by bit, cut by cut, to the new defense economy that was taking shape. Or they could go into corporate denial and refuse to hazard much at all in the way of strategic reformulation, playing the game out, hoping things would somehow turn around. Perhaps the federal government might intervene in the interest of "national security." So a brief period of suspended reckoning ensued, an expectant calm, as companies assessed their options, eyed their competitors, and waited for someone to make the first move. This liminal period was to be observed in every other industry that eventually consolidated.

The first move in the defense industry came from an unlikely source: General Dynamics (GD). The largest defense contractor when the industry crisis broke, and the only company making major weapons systems for all three branches of the U.S. military, GD produced the F-16 fighter aircraft, the M1 tank, nuclear submarines, and a variety of missile systems.[6] Sales had passed $10 billion in 1989 and the annual report that year proclaimed that GD, by virtue of its broad contract base, had attained "a unique advantage within the industry." But—the report went on to observe—geopolitical events would doubtless change the face of the industry. GD had reached the top just as the ground beneath it was beginning to erode precipitously.[7]

While peering somewhat uncertainly into the future, the company prepared for new leadership. In September 1989, GD brought in William Anders as vice chairman, grooming him to take over as CEO in 1991. Anders was an outsider, importing not only extended experience in the military and public sectors, but also a dozen years of private sector experience, including corporate positions with General Electric and Textron. He was coming from a very different business world, and coming in equipped to make forceful change: Anders pointedly negotiated a contract that would give him, as he put it, "the kind of independence I wanted so that I could make the changes that were needed," including compensation on a scale "so that I would be able to retire on the day I walked in here."[8]

After carefully reviewing the company's operations and strategic situation, Anders concluded that GD did indeed require a thorough overhaul. "The attitude was that as long as the company had the sales, revenues, and orders, everything was okay," he reported. "Everything was not okay. Productivity was low, and asset management was poor. I inherited a company with a major cultural problem."[9] GD was only slowly adapting to procurement reforms that were replacing "cost-plus build up" contracts with "fixed-price build down" project parameters. It was still instinctively pursuing growth for growth's sake, lunging at defense contracts without studying their profitability.[10] Most dangerously, the company was not coming to terms with the new realities of the post-Cold War marketplace. In-house calculations were projecting that sales would plummet by something like $5 billion over the coming five years, but the company's finance people were suggesting it would be able to sustain current operating levels for another two years, and the atmosphere at GD was one of complacency, not crisis.[11] Everyone seemed to assume that they were going to survive the shake-out more-or-less intact. From Anders' point of view, the situation was a little unreal, even unnerving: "the defense market had collapsed, and most of the people here couldn't emotionally deal with this fact."[12]

Anders himself was under no illusions. He knew GD needed a strategy to cope realistically with industry consolidation. More basically, he needed to "get this company to run more like a business."[13] He began by inviting in Wall Street analysts to lay out the company's situation in clear, hard-hitting terms—first for top management, then for the board, where the presentation did manage to instill a genuine sense of urgency. He made deep cuts in capital spending, brought inventory levels way down, and slashed plans for future spending. Meanwhile, to reorient strategic thinking within the company's managerial ranks, the company commissioned one-week seminars at Northwestern's Kellogg School of Management for 150 top managers, instructing them how to "think like business people, not like aerospace engineers."[14] Anders then restructured the company, breaking it down into distinct business areas and pushing operational authority down the chain of command. He redesigned GD's corporate compensation policy, setting up substantial incentives keyed to the company's stock performance. And he replaced 16 of the company's 25 senior managers over the first eight months of 1991, warning the survivors that any business unit failing to turn in at least a 15 percent return on investment would be divested or phased out.[15]

While his managers tightened up operations, Anders mulled over his strategic options. GD, he figured, would be able to sustain only those businesses that passed what Anders called the "critical mass test." In other words, the company had to ask itself, program by program, "Could we justify dedicated factories for these products based on the scale we could achieve?" By Anders' reckoning, the company's tank, submarine, and tactical aircraft programs qualified, and perhaps the space systems unit. The missiles programs did not. Missiles had become "a commodity business," Anders determined, in which "supply far exceeds demand." It was a grim reckoning, but once he worked out the numbers, Anders moved decisively, laying out guidelines for a "plan of contraction." In short order between 1992 and 1993, GD sold off its missile programs, a data systems unit, Cessna (a civilian aircraft operation), an electronics division, and the company's space systems unit.[16]

GD's decision to sell triggered a barrage of mergers, acquisitions, and sell-offs as the industry finally entered the throes of convulsive contraction. His rivals, Anders observed, "seem to be willing to risk increasing inefficiencies and eventual termination of their franchises by the marketplace simply to keep their 'nameplates' over the door." For his part, Anders cared less about whether GD came out on top than he did about maximizing value for his company's shareholders. And he was convinced that "the people who move first are going to be the winners. It doesn't matter from Wall Street's perspective whether you are a buyer or a seller. Just be one or the other."[17]

GD did explore possibilities for acquisition, possibilities that would build up what Anders called "critical mass." But when they fell apart, Anders quickly shifted positions and offered his company's programs for sale. Thus, GD first approached Hughes about purchasing its missiles programs, before agreeing to sell off its own. In Jay Dial's apt metaphor, "While other defense contractors engaged in a high-stakes game of musical chairs—hoping to be seated when the music stopped—GD pursued a strategy of offering its chair to the highest bidder."[18] The same basic pattern shaped GD's most dramatic divestiture: the sale of its fighter aircraft operations to Lockheed in November 1992. The F-16 program, for years a mainstay at GD, was winding down, and while the F-22 program (which GD shared with Boeing and Lockheed) remained profitable, overhead at Fort Worth (where both projects were located) was rising as F-16 operations tailed off. This was a core business, but one that would soon be operating at a small fraction of plant capacity: designed to build 256 F-16s annually, Fort Worth was building only 24 in 1992. "I went to [Lockheed chairman] Dan Tellep and badgered him to sell me his share of the F-22 program," Anders later recalled. "Tellep said, 'That sounds like a good theory, but I'm not—repeat not—willing to sell, so quit pestering me.' Then he turns around and says, 'Would you sell to me?' And I say, 'Holy Toledo.' I was trapped by my own theory."[19]

By January 1993, Anders had overseen the sale of $2.83 billion in business assets and was applying the bulk of the proceeds to repurchasing stock and making special payouts to shareholders. The stock, down to $25 two years before, was trading over $100. A year later, with the sale of space systems, GD was down to its tank and submarine programs and Anders was phasing himself out of company leadership, declaring "We have basically done the major part of the turnaround job for which this team was assembled."[20]

The first phase of consolidation in the defense industry left GD much smaller in size, but also strategically and operationally strengthened. Well in advance of many of its rivals, the company assessed the oncoming crisis and mapped its way out. While his competitors framed the situation as a "shakeout," a battle they had to survive at any cost, Anders forced his company to think and act in terms of shareholder value and business efficiency. While his rivals ate away at their contract backlogs and circled each other, waiting for someone to make the first move, it was Anders—as a seller, rather than a buyer—who gained the initiative and secured the strategic advantage.

Anders' willingness to part with core businesses began a sweeping process of consolidation in the industry. Soon, no business unit was sacred and each firm was willing to sell, buy, or swap any or all of its businesses to solidify their competitive position. By the end of the century, the industry had shaken out into a handful of integrated players. In almost every arena (shipbuilding, armaments, aerospace, etc.), the industry was left with two to three main competitors. Several mega-mergers drove this consolidation. Lockheed merged with Martin Marietta, Northrup merged with Grumman (and acquired Litton), and Boeing (after acquiring Rockwell's defense business) merged with McDonnell Douglas.

James Mellor succeeded Anders as CEO in 1993. Building on the strong balance sheet he had inherited from Anders, he led GD on an acquisition spree that once again made GD one of defense industry's large integrated players by the end of the century. After completing the planned sale of the company's space systems business to Martin Marietta, Mellor began building the company back up again. Under Mellor's leadership, GD bought shipbuilder Bath Iron Works (in 1995), Teledyne's combat vehicle unit (1996), Lockheed Martin's defense systems and armament systems units (1997) and defense electronics units from Ceridian and Lucent (1997).[21]

Mellor was succeeded in 1997 by Nicholas Chabraja, a director of Ceridian and former general counsel of GD. Chabraja continued the acquisition and consolidation program initiated by Mellon. In 1998, GD acquired National Steel and Shipbuilding and in 1999 made a $2 billion bid to acquire rival submarine and ship builder Newport News Shipbuilding. The Pentagon, however, had become concerned about the industry consolidation leading to monopolies. It rejected this bid, as it did Lockheed Martin Marietta's efforts to acquire Northrop-Grumman.[22]

Thwarted by the Pentagon, GD nevertheless continued its efforts to become one of the integrated majors in the industry. GD shored up its information systems business by buying GTE's military communications, electronics systems, and telecommunication services division. It reentered the commercial aviation market (after having sold Cessna) by acquiring business jet-maker Gulfstream Aerospace. GD's acquisitions continued in the year 2000 with smaller munitions companies like Saco Defense Corporation and Primer Technologies added to the fold.[23]

At the industry level, several other companies pursued a similar strategy, including Raytheon, Lockheed Martin, Boeing-McDonnell Douglas, and Northrop Grumman. Their goal was to become broadly integrated players—operating across the major segments of the industry with dominant positions in particular segments.

During this consolidation, many other players retreated entirely from the industry such as GM, GTE, and Rockwell International. Finally, some players focused on developing leading positions in specific niches such as GE in aircraft engines, TRW in defense subcomponents, Textron in Cessna airplanes and Bell Helicopters, ITT in defense subcomponents, and United Technologies in Sirkosky helicopters and Pratt and Whitney engines.

This pattern of consolidation is common across a large number of industries.[24] The industry coalesces around a handful of mega-integrated players that operate across almost every segment of the industry chain. At the same time, this process of integration opens up space for niche players who occupy the periphery of the industry and thrive by pursuing strategies of differentiation and distinction in their chosen field of operation.

Every one of the industries in which large industrial firms operate has experienced this trend toward consolidation. In some industries, consolidation came early. Steel and tires are good examples. By the end of the 1980s, these industries had already coalesced around a few major global players and a number of niche players. In tires, for example, there are now only three major global players (Goodyear, Michelin, and Bridgestone) of which only one is American and there are a few niche players like Cooper and Pirelli. Similarly, in steel and aluminum, of the 10 companies on the 1974 *Fortune* 100 list, only two were still standing by the end of the century, namely USX and Alcoa, though there are a number of niche players in specialty steels and other metals like Nucor.

In other industries, consolidation started in the 1990s and intensified by the end of the decade. The oil industry is an important example. In 1974, there were 19 oil companies on the *Fortune* 100 list. By 2000, there were only eight (and this on a list that includes only industrial companies). Megamergers including Exxon-Mobil, Chevron-Texaco, and BP-Amoco-Arco have completely reshaped the industry.

Take the case of Exxon-Mobil. In 1999, Exxon and Mobil merged to create the world's largest publicly traded oil company, with a market value of about $275 billion. The merger of these two oil giants was an unlikely match because the two companies possessed very different management styles: "While Exxon ran with icy command-and-control efficiency," a journalist observed, "Mobil behaved more like a high-tech start up: loose and informal. 'Exxon guys are more serious, Mobil guys more fun,' said a close observer of both companies."[25] Bringing these two different cultures together successfully appeared to be an arduous undertaking.

Despite these difficulties, Exxon Mobil appears to have been a very successful merger. The company's growth for 1999 and 2000 equaled $47 billion.[26] Lee Raymond, Chairman of Exxon Mobil, stated in 1999 that the merger would "achieve $3.8 billion in annual pretax savings [and] . . . the merger in coming years should add about three percentage points to Exxon's return on capital."[27] And in 2000, Exxon Mobil was the number one company in the *Fortune* 500 rankings, an honor Exxon held in 1974 and last received in 1984. Some of Exxon-Mobil's gains were undoubtedly due to higher oil prices because Chevron and Texaco also reported higher than average profits. Yet, even if oil prices were to fall, observers believe that there are good reasons for oil companies to merge. They contend that in the increasingly intense competition in the industry, larger corporations fare better. Mergers enable companies to have a broader scope and competitive advantage: "Petroleum is probably the only global business in which the industry's largest firms and best assets are controlled by governments. It may seem astonishing, but even the likes of Chevron and Texaco are midgets compared with the state-run oil giants like Saudi Arabia's Aramco, which alone produces a fifth of the world's oil exports. What is more, the industry's best, lowest-cost reserves are also controlled by governments. This leaves the private sector to fight ferociously over those oil and gas fields still left to be discovered . . . It is this frenzied hunt for the next big bonanza that is really behind recent mergers."[28] According to this argument, by coming together, Exxon and Mobil wield more power in the oil industry and can more effectively compete with the state-run oil enterprises.

Exxon and Mobil have not always been competitors. Both companies were initially a part of John D. Rockefeller's Standard Oil monopoly. With Standard Oil, Rockefeller established a "Trust, which held shares in each component company. Rockefeller was able to circumvent the laws which then prohibited a company in one state from owning shares in another; at the same time he could and did pretend that all the companies were independent."[29] However, in 1911 with the help of the Sherman

Antitrust Act, President Roosevelt forced Standard Oil and other similar trusts to break up their monopolies: Standard Oil was divided into several separate entities. The largest of them was the former holding company, Standard Oil of New Jersey. With nearly half the total net value, it eventually became Exxon. The next largest, with 9 percent of net value, was Standard Oil of New York, which ultimately became Mobil. Then there was Standard Oil (California), which eventually became Chevron; Standard Oil of Ohio, which became Sohio and later the American arm of British Petroleum; Standard Oil of Indiana, which became Amoco; Continental Oil, which became Conoco; and Atlantic, which became part of ARCO and eventually of Sun.[30]

The companies that once comprised Standard Oil had suddenly became direct competitors. In this new atmosphere, the oil companies began to alter the ways they targeted business: "There was also a new dimension in the competition. Oil companies were becoming marketers, for the first time selling automotive fuel at retail, directly to motorists, at the brand-name stations that were springing up all across the American landscape. Oil wars were not only being fought for supply and markets in foreign lands, but were also erupting in an equally fierce struggle for markets on the main streets of America."[31] The break up of Standard Oil meant that there was no longer one dominant American player in the oil industry.

The merger between Exxon and Mobil "reunites two parts of John D. Rockefeller's storied Standard Oil monopoly, 'Standard Oil had 90 percent of the U.S. market, while this company after the merger will have about 12 percent or 13 percent,' [FTC Chairman] Pitofsky said in an interview."[32] Exxon-Mobil is convinced that 12 percent to 13 percent of the market is enough to give them an advantage over the other oil companies. This has triggered other mergers in the industry as the remaining companies attempt to close the gap with Exxon-Mobil. Ninety years after the break up of Standard Oil, the pieces of the monopoly appear to be consolidating once again.

As the industry consolidates around a few globally integrated players, there are other firms like Unocal (focusing on oil exploration and production) and Sunoco (becoming an independent oil refiner and marketer) that are retreating into niches where they can prosper. This trend has left firms such as Phillips Petroleum and Occidental caught in the middle. The former recently announced a merger with Conoco (spun out from Du Pont) and the latter is trying to work itself out of the middle by forging a series of joint ventures.

We can observe a similar pattern in the food and consumer products industry. In the late 1980s, the LBO movement led to an initial wave of consolidation in the industry. A second more concerted wave has begun more recently with the acquisition of companies like Bestfoods by Unilever, Ralston-Purina by Nestle, and General Foods by Kraft. This has left companies like Sara Lee scrambling to decide whether to join the consolidators or retreat into a niche. At the same time, it has left players like Chiquita Brands and Fortune Brands (formerly American Brands) struggling to survive.

There is a final group of industries in which the trend to consolidate has only just begun. In some cases, once begun, consolidation has occurred quickly. The paper and paper products industry is a good example. In the United States, the industry is quickly consolidating around two integrated players, International Paper and Georgia-Pacific Group. Meanwhile, Weyerhauser—formerly an integrated player—has retreated into the lumber segment. The industry continues to have several makers of specialty papers like the 200-year-old Crane & Company. In other cases, like the chemical industry, the process of consolidation has yet to gather momentum. Beyond the Dow-Union Carbide merger, few other megamergers have yet been announced. To the extent that other industries are forerunners of a universal trend, the chemical industry may not be able to escape the consolidation squeeze for long.

Looking ahead, one strategy that large industrial corporations can pursue is to stay ahead of the consolidation curve. To win in this game, the rules are simple:

1. Eat or be eaten.
2. Enhance merger and post-merger integration capabilities.
3. Stay focused on increasing earnings through productivity gains. (Reengineer and downsize ruthlessly and continuously.)
4. If winning in the center of the field is not possible, identify and retreat quickly into a niche that can be dominated.

Growth through Innovation and Acquisition

The vast majority of companies in our study turned to consolidation or niche strategies as a way to compete in a contracting market. In sharp contrast, there are a handful of industrial firms that have attempted to keep growing through a focus on generating new products, either internally or through acquisitions. Among the *Fortune* 100 firms we studied, Johnson & Johnson, American Home Products, Philip Morris, Coca-Cola, Pepsico, Procter & Gamble, Colgate-Palmolive, Sara Lee, and 3M followed this trajectory. Notice that these firms were partly able to adopt this strategy because they produced nondurable consumer and industrial goods. These sectors may not have experienced explosive growth, but they were also not subject to the contraction pressures experienced by manufacturers of durable goods.

Johnson & Johnson has had the most consistent success on this trajectory. It has averaged a compounded sales growth of 5.9 percent per annum for the last 25 years, one of only two companies in our sample of *Fortune* 100 companies that was able to break the 5 percent per annum barrier over this period. The only other company was Philip Morris, which achieved its growth through mega-acquisitions including those of Kraft, General Foods, Nabisco, and Miller Brewing. Johnson & Johnson has about 99,000 employees across the world. According to its 1999 annual report, it is "the world's most comprehensive and broadly based manufacturer of health care products as well as a provider of related services, for the consumer, pharmaceutical, and professional markets."[33] The company's sales are divided between three main divisions. Consumer products consist of its traditional Band-Aid brand and other well-known products such as Tylenol. The pharmaceuticals group makes prescription drugs for cardiovascular treatments, contraception, and a variety of other therapies. The professional services division manufactures surgical equipment and related tools.[34]

Johnson & Johnson was founded in New Jersey in 1885 by James and Edward Mead Johnson. A year later, Robert Johnson joined the company, and in 1887 the company was incorporated with $100,000 in capital and 14 employees.[35] Two of the company's most popular products, Johnson & Johnson Baby Cream and Band-Aids, were introduced in 1921. Robert Johnson Jr., who ran the company from 1932 to 1963, created a system of decentralization that is still embedded in the Johnson & Johnson culture.[36] Decentralization allows each of Johnson & Johnson's businesses to manage themselves. Current CEO Ralph Larsen claims that decentralization works because it "gives people a sense of ownership and control—and the freedom to act more rapidly."[37] However, despite its long history, Larsen believes that unchecked decentralization can also be a danger for the company. "Decentralization is not an end unto itself," he said. "Any strength that is overused becomes a weakness, and we were overdoing the decentralization."[38]

In the 1940s, Johnson & Johnson launched its birth control line and sutures. In 1959, the company purchased McNeil Labs and introduced Tylenol in 1960. The company also acquired many foreign companies in the 1950s and 1960s. In the 1970s, Tylenol became the best-selling painkiller, which enabled Johnson & Johnson's consumer products division to surge.[39] In 1982, the company suffered a huge blow after several deaths occurred when some Tylenol capsules were laced with cyanide. The company reacted by removing Tylenol from the shelves. This response prompted the *Washington Post* to write that "Johnson & Johnson has succeeded in portraying itself to the public as a company willing to do what's right, regardless of cost."[40]

In the 1985 annual report, the company noted that it was a year of "exceptional recovery from the previous three years."[41] The company focused again on its strategy of innovation and acquisition. Indicative of this strategy was the theme of the 1988 annual report, termed "Strategies for Growth."[42] What is striking about this theme is how rarely it occurred among the other companies in our study. In keeping with this theory, several new products and companies were also added to the Johnson & Johnson fold, including Accuvue and LifeScan.

The "Strategies of Growth" continued in the 1990s with the acquisition of Neutrogena. Johnson & Johnson also purchased two medical companies to augment its professional business. Similarly, the company's internal innovation was also flourishing. In its 1996 annual report, the company claimed that "in terms of research spending, our investments place us among the top 10 companies in the United States."[43] Also in 1996 the company received the National Medal of Technology for its "continuous innovation in research and development."[44]

The theme of the 1997 annual report was innovation. In the letter to their shareholders, the company's chairmen claimed that "innovation . . . is of extraordinary importance to the future of Johnson & Johnson. We are convinced that long-term success in the new millennium will come only to those companies that value innovation and learn how to harness its power for growth."[45] In 1997, the company obtained the rights to Motrin, and in 1998 the FDA approved two new Johnson & Johnson products. The company also purchased DePuy and introduced a new product called Benecol.[46]

However, in its next annual report the company reported that "1998 was one of the more difficult years that Johnson & Johnson has encountered in a long time."[47] The company claimed that its problems were the result of the international economic crisis and the failure of many of its research projects.[48] To compensate, many jobs were cut and plants were shut down.

Despite the problems in 1998, the company returned to its acquisition and innovation strategy in 1999 and 2000. In 1999, it bought a skin care line from S.C. Johnson & Son and a biotechnology company. In 2000, Johnson & Johnson purchased a company that made equipment for sports medicine and established a health-care services joint venture with Merrill Lynch.[49]

1999 was Johnson & Johnson's sixty-seventh straight year of sales growth.[50] The company achieved this continued success through a combination of internal innovation and acquisitions. The chairman's 1999 letter to shareowners mentioned that this combination of "investments in a broad range of opportunities, both internally and outside the Company, have allowed us to grow at an accelerated rate and provide a strong platform for future growth."[51] The strategy gives Johnson & Johnson an extremely broad product scope. It has been argued that the company's success has as much to do with its "huge variety of operations and geographical diversity as it does to marketing. When knee-joint sales sag, pregnancy-detection kits might perk up. When U.S. drug sales are weak, foreign hospital product sales may be rising."[52] Essentially, Johnson & Johnson's products are so varied that a negative growth rate in one area can be absorbed by successes in other product areas.

As this history of mergers, acquisitions, and divestiture shows, Johnson & Johnson has been able to maintain its steady growth because it aggressively enters new growth markets. Equally, it has the discipline to quickly disband money losing or declining businesses. Johnson & Johnson has an acceptance for failure that has enabled it to continually pursue innovation regardless of outcome: "One of the things most striking about Johnson & Johnson is its tolerance for certain kinds of failure, which explains a lot about the company's culture."[53]

The other companies in this group have pursued similar strategies with minor variations. 3M has relied more on internally generated new products by encouraging its employees to spend 20 percent of their time pursuing new product ideas. It also ruthlessly monitors the fraction of revenues that come from products introduced in the last three to five years.

Like 3M, Colgate Palmolive also focuses on new product introductions. In 1999 alone, it introduced over 900 products and backed them with an advertising budget in excess of $1 billion. Under the leadership of Reuben Mark, the CEO of Colgate Palmolive since 1983, the company has given its shareholders a return of almost 3,000 percent. That's better than Jack Welch's GE over the same period, and certainly better than the S&P 500.[54] What was Reuben Mark's recipe? A constant search for new products, most home grown, combined with a relentless search for incremental productivity improvements. Sara Lee, in contrast, has relied somewhat more aggressively on acquisitions than internally generated growth.

As successful as this growth strategy has been, companies have found it hard to sustain over time. One slip and the markets can be punishing. In the spring of 2000, Procter & Gamble, the consumer products giant, discovered that when it comes to old industrial companies, the financial markets are more interested in continued productivity and earnings growth rather than in innovative plans to grow revenues. Impatient with progress on its 1996 goal to double revenues in the next 10 years ($70 billion by 2006), Procter & Gamble began restructuring in 1998 to focus on global business units rather than geographic regions. In 1999, Durk Jager took over as CEO "with hopes he would shake up the company's stodgy, 163-year-old corporate culture and rev up slowing sales and profits."[55] To reach this goal, Jager accelerated development of new products such as Swiffer (an innovative mop) and Dryel (a product for home dry cleaning of clothes).[56] At the same time, he quickened the pace of organizational change, announcing the elimination of 15,000 jobs and closing 10 plants.[57]

In 1999, Procter & Gamble acquired The Iams Company, a leading producer of nutritional pet foods and a complement to Procter & Gamble's growing interest in health care products.[58] The company was also rumored to be at the center of a mega-merger with American Home Products and Warner-Lambert, a deal that had it been consummated, would have made Procter & Gamble a major force in pharmaceuticals and over-the-counter drugs. When news of the deal leaked in January 2000, the value of Procter & Gamble's stock plunged about 15 percent. Meanwhile, the company was unable to meet its earnings expectations. In March 2000, the stock plunged by another 30 percent and a few months later, Jager resigned. Procter & Gamble's problems were blamed on its ambition: The company "undertook too much change too fast . . . We clearly took on more than we were able to execute."[59] The newly appointed CEO,

Alan G. Lafley, planned to "return to the more-conservative P&G way of doing things."[60] The Procter & Gamble case is a good illustration of how difficult it can be for an industrial giant to alter course and how severely markets can punish when they perceive management pushing growth at the expense of earnings.

To succeed on the growth trajectory, companies must embrace the following principles:

1. Relentlessly pursue related growth opportunities by investing in organic growth *and* acquisitions.
2. Ensure that products/services introduced in the past 3 to 5 years account for at least a quarter of current revenues.
3. Foster a culture of experimentation that promotes autonomy and supports innovation.
4. Don't punish failures, but be ruthless about weeding out failing initiatives.
5. While pursuing growth, continue to cut costs assiduously.

Metamorphosis

A third successful trajectory pursued by some of the companies in our sample was to exit entirely from their traditional industrial businesses and reinvest in businesses more closely associated with the post-industrial economy. We have already discussed two such examples of metamorphosis. The first, Westinghouse, withdrew from its industrial roots and reinvested its proceeds in its media and broadcasting subsidiary, CBS, which became the new name of the company. In 1999, Viacom, the media conglomerate run by Sumner Redstone, acquired CBS. If this combination is successful, Westinghouse will truly have redefined its identity, shedding the last vestiges of its industrial roots.

The second example we have discussed is Monsanto, which successfully exited the chemicals business. After being acquired by Pharmacia in 1999, its stock was reissued in 2001 and 2002 as a pure agricultural biotechnology company.

Of our original sample of 1974 *Fortune* 100 companies, only two other companies have been successfully able to slough off their industrial legacies—though none, so far, have done as well as either Westinghouse or Monsanto. One of these, Viad Corporation, was formerly known as the Greyhound Corporation. Greyhound Corporation began its diversification strategy long before the decline of the industrial economy. In the 1960s, the bus business faced great difficulties because flying and driving became more popular and cheaper. To combat this problem, Greyhound purchased several companies including Restaura, Travelers Express, and Exhibitgroup.[61] In 1970, Greyhound purchased Armour and Company, which diversified the company even further. In essence, "it was a conglomerate that had everything from buses to soap to meat."[62]

The company continued to broaden its business in the 1980s. In its 1984 annual report, CEO John Teets contended that "it is obvious that Greyhound Lines is confronting a new set of economic and competitive realities. The entire transportation industry, in fact, is suffering widespread dislocation and to endure, Greyhound Lines must become a different kind of company."[63] Essentially, Teets believed that it was necessary for Greyhound to evolve in order to survive. To achieve this end, Greyhound continued to purchase companies in the 1980s, including a travel agency, an airline catering company, and a cruise line. The company acquired a variety of different businesses to add to the Greyhound Corporation, which quite often, were completely unrelated to the company's traditional core business.

In 1987, Greyhound sold the Greyhound bus operations, claiming that the company was "divesting itself of operations which do not offer, and increasing its investment in areas which management believes will offer, desired growth or return on investment opportunities."[64] Teets argued that 1987 was the end of the company's five-year reorganization.[65] However, the reorganization was to continue. In 1991, the company changed its name to Dial Corporation, which was "selected to capitalize on the company's strong position in the consumer product markets . . . It is the start of a new era and further highlights our move into consumer products and services."[66] The corporate name change signified the extent of transformation the Greyhound Corporation had gone through since the 1960s. Teets was quoted as saying that the change was designed to "'sharpen investors' perception of Dial' and 'help shareholders better understand what they own.'"[67]

The paring down of businesses continued in the 1990s. In 1996, Dial was spun-off into two companies, Dial and Viad. Dial was comprised of the consumer products business while Viad held onto the service businesses.[68] While the company wanted to separate Viad and Dial to streamline its businesses, there were still concerns that the companies would fail. One concern was that despite ridding itself of the services division, Dial was still too large: "Dial, spun off from Viad, is still like a little conglomerate, with the consumer products and meats living together like the contents of a freshman's refrigerator."[69]

In 1996, the first year Viad issued an annual report, its CEO acknowledged the extreme changes the Greyhound Corporation had undergone in the past 15 years: "we have made the transition from The Greyhound Corporation conglomerate as we successfully sold or spun off a number of companies." Borrowing a page from Jack Welch, as so many others had, he proceeded to say, "We are now a corporation focused on niche markets in the services industry where our companies are either number one or two in their categories."[70] In 1997, Viad started to restructure itself by selling its travel agencies and cruise lines. In 1998 and 1999, the company continued to sell off more businesses, including its airline catering business and the majority of Restaura. Despite selling parts of the company, Viad's stock declined in 1999. In the 1999 annual report, Viad's CEO blamed this on the "tremendous outflows of money from funds focused on value and growth at reasonable price to technology and start-up funds." The second reason he gave was that the company had "to do a better job of communicating to potential and existing investors the real value and growth potential of our company."[71] Though it shed its industrial roots and refocused itself on faster growing service sectors, Viad had yet to find a firm footing in the new economy.

The other company in our sample that has fully exited its industrial roots is AT&T (which formerly owned Western Electric). Its computer business was spun off as NCR. Its telecommunications equipment business (the core of Western Electric) was spun off as Lucent Technologies. By shedding its industrial legacy, AT&T has become a pure telecommunications services company competing with the likes of Worldcom and Sprint.

Even though Westinghouse, Monsanto, Greyhound, and AT&T offer proof that some companies can shed their industrial legacy, their experience also makes clear how hard this is to do. Westinghouse and Monsanto both lost their independence, although Monsanto later regained it as a much smaller company. Viad (the renamed Greyhound) is still struggling to find its footing. And AT&T, despite all its efforts to shed its past, is still finding it difficult to compete against companies that were born as service providers. It is hard to escape the genetic heritage of being an industrial company.

The lessons that can be derived from companies that have sought metamorphosis are:

1. Metamorphosis does not occur overnight. It requires a long period of investment in building a radically different set of capabilities.
2. The growth of the targeted business must outpace the decline of the current business.
3. Acquisitions (of other companies and different kinds of senior executives) may be a part of acquiring new capabilities, but these capabilities need to be internalized before the final stage of metamorphosis.
4. Metamorphosis may be easier by merging with a larger company that grew up in the targeted business.

Combination

In an effort to survive in the new economy, some industrial giants have tried to chart an evolutionary path that combines their industrial core with new post-industrial businesses. The companies from our study that are most clearly attempting to do so are Ford, General Motors, General Electric, Xerox, IBM, and Kodak. These industrial giants are trying to combine their industrial heritage with products, services, and business practices more closely associated with the new economy. Their basic product does not change—GM is still trying to sell cars; however, they are trying to do so in the manner of Dell and Cisco. Because the majority of these transformations are ongoing, the ultimate success or failure of these undertakings is difficult to evaluate.

General Motors, for example, is attempting to rehaul its business in four major ways. The first is the creation of its e-commerce site GMBuyPower.com, which enables customers to order cars online. The second is the development of its OnStar technology, which, according to the company's 1999 annual report, will enable the first "Web car."[72] The third change is the development of a B2B auto parts exchange that allows GM to bid for auto parts online. Finally, the company is moving its internal processes, such as billing and inventory, online. GM estimates that each of these four undertakings will save an extraordinary amount of money and enable the company to prosper in the new economy.

There are many skeptics who believe that GM will not be able to successfully reinvent itself. Its recent history suggests that GM has had difficulties accomplishing this in the past.[73] In the 1980s, under the leadership of Roger Smith, GM tried to transform itself into the "21st Century Corporation."[74] The plan was to revamp all of the assembly plants and replace workers with robots and other forms of computerization. The company was to spend $40 billion on this project.[75] However, this project was a failure. As one former securities analyst noted, "None of this stuff worked the way it was supposed to."[76] This history seems especially relevant given GM's current attempts to create yet another model of the "21st Century Corporation." Is GM going down this same path again?

GM does not believe that these new changes will repeat the 1980s debacle. Rather, their executives see the Internet as the way of the future. The 1999 annual report states that the company believes ". . . that the potential of the Internet and other communications technologies is particularly great" for GM.[77]

One way GM is attempting to become more like Dell is by selling cars online.[78] Toward the end of 2000, GM began testing its consumer Web site, GMBuyPower.com, to bring customers online to purchase cars. The online system was designed to be much more efficient for consumers and for GM. First, it would reduce the amount of time customers had to wait for their car to arrive. A car ordered online would take only 15 to 20 days to reach the customer compared to the usual 55 to 60.[79] Customers could also go through the inventory at a variety of dealers and create a customized car if they could not find what they were looking for on the Web site.

However, GMBuyPower.com faces significant challenges. First, there are many people who believe that the public may want to buy computers online, but not cars.[80] Another challenge facing the company is that despite their efforts to create a company like Dell for the car industry "cars aren't anything like computers when it comes to manufacturing."[81] The efficiency of Dell cannot easily be achieved with cars, and it may be difficult for GM to follow such a strategy.

OnStar is the second way that GM is trying to transform itself. OnStar is "an on-board-communications service that GM is pushing at customers in a bid to become much more than the world's largest vehicle maker." GM believes that eventually subscribers to this service will be able to "use voice commands to reach the Internet and request in-car traffic updates, news headlines, weather reports, sports scores, stock quotes, and e-mail." On the face of it, OnStar has huge potential. There is no denying the popularity of cell phones and Internet services. And GM has a huge customer base that spends a great deal of time in the car.[82] Combining these two things may well make OnStar extremely popular.

However, there are several other aspects of Onstar that raise concerns that it might become the 1990s version of Roger Smith's robots. Entering the online communications market translates into significant added competition for GM. The company will no longer just compete with car companies; it will also have to battle cellular phone and other online communication companies. Similarly, there is the question of whether there is a demand for this type of service. As technology continually evolves, it is highly probable that the equipment placed in the car will become obsolete. Also, OnStar can only be used in the car, which may make it cumbersome for customers used to the easy accessibility of cell phones.[83]

GM is also attempting to revamp its business structure through the creation of a B2B exchange with auto parts suppliers. This system, initially called TradeXchange, was designed to bring suppliers online so that GM can purchase supplies. For a fee, suppliers were to use TradeXchange to "reduce their costs and pass on some of those savings to GM."[84] GM believed that they could save a great deal of money through this B2B exchange, and Chairman John Smith Jr. claimed that "we think e-business will have an even greater impact on the way we operate than e-commerce."[85] Besides saving money, TradeXchange was also designed to streamline production: "By sharing information electronically with the suppliers . . . auto makers know when to expect the parts needed to assemble a particular car, and they can schedule assembly accordingly. And suppliers can tap into the auto makers' order system to find out what's needed by the manufacturer even before the parts order comes through, so they have the part ready to ship as soon as the order is placed."[86] Here too, GM was attempting to replicate the new business models pioneered by companies like Dell and Cisco.

However, GM was not alone in the creation of a B2B exchange. Ford had created AutoXchange to do basically the same things, which forced the two firms to compete for suppliers.[87] Ford and GM also had disparate styles and software, which made it very difficult for suppliers to streamline their systems. To solve these problems, Ford, GM, and DaimlerChrysler agreed to join together to create one B2B supplier exchange.[88] This new service was named Covisint.

Issues have plagued Covisint since its inception. First, the Federal Trade Commission worried that the joint venture may lead to ". . . unlawful price signaling or coordination among buyers or sellers."[89] This issue has since been resolved and Covisint has been approved. Another potential problem that may hinder Covisint is that it requires the three companies to share a great deal of company knowledge, which might be difficult for three rivals.[90]

The third way that GM is transforming its business is by placing its internal processes online. Originally GM had different Web sites for its different types of cars; however, in 1999 the company decided to put all their Web sites under one organization. To streamline its relationships with dealers, GM created an agreement in May 2000 with Reynolds and Reynolds to move its dealers onto the network used by the GM Corporation. The goal of this restructuring was to "help simplify the mess of incompatible and redundant computer and communications systems at many dealerships, reducing costs overall. 'I've got a discombobulated monster here and it keeps growing' said . . . [one] dealer . . . 'I've got to get everything in one spot and on the Internet.' "[91] To handle other types of internal processes such as billing and expenses, GM used EDS, a systems integration company that it had once owned and subsequently divested. In November 2000, EDS launched an Internet system to handle billing and related services. Also in November, GM signed an agreement with EDS to manage its B2B and business-to-employee projects.[92]

The revenue growth and savings that GM executives predict have until now proved elusive, even in change adept companies like GE,[93] which may make it difficult for GM to meet its expectations.

Kodak is another company that is attempting to reinvent itself by shifting its products and services to the new economy. Through an emphasis on digital cameras and digital printing, Kodak is trying to transform itself from a "film dinosaur to digital powerhouse." Kodak's big dilemma is that while 80 percent of the company's revenue comes from traditional film products, that segment is growing at just 2 percent per year. One observer calls this "perhaps the most precarious moment in its 120-year history." To address this problem, Kodak has turned to digital cameras. In fact, Kodak CEO, Daniel Carp, "is betting the company on a digital strategy." Carp believes that digital cameras will increase sales by 8 percent to 12 percent a year.[94]

However, Kodak faces some serious challenges to its digital strategy. Like GM, Kodak has had a history of failure in adopting new technology. Former CEO George Fisher claimed that in 1997 digital cameras would break even; however, the company could not follow through on this. Also, by pushing digital cameras, Kodak will in effect be hurting parts of its traditional business, as digital cameras eliminate the need for photographic paper.[95] Although the company is developing a way to counteract this problem, Kodak's entry into the digital world will definitely be difficult.

The examples of General Motors and Kodak illustrate how industrial companies are attempting to evolve to survive and hopefully thrive in the new economy. Some people are optimistic about what these companies can do with the Internet. They believe that "the true force of the Internet revolution will be felt only when large companies embrace it."[96] By contrast others see this as merely a replay of the past, specifically for companies like Kodak, Xerox, and GM that have failed before at transforming themselves. These companies are in a precarious position. They must find ways, as only GE has successfully done, to build new businesses faster than the decline in their traditional business. The problem is that the success they might have in growing new businesses is uncertain, whereas the decline of the traditional business is inevitable.

To succeed in becoming a hybrid company, business leaders must pay attention to the following principles:

1. This is a difficult path to follow if the core business is losing money. The distractions of managing a failing business complicate the challenges of succeeding in a new one. Therefore, pursue the hybrid alternative before the core business deteriorates to crisis proportions.
2. Start by introducing services that complement existing products and combine them into solutions.
3. As services grow to sizeable proportions, treat them as an independent business rather than as an adjunct to the industrial core.
4. While it is important to have internally differentiated management practices to respond to differences among the industrial and post-industrial businesses, provide linking mechanisms to integrate them.

NECESSITY AND CHOICE

The foregoing discussion of the future of the large industrial corporation should make one point clear. The process of change that intensified a quarter century ago is not yet complete. The large industrial corporation must recognize and embrace the continuing necessity of change. As tempting as it might be to wish for a triumphant return to the glory days of the first half of the twentieth century, that will simply be wishful thinking. The role and prominence of the industrial corporation in the U.S. economy will continue to diminish—just as the role of agriculture diminished in relation to the industrial activity during the twentieth century. It is worth noting that at the end of World War II, agriculture still accounted for roughly 10 percent of the U.S. GDP. By the end of the century, this share had dropped to less than 2 percent.

The circumstances of the industrial corporation today are similar to those of the small family farm a few generations ago. The leaders of industrial companies must confront the same reality that their farmer predecessors did: There will simply be fewer of them in the years ahead. This is not to suggest that industrial output (measured in tons of steel or gallons of oil or numbers of cars) will decline. Indeed the output will certainly increase, but it will be produced more cheaply and using less labor.

The output of the four largest agricultural producers in the United States today far exceeds the output of hundreds, perhaps thousands, of farms at the end of the nineteenth century. Industrial companies will not see such staggering productivity gains, but they will nonetheless continue to grow more productive and efficient.

Johnathan Rauch provides some compelling data to support this trend in the oil industry. "From 1980 to 1990, the cost of analyzing a fifty-square mile [geological] survey fell from $8 million to $1 million. Now it is more like $90,000." Similarly, "the average cost of finding new oil fell from $12 to $16 a barrel in the 1970s and 1980s to $4 to $8 today." More oil has been discovered and drilled in the last 25 years than in the preceding hundred, despite this being a limited natural resource."[97] If we were to plot the productivity curves for other industrial activities, the shapes and slopes would be similar.

As inexorable and relentless as these trends—slowdown in demand, combined with continuing gains in productivity—appear to be, the history of change during the last several decades reveals an incredible capacity on the part of executives to deny them. They postpone cost cutting, consolidating, and downsizing until they have no choice. They try to diversify themselves out of their troubles, only to find themselves in new businesses that they barely understand. In due course, most of these new acquisitions are divested as well.

Eventually, most industrial executives recognize necessity and acknowledge that, during periods of decline, the invisible hand of markets gains the upper hand over the visible hand of management. Rather than fight market forces to protect organizational forms that are the legacy of long periods of growth, executives must embrace market forces and be willing to transform their organizations. This transformation must occur along multiple dimensions. Rather than craft strategies that enable revenue growth, executives must focus on strategies that cut costs and increase productivity. Rather than build ever more elaborate hierarchical multidivisional structures, they must constantly downsize and create flatter, more permeable, network-like structures. Rather than rely on centralized control systems, they must depend on distributed information systems. Rather than build long-term bonds of loyalty between the company and its employees, they must forge relationships that enable mutual flexibility. In short, executives must be willing to dismantle the M-Form organization that was ideally suited to achieve growth through the visible hand of management and replace it with an N-Form organization that is more open to market forces and better suited to increasing productivity.

The earlier a company recognized and dealt with the imperative to change, the better its choices about its future. The contrasting tales of GE and Westinghouse with which we started this book illustrate this point vividly. Under Jack Welch, GE confronted this necessity early and entered the twenty-first century as one of America's most valued and vibrant organizations. Westinghouse denied necessity until the 1990s and eventually lost its very identity. A part of Westinghouse may have a promising future as Viacom, but the now-scattered core businesses are casualties of the era of transformation, just as the small family farm all but disappeared in the transition from an agrarian to an industrial economy.

The pattern just observed—of sequential stages of denial, grudging acceptance, then determined (perhaps forced) acceptance and action—is characteristic in contexts of long waves of decline. Although the relative decline of industrial output began in the United States as early as the mid-1950s, it was consciously recognized only after the oil shocks of the 1970s. Moreover, as salient as this decline became during the last quarter century, it is important to recognize that it is not over. It continues. Even as we finish writing this book, the announcements keep rolling in: DaimlerChrysler announces it plans to eliminate 26,000 jobs, or 20 percent of its North American workforce, Lucent plans to cut 10,000 jobs, Sara Lee to cut 7,000 jobs, Textron to cut 3,600, LTV to cut 1,000 . . . it just goes on.

There is a lesson here for those interested in large industrial corporations. The fundamental structural changes in the economy that we have been experiencing for the past half-century are still ongoing. As weary as we might be, we cannot rest. We must continue to wrestle with necessity and make difficult choices.

There may also be a lesson here for the pioneers of the post-industrial economy—the providers of IT hardware and software, telecommunications, pharmaceuticals, financial services, and retail stores. They may soon approach precisely the same point that industrial corporations reached during the 1950s—at their peak, unaware of their imminent decline. They too may soon have to confront the necessity of contraction, of making choices as they slowly, yet inevitably give way to the next economy—whatever that might be.

The strength of the capitalist system lies in its constant and continuing ability to reallocate resources from existing companies that pay diminishing returns to emerging enterprises that pay rising returns. Although markets play a central role in this dynamic of progress, management plays an equally vital role. The importance of entrepreneurs and managers as agents of innovation and architects of growth has been recognized and celebrated by writers like Schumpeter and Chandler. But let us not forget the importance of leaders also during periods of decline. These may not be the same kinds of heroes as those who build great new companies, but they are no less important to the functioning of a healthy capitalist economy. The fates of the companies in our study hinged to a great extent on their leadership. Nowhere is this clearer than in the contrasting cases of GE and Westinghouse. But we see the importance of leaders in all the other cases as well.

At first blush, this conclusion might seem at odds with our view that in contexts of decline, markets gain the upper hand over management. Although we maintain this view, we also believe that the industrial economy still needs leaders who understand market forces and are willing to act accordingly. These leaders must differ from their predecessors who managed the growth of large industrial enterprises.

They must be willing to make hard and unpalatable decisions—it is not easy to preside over prolonged downsizing, for example. Leaders may have to endure years of vilification. Recall that during the early years of his tenure Jack Welch was called, derisively, "Neutron Jack." Leaders who can successfully manage decline are highly disciplined and relentless about setting and monitoring progress towards demanding performance standards. They don't deny reality. Instead, they quickly confront it. They understand that the best hope for a more promising future lies first in dealing with the difficult actions that are necessary in decline. Yet pragmatic as they are, these leaders also display an optimistic bent—they believe in a light at the end of the tunnel. They recognize that in business, fortunes are always changing and opportunities are always available, if the right choices can be made

THE LEGACY OF THE LARGE INDUSTRIAL CORPORATION

The winds of transformative change have blown across the economic landscape of the United States—and of nations everywhere—for centuries, and they will continue to blast so long as humankind is engaged in producing goods and services and pursuing a better life. Economic institutions, and ways of organizing and managing them, come and go. For nearly a century, from the 1880s to the 1970s, the large industrial corporation dominated the American economy. It proved an extraordinarily efficient and reliable vehicle for mobilizing large pools of capital, managing the complex tasks of converting raw materials into finished goods on a large scale, and making these goods available to masses of people. It produced fortunes for its owners and investors, rising real incomes and benefits to increasing numbers of employees, ever-improving and cheaper goods to customers and consumers, and a multitude of benefits and services to local communities.

As the basis of the American economy evolves from manufacturing of traditional goods toward delivery of services and production of higher technology goods, the role and function of the large industrial corporation is inevitably changing. It remains, nonetheless, a powerful force in the post-industrial economy. Basic economic principles—economies of scale and scope in production and distribution—will ensure that certain types of goods can only be produced efficiently by big enterprises. A few years ago, it was fashionable in some circles to trumpet "small is better," even in mass production. Examples cited as proof included the autonomous work groups that replaced assembly-line workers in manufacturing Volvos and the northern Italian mini-mills that made specialty steel, fabrics, and garments. Such alternatives may be viable in some niche markets—although GM's absorption of Volvo strikes a cautionary note—but the basic fact remains that small cannot compete with large in high-volume or mass-distributed products. Cars, primary materials, chemicals, electrical and electronic equipment, mass-market consumer items, and many other products required in big numbers will be made by big companies into the indefinite future. Upstart companies like Intel, Dell Computer, and Cisco Systems have already become big and use their large size as a competitive weapon—a pattern that will recur in the twenty-first century as the eventual winners in the biotechnology industry emerge.

Although the large industrial corporation will not disappear anytime soon, it will grow ever leaner and more productive. It is unlikely ever again to generate the large-scale benefits to society that it seemed for so long to guarantee. This need not be cause for undue concern. As long as the new sectors of the economy grow at a pace fast enough to absorb the resources released from the industrial sector, society will prosper. This proved true during the final decade of the twentieth century, when aggregate U.S. unemployment reached historic lows even as the manufacturing sector continued to shed millions of jobs. However, should growth in the emerging economic sectors slow dramatically, as it appears to have recently, the waning of the industrial sector will impose greater social costs. We have only to recall the early 1990s, when so many families affected by layoffs and downsizing experienced financial distress and associated anxieties. With fraying social security and health-care systems, it is important from a social standpoint to make sure that the rate in the decline of the industrial sector is closely matched to the rate of growth of the new sectors of the economy. We are not suggesting that the government prop up the industrial sector with subsidies. Rather, we are suggesting that we prepare for "sustainable downsizing"—helping people and communities manage and adjust to the transition from an industrial to a post-industrial economy.

In a society that places great emphasis on individual responsibility, the lesson of industrial decline for individuals is to recognize the importance of investing in skills that will be more relevant and valued in the post-industrial economy—computer skills, collaborative skills, and knowledge work. The comfort of long-term or permanent employment is unlikely to return any time soon. At the same time, individuals must take more responsibility for managing their own careers, which are likely to include several, perhaps many, different employers, and for planning for their own retirement, which employer pension benefits may only partly underwrite. Perhaps once the post-industrial economy matures and takes on more definite dimensions, big companies might once more be counted upon to provide stable employment and retirement security. But for those presently employed in large industrial corporations, the long economic boom of the last decade did not ensure these benefits, and the next upturn will not bring them back.

Finally, we should appreciate the extraordinary influence of the large industrial corporation on our civic and public lives during the twentieth century. These institutions have been at the center of every facet of our lives—from the structures we inhabit to the philanthropies that support myriad social and cultural activities. The names of the buildings that define America's urban skylines may have changed but let us remember their origins in the fortunes of GE and Westinghouse, Du Pont and Union Carbide, GM and Chrysler, U.S. Steel, IBM, and Kodak. Let us not forget Carnegie's libraries, Rockefeller's music halls, or Whitney's museums. Eventually, the large industrial corporation will be replaced in these spheres as well. It is already happening as nonindustrial and post-industrial fortunes underwrite philanthropic organizations like the Bill and Melinda Gates Foundation, the Open Society Institute, or the California Endowment, and as America's sports venues are being renamed Qualcomm Stadium, CMGI Field, or the Edward Jones Dome. While the leading enterprises of the post-industrial economy will certainly come to play a more central role in our public lives, let us not forget that we will still be using the products and enjoying the heritage of large industrial corporations for generations to come.

ACKNOWLEDGMENTS

Authors incur many lasting debts in their work. The Division of Research at Harvard Business School under Deans John McArthur and Kim B. Clark and Research Directors Richard Tedlow and Teresa Amabile underwrote Nohria's original research and provided major support for this volume. The Winthrop Group, Inc. also supported the research as the study broadened and moved toward completion. We are grateful for this generosity, as well as the enthusiastic encouragement of our colleagues in these institutions.

Sandy Green, Rakesh Khurana, Geoff Love, and Misiek Piskorski contributed to Nohria's original study, and the database of *Fortune* 100 companies they collectively built became the major resource for the quantitative and statistical information and analysis in this book. Sarah Erikson, manager of research services at Baker Library, Harvard Business School, provided invaluable assistance to this project. Chris Allen and Sarah Woolverton, business information analysts at Baker Library, generated much of the time-series data and met numerous queries with timely and accurate responses. Amanda Johnson helped to prepare initial versions of many charts and tables and, as the project neared the finish line, Jill MacQuarrie took on the onerous tasks of producing most of these in final form and answering countless last-minute questions. Tony Mayo, a Dean's Research Fellow, and Bridget Gurtler, a research associate at Harvard Business School, helped greatly in preparing Chapter 8. Diane Line and Joan McDonald, Nohria's assistants, provided excellent administrative support to the project throughout its duration.

We are grateful to friends, colleagues, and family members who gave generously of their time to discuss this work as it gestated and/or subjected drafts of the manuscript (or portions thereof) to close reading. We wish particularly to thank Christopher Bartlett, Joseph Bower, Alfred Chandler, Robert Dalzell, David Garvin, Sumantra Ghoshal, Margaret Graham, Janice McCormick, Thomas McCraw, George Smith, and Richard Tedlow for their insights, criticisms, comments, and suggestions.

Our agent, Raphael Sagalyn, helped to place the book with John Wiley & Sons. Our editors at Wiley, Karen Hansen and Airie Dekidjiev, and our production team at Publications Development Company of Texas, especially Pam Blackmon and Nancy Land, exhibited exemplary patience with dilatory authors and ably guided the always miraculous process of turning the manuscript into a book.

Finally, we wish to thank our families for the support and encouragement that helped to keep us going during the long hours of research, thinking, writing, and rewriting. The unsung (but now acknowledged) heroes of this project are named Monica, Reva, Ambika, Janice, Ricky, Bella, Mary-Elise, Abby, and Molly.

NOTES

Preface

1. Chandler has been an extraordinarily productive and influential author, with many significant publications to his credit and a list that continues to accumulate. For our purposes, his main works include: *Strategy and Structure: Chapters in the History of the American Industrial Enterprise* (Cambridge, MA: MIT Press, 1962); *The Visible Hand: The Managerial Revolution in American Business* (Cambridge, MA: Harvard University Press, 1977); and *Scale and Scope: The Dynamics of Industrial Capitalism* (Cambridge, MA: Harvard University Press, 1990). See also, Thomas K. McCraw, Ed., *The Essential Alfred Chandler* (Boston: Harvard Business School Press, 1988).
2. Nitin Nohria, "From the M-Form to the N-Form: Taking Stock of Changes in the Large Industrial Corporation," Harvard Business School Working Paper 96–054 (1996).

Chapter 1

1. *Wall Street Journal,* October 30, 1998.
2. The remaining pieces of Westinghouse Electric were sold to Emerson Electric Co., and to a joint venture between Morrison Knudsen Corp. and British Nuclear Fuels in 1998 and 1999. The joint venture kept the name Westinghouse Electric Corp., but it was a shadow of its former self. The sequel at CBS came in 2000, when it merged into the media conglomerate Viacom under terms that position Karmazin as a possible successor to legendary CEO Sumner Redstone.
3. E.g., Steve Massey, "Who Killed Westinghouse?," a six-part series published in the *Pittsburgh Post-Gazette,* available online at www.post-gazette.com/westinghouse/prologue.asp.
4. The stock surged still higher in 1998 when Karmazin succeeded Jordan.
5. *Moody's Industrial Manual,* 1973, 2:3373–3375.
6. *Fortune,* August 1976, pp. 148, 150–152.
7. *New York Times,* June 9, 1974, 3:1, p. 11.
8. "Westinghouse Electric Corporation: The Elusive Winner's Circle," London Business School case, 1994, 7–8; *Business Week,* December 5, 1983.
9. *Financial World,* May 28, 1975, p. 15; *Forbes,* May 15, 1975, p. 107.
10. *Business Week,* December 5, 1983.
11. *Wall Street Journal,* April 28, 1983.
12. Quoted in "Westinghouse Electric Corporation: The Elusive Winner's Circle," p. 9.
13. *Business Week,* July 28, 1986; *Wall Street Journal,* November 6, 1990.

14. *Wall Street Journal,* November 6, 1990.
15. *Business Week,* March 8, 1993.
16. "Westinghouse Electric Corporation: The Elusive Winner's Circle," p. 13; *Forbes,* April 4, 1988.
17. *Wall Street Journal,* July 30, 1987.
18. *Business Week,* March 28, 1988.
19. See Westinghouse, Annual Report, 1987.
20. *Business Week,* February 17, 1992.
21. *Business Week,* February 17, 1992.
22. *Business Week,* December 7, 1992.
23. *Wall Street Journal,* November 17 and 24, 1992.
24. *Wall Street Journal,* November 24 and December 4, 1992.
25. *Business Week,* July 8, 1972, pp. 52–54; Norman Bartczak, "General Electric Company: Quality of Earnings Analysis," Harvard Business School case, 1982, p. 6.
26. "General Electric Company: Quality of Earnings Analysis," p. 5.
27. General Electric Co., Annual Report, 1976; *Wall Street Journal,* December 16 and 18, 1975.
28. Quoted in *Washington Post,* October 7, 1984.
29. Robert Slater, *The New GE: How Jack Welch Revived an American Institution* (Homewood, IL: Business One Irwin, 1993), pp. 64–65; Francis Aguilar and Richard Hamermesh, "General Electric: Strategic Position—1981," Harvard Business School case, 1981.
30. *Wall Street Journal,* April 13, 2000.
31. Francis Aguilar, Richard Hamermash, and Caroline Brainard, "General Electric: Reg Jones and Jack Welch," Harvard Business School case, 1991; *Wall Street Journal,* December 4, 1984, p. 41.
32. *Wall Street Journal,* January 31, 1983.
33. "General Electric: Reg Jones and Jack Welch," 14. *Forbes* printed Welch's sketch laying out the three circles in March 26, 1984, p. 106.
34. *Wall Street Journal,* December 12, 1985.
35. *Business Week,* June 30, 1986.
36. Slater, *New GE,* p. 195.
37. *Business Week,* June 30, 1986.
38. *Forbes,* January 1, 1996; *Business Week,* October 2, 1995.
39. General Electric, Annual Report, 1997.
40. *Fortune,* November 10, 1997.
41. See, for example, General Electric, Annual Report, 1990; *Fortune,* March 26, 1990.
42. Slater, *New GE,* p. 198.
43. *Wall Street Journal,* April 13, 2000.
44. General Electric, Annual Report, 1999, Letter to Shareowners; "GE Bucks Trend to Keep Up IT Spending," *Financial Times,* January 18, 2001.
45. *Fortune,* April 17, 2000.
46. General Electric, Annual Report, 2000.
47. Thomas A. Stewart, "A New 500 for the New Economy," *Fortune,* May 15, 1995, p. 166.

48. http://averages.dowjones.com/in_out.html.
49. The best collection of essays on the dynamics of institutionalization, by which innovative practices get imitated and commonly understood can be found in Walter W. Powell and Paul J. DiMaggio (editors), *The New Institutionalism in Organizational Analysis* (Chicago: University of Chicago Press, 1991).
50. See Marshall McLuhan and Bruce R. Powers, *The Global Village: Transformations in World Life and Media in the 21st Century* (New York: Cambridge University Press, 1992).
51. See Chapter 9 in Robert G. Eccles and Nitin Nohria, *Beyond the Hype: Rediscovering the Essence of Management* (Boston, MA: Harvard Business School Press, 1992).
52. For the case of Korea, which is emblematic of late industrializers, see Alice H. Amsden, *Asia's Next Giant: South Korea and Late Industrialization* (New York: Oxford University Press, 1989).
53. The distinction between value-created and value-captured is highlighted in Adam Brandenburger and Barry Nalebuff, *Coopetition* (New York: Doubleday, 1997), which documents many examples in which a company that creates economic value does not necessarily capture it.
54. See Michael L. Dertouzos, Richard K. Lester, and Robert M. Solow, *Made in America: Regaining the Productive Edge* (Cambridge, MA: MIT Press, 1989).
55. See Alfred D. Chandler Jr., *The Visible Hand: The Managerial Revolution in American Business* (Cambridge: MA: Harvard University Press, 1977).
56. This argument for the benefits of managerial coordination is also implicit in the theory of the firm advanced by Ronald Coase, which has been further elaborated by Oliver E. Williamson in *The Economic Institutions of Capitalism* (New York: Free Press, 1985).
57. See a collection of essays edited by John W. Pratt and Richard J. Zeckhauser, *Principals and Agents: The Structure of Business* (Boston, MA: Harvard Business School Press, 1985) for an overview of the principal-agent framework.
58. See Chandler, *The Visible Hand,* p. 460; Williamson, *Economic Institutions,* p. 281.
59. In addition to notes 55 and 56, see Joseph L. Bower, *Managing the Resource Allocation Process* (Boston, MA: Harvard Business School Press, 1986).
60. In addition to note 55, also see Adolph A. Berle Jr. and Gardiner C. Means, *The Modern Corporation and Private Property* (New York: Harcourt, 1932).
61. See Michael Useem, *The Inner Circle: Large Corporations and the Rise of Business Political Activity in the U.S. and U.K.* (New York: Oxford University Press, 1984).
62. See Chandler, *Visible Hand.*
63. See Richard F. Vancil, *Decentralization: Managerial Ambiguity by Design* (Homewood, IL: Irwin, 1979).
64. See Williamson, *Economic Institutions,* pp. 286–290.
65. See Michael Useem, *Executive Defense: Shareholder Power and Corporate Reorganization* (Cambridge, MA: Harvard University Press, 1993).
66. See Neil Fligstein, *The Transformation of Corporate Control* (Cambridge, MA: Harvard University Press, 1990).
67. For the relationship between contracting problems and the boundaries of the firm, see Sanford Grossman and Oliver Hart, "The costs and benefits of ownership: a theory of vertical and lateral integration," *Journal of Political Economy* (1986), 94:691–719.

68. C. K. Prahalad and Gary Hamel, "The Core Competence of the Corporation." *Harvard Business Review,* 1990, 68(3), pp. 79–92.
69. See Shoshana Zuboff, *In the Age of the Smart Machine: The Future of Work and Power.* (New York: Basic Books, 1988).
70. Harrison White, "Where do markets come from?" *American Journal of Sociology,* 1981, 87, pp. 517–547.
71. The tit-for-tat dynamics of oligopolistic imitation have been highlighted by F. T. Knickerbocker, *Oligopolistic Reaction and the Multinational Enterprise* (Cambridge: MA: Harvard University Press, 1973).
72. Joel M. Podolony, "A status-based model of market competition," *American Journal of Sociology,* 1993, 98, pp. 829–872.
73. See Brian J. Hall and Jeffrey B. Liebman, "Are CEOs really paid like bureaucrats?" *Quarterly Journal of Economics,* 1998, pp. 653–691.
74. In terms of Michael C. Jensen and William H. Meckling's influential paper, "Specific and general knowledge, and organizational structure," in L. Werin and H. Wijkander (editors), *Contract Economics* (Oxford, UK: Basil Blackwell, 1992); the emphasis shifts from the general knowledge possessed by corporate strategists to the specific knowledge possessed by operating managers.

Chapter 2

1. Manufacturing, unlike agriculture, never accounted for a majority of GDP or national employment. It became by far the biggest and wealthiest component of national income in the late nineteenth century and peaked in influence in the years between 1953 and 1957. See U.S. Bureau of the Census, *Historical Statistics of the United States, Colonial Times to 1970* (Washington, DC, 1975), Series F 250–261.
2. It's worth noting the publication date of Daniel Bell's *The Coming of Post-Industrial Society* (New York: Basic Books, 1973), a difficult book that nonetheless began to shape awareness of the fundamental economic shift.
3. A case in point is the *Oxford History of the United States:* James T. Patterson, *Grand Expectations: The United States, 1945–1974* (New York: Oxford University Press, 1996). Among economists, see Wallace C. Peterson, *Silent Depression: Twenty-five Years of Wage Squeeze and Middle Class Decline* (New York: W.W. Norton, 1994), Chapter 2.
4. For a similar analysis, see Alfred D. Chandler Jr. and Takashi Hikino, "The Large Industrial Enterprise and the Dynamics of Modern Economic Growth," in Alfred D. Chandler Jr., Franco Amatori, and Takashi Hikino, *Big Business and the Wealth of Nations* (New York: Cambridge University Press, 1997), p. 40; and Alfred D. Chandler Jr., *Scale and Scope: The Dynamics of Industrial Capitalism* (Cambridge, MA: Harvard University Press, 1990), Appendices. Chandler documents the continuing dominance of the large industrial corporation in certain industries around the world, as well as the trend in the United States of the largest firms into knowledge-intensive, as opposed to capital-intensive, industries. We agree with his conclusions but are concerned with a different point: the changing composition of the top industrials, as well as the relative decline of this sector of the economy.
5. Chandler and Hikino, "The Large Industrial Enterprise," pp. 37–50.

6. See note 1.
7. Alfred D. Chandler Jr., "The Competitive Performance of U.S. Industrial Enterprise since the Second World War," *Business History Review* (Spring 1994), pp. 5–6.
8. Edward F. Dennison, *Trends in American Economic Growth, 1929–1982* (Washington, DC, 1985), p. 4, based on data furnished by the U.S. Census Bureau.
9. Carl Kaysen, Ed., *The American Corporation Today* (New York: Oxford University Press, 1996), p. 6.
10. Wallace C. Peterson, *Silent Depression: The Fate of the American Dream* (New York: W.W. Norton, 1994), Chapter 2.
11. Quoted in Ed Cray, *Chrome Colossus* (New York: McGraw-Hill, 1980). The statement is widely cited although not normally in its entirety.
12. The heavy manufacturers dominated the Dow Jones Industrial Average in the 1950s and 1960s, another indication of their economic salience. For the changing composition of the DJIA, see http://averages.dowjones.com.
13. Edward S. Mason, *The Corporation in Modern Society* (Cambridge, MA: Harvard University Press, 1959); cf. Kaysen, *American Corporation Today,* Introduction.
14. John Kenneth Galbraith, *The New Industrial State* (Boston: Houghton Mifflin, 1967); Jean Jacques Servan-Schreiber, *Le defi americain* (Paris: Denoel, 1967), translated by Ronald Steel and featuring an introduction by Arthur Schlesinger Jr. (New York: Atheneum, 1968). See also George David Smith and Davis Dyer, "The Rise and Transformation of the American Corporation," in Kaysen, *American Corporation Today,* Chapter 2. In the early 1970s, other works continued to mine the vein, for example, Richard J. Barnet and Ronald E. Muller, *Global Reach: The Power of Multinational Corporations* (New York: Simon & Schuster, 1974).
15. Neil Fligstein, *The Transformation of Corporate Control* (Cambridge, MA: Harvard University Press, 1990), pp. 201–202; Davis Dyer, *TRW: Pioneering Technology and Innovation since 1900* (Boston: Harvard Business School Press, 1990), pp. 244–245.
16. Dyer, *TRW,* p. 261; Norman A. Berg, *General Management: An Analytical Approach* (Homewood, IL: Irwin, 1984), pp. 123–125; Kenneth A. Davidson, *Megamergers: Corporate America's Billion Dollar Takeovers* (Cambridge, MA: Ballinger, 1985), pp. 138–143; Chandler, "Competitive Performance," pp. 16–19.
17. David Vogel, "The 'New' Social Regulation in Historical and Comparative Perspective," in Thomas K. McCraw, ed., *Regulation in Perspective: Historical Essays* (Cambridge, MA: Harvard University Press, 1981), pp. 155–185.
18. Patterson, *Grand Expectations,* pp. 740–741 and 783–785; Barry Eichengreen, *Globalizing Capital: A History of the International Monetary System* (Princeton: Princeton University Press, 1996), pp. 130–133.
19. U.S. Department of Commerce, Economics and Statistics Division, Bureau of the Census, *Statistical Abstract of the United States 2000* (Washington, DC, 2001).
20. John Cassidy, "The Productivity Mirage," *New Yorker,* November 27, 2000, p. 109.
21. David B. Sicilia, "Distant Proximity: Writing the History of American Business since 1945," *Business and Economic History,* Fall 1997, 26, p. 269; and Peterson, *Silent Depression,* Chapter 2.
22. ftp://ftp.bls.gov/pub/special.requests/ForeignLabor/flsforc.txt
23. http://averages.dowjones.com.

24. http://averages.dowjones.com.
25. Alan Greenspan, Congressional testimony, 2000.
26. Robert G. Eccles and Nitin Nohria, with James D. Berkley, *Beyond the Hype: Rediscovering the Essence of Management* (Boston: Harvard Business School Press, 1992), pp. 19, 23.
27. Richard L. Nolan, "Information Technology Management since 1960," in Alfred D. Chandler Jr. and James W. Cortada, Eds., *A Nation Transformed by Information: How Information Has Shaped the United States from Colonial Times to the Present* (New York: Oxford University Press, 2000), pp. 217–256, esp. pp. 250–251 and 253–254.
28. The revolutionary potential and ultimate limits of IT in affecting business are evident in two widely spaced articles by Michael E. Porter: (with Victor E. Millar), "How Information Technology Gives You Competitive Advantage," *Harvard Business Review* (July–August 1985); and "Strategy and the Internet," *Harvard Business Review* (March 2001).
29. *Information Technology Industry Data Book,* 2000.
30. Bhaskar Chakravorti, *Financial Times,* May 24, 1998.
31. Nolan, "Information Technology Management since 1960," pp. 250–251 and 253–254.
32. *Business Week,* March 26, 2001, p. 118; Nolan, "Information Technology Management since 1960," p. 253.
33. John Newhouse, *The Sporty Game* (New York: Knopf, 1982).
34. Alfred D. Chandler Jr., *The Visible Hand: The Managerial Revolution in American Business* (Cambridge, MA: Harvard University Press, 1977).
35. Landon Y. Jones, *Great Expectations: America and the Baby Boom Generation* (New York, Ballantine Books, 1981). For the values and expectations of baby boomers, see Daniel Yankelovich, *New Rules: Searching for Self-Fulfillment in a World Turned Upside Down* (New York: Random House, 1981); Rosabeth Moss Kanter, "Work in a New America," *Daedalus* (Summer, 1977).
36. Peter G. Peterson, *Gray Dawn: How the Coming Age Wave Will Transform America and the World* (New York: Three Rivers Press, 1999).
37. Thomas A. Kochan, "The American Corporation as Employer: Past, Present, and Future Possibilities," in Kaysen, Ed., *The American Corporation Today,* pp. 242–268; William B. Johnston and Arnold E. Packer, *Workforce 2000: Work and Workers for the 21st Century* (Indianapolis, IN: Hudson Institute, 1987).
38. Mabel Newcomer, *The Big Business Executive: Factors That Make Him, 1900–1950* (New York: Columbia University Press, 1965).
39. Michael T. Jacobs, *Short-Term America: The Causes and Cures of Our Business Myopia* (Boston: Harvard Business School Press, 1991); Chandler, "Competitive Performance," pp. 21–22; Michael Useem, *Investor Capitalism: How Money Managers Are Changing the Face of Corporate America* (New York: Basic Books, 1996), passim.
40. http://www.nyse.com; *New York Stock Exchange Fact Book* (2000), p. 101.

Chapter 3

1. *Wall Street Journal,* March 20, 1998, A4.
2. On consolidation pressures within the industry, see e.g., *Chemical Market Reporter,* August 9, 1999, p. 1; *Chemical Week,* August 11, 1999, p. 5.

3. *Chemical Week,* August 11, 1999, p. 5.
4. In October 2000, Pharmacia sold a 15 percent interest in Monsanto via an initial public offering. As of early 2002, Pharmacia still retained its 85 percent stake, though plans to divest the holding reportedly remained on track for later this year.
5. Joseph L. Bower, *When Markets Quake: The Management Challenge of Restructuring Industry* (Boston: Harvard Business School Press, 1986), p. 19. Alfred D. Chandler Jr. explores the implications of the energy shocks for chemical companies in his *Shaping the Industrial Century: The Chemical and Pharmaceutical Industries* (New York: The Free Press, forthcoming 2003). We are grateful to Professor Chandler for affording us an early look at this important work.
6. The definitive historical account of this story is Alfred D. Chandler Jr., *Strategy and Structure: Chapters in the History of the American Industrial Enterprise* (Cambridge, MA: MIT Press, 1962), Part II. See also David A. Hounshell and John Kenly Smith Jr., *Science and Corporate Strategy: Du Pont, 1902–1980* (New York: Cambridge University Press, 1988); and Davis Dyer and David B. Sicilia, *Labors of a Modern Hercules: The Evolution of a Chemical Company* (Boston: Harvard Business School Press, 1990).
7. Intangible assets such as technology, brand identity, and managerial capabilities are subject to market failure. As Teece points out, these assets are thus best exploited through diversification within the boundaries of the firm: D. J. Teece, "Toward an Economic Theory of the Multiproduct Firm," *Journal of Economic Behavior and Organization,* March 1982, pp. 39–63.
8. Teece, "Toward an Economic Theory of the Multiproduct Firm."
9. For a succinct review, see Cynthia A. Montgomery, "Corporate Diversification," *Journal of Economic Perspectives,* 8 (1994), pp. 163–178.
10. See Neil Fligstein, *The Transformation of Corporate Control* (Cambridge, MA: Harvard University Press, 1990); and G. F. Davis, K. A. Dieckmann, and C. H. Tinsley, "The Decline and Fall of the Conglomerate Firm in the 1980s: A Study in the Deinstitutionalization of an Organizational Form," *American Sociological Review,* 1994, 59, pp. 547–571.
11. Davis, "The Decline and Fall."
12. See Y. Amihud and B. Lev, "Risk Reduction as a Managerial Motive for Conglomerate Merger," *Bell Journal of Economics,* 1981, 12, pp. 605–617.
13. See Oliver E. Williamson, *Corporate Control and Business Behavior* (Englewood Cliffs, NJ: Prentice-Hall, 1970); and Williamson, *The Economic Institutions of Capitalism* (New York: Free Press, 1985).
14. See Thomas E. Copeland and J. Fred Weston, *Financial Theory and Corporate Policy* (Reading, MA: Addison-Wesley, 1979); and Bower, *When Markets Quake,* pp. 42–43.
15. Du Pont, Annual Report, 1985.
16. On Dow's growth strategy, see *Fortune,* May 1977, 312 ff; *Forbes,* July 4, 1994, p. 44 ff; and the company's commissioned history, E. N. Brandt, *Growth Company: Dow Chemical's First Century* (East Lansing, MI: Michigan State University Press, 1997).
17. For a general account, see *Chemical Week,* November 19, 1980.
18. Quoted in *Fortune,* September 10, 1979.
19. Dow Chemical, Annual Report, 1973, Consolidated Statement of Income, p. 12. On the development of Saran Wrap®, see Brandt, *Growth Company,* 288–289.

20. *Fortune,* May 1977, 312 ff.
21. See Bower, *When Markets Quake,* Chapter 6.
22. Quoted in Brandt, *Growth Company,* 531–532; see also *Chemical Week,* November 11, 1980.
23. Quoted in Brandt, *Growth Company,* 538; see also Bower, *When Markets Quake,* 105–106.
24. Dow Chemical, Annual Report, 1983.
25. Brandt, *Growth Company,* 532.
26. Drexel, Burnham, and Lambert report on the chemical industry, 1990.
27. Bower, *When Markets Quake,* 101.
28. Union Carbide, Annual Report, 1974, p. 2.
29. Quoted in *Forbes,* April 28, 1980.
30. Quoted in *Forbes,* April 28, 1980.
31. Union Carbide, Annual Report, 1982, p. 7.
32. See *Chemical Week,* October 26, 1983, p. 44.
33. See e.g., "Union Carbide Could Face Staggering Gas-Leak Damage Claims, Experts Say," *Wall Street Journal,* December 6, 1984.
34. *Wall Street Journal,* April 13, 1988 and June 24, 1988.
35. Union Carbide, Annual Report, 1990, p. 2.
36. *Forbes,* December 18, 1995.
37. Union Carbide, Annual Report, 1991, p. 2.
38. *Chemical Week,* October 29, 1997, p. 8.
39. Brandt, *Growth Company,* p. 557.
40. *Chemical Week,* May 18, 1994.
41. Brandt, *Growth Company,* p. 556.
42. Brandt, *Growth Company,* p. 556.
43. Brandt, *Growth Company,* p. 563.
44. Brandt, *Growth Company,* p. 563.
45. Brandt, *Growth Company,* p. 563.
46. Dow Chemical, Annual Report, 1997.
47. See Andrew Campbell, "Tailored, Not Benchmarked: A Fresh Look at Corporate Planning," *Harvard Business Review* (March–April 1999), pp. 41–50.
48. Davis et al., "Decline and Fall."
49. Alfred D. Chandler Jr., *Scale and Scope: The Dynamics of Industrial Capitalism* (Cambridge, MA: Harvard University Press, 1990).
50. See D. LeBaron and L. S. Speidel, "Why Are the Parts Worth More than the Sum? Chop Shop, a Corporate Valuation Model," in L. E. Browne and E. S. Rosengren, Eds., *The Merger Boom* (Boston: Federal Reserve Bank of Boston, 1987), pp. 78–101.
51. C. Markides, "Diversification, Restructuring and Economic Performance," *Strategic Management Journal,* 1995, 16, pp. 101–118: J. Leibskind and T. C. Opler, "The Cause of Corporate Refocusing," working paper, University of Southern California, 1992.
52. Amar Bhide, "The Causes and Consequences of Hostile Takeovers," *Journal of Applied Corporate Finance,* 9 (Summer 1989).

53. B. Wernerfelt, "A Resource-based View of the Firm," *Strategic Management Journal,* 1984, 5, pp. 171–180.
54. See esp. C. K. Prahalad and Gary Hamel, "The Core Competence of the Corporation," *Harvard Business Review* (May–June 1990), pp. 79–92.
55. *Chemical Week,* June 21, 1995, p. 21.
56. Union Carbide, Annual Report, 1993.
57. Union Carbide, Annual Report, 1993; on the Elf Autochem joint venture, see Annual Report, 1994.
58. *Chemical Week,* June 21, 1995, pp. 21 ff.
59. *Chemical Week,* February 8, 1995; April 17, 1996.
60. E. Anderson, "Two Firms, One Frontier," *Sloan Management Review* (1990), 19–30.
61. See B. Kogut, "Joint Ventures and the Option to Expand and Acquire," *Management Science,* 1991, 37, pp. 19–33; P. Mohanram and A. Nanda, "When do Joint Ventures Create Value," working paper #96–028, Harvard Business School, 1996; and Nitin Nohria and M. J. Piskorski, "Focus and Diversification: the Effects of Changes in the Scope of Large Industrial Corporations," Working Paper #96–058, Harvard Business School, 1996, for reviews.
62. B. Anand and T. Khanna, "On the Market Value of Inter-firm Agreements: the Computer and Telecommunication Industries, 1990–1993," working paper, Harvard Business School, 1995; Nohria and Piskorski, "Focus and Diversification."
63. "Monsanto's March into Biotechnology (A)," case no. 9–690–009, Harvard Business School, p. 2; *Wall Street Journal,* November 5, 1985; Dow Jones Newswires, November 5, 1980.
64. "Monsanto's March into Biotechnology (A)."
65. *Chemical Week,* October 26, 1983, p. 58.
66. "Monsanto's March into Biotechnology (A)," p. 5.
67. "Monsanto's March into Biotechnology (A)," pp. 7–8.
68. *Chemical Week,* October 26, 1983, p. 53.
69. *Wall Street Journal,* July 19, 1985.
70. *Wall Street Journal,* July 19, 1985; see also *Wall Street Journal,* November 9, 1984; January 7, 1985; July 22, 1985; and Harvard Business School, "Monsanto's March into Biotechnology (A)," p. 8.
71. *Wall Street Journal,* August 4, 1986.
72. *Wall Street Journal,* September 14, 1994.
73. *Wall Street Journal,* September 14, 1994; February 24, 1997.
74. *Wall Street Journal,* October 24, 1996.
75. *Fortune,* April 14, 1997.
76. *Forbes,* March 10, 1997.
77. Monsanto, Annual Report, 1997, "A Network of Partnerships."
78. *Business Week,* May 25, 1998.
79. *Business Week,* November 30, 1998, 40; on the AHP merger proposal, see also *Economist,* U.S. edition, October 17, 1998.
80. *Wall Street Journal,* February 10, 1999.
81. *Chemical Week,* August 11, 1999, p. 5.

82. *Los Angeles Times,* August 5, 1999, p. C1.
83. *Wall Street Journal,* August 5, 1999, p. A3.
84. Thomas R. Kelly, an analyst at Standard & Poors, as quoted in *Chemical Week,* February 14, 2001, online version.

Chapter 4

1. The definitive account is Alfred D. Chandler Jr., *Strategy and Structure: Chapters in the History of the American Industrial Enterprise* (Cambridge, MA: Massachusetts Institute of Technology Press, 1962), Part 3.
2. Alfred P. Sloan Jr., *My Years with General Motors* (Garden City, NY: Doubleday & Company, 1964), 42. For a detailed account of GM's transformation over the 1920s, see esp. Arthur J. Kuhn, *GM Passes Ford, 1918–1938: Designing the General Motors Performance-Control System* (University Park, PA: Pennsylvania State University Press, 1986).
3. On this critical aspect of GM's rise to dominance, see esp. Richard S. Tedlow, *New and Improved: The Story of Mass Marketing in America* (Boston: Harvard Business School Press, 1996).
4. See Chandler, *Strategy and Structure,* Part 5.
5. Peter F. Drucker, *Concept of the Corporation* (rev. ed., New York: John Day Co., 1972), p. 298.
6. See Richard Vancil, *Decentralization: Managerial Ambiguity by Design* (Homewood, IL: Irwin, 1979).
7. Davis Dyer, Malcolm S. Salter, and Alan M. Webber, *Changing Alliances: The Harvard Business School Project on the Auto Industry and the American Economy* (Boston: Harvard Business School Press, 1987), p. 30; Susan Helper, "Strategy and Irreversibility in Supplier Relations: The Case of the U.S. Automobile Industry," *Business History Review,* vol. 65, pp. 781–824.
8. See William Serrin, *The Company and the Union: The "Civilized Relationship" of the General Motors Corporation and the United Automobile Workers* (New York: Knopf, 1970).
9. Robert Sobel, *Car Wars: The Untold Story* (New York: Dutton, 1984), p. 227.
10. General Motors, Annual Report, 1973, p. 2.
11. Roger Smith quoted in MaryAnn Keller, *Rude Awakening: The Rise, Fall, and Struggle for Recovery of General Motors* (New York: Morrow, 1989), p. 101.
12. Keller, *Rude Awakening,* p. 113.
13. Quoted in John Paul MacDuffie, "Automotive White Collar: The Changing Status and Roles of Salaried Employees in the North American Auto Industry," in Paul Osterman, ed., *Broken Ladders: Managerial Careers in the New Economy* (New York: Oxford University Press, 1996), p. 97.
14. John Z. De Lorean with J. Patrick Wright, *On a Clear Day You Can See General Motors* (Grosse Pointe, MI: Wright Enterprises, 1979).
15. General Motors, Annual Report, 1980; *Ward's Automotive Yearbook,* 1981. The company did prune out 13,000 salaried employees in 1980, mainly by attrition, but not so as to fundamentally reroute its channels and patterns of management. *Fortune,* March 9, 1981.

16. *Fortune,* March 9, 1981.
17. Sobel, *Car Wars,* pp. 281–282.
18. For an account of the breakdown of the automation drive, see Keller, *Rude Awakening,* pp. 202–211.
19. Joseph L. Badarocco, "General Motors in 1988," Harvard Business School Case, 1988, pp. 5–6.
20. Quoted in Keller, *Rude Awakening,* p. 94. Emphasis in the original.
21. Anita McGahan and Greg Keller, "Saturn: A Different Kind of Car Company," Harvard Business School Case, 1994, p. 14.
22. Quoted in Albert Lee, *Call Me Roger* (Chicago: Contemporary Books), pp. 243–244.
23. *Wall Street Journal,* January 11, 1984.
24. *Automotive News,* January 16, 1984, p. 57.
25. *Automotive News,* February 27, 1984, p. 40.
26. *Automotive News,* January 16, 1984.
27. *Automotive News,* January 16, 1984.
28. Donald E. Petersen and John Hillkirk, *A Better Idea: Redefining the Way Americans Work* (Boston: Houghton Mifflin Company, 1991), p. 5.
29. Petersen and Hillkirk, *Better Idea,* p. 20.
30. Quoted in Richard T. Pascale, *Managing on the Edge: How the Smartest Companies Use Conflict to Stay Ahead* (New York: Simon & Schuster, 1990), p. 133.
31. Quoted in Pascale, *Managing on the Edge,* p. 136.
32. Quoted in Harvard Business School, "Transformation at Ford," p. 11.
33. Quoted in Pascale, *Managing on the Edge,* p. 136.
34. Quoted in Pascale, *Managing on the Edge,* p. 122.
35. Petersen and Hillkirk, *Better Idea,* p. 49.
36. Quoted in Pascale, *Managing on the Edge,* p. 130.
37. Quoted in Mark Pelofsky, "Transformation at Ford," Harvard Business School Case, 1986, revised 1991, p. 8.
38. Petersen and Hillkirk, *Better Idea,* p. 69.
39. See Robert L. Shook, *Turnaround: The New Ford Motor Company* (New York: Prentice Hall Press, 1990), pp. 139–145.
40. Quoted in Shook, *Turnaround,* p. 150.
41. Shook, *Turnaround,* p. 151.
42. Petersen and Hillkirk, *Better Idea,* p. 70.
43. Shook, *Turnaround,* pp. 152–153.
44. Petersen and Hillkirk, *Better Idea,* p. 75.
45. The account that follows draws heavily from Jeffrey H. Dyer, "How Chrysler Created an American Keiretsu," *Harvard Business Review,* July–August 1996.
46. Cary Reich, "The Creative Mind; The Innovator," *New York Times Magazine,* April 21, 1985.
47. *Fortune,* April 9, 1990.
48. Micheline Maynard, *Collision Course: Inside the Battle for General Motors* (New York: Carol Publ. Group, 1995), pp. 144–145.
49. *Fortune,* April 9, 1990.

50. See, e.g., *Wall Street Journal,* May 14, 1984; January 10, 1985; Lee, *Call Me Roger,* pp. 241–242.
51. *Fortune,* February 15, 1988.
52. C. Sabel, "Moebius-Strip Organizations and Open Labor Markets," in J. Coleman and P. Bourdie, Eds., *Social Theory for a Changing Society* (Boulder, CO: Westview Press, 1991). Note that of 410 pared out, 300 were redistributed in line operations; 110 were permanently laid off. "M-Form," p. 22.
53. *Aviation Week and Space Technology,* May 31, 1993, p. 81.
54. *Fortune,* November 30, 1992.
55. Quoted in *Fortune,* November 6, 1989, p. 34.
56. See General Electric, Annual Report, 1990.
57. *Wall Street Journal,* April 27, 1992, A3 and October 26, 1992; General Motors, Annual Report, 1992; *Automotive News,* October 26, 1992.
58. *Wall Street Journal,* August 4, 1998.
59. Ibid.
60. See *Ward's Auto World,* August 1, 1995; *Wall Street Journal,* March 23, 1993.
61. For an account of the DaimlerChrysler merger, see Bill Vlasic and Bradley A. Stertz, *Taken for a Ride: How Daimler-Benz Drove Off with Chrysler* (New York: HarperBusiness, 2000).

Chapter 5

1. *Business Week,* September 19, 1959, p. 88.
2. Quote from Harvard Business School case, "Xerox Corporation: Leadership Through Quality (A)," p. 1. For a colorful account of Xerox's meteoric rise and the "mania" of copying that fueled it, see John Brooks, "Xerox Xerox Xerox Xerox," *Business Adventures* (New York: Weybright & Talley, 1969), pp. 145–175.
3. The best account remains T. A. Wise, "IBM's $5,000,000,000 Gamble," *Fortune,* September 1966; but see also Robert Sobel, *IBM: Colossus in Transition* (New York: Times Books, 1981).
4. T. A. Wise, "IBM's $5,000,000,000 Gamble," *Fortune,* September 1966, p. 119.
5. Quoted in JoAnne Yates, *Control through Communication: the Rise of System in American Management* (Baltimore: Johns Hopkins University Press, 1989), p. 41.
6. On the sudden surge in industrial scale and increase in managerial complexity, see Alfred D. Chandler Jr., *The Visible Hand: The Managerial Revolution in American Business* (Cambridge, MA: Harvard University Press, 1977). On the emergence of industrial systems, see James R. Beniger, *The Control Revolution: Technological and Economic Origins of the Information Society* (Cambridge, MA: Harvard University Press, 1986), as well as Yates, *Control through Communication*; and James Cortada, *Before the Computer: IBM, NCR, Burroughs, and Remington Rand and the Industry They Created, 1865–1956* (Princeton: Princeton University Press, 1993).
7. Thomas J. Watson Jr. and Peter Petre, *Father, Son & Co: My Life at IBM and Beyond* (New York: Bantam Books, 1990), pp. 357–358, emphasis Watson's.
8. Yates, *Control through Communication,* pp. 56–57.

9. "The Dynamo and the Virgin," in Henry Adams, *The Education of Henry Adams* (New York: Oxford University Press, 1999).
10. See Joseph L. Bower, *Managing the Resource Allocation Process: A Study of Corporate Planning and Investment* (Boston: Harvard Business School Press, 1986).
11. See Richard L. Nolan, "Plight of the EDP Manager," *Harvard Business Review* (May–June 1973), pp. 143–152.
12. M. C. Jensen and W. H. Meckling posit the theoretical distinction between specific and general knowledge, and explore its impact on the structure and control systems of organizations, in "Specific and General Knowledge, and Organizational Structure," in L. Werin and H. Wijkander, Eds., *Contract Economics* (Oxford: Basil Blackwell, 1992).
13. See L. D. Schall, G. L. Sundem and W. R. Geijsbeek Jr., "Survey and Analysis of Capital Budgeting Methods," *Journal of Finance,* 33 (1) (1978), pp. 281–287.
14. Carliss Y. Baldwin and Kim B. Clark, "Capabilities and Capital Investment: New Perspectives on Capital Budgeting," Working Paper #92–004, Harvard Business School, 1991; Robert H. Hayes and William J. Abernathy, "Managing Our Way to Economic Decline," *Harvard Business Review* (July–August, 1980), pp. 67–77.
15. See O. E. Williamson, *The Economic Institutions of Capitalism* (New York: Free Press, 1985).
16. David T. Kearns, *Prophets in the Dark: How Xerox Reinvented Itself and Beat Back the Japanese* (New York: Harper Business, 1992), p. 55. See also Gary Jacobson and John Hillkirk, *Xerox, American Samurai* (New York: Macmillan, 1986), p. 178.
17. See John A. Byrne, *The Whiz Kids: Ten Founding Fathers of American Business—and the Legacy They Left Us* (New York: Doubleday, 1993), pp. 433–434.
18. Julio Bucatinsky (Program Administrator, Management Planning Systems, Data Processing Division, IBM), "Use a Computer to Improve your Decision Making," *Automation,* 20 (July 1973), pp. 34–38.
19. See Richard L. Nolan, "Information Technology Management Since 1960," in Alfred D. Chandler Jr. and James W. Cortada, Eds., *A Nation Transformed by Information: How Information Has Shaped the United States from Colonial Times to the Present* (New York: Oxford University Press, 2000), pp. 232–235, for a concise summary of corporate mainframe computing usage during this era.
20. For a vivid testament of Xerox's faith in the imminent coming of the "office of the future," see the company's Annual Report, 1977. On the last 914: Annual Report, 1976, p. 5; on the emergence of the ethernet see Richard Nolan, "Information Technology Management Since 1960," p. 229, and Xerox's Annual Report, 1977, p. 22.
21. See Michael Porter and Yoko Ishikura, "Note on the World Copier Industry in 1983," Harvard Business School case, 1988.
22. See Kearns, *Prophets in the Dark,* pp. 75–76.
23. Kearns, *Prophets in the Dark,* p. 135.
24. Kearns, *Prophets in the Dark,* p. 89. Savin, a U.S. company, was marketing the copier; Ricoh was the manufacturer.
25. "Xerox Corporation: Leadership Through Quality (A)," Harvard Business School case, pp. 2–3.

26. Kearns, *Prophets in the Dark*, p. 75.
27. See Joseph Juran, "Made in U.S.A.: A Renaissance in Quality," *Harvard Business Review* (July–August, 1993); Kearns, *Prophets in the Dark*, esp. pp. 76–87, quote from p. 76.
28. Kearns, *Prophets in the Dark*, p. 90.
29. Kearns, *Prophets in the Dark*, pp. 90–91.
30. *Fortune*, October 19, 1992; *Prophets in the Dark*, pp. 121–122.
31. The body of literature reporting on and proselytizing for Total Quality Management is voluminous. One of the key texts, a business bestseller in Japan by a leading authority on the subject, was subsequently translated and published in the U.S. as Kaoru Ishikawa's *What Is Total Quality Control? The Japanese Way* (Englewood Cliffs: Prentice-Hall, 1985, David J. Lu, trans.). See also James P. Womack, Daniel T. Jones, and Daniel Roos, *The Machine That Changed the World* (New York: Rawson Associates, 1990), for an accessible and authoritative account of the evolution of TQM by Toyota and its transfer to the American auto industry.
32. Kearns, *Prophets in the Dark*, p. 133.
33. Kearns, *Prophets in the Dark*, pp. 201–204.
34. This shift in decision rights is highlighted by M.W. Meyer, "Turning Evolution Inside the Organization," in J. A. C. Baum and J. V. Singh, Eds., *Evolutionary Dynamics of Organizations* (New York: Oxford University Press, 1994), p. 115.
35. Jacobson and Hillkirk, *American Samurai*, p. 254.
36. Jacobson and Hillkirk, *American Samurai*, pp. 253–255.
37. *Industry Week*, October 15, 1990.
38. Kearns, *Prophets in the Dark*, pp. 170–171.
39. *Business Week*, November 13, 1989, p. 136; "David Kearns: How I Saved the Titanic," *Fortune*, May 4, 1992, p. 117; David A. Garvin, "How the Baldrige Award Really Works," *Harvard Business Review* (November–December, 1991).
40. On the origins of the Ethernet, see Katie Hafner and Matthew Lyon, *Where Wizards Stay Up Late: The Origins of the Internet* (New York: Simon & Schuster, 1996), pp. 237–240.
41. Lynda Applegate and Donna Stoddard, "Xerox Corporation: Leadership of the Information Technology Function (A)," Harvard Business School case, 1995, p 1.
42. Applegate and Stoddard, "Leadership of the Information Technology Function," p. 3.
43. Michael Hammer, "Reengineering Work: Don't Automate, Obliterate," *Harvard Business Review* (July–August 1990); Hammer and James Champy, *Reengineering the Corporation: A Manifesto for Business Revolution* (New York: Harper Business, 1993).
44. Adoption rates among the F100 based on telephone interviews with senior executives in each F100 company. For reengineering at IBM, see *Industry Week*, October 15, 1990, and David P. Andros, J. Owen Cherrington, and Eric L. Denna, "Reengineer Your Accounting, the IBM Way," *Financial Executive* (July–August 1992). For the limitations of reengineering, see James Champy, *Reengineering Management: The Mandate for New Leadership* (New York: Harper Business, 1995).
45. Joel M. Stern and John S. Shiely, *The EVA Challenge: Implementing Value-Added Change in an Organization* (New York: John Wiley & Sons, 2001), p. 15; Shawn Tully, "The Real Key to Creating Wealth," *Fortune*, September 20, 1993, p. 38.

46. For the rise of traditional cost accounting, see H. Thomas Johnson and Robert S. Kaplan, *Relevance Lost: The Rise and Fall of Management Accounting* (Boston: Harvard Business School Press, 1987). On the advent and value of ABC accounting, see Peter F. Drucker, *Management Challenges for the 21st Century* (New York: Harper Business, 1999), pp. 111–112.
47. Peter Senge, *The Fifth Discipline* (New York: Doubleday, 1990); Thomas A. Stewart, *Intellectual Capital*; David A. Garvin, *Learning in Action: A Guide to Putting the Learning Organization to Work* (Boston: Harvard Business School Press, 2000).
48. Jeremy Main, "How to Steal the Best Ideas Around," *Fortune,* October 19, 1992; Robert Camp, *Benchmarking: The Search for Best Practices That Lead to Superior Performance* (Milwaukee: ASQC Quality Press, 1989).
49. Robert S. Kaplan and David P. Norton, "The Balanced Scorecard: Measures That Drive Performance," *Harvard Business Review* (January–February 1992). See also Kaplan and Norton, *Translating Strategy into Action: The Balanced Scorecard* (Boston: Harvard Business School Press, 1996).
50. Robert Howard, "The CEO as Organizational Architect: An Interview with Xerox's Paul Allaire," *Harvard Business Review* (September–October 1992), p. 108.
51. Howard, "The CEO as Organizational Architect," p. 112.
52. Howard, "The CEO as Organizational Architect," pp. 111, 120; "The Search for the Organization of Tomorrow," *Fortune,* May 18, 1992.
53. Richard L. Nolan and David C. Croson, *Creative Destruction: A Six-Stage Process for Transforming the Organization* (Boston: Harvard Business School Press, 1995).
54. Mike Graen, "Technology in Manufacturer/Retailer Integration: Wal-Mart and Procter & Gamble," *Velocity* (Spring 1999).
55. See Gary Folger, "Jeep Puts JIT in High Gear," *Modern Materials Management,* January 1993, pp. 42 ff.; Jeffrey Dyer, "How Chrysler Created an American Keiretsu," *Harvard Business Review,* July–August 1996.
56. Bill Gates, *Business @ the Speed of Thought: Using a Digital Nervous System* (New York: Warner Books, 1999), p. 15. See also Jeffrey F. Rayport and Bernard J. Jaworski, *e-Commerce* (Boston: McGraw-Hill/Irwin, 2001), p. 347.
57. Rayport and Jaworski, *e-Commerce,* p. 347; Nolan, "Information Technology Management since 1960," p. 248.
58. For useful overviews of knowledge management, see Thomas H. Davenport and Laurence Prusak, *Working Knowledge: How Organizations Manage What They Know* (Boston: Harvard Business School Press, 1998); and Amrit Tiwana, *The Knowledge Management Toolkit: Practical Techniques for Building a Knowledge Management System* (Upper Saddle River, NJ: Prentice Hall PTR, 2000).
59. *Economist,* "Business and Internet Survey," July 2, 1999, pp. 11, 12, 17; *Wall Street Journal,* May 10, 1999.
60. Dow Jones News Service, Press Release, September 10, 1998; Business Wire, September 10, 1998; *Wall Street Journal,* September 10, 1998.
61. *Rochester Business Journal,* January 8, 1999, p. 1.
62. *Wall Street Journal,* May 15, 2000.
63. *Irish Times,* September 18, 1998.

64. *Wall Street Journal,* January 26, 2000.
65. *Wall Street Journal,* January 20, 2000.
66. Xerox Corporation, Press Release, May 1, 2001; Donna Fuscaldo, "Tales of the Tape: After Restructuring, Xerox Pushes Growth," Dow Jones New Service, December 3, 2001.
67. Telephone interviews with senior executives in each F100 company.
68. Johnson and Kaplan, *Relevance Lost,* passim; Thomas A. Stewart, *The Wealth of Knowledge* (New York: Currency Doubleday, 2001), especially Chapters 13–14.

Chapter 6

1. For a short, lively account of the floating of U.S. Steel, see George David Smith and Richard Sylla, "The Deal of the Century," *Audacity* (Fall 1993), pp. 26–31. The Wall Street veteran, investment banker Isaac Seligman, is quoted on p. 28.
2. Horace L. Wilgus, *A Study of the United States Steel Corporation in its Industrial and Legal Aspects* (Chicago: Callaghan & Company, 1901), p. 4.
3. Jay W. Lorsch and Elizabeth MacIver, *Pawns or Potentates: The Reality of America's Corporate Boards* (Boston, MA: Harvard Business School Press, 1989).
4. Albert O. Hirschman, *Exit, Voice, and Loyalty: Responses to Decline in Firms, Organizations, and States* (Cambridge, MA: Harvard University Press, 1972).
5. For a study of takeover defenses, see Sandy E. Green Jr., *Rhetoric and the Institutionalization of Takeover Defenses in the S&P 1500 from 1975–1998.* Unpublished Ph.D. dissertation, Harvard University, 2001.
6. Quoted in James Howard Bridge, *The Inside History of the Carnegie Steel Company: A Romance of Millions* (New York: Aldine Book Company, 1903), pp. 117–118.
7. Quoted in Joseph Frazier Wall, *Andrew Carnegie* (New York: Oxford University Press, 1970), p. 665.
8. Wall, *Andrew Carnegie,* pp. 664–666; Bridge, *Inside History,* pp. 124–125.
9. Quoted in Wall, *Andrew Carnegie,* p. 727.
10. See Wilgus, *A Study of the United States Steel Corporation,* pp. 52–53.
11. *Fortune,* "The Corporation," March 1936, p. 152.
12. See *Fortune,* "The Corporation," March 1936.
13. *Fortune,*"The Corporation," March 1936.
14. Alfred D. Chandler Jr., *The Visible Hand: The Managerial Revolution in American Business* (Cambridge, MA: Harvard University Press, 1977).
15. See, for example, the reports on the state of American management by R. A. Gordon and J. E. Howell, *Higher Education for Business* (New York: Columbia University Press, 1959); and L. W. Porter and L. E. McKibbin, *Management Education and Development: Drift or Thrust into the 21st Century?* (New York: McGraw-Hill, 1988).
16. See Hirschman, *Exit, Voice, and Loyalty.*
17. See Michael Useem, *The Inner Circle: Large Corporations and the Rise of Business Political Activity in the U.S. and U.K.* (New York: Oxford University Press, 1984).
18. R. J. Larner, "Ownership and Control in the 200 Largest Non-Financial Corporations, 1929 and 1963," *American Economic Review,* 56 (September 1966).
19. For an early warning, see Adolf A. Berle Jr. and Gardiner C. Means, *Concentration of Economic Power* (Princeton, NJ: Princeton University Press, 1932). This managerial

discretionary power opens the door to what Jensen and Meckling have called agency costs, borne by principals when managers use their discretion to pursue strategies that do not maximize the principals' interests also. See also A. Shleifer and R. W. Vishny, A Survey of Corporate Governance, Cambridge, MA: Harvard Institute for Economic Research, 1995, Discussion Paper #1741.

20. *Business Week,* February 25, 1985.
21. For a vivid portrait, see Ralph Nader and William Taylor, *The Big Boys: Power and Position in American Business* (New York: Pantheon, 1986).
22. *Business Week,* February 25, 1985; Nader and Taylor, *The Big Boys,* pp. 16–17.
23. U.S. Steel, Annual Report, 1979.
24. U.S. Steel, Annual Report, 1980.
25. U.S. Steel, Annual Report, 1982.
26. *Wall Street Journal,* January 7, 1982.
27. On Pickens, see T. Boone Pickens Jr., *Boone* (Boston: Houghton Mifflin, 1987).
28. On Icahn, see, e.g., *Business Week,* October 27, 1986, p. 98 ff.
29. *Wall Street Journal,* March 19, 1984.
30. *Wall Street Journal,* August 19, 1985.
31. *Wall Street Journal,* October 31, 1985.
32. *Wall Street Journal,* December 6, 1985.
33. *Business Week,* December 2, 1985, p. 132.
34. *Wall Street Journal,* December 6, 1985.
35. *Business Week,* December 2, 1985, p. 132.
36. *Business Week,* November 11, 1985, p. 34.
37. *Wall Street Journal,* December 6, 1985.
38. USX, Annual Report, 1986, p. 6.
39. *Wall Street Journal,* September 19 and October 6, 1986.
40. *Wall Street Journal,* October 7, 1986.
41. *Wall Street Journal,* October 6, October 7, October 22, and October 30, 1986; *Business Week,* November 3, 1986.
42. *Wall Street Journal,* January 9 and January 28, 1987; *Business Week,* February 2, 1987.
43. *Business Week,* October 16, 1989, p. 37.
44. *Wall Street Journal,* October 25, 1989.
45. *Wall Street Journal,* October 25 and December 5, 1989.
46. *Wall Street Journal,* March 9, 1990.
47. *Wall Street Journal,* March 14, March 22, April 6, April 25, and May 4, 1990.
48. *Wall Street Journal,* April 4, 1990.
49. *Wall Street Journal,* May 2, 1990.
50. *Wall Street Journal,* May 8, 1990.
51. *Wall Street Journal,* May 15, 1991.
52. G. F. Davis and S. K. Stout, "Organization Theory and the Market for Corporate Control: A Dynamic Analysis of Large Takeover Targets, 1980–1990," *Administrative Science Quarterly,* 37 (1992), pp. 605–634.
53. Michael Useem, *Executive Defense: Shareholder Power and Corporate Reorganization* (Cambridge, MA: Harvard University Press, 1993), p. 23.

54. George P. Baker, "Beatrice: A Study in the Creation and Destruction of Value," *Journal of Finance* (July 1992), pp. 1081–1119.
55. See Baker, "Beatrice," pp. 1100–1101.
56. Quoted in Baker, "Beatrice," p. 1104.
57. Baker, "Beatrice," p. 1099.
58. Despite somewhat disappointing numbers for the final sale, the deal as a whole made substantial profits for KKR's constituents, generating an annual compounded return on equity of 83 percent.
59. In addition to Baker, see George P. Baker and George David Smith, *The New Financial Capitalists: Kohlberg, Kravis Roberts and the Creation of Corporate Value* (New York: Cambridge University Press, 1998), pp. 83–85.
60. *Fortune,* September 12, 1988, p. 140.
61. Michael Useem, *Investor Capitalism: How Money Managers Are Changing the Face of Corporate America* (New York: Basic Books, 1996), p. 31.
62. *Fortune,* September 12, 1988, p. 140.
63. *Fortune,* September 12, 1988.
64. *Business Week,* July 22, 1991.
65. *Fortune,* January 16, 1989.
66. *Fortune,* September 12, 1988.
67. *Fortune,* September 12, 1988.
68. *Fortune,* September 12, 1988.
69. *Wall Street Journal,* April 3, 1990.
70. *Los Angeles Times,* January 25, 1989; *Fortune,* February 27, 1989.
71. *Business Week,* July 22, 1991.
72. *Wall Street Journal,* April 3, 1990.
73. *Fortune,* February 27, 1989.
74. Quoted in *Fortune,* September 12, 1988.
75. Quoted in *Wall Street Journal,* May 15, 1989.
76. Quoted in *Fortune,* September 12, 1988. For a early overview of the phenomenon of institutional investor activism, see, e.g., Hilary Rosenberg, "The Revolt of the Institutional Shareholder, *Institutional Investor,* May 1987, pp. 131–142.
77. *Dallas Morning News,* April 15, 1990.
78. *Los Angeles Times,* May 30, 1990, Home section, p. 15.
79. On Occidental, see *Wall Street Journal,* March 22, 1990; *Business Week,* March 19, 1990. On Lockheed, see *Wall Street Journal,* March 27, 1990.
80. Fran Hawthorne, "Outside Directors Feel the Heat," *Institutional Investor,* April 1989, p. 59.
81. *Wall Street Journal,* April 3, 1990.
82. Quoted in Useem, *Investor Capitalism,* p. 24.
83. *Institutional Investor,* March 1, 1991.
84. See Useem, *Investor Capitalism.*
85. See M. C. Jensen and R. S. Ruback, "The Market for Corporate Control: The Scientific Evidence," *Journal of Financial Economics,* 11 (1983), pp. 5–50; and Jensen, "The Eclipse of the Public Corporation," *Harvard Business Review* (September–October 1989), pp. 61–74.

86. See, e.g., "Best of a Breed," *The Economist,* September 30, 1989, pp. 86 ff.
87. Useem, *Executive Defense.*

Chapter 7

1. On the "Kodak Moment" campaign, see *Advertising Age,* March 29, 1993. For market share data, see *Wall Street Journal,* January 26, 1994, p. A3; Robert Dolan, "Eastman Kodak Company: Funtime Film," Harvard Business School case, 1995, p. 2.
2. On critical reactions to "A Kodak Moment," see *Advertising Age,* August 23, 1993.
3. *Wall Street Journal,* November 19, 1992, p. C1.
4. See for example *Wall Street Journal,* April 8, 1992, p. B4; *Business Week,* December 7, 1992, pp. 100ff.
5. On "free agency," see Bruce Tulgan, *Winning the Talent Wars* (New York: Norton & Company, 2001); Charles Woodruff, *Winning the Talent War: A Strategic Approach to Attracting, Developing, and Retaining the Best People* (New York: Wiley, 1999); and Daniel H. Pink, *Free Agent Nation: How America's Independent Workers Are Transforming the Way We Live* (New York: Warner Books, 2001).
6. On the concept of the "Organization Man," see William H. Whyte Jr., *The Organization Man* (New York: Simon & Schuster, 1956). Perhaps the best, most evocative study of the experience of Whyte's "Organization Man" in the midst of corporate downsizing is Charles Heckscher *White Collar Blues* (New York: Basic Books, 1995).
7. Sanford Jacoby's *Modern Manors: Welfare Capitalism since the New Deal* (Princeton: Princeton University Press, 1997) is a key source. For a view closer to the scene, see John E. Webber, "Making Kodaks and Contentment," *American Industries,* 25 (November 1924), pp. 27–34.
8. Quoted in Jacoby, *Modern Manors,* pp. 64–65.
9. See Jacoby, *Modern Manors,* pp. 66–67, 71–75.
10. Jacoby, *Modern Manors,* pp. 79–80.
11. Michael J. Piore and Charles F. Sabel, *The Second Industrial Divide: Possibilities for Prosperity* (New York: Basic Books, 1984).
12. See Piore and Sabel, *The Second Industrial Divide.*
13. James D. Thompson, *Organizations in Action* (New York: McGraw-Hill, 1967).
14. David J. Teece and Gary Pisano, "The Dynamic Capabilities of Firms," *Industrial and Corporate Change,* vol. 3, pp. 537–556.
15. *Wall Street Journal,* October 28, 1992, p. A9; January 12, 1993, p. A3.
16. See *Wall Street Journal,* January 8, 1993.
17. *Rochester Democrat and Chronicle,* January 20, 1993, p. 12A.
18. *Rochester Democrat and Chronicle,* January 20, 1993, p. 6B.
19. *Rochester Democrat and Chronicle,* January 20, 1993, p. 10B.
20. *Wall Street Journal,* January 21, 1993, p. C1.
21. Kodak, Annual Report, 1992.
22. Kodak, Annual Report, 1992.
23. Jack Blackstock (First Boston Corp), *Wall Street Journal,* January 12, 1993, p. A3.
24. *Wall Street Journal,* January 12, 1993, p. A3.
25. *Wall Street Journal,* April 28, 1993, p. A1.

26. *Wall Street Journal,* April 28,1993, p. A1; *Forbes,* August 30, 1993, p. 40.
27. *Rochester Business Journal,* April 30, 1993, p. 1.
28. *Rochester Business Journal,* April 30, 1993, p. 1.
29. *Wall Street Journal,* April 29, 1993, p. A3. See also *Rochester Democrat & Chronicle,* May 2, 1993, p. 11A.
30. *Wall Street Journal,* April 29, 1993, p. A3; *New York Times,* May 3, 1993, p. D1.
31. *Rochester Democrat & Chronicle,* May 2, 1993, p. 11A.
32. *Wall Street Journal,* April 29, 1993, p. A3.
33. *Rochester Democrat & Chronicle,* May 2, 1993, p. 1A.
34. *Wall Street Journal,* April 30, 1993, p. A4.
35. *Wall Street Journal,* May 6, 1993, p. A4.
36. *Wall Street Journal,* May 4, 1993, p. A3.
37. *Rochester Democrat & Chronicle,* May 13, 1993, p. 1A.
38. *Wall Street Journal,* May 13, 1993, p. A3 and May 18, 1993, p. C1; *Rochester Democrat & Chronicle,* May 13, 1993, p. 4A.
39. *Rochester Democrat & Chronicle,* May 13, 1993, p. 1A.
40. *Wall Street Journal,* May 18, 1993, p. C1.
41. *Rochester Democrat & Chronicle,* May 12, 1993, p. 1A.
42. *Rochester Democrat & Chronicle,* May 13, 1993, p. 4A.
43. *Rochester Democrat & Chronicle,* May 13, 1993, p. 14A.
44. *Rochester Democrat & Chronicle,* August 7, 1993, p. 6A.
45. *Rochester Democrat & Chronicle,* May 13, 1993, p. 14A.
46. See, e.g., *New York Times,* August 9, 1993, p. D1.
47. *Rochester Democrat & Chronicle,* August 7, 1993, p. A1.
48. *Buffalo News,* August 8, 1993; *Wall Street Journal,* August 6, 1993, p. A3; August 9, 1993, p. A3.
49. *Buffalo News,* August 8, 1993.
50. *Rochester Democrat & Chronicle,* August 8, 1993, p. 1A.
51. *New York Times,* August 19, 1993, p. D1.
52. *Rochester Democrat & Chronicle,* August 7, 1993, p. 8A.
53. *Rochester Democrat & Chronicle,* August 7, 1993, p. 8A.
54. *Rochester Democrat & Chronicle,* August 7, 1993, p. 7A.
55. *Rochester Democrat & Chronicle,* August 7, 1993, p. 8A.
56. *Rochester Democrat & Chronicle,* August 7, 1993, p. 7A.
57. *Rochester Democrat & Chronicle,* August 7, 1993, p. 10A.
58. *Rochester Democrat & Chronicle,* August 7, 1993, p. 10A.
59. *New York Times,* August 19, 1993, p. D1.
60. *New York Times,* August 19, 1993, p. D1; *Wall Street Journal,* August 19, 1993, p. A3.
61. *Wall Street Journal,* August 29, 1993, p. A1.
62. Kodak, Annual Report, 1993.
63. *Wall Street Journal,* December 16, 1993, p. 2A.
64. Quoted in *Forbes,* January 13, 1997.
65. *Fortune,* October 27, 1997; *Business Week,* October 27, 1997.
66. *Rochester Democrat & Chronicle,* September 16, 1997, pp. 1A, 9A.

67. Employment numbers from *Buffalo News,* July 5, 1998, p. H1.
68. *Rochester Business Journal,* December 9, 1994, p. 10.
69. *Fortune,* January 13, 1997, p. 76.
70. *Fortune,* January 13, 1997, p. 76.
71. On EVA, see, e.g., Shawn Tully's account in *Fortune,* September 9, 1993. For Kodak and EVA, see *Fortune,* January 13, 1997, p. 76.
72. Raymond Hernandez, "Deferring to 'Great Yellow Father,' " *New York Times,* November 16, 1997, Section 1, pp. 41 ff.
73. Raymond Hernandez, "Deferring to 'Great Yellow Father,' " *New York Times,* November 16, 1997, Section 1, pp. 41 ff; *Buffalo News,* July 5, 1998, p. H1.
74. For Sharlow's story, see Rick Bragg, "The Downsizing of America," *The New York Times,* March 5, 1996, pp. A1 ff.

Chapter 8

1. Theresa Eiben & Joyce E. Davis, "A New List for the New Economy," *Fortune,* May 15, 1995, pp. 166–170.
2. For discussion of the effect of the repeal of Glass-Stegall on industry, see Margaret Boitano, "An Old Law's Repeal, A New Wave of M&A," *Fortune,* January 24, 2000.
3. See Daniel, M. G., Raff and Walter J. Salmon, "Economies of Speed and Retailing: The History, Pathology, and Future of Department Stores," Harvard Business School Working Paper, 1997, pp. 1–5.
4. Raff and Salmon, "Economies of Speed and Retailing," pp. 1–5.
5. Carol J. Loomis, "Sam Would Be Proud," *Fortune,* April 17, 2000, p. 132.
6. See Sam Walton, *Sam Walton, Made in America: My Story* (New York: Doubleday, 1992).
7. For further information, see "Wal-Mart Stores, Inc.," Harvard Business School case No. 794-024 (1996).
8. *Forbes,* August 16, 1982, p. 43.
9. For further information, see "Wal-Mart Stores, Inc.," Harvard Business School case No. 794-024 (1996).
10. Richard S. Tedlow, *Giants of Enterprise: Seven Business Innovators and the Empires They Built* (New York: HarperCollins, 2001).
11. "Wall Street's old order changes: Chase Manhattan's acquisition of J. P. Morgan puts Wall Street's most aristocratic bank in the hands of ruthless meritocrats," *Economist,* September 16, 1990, pp. 81–83.
12. John Donald Wilson, *The Chase: The Chase Manhattan Bank, N.A. 1945–1985* (Boston: Harvard Business School Press, 1986), p. 57.
13. Wilson, *The Chase,* p. 57.
14. Stuart Gilson and Cedric Escalle, "Chase Manhattan Corporation: The Making of America's Largest Bank," Harvard Business School case, 1998.
15. "Wall Street's old order changes: Chase Manhattan's acquisition of J. P. Morgan puts Wall Street's most aristocratic bank in the hands of ruthless meritocrats," *Economist,* September 16, 2000, pp. 81–83.
16. *Economist,* September 16, 2000, pp. 81–83.

17. Stuart Gilson and Cedric Escalle, "Chase Manhattan Corporation: The Making of America's Largest Bank," Harvard Business School Case, 1998.
18. *Euromoney,* November 2000, p. 5.
19. Wilson, *The Chase,* p. 72.
20. John Massey, Healthcare: Managed Care, Standard & Poor's Industry Surveys, February 22, 2001, p. 1
21. Herman Saftlas and Bradley Worrell, Healthcare: Pharmaceuticals, Standard & Poor's Industry Surveys, June 29, 2001, p. 1.
22. Saftlas and Worrell, Ibid., p. 4.
23. The Merck story draws extensively on Matthew Lynn, *The Billion Dollar Battle: Merck v. Glaxo* (London: Heinemann, 1991).
24. Lynn, *Billion Dollar Battle,* p. 86.
25. The story of this incident and Merck's involvement in it draws upon Linda Marsa, *Prescription for Profits* (New York: Scribner, 1997), pp. 16–22.
26. Marsa, *Prescription.*
27. For background on drug development, see Gary Pisano, *The Development Factory: Unlocking the Potential of Process Innovation* (Boston: Harvard Business School Press, 1996).
28. Saftlas and Worrell, Healthcare, pp. 1–5.
29. The following account of WorldCom draws principally on the historical background provided at http://www.hoovers.com.
30. The account that follows draws principally from Kara Swisher, *AOL.COM: How Steve Case Beat Bill Gates, Nailed the Netheads, and Made Millions in the War for the Web* (New York: Times Business, 1998).
31. For background on Netscape, see Kaplan, *The Silicon Boys,* pp. 226–236.
32. Kaplan, *The Silicon Boys,* p. 267.
33. Kaplan, *The Silicon Boys,* pp. 249–252.
34. For more information on the development of the transistor, see Kaplan, *The Silicon Boys,* pp. 40–43.
35. In addition to Kaplan, see also Richard Tedlow, *Giants of Enterprise: Seven Business Innovators and the Empires They Built* (New York: HarperBusiness, 2001).
36. *Worldwide Computer News Products News,* January 9, 2002.
37. For information on Moore's Law, see Kaplan, *Silicon Boys,* pp. 69–71.
38. Information on Michael Dell and Dell Computer Corporation drawn from Hoover's Online, Dell Computer Corporation profile, and from V. Kasturi Rangan, "Dell Online," Harvard Business School Case, 1999.
39. Nancy F. Koehn, *Brand New: How Entrepreneurs Earned Consumers' Trust from Wedgewood to Dell* (Boston: Harvard Business School Press, 2001), p. 304.
40. The history of Apple is based on John Sculley with John A. Byrne, *Odyssey: Pepsi to Apple, A Journey of Adventure, Ideas and the Future* (New York: Harper and Row, 1987) and David A. Kaplan, *The Silicon Boys and Their Valley of Dreams* (New York: William Morrow, 1999).
41. Kaplan, *Silicon Boys,* p. 81.
42. The following account of Apple's founding draws primarily on Kaplan, *Silicon Boys,* pp. 82–104.

43. For the competitive implications of modularity, see Carliss Baldwin and Kim Clark, *Design Rules* (Cambridge, MA: MIT Press, 2000).
44. For historical background on Compaq, see E. Geoffrey Love and Robert G. Eccles, "Compaq Computer Corporation," Harvard Business School Case, 1991.
45. For Microsoft's story, see Kaplan, *Silicon Boys;* and Michael Cusumano, *Microsoft Secrets: How the World's Most Powerful Software Company Creates Technology, Shapes Markets, and Manages People* (New York: Simon & Schuster, 1998).
46. See Kaplan, *Silicon Boys.*

Chapter 9

1. See Robert J. Shiller, *Irrational Exuberance* (New York: Broadway Books, 2001).
2. For a an even gloomier forecast, see Michael Mandel's, *The Coming Internet Depression: Why the High-Tech Boom Will Go Bust, Why The Crash Will be Worse Than You Think, and How to Prosper Afterwards* (New York: Basic Books, 2000).
3. These data and discussion of the changing structure of the U.S. economy were obtained from the Commerce Department Web site: http://www.bea.doc.gov.
4. See Peter Drucker, "Beyond the Information Revolution," *Atlantic Monthly* (October, 1999), p. 47 ff.
5. Ann Markusen, "The Post-Cold War American Defence Industry: Options, Policies and Probable Outcomes," in Efraim Inbar and Benzion Zilberfarb, Eds., *The Politics and Economics of Defence Industries* (London: Frank Cass, 1998), p. 58.
6. "General Dynamics: Compensation and Strategy (A)," Harvard Business School case, p. 2. For a general account of GD through the late 1980s, see Jacob Goodwin, *Brotherhood of Arms: General Dynamics and the Business of Defending America* (New York: Times Books, 1985).
7. All quotes from the General Dynamics, Annual Report, 1989.
8. "General Dynamics: Compensation and Strategy (A)," Harvard Business School case, p. 3.
9. *Aviation Week and Space Technology,* August 5, 1991, p. 38.
10. "General Dynamics: Compensation and Strategy (A)," Harvard Business School case, p. 8.
11. Sales projections and backlog data from *Business Month,* June 1990.
12. "General Dynamics: Compensation and Strategy (A)," Harvard Business School case, p. 8.
13. *Aviation Week and Space Technology,* August 5, 1991, p. 38.
14. "General Dynamics: Compensation and Strategy (A)," Harvard Business School case, p. 8.
15. *Aviation Week and Space Technology,* August 5, 1991, p. 38.
16. Jay Dial and Kevin Murphy, "Incentives, Downsizing, and Value Creation at General Dynamics," *Journal of Financial Economics,* 37 (1995), p. 286; *Wall Street Journal,* May 7, 1993; *Aviation Week and Space Technology,* May 11, 1992.
17. *Aviation Week and Space Technology,* November 2, 1992; *Fortune,* January 11, 1993.
18. See note 16, Dial and Murphy, "Incentives," p. 297.
19. *Aviation Week and Space Technology,* November 2, 1992; *Fortune,* January 11, 1993.

20. *Wall Street Journal,* March 19, 1993.
21. Facts taken from Hoovers Online.
22. Facts taken from Hoovers Online.
23. Facts taken from Hoovers Online.
24. Michael T. Hannan and Glenn R. Carroll, *Dynamics of Organizational Population* (New York: Oxford University Press, 1992).
25. Alex Taylor III, *Fortune,* April 16, 2001, p. 156.
26. Ibid. p. 150.
27. *Wall Street Journal,* December 16, 1999.
28. *Economist,* October 21, 2000.
29. Anthony Sampson, *The Seven Sisters: The Great Oil Companies and the World They Made* (New York: Viking Press, 1975), p. 25.
30. Daniel Yergin, *The Prize: The Epic Quest for Oil, Money, and Power* (New York: Simon & Schuster, 1991), p. 110.
31. Yergin, *The Prize,* pp. 224–225.
32. *Wall Street Journal,* December 1, 1999.
33. Johnson & Johnson, Annual Report, 1999.
34. Information on the three product divisions taken from Hoovers Online and "Dusting the Opposition," *Economist,* April 29, 1995.
35. Francis J. Aguilar and Arvind Bhambri, "Johnson & Johnson (A): Philosophy and Culture," Harvard Business School case, 1983, p. 2.
36. For a fascinating history, see Lawrence G. Foster, *Robert W. Johnson: The Gentleman Rebel* (Ashland, OH: Lillian Press, 1999).
37. Ralph Larsen, as quoted in "Dusting the Opposition," *Economist,* April 29, 1995, p. 71.
38. Larsen, as quoted in Johanna Hurstak, *Johnson & Johnson in the 1990s,* Harvard Business School case study, 1992, p. 2.
39. Facts taken from Hoovers Online.
40. Aguilar and Arvind Bhambri, Johnson & Johnson (A), p. 6.
41. Johnson & Johnson, Annual Report, 1985.
42. Johnson & Johnson, Annual Report, 1988.
43. Johnson & Johnson, Annual Report, 1986.
44. Johnson & Johnson, Annual Report, 1986.
45. Johnson & Johnson, Annual Report, 1997.
46. Data taken from Hoovers Online.
47. Johnson & Johnson, Annual Report, 1998.
48. Johnson & Johnson, Annual Report, 1998.
49. Data taken from Hoovers Online.
50. Johnson & Johnson, Investor Fact Sheet (1999).
51. Johnson & Johnson, Annual Report, 1999.
52. *Fortune,* December 26, 1994, p. 184.
53. *Fortune,* December 26, 1994, p. 186.
54. *Fortune,* April 25, 2001.
55. *Wall Street Journal Europe,* June 6, 2000.
56. *Pittsburgh Post-Gazette,* June 9, 2000.

57. Hoovers Online and *Pittsburgh Post-Gazette,* June 9, 2000.
58. Data from Hoovers Online.
59. John E. Pepper as quoted in *Wall Street Journal Europe,* June 6, 2000.
60. *Wall Street Journal Europe,* June 6, 2000.
61. Data from Hoovers Online.
62. *The Arizona Republic,* October 25, 2000.
63. Greyhound Corporation, Annual Report, 1984.
64. Greyhound Corporation, Form 10K, 1987.
65. Greyhound Corporation, Annual Report, 1987.
66. Greyhound-Dial Corporation, Annual Report, 1991.
67. John Teets as quoted in *Wall Street Journal,* October 30, 1991, p. C9.
68. Hoovers Online and *Wall Street Journal,* November 22, 1996.
69. *The Arizona Republic,* October 25, 2000.
70. Viad, Annual Report, 1996.
71. Viad, Annual Report, 1999.
72. General Motors, Annual Report, 1999.
73. Dale Buss, "Wishing on an OnStar," *Context,* October–November 2000, p. 54.
74. Sandy E. Green and Nitin Nohria, "General Motors: Smith's Dilemma," Harvard Business School case study, 1993, p. 2.
75. Green and Nohria, "Smith's Dilemma," and Buss, "Wishing on an OnStar," p. 54.
76. MaryAnn Keller as quoted in Buss, "Wishing on an OnStar," p. 54.
77. General Motors, Annual Report, 1999.
78. *Wall Street Journal,* February 22, 2000, p. B23.
79. *Wall Street Journal,* November, 17, 2000, p. A4.
80. *Wall Street Journal,* November, 17, 2000, p. A4.
81. *Wall Street Journal,* February 22, 2000, p. B23.
82. Buss, "Wishing on an OnStar," p. 52.
83. Buss, "Wishing on an OnStar," p. 53.1.
84. *Wall Street Journal,* January 20, 2000, p. B18.
85. *Wall Street Journal,* January 18, 2000, p. B14.
86. *Wall Street Journal,* July 12, 1999.
87. *Wall Street Journal,* January 20, 2000.
88. *Wall Street Journal,* December 12, 2000.
89. *Wall Street Journal,* April 17, 2000.
90. *Wall Street Journal,* April 17, 2000.
91. *Wall Street Journal,* May 17, 2000.
92. "EDS Lands $1 Billion in New Business; IT Services Leader on Course for Another Record Contract Signings," PR Newswire, November 14, 2000.
93. Mark Roberti, "GE's Spin Machine," *The Industry Standard,* January 22, 2001.
94. *Forbes,* August 21, 2000, p. 106.
95. *Forbes,* August 21, 2000, p. 106.
96. "The House that Jack Built," *Economist,* September 18, 1999, p. 25.
97. Jonathan Rauch, "Oil, Computers, and the Reinvention of the Earth," *Atlantic Monthly,* January 2001.

INDEX